Wine

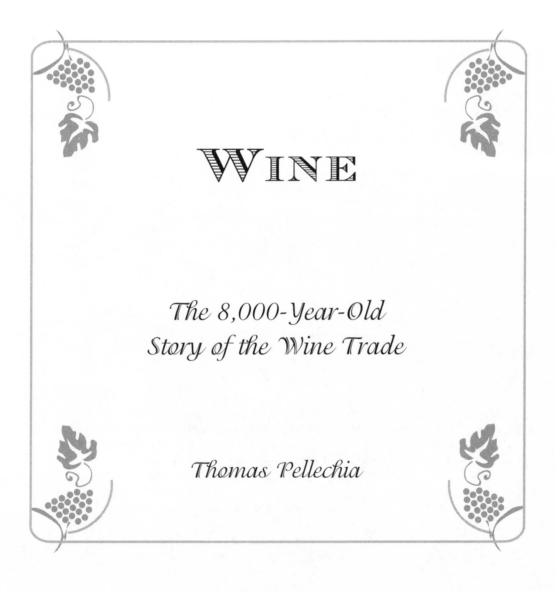

WINE

The 8,000-Year-Old Story of the Wine Trade

Thomas Pellechia

THUNDER'S MOUTH PRESS
NEW YORK

WINE

The 8,000-Year-Old Story of the Wine Trade

Published by
Thunder's Mouth Press
An Imprint of Avalon Publishing Group, Inc.
245 West 17th Street, 11th floor
New York, NY 10011

AVALON
publishing group incorporated

Illustrations by Anne Kiley

First printing, August 2006

Library of Congress Cataloging-in-Publication Data is available.

ISBN-10: 1-56025-871-3
ISBN-13: 978-1-56025-871-1

9 8 7 6 5 4 3 2 1

Book design by Maria Elias

Printed in the United States of America
Distributed by Publishers Group West

This book is dedicated to that wine merchant nearby, the one with the great selection of wines augmented by a pleasant, passionate, knowledgeable staff—you know the shop I mean.

Table of Contents

PART IV:
Northern Europe Seizes the Wine Trade

PART V:
The Recent Past

PART VI
Post-World War II

Acknowledgments

An author whose book draws from various sources would be remiss not to acknowledge his massive debt owed to those sources. So, to all the authors of all the books I have read or have used in my research, and whose titles appear in the bibliography of this book, I have nothing but admiration and reverence. Thank you for hundreds of hours of enjoyment and education. Particular mention goes to authors Patrick McGovern, Tim Unwin, Edward Hyams, H. Warner Allen, Thomas Pinney, and Leo A. Loubère.

Had I kept count of the hours gone by as I read the many books and documents that got me to this point I am sure I would be wondering how I had time for anything else. But I did have time left over, much of which I spent in the wine profession.

Next to the wine itself, the best thing about the wine profession is working with and meeting so many wonderful wine people: the retailers and restaurateurs who had been my customers when I sold wine at wholesale, the distributors and importers who sold me wine for my retail shop, the wine producers both at home and abroad who are always willing to share what they know, the wine consumers who allowed me the indulgence of selling my wine discoveries to them, and the students who have attended my wine classes and listened to me ramble on about what I think I know. I thank them all for their collective influence on what I have learned about wine and will continue to learn about the subject.

I also thank the many characters that have formed throughout the ages the building blocks for this story of the wine trade. Of course, I did not personally know the ones from the past, but I want to thank those of my contemporaries with whom I spoke or corresponded with for clarification and information, especially the buoyantly helpful *Decanter Magazine* editor Amy Wislocki, the innovative wine retailer Joshua Wesson, the energetic wine educator Edmund Osterland, and noted wine critic Robert M. Parker.

Last, I thank my wife, Anne Kiley, for her encouragement, research help, and the marvelous maps and graphics that she created to grace this book.

Introduction

In a much-repeated story, King Jam-Sheed, founder and ruler of the city of Persepolis, came to look with disfavor on a former beauty of his harem and banished her. She became despondent and decided to end her life. The woman came upon the king's warehouse in which he had stored his favorite food—grapes—in a jar marked "poison" so that no one else would eat them. The king's grapes had broken down into a liquid, so she decided to drink the "poison."

To her pleasant surprise, the drink had quite the opposite effect from that which the young woman had intended. Her spirit was revived and life took on new meaning. Excited by what had happened, she brought a cup of the liquid to the king, who upon tasting it took her back into his harem and decreed that from then on the purpose of grapes in Persepolis would be to make wine.

According to another story, ancient Persian traders would not enter into a contract without the benefit of wine to give them better insight into the validity of the deal. First they scrutinized the matter without wine; then they drank. If, after they had consumed the wine, the deal held up to scrutiny as it had earlier, it was consummated.

These are legends, of course, but it is true that wine had reached major importance in Persia by the fifth century B.C., when the empire controlled the area from the southern shores of the Caspian Sea to the Persian Gulf. There is evidence that ancient Persians, especially royalty, drank wine to great excess. This was 2,500 years ago and wine had already enjoyed a long history of at least 5,500 years; it might even have been traded before then.

> First of all it is to the wine-merchant
> that the libertines drink . . .
> may those who slander us be cursed
>
> —Carl Orff, *Carmina Burana*
> (English translation of part II,
> "In the Tavern," stanza 14)

The noted archaeologist, Patrick McGovern, of the University of Pennsylvania, studies the origins of wine. In his book, *Ancient Wine: The Search for the Origins of Viniculture,* McGovern makes the case that, although the Transcaucusus Mountains are home to the wild grapevine *Vitis vinifera sylvestris,* grapevines did not grow naturally everywhere in the region. Yet, within a relatively short period of time, ancient viniculture spread from Mesopotamia in all directions of the known world, something that could not have happened without trade of some sort. Along with grain and minerals, wine is among the earliest trading commodities, and when it was traded, wine often became an economic as well as a cultural powerhouse.

Throughout the ages most knowledge about wine has come our way from scientists like McGovern and from agrarians, historians, religious leaders, poets, and even politicians. Volumes have been written about the places where wine has been produced over the centuries, how it is produced, and sometimes why it is produced. I have read hundreds of such books. They cover the universals connected to wine—archaeology, culture, cooking, religion, and so on—but with the exception of a few personal stories or biographies and one particular book, *Wine and the Vine,* by Tim Unwin, wine merchants are neither celebrated nor condemned. They are just there.

Wine merchants do the legwork; they find the product, move it, store it, and get it to us. Depending upon the period of history, wine merchants sometimes accomplished these things against great cultural odds. Telling the wine story from the perspective of its commerce can lead us—if not to an understanding of caste, exploration, discovery, invention, climate, food, war, religion, and the endless human spirit, at least to marvel at it all.

In Britain, *merchant* is the word used for those who engage in either wholesale or retail trade. In the American vernacular, *merchant* has taken on a less than honorable cloak. The success of one major American wine critic is in part built on the belief by some that wine merchants can't be trusted to recommend the best wines because they have a vested interest in making the sale.

From what I know of the wine trade, sure, some wine merchants have been less than on the up-and-up, and some have been inscrutable, but some have been incorruptible and some have even been innovative. In other words, wine merchants are human, too, and none of us can deny that without them we—the consumers—would have a tough time getting our wine.

Having said that, I sometimes find myself wondering if the wine merchant really is like everyone else. First, the availability and the price of wine are at the whim of both nature and governments, which makes it tough to earn a good living as a wine merchant. Second, there is the customer, that fickle species that will fast understand the emptiness of a passionless recommendation from a merchant and thus will not return. Third, it takes most people years to become educated wine consumers; likewise, you don't just wake up one morning and say, "I want to become a wine merchant." With wine, that kind of epiphany arrives only after something much deeper in the human soul has taken place.

My wine epiphany took place when I was quite young, in the cellar of an immigrant Italian who, like my family, wound up in Brooklyn. I loved Anton—the winemaker—for what he taught me about wine and about living. I used to help Anton load boxes of grapes in autumn and I used to love to sniff his barrels just after they had been emptied of the wine he had recently bottled. Most of all, I loved the old man's wine, which I first tasted when I was six and then drank thereafter, cut with water, at many family dinners. I had no idea how strong Anton's influence would be on me as an adult, and it certainly took me a long time to find out.

Having a head for numbers, I was somehow persuaded in high school that I should be a CPA. After graduation, and because there was no money in the family for college, I went to night school to study accounting, paying for classes out of my day job paycheck. I worked in the cost accounting department of a local industrial air conditioner manufacturing company. Part of my job was to measure and evaluate work efficiency, a task that began with me standing in a production department armed with a stopwatch and a clipboard, and recording the time and steps it took to perform individual production tasks. Some of the workers in the factory were people I had grown up with in the neighborhood; they thought I was a traitor.

My task was completed at my desk, as I calculated the actual time against the standard time allowed to complete production, and what it had actually cost the company to produce each portion of an air conditioner and, hence, the cost of building the whole thing. The cost of production had exceeded revenue so often that the air-conditioning company was on its way to going bust. No matter: I probably would have been dead of boredom by the age of twenty, the age I had reached when I was called to military service.

Not wanting to be obliterated on the ground in Vietnam, I joined the U.S. Air Force.

The air force also recognized my head for numbers. I received training in the first ever high-tech computerized inventory control system. For the next four years I was again bored and frustrated at work, but my time off was quite the opposite. Before I had left for military duty I had begun to develop a taste for wine and for dining out, which I did with a few close friends and which I continued with a few close military associates.

In the air force, I was lucky to have worked under two particular individuals who really were my superiors both in rank and in experience. Each introduced me to new heights of wine and food enjoyment.

One of the men was a tech sergeant—five stripes—and a Southern black man with a Southern black wife. At their home, I got my first taste of collards and pig parts that I had never heard of, washed down with some of the best-tasting Rhône wines I can remember.

The other man was a warrant officer who had grown up in the old Germantown in upper Manhattan. He introduced me to hot peppers and other spicy foods, paired with Riesling, a grape and wine that, in my opinion, is the most elegant and noble of all.

When the air force discharged me in 1970, I was adrift. All I knew was that working with numbers was no career choice for me. I went back to college to study journalism but soon dropped out for lack of funds. I took a series of inventory control jobs, and I even drove a taxi in New York City for six months. All the while, my love for wine and for knowledge about wine had continued to emerge. It scared a few of my taxi passengers after they discovered the Spanish wine sack that always accompanied me—full at the beginning of my shift, drained by its end.

I began to read about wine, to save bottles and labels from wines I had consumed, to dream about traveling to wine countries. And in the mid-1970s, during a two-year stay in Iran working under contract with a computer company as—what else?—an inventory control advisor to the Iranian air force, I began to get the feel for the ancient roots of grapevine cultivation. During the time I lived in Iran, I made trips to Europe and to wine regions. I also made a decision to direct my energies toward the wine industry.

Back in the United States, I took winemaking classes and began to make wine at home; while holding down an accounting job, I worked part-time at night and on weekends in a local wine shop; I traveled to winemaking regions in America and abroad; I joined a wine association and began to network—to meet wine professionals who lectured at club meetings. In 1984 I made a major leap when I somehow got my wife to agree that we should buy property in the Finger Lakes region of New York State and start up a small winery. I also began what has become a twenty-year career, writing about wine and food.

After closing my winery business in 1993 I first did some wine sales work for a small local winery and then went on the road as a wine salesman for a major East Coast distributor. In that position, I began to notice both the mistakes and the successes of wine retailers. The job also gave me a firsthand view of what at the time had been happening and had been written about: a sharp increase in an interest in wine in America, which led me in 2000 to open, with a partner, a small wine shop in Manhattan.

Finally, I had joined the ranks of what perhaps is really the oldest profession: the wine merchant.

As a wine professional, I understand that wine is an ongoing pursuit. I have never stopped pursuing, and likely will never stop studying, wine. With each new book I read, with each new piece of information I uncover, I find that wine has so much to offer inside and outside the glass.

This chronicle is my attempt to introduce you to what I have learned from others about the historical importance and influence of the wine trade. My task was to glean from the books I have read, and from my personal experience and research, those areas of the wine story that pertain mostly to trade—to the role of merchants, complete with their hardships and their innovations. The story of the wine trade is to me as exciting as any thriller. I hope that by reading this book you will be spurred to dig deeper into other books, the ones that, taken together, provide the complete and glorious history of wine. If you take the bait I promise that you will be richly rewarded, especially if you start your search with my bibliography.

PART I

Origins

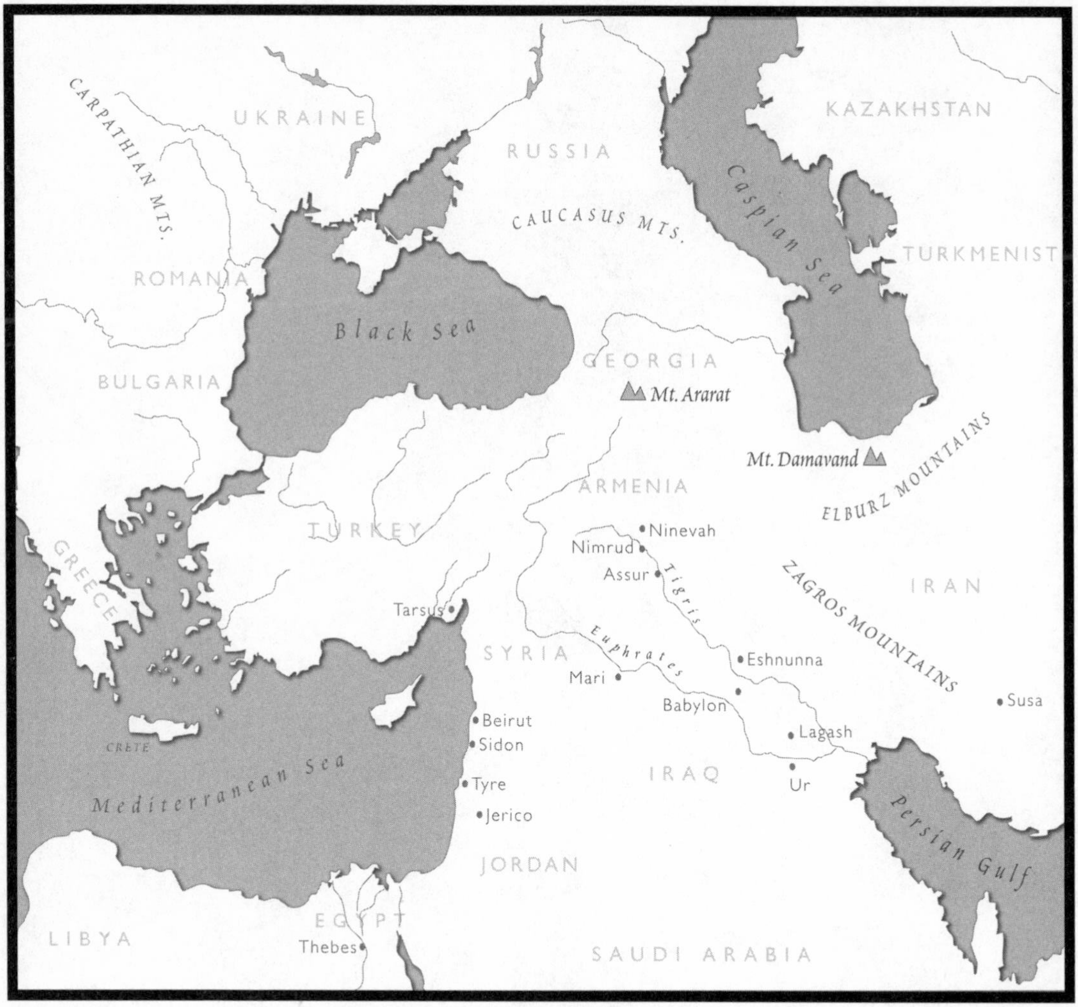

The prehistoric world circa 2000 BC

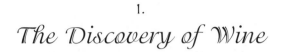

1.

The Discovery of Wine

As intriguing and often exciting as the stories of the origins of viniculture are, this tangled "vineyard" needs to be trod with caution.

—Patrick McGovern, *Ancient Wine: The Search for the Origins of Viniculture*

As March approaches and the snow that covers the Elburz Mountains to the north of Tehran begins to melt, water that is not diverted to reservoirs and cisterns flows violently south and down the city's streets. The Iranian word for the wide-open concrete trench that carries the water is *jube*. It is a sewer system that dates to Alexander the Great and his conquest of the Persian Empire, and if it were not in place, southern Tehran would likely be flooded a few times a year. What begins in March as a quiet trickle, by April becomes a roar; yet, even with all the water flowing from the northern mountains, Tehran—and much of the Near East for that matter—has a desert climate. By mid-summer the *jubes* are nearly dry and only the highest peaks of the mountains are white, like the 18,000-foot Mount Damavand. Dry is generally how things remain until the wet winter season when rain or sleet falls on the city and snow again covers the mountains to the north.

A few hundred miles southwest of Tehran, the 15,000-foot Zagros Mountains separate Iran from Turkey, Armenia, and Iraq; they are not too far east of the biblical Mount Ararat. Like the Elburz Mountains, the Zagros have historically supplied liquid to Iran—but not water. In 1997 an archaeological research team led by Patrick McGovern analyzed pottery vessels from a site they believed to have been the kitchen of a square mud-brick building. Inside the ancient pottery were traces of a residue that proved in the lab to be made up mostly of tartaric acid. McGovern had earlier discovered that grapevines were the only source for tartaric acid in the ancient Middle and Near East, and so the discovery of the acid proved that wine had been stored in that pottery. The team dated the finding to about 5600 BC. At the time, it was the oldest wine-related finding and seemed to suggest that the Persian's ancient ancestors, the Aryans, had something to do with the development of wine. The trouble is, wine could have been developed anywhere between the caves of Europe and the mountains of Iran. In fact, McGovern's archaeological team has more recently discovered a wine storage vessel in the Republic of Georgia. The team dated that finding to eight thousand years ago, making it the oldest by a few hundred years.

These findings take us back to approximately 6000 BC, but grapes have been around much longer than that; in fact, they predate humans. Fossils of a vine genus named *Vitis* survived in subtropical forests of eastern France about 37 million years ago. From there, various subgenera of *Vitis* spread across the globe. By the time humans arrived about 2 million years ago, *Vitis vinifera sylvestris,* a wild grapevine specie, had survived everything, even ice ages, and established itself in the Transcaucusus, in the vicinity of 17,000-foot Mount Ararat.

Grape-seed remnants have been discovered on the European continent in Paleolithic (Stone Age) caves, and they were left there well before the wine residues in the Zagros Mountains. The grape-seed remnants offer little clue as to the form in which the grapes had been consumed. But anyone who makes wine knows that freshly picked grapes will ferment into wine if left untended in a temperate dark place like a wine cellar—or a cave. The grapes would have had on their skins the yeast necessary for fermentation. It is not much of a stretch to imagine that a few curious cave dwellers, mystified by the microbial activity before them, might have tasted the resulting juice and discovered its inexplicable powers over mind and spirit. But we are left to speculate: did the grapes give sustenance to Paleolithics as a dessert of wild fruit and nuts after they ate some wild game, or did the enticing aroma, robust color, and forward flavors of wine accompany their—mostly—meat dinner? Or perhaps a skin of wine was passed around and shared by members of the tribe while they viewed and critiqued the most recent cave drawings.

If available, wine's ability to warm and to make the drabness of cave life palatable would have been among the most pleasing of the hallucinogenics enjoyed by these people. But would it have been traded?

European Paleolithic time is marked by the dual activity of trade and war, the former often being the cause of the latter, which sadly proves how little we have evolved. The nature of the wild grapevine, however, makes it unlikely that wine was a commodity in the Stone Age. Instead, wine would have been quite rare.

Wild grapevines produce either male or female flowers. Male flowers alone cannot produce fruit and female flowers cannot produce fruit until they have been pollinated. Pollination requires a confluence of conditions that include the proper climate, proximity to pollinating insects, and so on. Even when pollination is successful, not all the flowers on a wild female grapevine are pollinated and those that are must then endure potential disease or adverse weather conditions in order for the fruit to survive. In addition, the natural tendency for most wild plants is to produce an excess of leaves and wood as protection for their long-term survival. The more wood and leaf produced, the less chance there is for the development of full, juicy, ripe fruit. Under these conditions, only some of the sparsely pollinated flowers on a wild grapevine survive a growing season, which in the Stone Age would have made fruit production inconsistent and thus rare.

About 12,000 years ago, much of the earth was still cold but starting to warm after the last ice age. Massive ice shields that blanketed the globe from the Alps to the Adirondacks slowly receded. The retreating ice cut into the earth, leaving behind mountains, valleys, and waterways. When Paleolithic cave dwellers went out to hunt and felt the new warmth in the air they must have liked it a lot. Game animals also liked the warming trend; they traveled to better and more distant grazing land, a fact that the hunters probably did not like, as they were forced to wake up earlier and to seek farther afield to find food—a grueling schedule. Their success at putting food on the table surely was far less certain than a weekly paycheck. Large, latter-day Paleolithic communities of hunters covered such great distances to hunt that they began to split and to scatter into many communities. When community groups established themselves across boundaries and across continents it was the beginning of Mesolithic life in Europe and Neolithic life in the Middle East—two periods that converged. Out from their caves and living in a variety of dwellings 10,000 years ago, humans were hunter-gatherers but not for much longer.

Generally, the men hunted and the women gathered. In their gathering role women must have discovered the benefit of growing crops from seed. They probably easily coaxed the men to stay home and put their tool-making talent to use—to make the newly discovered practice of farming less labor intensive. Soon enough, animals were domesticated both to help out on the farm and to provide meals; the development of agriculture was the start of communal village life. Humans made the conversion from hunter-gatherers to farmers somewhere between 8000 and 6000 BC, which is a period that coincides with Patrick McGovern's wine residue discoveries.

2.

Of Water, Wine, and Early Civilization

And a river went out of Eden to water the garden; and from thence it was parted, and became into four heads. The name of the first is Pison. . . . And the name of the second river is Gihon . . . And the name of the third river is Hiddekel. . . And the fourth river is Euphrates.

—Genesis 2

Desertlike conditions exist today between the southeast shores of the Black Sea and northwest of the Persian Gulf, in parts of Turkey, Armenia, Iran, and Iraq, but eight thousand years ago the region was a verdant paradise. What is referred to in the Old Testament as Eden is known in history books as the Fertile Crescent. Prior to World War I, we called the place Mesopotamia; today it is the Middle and Near East.

The placement of the Garden of Eden in Genesis 2 is described as being between four rivers created by a swelling body of water that broke into branches. Geological evidence confirms that flooding did occur often thousands of years ago in the southern Mesopotamian region. Recent geological evidence suggests the flooding can be attributed to an overflowing Mediterranean Sea that, scientists speculate, might account for the sand deposits that now blanket a great deal of the Middle and Near East. Despite periodic devastation through flooding, it was here, near the Euphrates and Tigris rivers, where the practices of agriculture, husbandry, and viticulture probably started.

Ancient Mesopotamians are believed to have migrated from central Asia, settling between the Euphrates and Tigris rivers. One of the earliest groups to settle there called it Sumer—the Land of the Two Rivers. They relied for survival on the bounty of date palms, nut trees, wild vines, and wild grains. Barley was an important crop, important enough for it to be used first as food and later as currency. Although wine is often referred to as the first drink of civilization that title likely belongs to barley beer. Neolithic farmers consumed a lot of beer. (In classical Greek mythology the wine god, Dionysus, is said to have fled from Mesopotamia because its inhabitants preferred beer.) But then McGovern makes the case that split grapes went into the ancient mix to jump-start all fermentations, including beer from barley, dates, and pomegranates.

To prove his case, McGovern makes the important point that grapes were the only fruit of the region that contained the necessary yeast (*Saccharomyces cerevisiae*) that could effectively do the job.

McGovern also points out that the yeast could only start its work when it had access to the sweet pulp inside grape skins, and that could happen only after the skins had been broken. He believes that honey or dates or both went into the mix of most fermentations as sources of added sugar to feed the process.

Wine eventually would be produced from only grapes, but that wine remained rare and revered, used by rulers and high priests, first for spiritual enlightenment and offering to the gods, and then as a valuable trading commodity.

The agrarian Mesopotamian community was hierarchical and patriarchal. The male offspring or relatives of previous male leaders led the Sumerian community. Community rulers controlled the land and allotted portions of it to their subjects. At harvest, the ruler determined how much of the crop went to each family; the rest of the harvest went to him, to his priests, and to trade. Sumerians accumulated great wealth, which facilitated trading among their spreading communities.

The trade portion of a Sumerian harvest that went into warehouses was the responsibility of the ruler's priests. As a community grew, so did the warehouses and the volume of commodities in storage. The principal commodities of Sumer were metals like silver and copper, plus clay pottery produced without the benefit of a potter's wheel. Pretty shell and stone arrangements seem also to have been produced in great quantity. All of it was traded. To control the flow of goods, priests created an inventory system made up of symbols, or pictures (pictographs), etched in clay tablets to represent the items in storage and their quantity. Highly prized wine was stored in the warehouses, too.

Like their Stone Age ancestors, Sumerian families suffered many differences, most of them brought on by disappointment over the distribution of wealth and power. These differences led to the development of breakaway communities. Each new community became both a trading partner and a potential foe. Some of the idyllic landscape that the Sumerians turned into farms also became a place for bivouacking as each community was forced to develop a military for protection. Wars were often sparked by trade disagreements that developed when merchants traveling to distant communities found the local ruling class coveting their wares and their wealth.

A story dated around 2500 BC tells of a series of wars that stemmed from a Sumerian city-state named Lagash. The wars made it necessary for the government to raise taxes to pay for arms. When peacetime returned, the bureaucrats relinquished neither power nor sources of revenue. They also proceeded to diminish the personal rights of the citizenry. To pay the taxes citizens had their boats, cattle, and private important fisheries seized. When a shepherd was forced to have his sheep sheared for wool, he paid an extra tax if it turned out to be white wool. And when the bureaucrats took control of the temple and its grounds, they stole the community's important grain and wine warehouses. A citizen by the name of Urukugina took control. He managed to reduce taxes and to free the culture, but he lasted only a decade or so and Lagash once again sank into devastating wars.

To accommodate these growing complexities of Mesopotamian life the pictographs that started out recording warehouse inventory evolved into a written language we know as cuneiform. The new script was the basis for the first literature, putting into written form what had been passed down for ages in the art of story telling.

A breakthrough cuneiform poem appeared in Babylon around 1800 BC. It was etched in clay and it is among the earliest pieces of literature to have been discovered. The epic poem of Gilgamesh tells of a major civil war in Mesopotamia, but it also tells of a man's journey in an attempt to elude the Babylonian fate of the dead—to spend eternity as a wandering spirit. In an important passage of the poem, Gilgamesh meets with an old ruler named Utanapishtim who recounts the story of a great flood that struck southern Mesopotamia around 5000 BC. The flood forced Utanapishtim to gather his family and flock and to flee upstream along the Two Rivers, to the high ground of the north. This story is a rewrite of a Sumerian tablet discovered in 1914 that was believed to have been one source for the Gilgamesh epic. In the earlier Mesopotamian story, the name of the man who flees from the flood with his flock is Ziusudra. In the book of Genesis, which came later, the man who flees a similar flood is named Noah.

> And the LORD said unto Noah, "Come thou and all thy house into the ark . . . Of every clean beast thou shalt take to thee by sevens, the male and his female: and of beasts that are not clean by two, the male and his female; of fowls also of the air by sevens, the male and the female; to keep seed alive upon the face of all the earth. For yet seven days, and I will cause it to rain upon the earth forty days and forty nights; and every living substance that I have made will I destroy from off the face of the earth."
>
> —Genesis 7

When the dove bearing an olive leaf appeared as a sign that the great floods had receded, Noah found himself on the high, cool plains of Mount Ararat. He quickly got to work to establish his livestock, and to plant a vineyard. Noah's activities offer proof that Mesopotamians valued wine, but if archaeologists are correct that Mount Ararat is a natural home of the wild grapevine species, *Vitis vinifera sylvestris,* why would Noah have had to plant a vineyard there?

Sumerians must have propagated new vineyards first by planting grape seeds or cuttings from wild grapevines. If so, they would have had to live with the inconsistent fruit production of wild vines. But nature is known to produce freaks. In this case, the Sumerians might have noticed some freak vines with both male and female flowers—self-pollinating hermaphrodites. Observant

Sumerian farmers would have noticed that fruit production was consistent from these vines, and they obviously would have wanted to duplicate that situation. They would have abandoned the inconsistent producers and favored seeds or cuttings from the hermaphrodite vines. Judging by the results, that is likely what happened. The transition led to a new and separate grapevine specie, *Vitis vinifera sativum,* the cultivated wine vines that remain in use today throughout the world.

By planting his own grapevines on Mount Ararat, Noah offers proof that ancient Mesopotamians had figured out how to cultivate grapevines.

PART II

From Feeding the Provincial Spirit to Trade

Phoenician trading markets – first millennium BC

The Classic Greek world – circa 600 BC

3.

The Wine Trade Crosses the Seas

Wine and the domesticated Eurasian grapevine had already begun their odyssey southward from the highlands of the Caucasus, Taurus, and Zagros Mountains during the Neolithic period.

—Patrick McGovern, *Ancient Wine: The Search for Ancient Viniculture*

Grapevines survive neither in the Arctic nor at the equator. In places where they do survive, grapevines—and their fruit—can still suffer from temperature extremes. In southern wine regions, where summers can be quite hot, over-ripened grapes can result in limpid, flat juice and wine. On the other hand, grapes grown in a cool climate are naturally high in acidity—sometimes too high in a shortened growing season. The best way to ensure consistently enjoyable wine is through careful grapevine cultivation, by propagating and selecting particular grape varieties suitable for particular climates, through proper site selection for sun exposure and air and water drainage, and by good vine maintenance to manage crop size.

Today, the methods for the best vineyard practices and the most suitable grapevines for specific regions are researched at agricultural universities and extension services across the globe and then made available to the wine industry. In ancient Mesopotamia, research was accomplished by trial and error in the field, and evidence suggests that Mesopotamians knew a thing or two about quality control in the vineyard.

In southern Mesopotamia, where floods were often devastating, farmers laboriously gathered great quantities of earth to build large hills at the top of which they planted grapevines. Their motivation to move enough earth to create these little mountains was in part to protect their crops from flooding but it was also to emulate what had been recognized as favorable growing conditions in the north. Through clashes and rivalry between northern and southern wine regions, history seems to bear witness to the delicacy and thereby more interesting qualities of the former over the latter. Northern Mesopotamian wines were highly prized for being more interesting, more consistent, more delicate, and sometimes longer lasting. The cool northern Mesopotamian evenings, when grapevines require rest from the heat of the day, were in large measure responsible for the success of its wines.

Unfortunately for them, the great effort of southern Mesopotamian viticulturists met with limited success. If periodic flooding did not drown the vines, the continual reconstituting of the soil made it too fertile, resulting in overfeeding of the grapevines' extensive root system. Plus, farmers could not build hills tall enough to duplicate the climatic conditions of the mountainous north. By the time of Babylon, wine production south of those cool mountain ranges had all but been abandoned, but the thirst for wine had not.

In the city-state at Babylon—located not far from the place we know today as Baghdad—hardly any wine was produced, but wine certainly was bought and sold. In the Code of Hammurabi, a Babylonian legal document established around 1800 BC, rules governing the wine trade included a simple punishment for a fraudulent wine seller: he was to be dumped into the river. It was an easy sentence to administer since the trade took place right next to the two great rivers of the region—the Tigris and the Euphrates.

Hammurabi's code also disdained public drunkenness. The drunk and unruly in neighborhood taverns—which were operated mainly by women—were subject to the same fate as frauds.

Trade of all kinds was brisk in Babylon, resulting in a growing merchant citizenry. Much of the economic wealth was in the hands of families who had built fortunes in the wine and spice trades. An account of how wine was handled about four thousand years ago when shipped to Babylon is found in the writings of Herodotus, the controversial fourth-century historian. He described how Armenian traders built a circular raft from animal skin and then made a frame for the raft from willow wood. They placed a layer of straw over the skin to protect it from their cargo, which was wine stored in casks made of date palm wood. Taking with them one donkey, a couple of Armenian salesmen rowed and floated close to the shores of the Tigris. In Babylon, they sold the casks of wine and the frame of the vessel at market. Afterwards, the tradesmen wrapped provisions in the skin, rolled it up, loaded it onto the donkey and set out for home.

By the time of Babylon, Sumerians had reached their nadir and Arabian Semites had become the dominant group some of whom migrated to settle in what is now northern Syria, a mountainous climate quite suitable for grape growing. Wine was shipped down the Euphrates from northern Syria's border with Anatolia (now part of Turkey) to a city called Mari that was later burned by the Babylonians. Various tolls along the Euphrates were charged for the right to pass—a cost that was built into the price of the wine cargo. The cost of the raft on which wine was floated down the river to market was also included. By the time wine from Mari had made it to market the price in shekels was the equivalent of about $12 for a bottle of wine in our modern market. Back then, only kings, queens, and their priests could afford to pay for wine.

The wine-profitable region of Anatolia is where the phrase "eat, drink, and be merry" has its roots, from fourteenth-century BC Hittite culture. At the time, wine traders tracked along caravan routes from Mesopotamia, southwest into Egypt, and east to Asia. The value of that wine is reflected in the high price of vineyard land under Hittite rule, which has been estimated to be as much as forty times over other arable plots. Anyone who did something stupid that resulted in losses, either in the number of vines or in crop size, faced serious corporal or monetary reprisal or both; the severe fines were paid in barley and could exceed six months' worth of income.

The wine trade of northern Syria followed the same caravan routes and was equally profitable. The most revered of Syrian wines was a lush, sweet Chalybion that was shipped from Damascus over mountainous ranges to eagerly awaiting Persian kings. Syrian wines made their way farther east, to what is now Afghanistan and was then part of India, and to northwestern China. But wine in Asia was mostly a curiosity that never became part of the culture, even when it was later traded along the famous Silk Road in the second century BC. Perhaps Asian indifference gave Mesopotamian wine traders more reason to turn their focus to the west and southwest.

One particularly successful group of wine traders—Phoenicians—is believed to have arrived in the Levant from Asia Minor, an area that included north Syria and Turkey. When the Phoenicians settled in what is now Lebanon they quickly saw the trade advantages offered by the shores of the Mediterranean; they were among the earliest to chart the seas. Their wine merchants invested heavily in Hebron, making it a premium wine-producing region.

The Phoenicians and Minoans of Crete may have been the same people—some scholars offer their collective mastery of waterway navigation as proof. Others speculate that the Phoenicians might have been direct descendants of the Canaanites, a wine culture referred to in the Old Testament's book of Numbers.

In Semitic languages like the one Phoenicians spoke, one-word nouns were often used to represent whole phrases that described outstanding or complex attributes. The word *hebron*, stems from the phrase "Valley of Grapes." The modern-day English word "wine" is believed rooted in the Semitic *yain*. In Arabic today the word is *wain*; in Greek it is *oinos*; in the Romance languages *vin, vino, vina, vinho*; Germans say *wein*. The word may have been used to describe the uniqueness of the grape, which is the only fruit that on its own is capable of providing the proper nutrition for the yeast on its skin and sugar in its juice to ferment into a beverage with an alcoholic content beyond 8 percent by volume.

Phoenicians eschewed vast land holdings, preferring instead to establish their homes in great city-states such as Aradus, Beirut, and Sidon. A Phoenician city was often surrounded with small tracts of land, not enough to raise vital grain crops, but just enough for efficient viticulture. Wine merchants traded high-quality wine throughout the Mediterranean for grain and other necessities. Two of the most important Phoenician trading posts were at the world-renowned Byblos, located about midway between Beirut and Tripoli, and at the fortress city of Tyre, where potable water had to be brought in by ship. (Even so, there was plenty of wine to go around.)

Phoenicians set up trading stations along the south coast of Iberia with Celt-Iberians, on Sicily's coast, on other Mediterranean islands, and along the coast of North Africa. In *A History of Wine,* H. Warner Allen recounts an unusual trading practice between Phoenicians and North Africans that he uncovered in the texts of the Greek historian, Herodotus, known for flights of historical fancy. According to Herodotus, Tyrian seamen placed trade goods on a beach at a North African trading site and then withdrew to their ships. They waited off the Mediterranean coast for the North African natives to come down to the beach to examine the goods. If they liked what they saw, the natives placed an amount of gold next to the goods and then they withdrew inland. The Tyrians would go ashore again. If satisfied with the amount of gold offered for their goods they departed, leaving the goods for the natives to take home. If, however, the Phoenician traders thought the goods were worth more, they left the gold there as a signal that they wanted an increased payment, and again they waited off shore, giving the natives time to reconsider and, hopefully, add to the pile of gold.

If Herodotus gave us the facts, then the trade between these two cultures could be viewed as a wonderful morality story of trust. In any event, it must have taken a large amount of gold to satisfy Tyrian Phoenicians; their wine trade produced great wealth for them, so much that it inevitably produced enmity in others. Beginning in the ninth century BC, the Assyrians, believed to have been descendants of Babylonians, went on military expeditions throughout the Near East. In the eighth century BC they hit the Levant with great military might, forcing the merchant-class Phoenicians out of Tyre and taking over the coveted wine trade. Soon thereafter a wine called Byblian, which had vanished from the market during the turmoil, showed up again. But this time Phoenicians had not produced it. The fake Byblian wine had possibly been produced in Greece or in Sicily and the Assyrians had marketed it.

Meanwhile, fleeing Phoenicians established colonies at their old trading posts in North Africa, in Carthage (Tunisia). As they had in the Levant, Phoenician merchants first owned no land in Carthage, preferring instead to lease from the natives, paying the lease fees in kind. But after they had once again amassed great wealth through their wine trade, the new Carthaginians, perhaps learning from history, took ownership of the land and then expanded their wine trade along the western Mediterranean shores of Africa and Europe, a move that put an end to their reliance on what had become a dangerous trade with Assyrian-controlled Tyre and Byblos and in Egypt. At that point, Carthaginian traders took grapevines farther west than any Middle Eastern wine merchants had gone; they traveled to the far reaches of northwest Africa, to the western shores of the Iberian Peninsula, and into the islands of the Atlantic. Some historians claim that Carthaginians even landed in Central America, basing the claim on recently discovered sculptures in Mexico.

The wealth Carthaginians had amassed supported an ever-expanding class of merchant rulers. They eventually gave up the sea and built large landed estates where they grew fat as land-owning oligarchs and gentlemen farmers. They also controlled massive plots of vineyard lands that were worked by slaves. Carthage developed sophisticated, legendary vineyard management practices and for their efforts they reaped great rewards from their wines. It was a success that lasted hundreds of years.

Phoenician/Carthaginian viticulture had also made a great impact on Egypt.

4.

Egypt

And wherefore have ye made us to come up out of Egypt, to bring us in unto this evil place? It is no place of seed, or of figs, or of vines . . .

Numbers 20:5

Forty years is a long time to go without good food and wine, which explains why, despite their escape from oppression and enslavement, the Israelites sometimes despaired over the seemingly endless journey on which Moses led them toward the Promised Land.

When the Israelites re-conquered Canaan they also re-discovered wines that were as fine as any they had known in Egypt—and why not? According to the Bible, Esau brought the Israelites' ancestors into Egypt from Palestine. Coming

A nomadic group known as Rechabites had challenged the Canaanites. *Rechabite* is one-word Semitic noun, meaning a "splendid company of riders." The Rechabites owned only cattle and horses, atop the latter they swept into Mediterranean communities to persuade Semitic peoples toward a life of spirituality, claiming that teeming cities, great wealth and wine were signs of depravity. The Canaanites were unaffected by this argument.

from a place known for its fabulous wine, he certainly would have brought wine with him to Egypt. The Egyptians would have liked that, and perhaps that was how wine had been introduced in Egypt. But archeologists and historians say that Egyptians had imported wine both from Mesopotamia and from the Levant before they began their own wine production; to support the theory, they point out that the Egyptian language had a word for wine before it had a word for the vine.

Egyptians are believed to have controlled a timber-cutting factory at Byblos, cutting the famous Cedars of Lebanon under the reign of Sneferu almost five thousand years ago. The location of the timber factory is also the mythical burial site of the Egyptian god of wine, Osiris, a coincidence that reinforced the belief that the Egyptians had discovered wine through their trade in the Levant. There is further evidence that Egyptians traded in northern Syria, at Tyre, and at Sidon around 3000 BC. Based on evidence McGovern found, in around 1750 BC Palestine export ships delivered hundreds of liters of wine each day to Egypt. Export activity of wine from Canaan alone is estimated to have lasted 250 years, and the shipments were on the order of twenty jars a day containing about thirty liters of wine per jar. The Egyptians traded in exotic tree resins like myrrh, to use as incense, medicine and for embalming. This trade is likely the origin of the ancient practice of adding resin to wine as a preservative; the first excavated evidence of these preservatives in wine appeared on jars bound for Egypt from Palestine.

Wine certainly was precious to the early Egyptian culture, fit mainly for royalty and its court. When they began producing their own wine it was from the king's own vineyards or from vineyards of the temple priests and other nobility. A great deal of Egyptian wine drinking was confined to ceremonial purposes and for elaborate funerals of princes which, based on the volume imported, tells us a lot about royal Egyptian daily life; if they weren't celebrating at court they were mourning. As in Mesopotamia, Egyptian commoners drank juice of fermented barley, or pomegranate and date palm "wine." On special occasions, upper-class Egyptians offered their workers bonuses that might include imported beer or, once in a while, the always-appreciated wines from the Levant.

Also, as in Mesopotamia, periodic floods of the Nile delta demanded great amounts of human labor to raise vineyard plots. The Egyptians proved it was well worth the effort. By the Fifth and Sixth Dynasties, some four thousand years ago, the Nile delta gained official sanction as a wine-producing region of Lower Egypt. The western delta became the premier spot for wine production; local kings in that part of the delta were accustomed to their wives handling the money. With financial control, Egyptian queens of the region engaged in the high-status ventures of commercial wine production and trade.

Egyptian wine production was apparently as sophisticated as in Carthage but with a twist: the orderly and tasteful Egyptians confined much of their well-tended vineyards to walled-in gardens. Their vines were trained to trellis, planted close, and arranged in a colonnade that archaeologists believe was a method to protect against evaporation in the hot environment as well as being an aesthetic: Egyptians were avid gardeners. One particular viticultural innovation credited to ancient Egyptians, and still practiced today, is to subject grapevines to severe pruning during their dormant stage, a practice that decreases wood development and new shoot growth so that the vines' energy could best be reserved for quality fruit production. The practice also helps to lower crop yield—a known way of increasing wine quality.

Egyptian princes retained wealth by trading their best wines. A widely recognized white wine was produced south of Alexandria in the northwest delta, near Lake Mareotis. The wine appears in both Greek and Roman classical literature and it is obvious that the writers had an effect on the status and value of the wines.

Author Tim Unwin notes in *Wine and the Vine* that in the first century BC, the Roman poet Virgil claimed that Mareotic vines were unaccustomed to rich soil, perhaps indicating that wine quality suffered from soil being too fertile. Horace thought Mareotic had negatively affected Cleopatra's brain, and Athenaeus thought Mareotic was "excellent." Although he praised Mareotic, Athenaeus preferred a wine produced southwest of Alexandria: Taeniotic.

Egyptian grapes were harvested into baskets carried by laborers on their heads and shoulders or carried by slaves on a yoke (there is evidence that trained monkeys sometimes assisted in fruit harvests). Table grapes for eating were selectively placed in flat baskets and protected from the sun by a layer of palm leaves. The rest of the grapes were slated for a trip to the winepress—a bag that hung between two poles. After filling the bag with grapes, workers holding the poles walked and turned in opposite directions. The poles squeezed the bag to release juices into a vat that was placed underneath. For larger harvests a stone foot press was placed over a trough. Ropes suspended from rooftops supported laborers as they pushed down on the foot press. Greeks and Romans later used both the bag and the foot press techniques.

In his book, *King Tut's Wine Cellar,* Leonard J. Lasko details wine labels of many early Egyptian dynasties, which, he says, were as informative as modern-day labels—maybe more so. Records of these practices were relatively easy to identify once Egyptian tombs had been discovered and chronicled because wine was one of the important items that accompanied princes on their final journey; it was placed in tombs alongside olives and spices as offerings and for sustenance. One recent excavation points to hundreds of wine jars stored 2,500 years ago in the compound at Thebes of Amenhotep III. From this finding, archeologists learned that the average farming estate that supplied wine to Thebes included ten male children or adolescents, plus eleven adult males to produce annually the equivalent of 48,000 liters of wine. The vineyard estate name, or the name of its owner, was often inscribed on a massive mud stopper that sealed the wine jars, and the wine bottling date was often written down the side of the jars.

The tomb of the Pharaoh, Pepi, of the Sixth Dynasty (2345–2181 BC), included hieroglyphic names on jars of five different kinds of wine. Following Pepi by a thousand years, the tomb of the child king, Tutankhamen, discovered in 1922, included about three dozen wine bottles. More than two dozen of King Tut's bottles had been labeled with the vintage year, name of the estate and, often, the name of the estate's owner and chief vintner—these were the premium wines. Other wines in the tomb were either labeled as of good quality, or they were simply identified by the house that had produced them. This was the Egyptian version of today's *vin de pays* of France or *vino di tavola* of Italy—quaffing wine.

The earliest Egyptian documents referring to the existence of a tax on wine date from about 2500 BC. But where there is a tax there is either a loophole or downright evasion. As wine slowly became part of the economy, the elite shifted the tax burden to a small but growing group of viticulturist farmers who represented neither temple priests nor the state. The ruling class appointed a public official to the job of tasting and evaluating common wine. His title was "Inspector of the Wine Test." Only when it passed his test could the wine be stored or sold. Methods to establish and judge the quality were given official sanction and the taxes were applied according to the level of quality a wine was assigned by the government officials. Better wine equaled higher taxes. Historian Lasko found that in western Thebes the purpose of the wine was often written on labels, such as *"wine for offerings," "wine for merrymaking," "wine for a happy return."* One particular purpose he found on a label hints at potential tax fraud. Egyptian vintners were supposed to pay state taxes in cash or in jewels, yet the particular label that Lasko had found read, *"wine for taxes,"* which the author assumes to have been a bribe.

Egyptian wine production remained largely part of the foundation of the wealth of kingdoms and princedoms, yet the wine trade between Egypt and the Levant produced great wealth in Palestine for hundreds of years. In the twelfth century BC, however, the reigning Ramesses III engaged in military campaigns into the Levant, weakening and then cutting down the wine trade. Soon thereafter, a new and dynamic wine trade had emerged across the Mediterranean.

5.

Classical Greece and Etruria

Behold, God's son is come into this land
Of Thebes, even I, Dionysus, whom the brand
Of Heaven's hot splendor lit to life, when she
Who bore me, Cadmus' daughter, Semele, died here.
So, changed in shape from God to man . . .

—Euripides: *The Bacchae*

When you get off the plane at Athens airport the first thing you notice is that this is not a quiet place. If they are anything, Greeks are a bustling, energetic people with a love for life mingled with a sense of foreboding. Perhaps they are entitled to seem to be carrying the weight of the world. After all, Greece is where philosophy, democracy, and pharmacy have their origins. One particular cultural development the Greeks can be proud of is the concept of three square meals a day, with wine, of course. They had established that pattern by the time of Homer.

By Homer's time—the eighth century BC—the cult of Dionysus had not yet spread into Greek life. Even so, wine had already become a common drink. In fact, Homeric Greeks may have been too serious about wine. In the *Odyssey*, after the fall of Troy, Odysseus sailed north to the coast of Thrace. His crew sacked the town and then proceeded to consume the local wine for some hours. The crew's preoccupation with gathering up wine gave the locals time to regroup and fight back with great force. Crewmembers who managed to escape to the ships did so in spite of the extra time it took them to periodically stop to gather up plenty more of the local wine while they retreated.

Written three hundred years after Homer, a most important character in Euripides' *The Bacchae* is the god of wine, Dionysus, offspring of the god Zeus and Semele, a mortal woman. Semele had bid Zeus to visit her, not in earthly form but as an immortal god. Zeus arrived as a bolt of lightening that killed Semele but not her fetus. Zeus took the child from her womb and sewed it into his thigh; then, he fled to the fabled Mount Nysa, in Asia Minor to give birth to the Vine, the immortal Dionysus.

In *The Bacchae,* Euripides tells us that Cadmus was Semele's father. The historical Cadmus was a Phoenician, and the man who founded the Grecian city of Thebes. Cadmus also lived for a time in Thrace. Despite having had wild grapevines nearby, the Greek love of wine was less the result of a natural tendency than it was something that they had learned from their Phoenician trading partners at Thrace around 1300 BC Although Greeks considered Thracians barbarians, they traded grain and oil with them for gold, silver, and Phoenician wine.

The earliest literary evidence regarding Greek agriculture dates to the seventh century BC. In *Works and Days,* Hesiod confirmed the existence of a vibrant viticultural and winemaking chunk of the Greek economy. He described practices such as vine pruning, timing of the vintage and even a brief mention of vinification methods, as well as the benefits of the amphora, a large airtight pottery vessel that came to a point at its bottom to stick in the earth for storage. In the hold of Greek ships, long planks with holes cut into them held the pointed ends of amphorae during their merchant voyage. (When the efficient Egyptians emptied an imported wine amphora they often saved it to use for carrying and storing water.)

In cultures that preceded Greek ascendancy wine had been the drink of rulers and high priests. By Hesiod's time, a century after Homer, Greeks from the lower to the upper rungs of society had regular access to wine as a basic daily food. Wherever Greeks traveled to expand their colonial power, viticulture traveled with them: to Macedonia for the great wines of Acanthus and Mende; east to the Asias; west to the Italic peninsula; and through such Greek islands as like Rhodos, Lesbos, and an island where the wines had been deemed superior, Homer's birthplace, Chios.

Under Roman rule, in the second century, the author Athenaeus published *Banquet of the Sophists*. In the book, he claimed that Chios was where the written dinner menu had been introduced. He noted that a custom developed on the island that once diners had reclined they were given a "tablet" listing the dishes the cook would be presenting; obviously, one or more of Chios's famed wines surely accompanied these earliest menus.

Greeks landed on the shores of the Italic peninsula between 1000 and 800 BC. As they navigated its massive Adriatic and Mediterranean coastline, the

Greeks must have been overwhelmed by what appeared to be a vast, verdant island of rolling hills. When they ventured into these hills, Greeks encountered Indo-European shepherds. In the southern part of the peninsula, in a region rich with grapevines, the people who lived there preferred dairy.

At first, the Greeks traded wine and grain for local cheese. Over the following centuries, Greek colonies sprang up at places like Cumae near Naples, and Syracuse in Sicily. Superior grain and wine were produced at each Greek outpost. Soon Mediterranean traffic in grain, wine, and olive oil became the commercial thread that held Greece's colonies together.

On the Greek mainland, the picture was no different. A Hellenic family farm sustained the household with crops of grains, olives, and vines. Paradoxically, the measure of distinction of a citizen of Classical Greece had become his leisure time. Freedom from work allowed Greeks to think and to engage in military and civic activities, which formed the basis for Greek democracy. Slaves performed the bulk of the labor on mainland family farms and their efficiency produced surplus crops. As the Greek city-state system grew, encircled by rural farms, the new urbanity created greater demand for wine and the family farms exported their surplus to the cities.

Athenian commoners bought from street vendors cheap wine that the merchants had cut with seawater. In an effort to ensure high quality some wealthy Athenians tried their hand at viticulture, but not many; the Greek form of high culture included a large measure of status-consciousness. Wealthy Athenians generally considered imports superior to domestic products. The island colonies were their preferred wine suppliers. Mountain viticulture on the islands was responsible for the highest quality; in the Peloponnese, the southern part of the Greek mainland, wines waiting to be shipped to the valuable mainland market were buried in mountain snow to keep them cool and preserved.

Secure in the knowledge that fraud was kept in check by the authorities,

H. Warner Allen claims that between the sixth and second centuries BC, well before the advent of the printing press, colonies and protectorates doing business with Greece were reminded daily of the extensive Greek wine export trade by vine and wine symbols, logos, and descriptions imprinted on coins. The images and designs used on the coins were duplicated for use on wine amphorae seals and stoppers.

the elite paid a high price in Athens for their prized island wines, which they drank neat. They knew that at Thasos, a strategic Greek island facing the boundary between Macedonia and Thrace, the law prohibited merchants from watering down wine, nor were they allowed to sell small quantities of wine in large containers; and before they could sell any wine at all, they had to seal it inside a large-mouthed, airtight *pithoi* (amphora). Merchants paid a hefty fine if caught selling either grape juice or wine on consignment or on futures, while the crop was still on the vine. To ensure the true origin of local wine, traffic in foreign wine was forbidden on board Thasian ships. Greeks knew that most of these types of wine regulations had been duplicated and strictly enforced on all the Aegean islands.

Some historians credit the Greeks with being the first people to set sails on large ships. While it is true that many of the ancients before Classical Greece mainly floated and used oars for locomotion, staying close to the shoreline, the Phoenicians made their way to Cadiz, about fifteen hundred or so years before the birth of Christ, from their base in Carthage. It seems unlikely they floated that distance using oars. In any event, Phoenician vessels surely had not been as large as third-century BC Greek ships, which averaged up to five hundred tons. Two or three sailing masts had become common by then. Trading ships were made of wood, were as much as sixty feet long, and had deep hulls to hold a large volume of amphorae that had to be stood upright and through holes in platforms during passage. The ships' sails were stationary; with no way to work the sails, Greeks situated the ships with their backs to the wind. Without a steering mechanism, their sailing was hardly ever in a straight line but more resembled a herringbone pattern, which required covering the distance of two trips for every one, and obviously increased the cost of the wine onboard.

When they founded Massilia (Marseilles) in the sixth century BC the Greeks established the first commercial wine trade in Gaul. From there they traded wine throughout Gallic territory, through the Mediterranean, and to the Black Sea, as well as to Egypt. A century later they added the Danube region to their trade routes.

By the third century BC the philosopher Theophrastus, who was the first to document agricultural plant life, published an account of Greek viticulture in his largely philosophical but also practical book, *Causes of Plants*. In this work, Theophrastus explained the grapevine's makeup and environmental needs and also techniques for its propagation and pruning. He identified certain vineyard pests and diseases. He recommended which soil suited which grapevine and he advised cultivating methods that included the certainly controversial practice of planting grapevines on low ground and in regular rows over relatively flat plains as it was commonly believed that higher elevation, mountainous vineyards produced the highest quality wines. In any event, many of his recommended viticultural practices were in effect in the Greek wine regions that enjoyed the highest status; much of Theophrastus's practices resembled the viticulture of Carthage.

In the second century AD Athenaeus listed premium Greek wine regions that were believed to still be following the viticultural practices recommended by Theophrastus five hundred years earlier: Chios, Thasos, Peparethos, Mende, Icaria, Euboea, Naxos, Rhodos, Corcyra, and Lesbos. Lesbos became famous for its seductively sweet Pramnian Essence, produced from the juice that ran free under the grapes' own weight. The wine was fortified with honey, and it is the source of Nestor's Cup that was served to him in Book XI of Homer's *Iliad*. Pramnian Essence maintained its mythical status for healing wounds and was consumed by Alexander the Great of Macedon (and his father before him) for that purpose.

When the historian Herodotus recounted in the fifth century BC the Greek landing in the southern region of the Italic peninsula, he referred to the region as Oenotria (the land of vines). By Herodotus's time, the Greeks had introduced dozens of grape varieties to the south and no one is sure whether the historian was referring to the abundance of vines that he saw or to the abundance of vines that the Greeks saw when they first set eyes on the land. No matter: Greek influence in Sicily was responsible for great quantities of highly regarded Sicilian wines, much of which was being shipped to Gaul, despite the fact that the Greeks had earlier established a wine industry at Massilia. In contrast to the advice of Theophrastus, the grapes were grown in mountain areas, yet Sicilian wine was better and in more demand than the Massilian wines of the flat, hot plains. This rivalry between Sicily and Gaul was the precursor of rivalries between Italic and Gallic wine merchants that would develop under Roman rule. But before that day came, both Greeks and Romans were forced to deal with a particular group of people that had settled in the northern part of the Italic peninsula.

Semele, mother of Dionysus, was also the mythological mother of the Etruscan wine god with the incredible name of Fluflunss. The Etruscans, who seem to have originated in Asia Minor, had settled in the northern reaches of the Italic peninsula in about 900 BC.

Visitors to northern Italy, especially Tuscany, often talk about the beauty of the stone and masonry work in the region. Those Tuscan bridges, pathways, and building foundations are the only things that remain of the industrious, superstitious, mysterious group of settlers who lived north of the Tibor and Arno rivers for half a millennium. Of all the ancient groups that have inhabited the earth, the Etruscans have to be counted among the most mysterious.

The poet Virgil said the Etruscans descended from Aeneas, after his flight from the battle of Troy. Some historians speculate that the Etruscans were direct descendents of the Phoenicians, which would have made them all or in part Semitic. This belief might stem from a later alliance between Etruscans and Carthaginians, the latter having certainly been direct descendents of Phoenicians, or it may be the result of the Etruscans' historical seafaring prowess, a trait shared with Phoenicians and Minoans.

Linguists view the written Etruscan language as a close relative of the Greek alphabet, yet its grammar was unlike any other regional language of the period. More important, Etruscan culture was not like Greek culture. Greeks sought knowledge and refinement; Etruscans worked and played hard (the Bacchic cult had its roots in Etruria). Yet the difference in languages and the fact that Greeks considered Etruscans barbarous did nothing to prevent the two from engaging in mutual trade. Etruscan wealth was built on mining rather than on agriculture, trading with Greeks (as well as Latins and North Africans) for food with the iron, copper, tin, silver, and lead that they mined in the mountainous north of the peninsula. It is believed that some Greek wine traders had established enclaves inside Etruria, and this may be how Etruscans came to viticulture.

In the *Aeneid*, Virgils' first-century BC account of the Etruscan defeat in Latium, Etruria's King Caere surrenders an entire vintage to the Romans. Surely by Virgil's time Romans appreciated the thought of a vintage being surrendered as a spoil of war, but Romans four hundred years before Virgil had yet to embrace wine. There is a theory in academic circles that at the same time that the Republic of Rome had begun to emerge, Western Europe entered into a five-hundred-year climate shift that brought warmer, more hospitable weather to the north. According to this theory, the climate shift was instrumental in establishing Roman interest in viticulture. Perhaps, but it appears that Virgil's account of wine having been passed from Etruscans to Romans may contain a kernel of truth.

Early Romans were simple agrarians and dairy farmers. True to his Roman roots, Romulus, the fabled part-founder of Rome, is said to have made the libation to the gods with milk. Like the Greeks, Romans harbored a certain distaste for the Etruscans, and especially for their religious belief in the importance of the hereafter; Romans took more seriously the religion of the here and now. They did, however, adopt divination, the Etruscan religious practice of reading the entrails of animals for signs to foretell the future and know the will of the gods. You have to wonder if the Etruscans missed a few signs of the entrails, the ones that might have forewarned of disaster facing them in 509 BC. That was the year the Etruscan king Tarquin was booted out of Rome and the republic was born. True to their simple dairy roots, in the early laws of the Roman Republic women and men under thirty were prohibited from consuming wine. Of course, none of that foolishness lasted for very long.

Known as "the emperor who shook," Roman emperor Claudius was born with birth defects. Everyone thought he lacked intelligence, but he was quite learned and he spoke a few languages, Etruscan among them. Claudius is the last known person to have spoken Etruscan; when he died in AD 51 it was the end of the Caesar bloodline (Caesar being a family surname that only later became a word for "king") as well as the end of the Etruscan language.

When, in the fourth century BC, war broke out between the major powers of the peninsula—Celts in Gaul, Romans, and Etruscans—the Celts kept the Romans in check as they pushed the Etruscans east to the Adriatic coast. Although 250-year-old vineyards had been wiped out as a consequence of the battle that stretched across a vast region in the Po Valley and rice became the major crop there, the culture of the vine managed to survive in the north; both Romans and Greeks took over what vineyards remained after the Celts finally got pushed out.

Even though the Romans revolted against them and, like the Greeks, considered them barbarous, it would be foolish to dismiss the Etruscan influence over Rome. Etruscans built the city, complete with pavement and sewers, and then made Rome the crossroads of their trade. They gave to Rome the twelve-month calendar, the practice of using surnames, the craft of vase making, engineering prowess, and the concept of military strategy; Rome excelled at the last two endeavors. The Etruscans also left vineyards behind and probably viticulturists who worked for Romans.

After winning a military victory, Romans built on their strength by forgiving their enemies and thereby creating loyalty and alliances. They did the same for the Etruscans, tolerating them and allowing them to live out their existence at their new home along the Adriatic for a few hundred years, until they allied themselves with an enemy of Rome.

Part III:

Rome

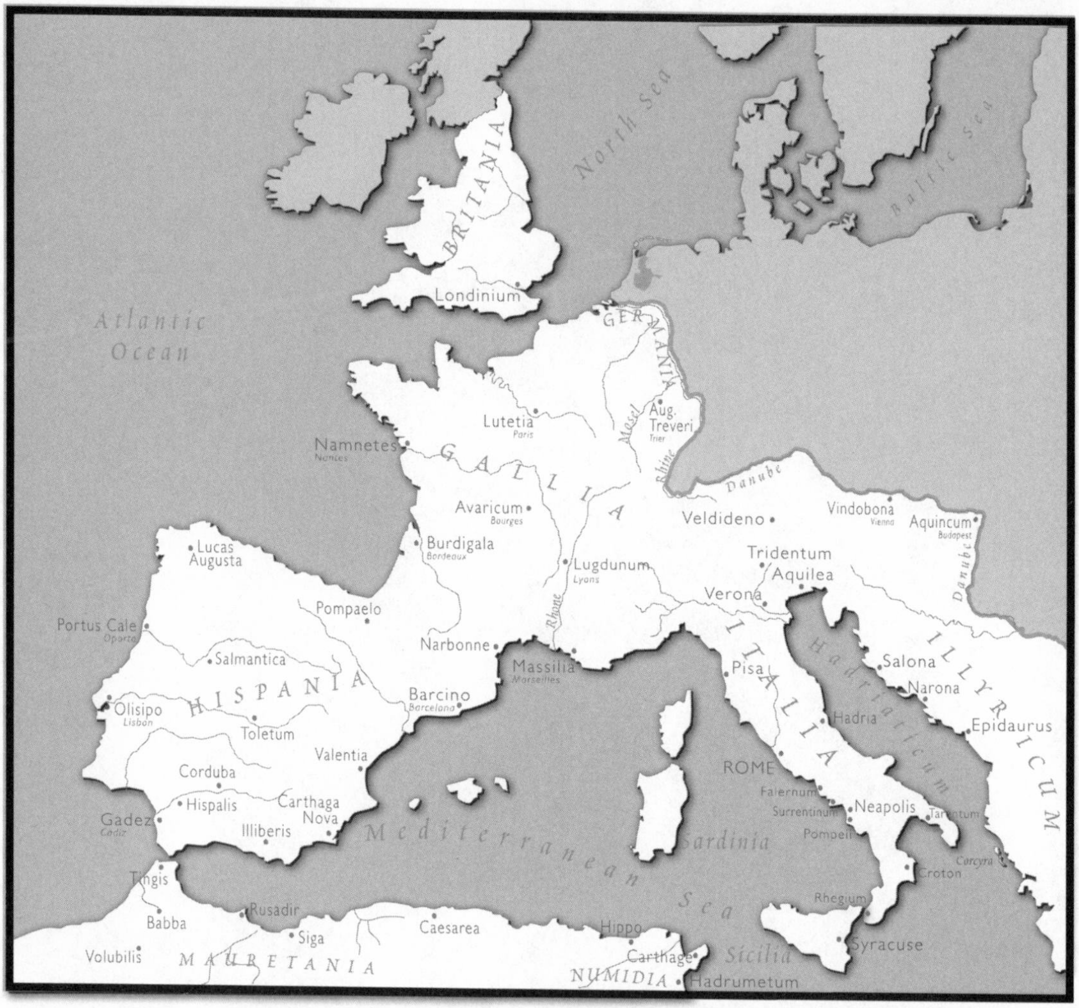

Western Roman Empire, first century AD

6.

The Rise

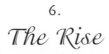

Gather the early grapes when they are quite ripe, rejecting the berries which are moldy or damaged. Fix in the ground forks or stakes four feet apart for supporting reeds and yoke them together with poles, then put reeds on the top of them and spread out the grapes in the sun, covering them at night so that the dew may not fall on them. When they have dried, pluck the berries and throw them into a barrel or wine jar and add the best possible must thereto so that the grapes are submerged. When they have absorbed the must and are saturated with it, on the sixth day put them all together in a bag and squeeze them in a wine press and remove the raisin wine. Next tread the wineskins, adding fresh must, made from other grapes that you have dried for three days in the sun; then mix together and put the whole kneaded mass under the press and immediately put this raisin-wine of the second pressing in sealed vessels so that it may not become too rough; then, twenty or thirty days later, when it has finished fermenting, strain it into other vessels and plaster down the lids immediately and cover them with skins . . .

—Lucius Columella, first century Roman agrarian

Having no infrastructure of its own, the early Roman Republic had little ability to trade. Grain shortages immediately sent its economy into depression. Guided by its policy of keeping the gods happy, Rome managed to steady itself by administering oaths of honor among citizens and soldiers not to steal or slack off, for fear of stirring the gods against them. It took alliances with other Latin states for the republic to come out of its economic woes. Meanwhile, Greece was still an economic force in grain, olives, and wine from its southern Italic peninsula colonies.

Roman viticulture was first concentrated in the areas that once were Etruria and it was but a small segment of Roman farming. Citizens consumed home-grown wines and the new Roman elite drank prized Greek wines. But by observing the success of the Greek wine trade, the diligent Romans slowly came to understand wine's commercial possibilities; they began to study Greek technical and economic documents pertaining to the wine trade.

By the sixth century BC Rome had penetrated into just about all the Italic peninsula and Sicily. It also traded, reluctantly, with Carthage. Greece had recently lost its grain production supremacy to Carthage and, in response, a chief Greek civil servant named Solon had created legislation in Attica designed to strengthen its olive industry. Over the next few hundred years, no longer involved in grain production, the Greeks dominated olive production in the Mediterranean. They also continued to supply wine to a growing Roman culture, but their overall economic power was already in decline, ready to be subsumed by Rome.

Over the next few centuries, as they pushed their way into power along

> The three major wars between Rome and Carthage are referred to as the Punic Wars, derived from the Latin Poeni, the word for Phoenician. In one of the wars, the Carthaginian Hannibal proved a formidable, but not unbeatable, foe.

the Italic peninsula and beyond in search of further economic and colonial advantage, Romans took a sinister interest in the efficient and commercially successful Carthage on the coast of North Africa. In the middle of the third century BC, Rome invaded Carthage, ostensibly to help protect Mamertine mercenaries in Sicily. The war lasted about two decades before Rome managed to pierce Carthage's superior sea power. Having gained Sicily, Rome quickly usurped grain production from its new colony to feed its growing population and legions.

About fifty years later Carthage and Rome fought again, this time over Iberia, which was under the command of the young Hannibal. The fierce Hannibal led armies right into Roman territory on the peninsula, trampling much with his elephants—including vineyards—for sixteen years before he was defeated. Rome's ultimate victory over Hannibal solidified its dominant power over the known Western world, but that did not mean Rome was suddenly omnipotent. The war with Hannibal also created conditions for a long series of civil wars that led ultimately to the fall of the Roman Republic and the rise of a new Roman Empire—but that was still in the future. After the second defeat of Carthage, wine's destiny hinged on Roman hegemony.

While Rome spent the next half-century expanding into the Hellenistic world and brutalizing Iberia into submission, Carthage rebuilt its commercial power, but it owed a war debt to Rome, and it had given a promise not to engage in further wars. Still, there were Romans who hated them, and waited for a chance to clear the globe of Carthaginians. The next opportunity came in 149 BC, after Carthage went to war with Numidia. Rome had been an instigator in the war, and it used the situation as an excuse to sack and burn Carthage into near extinction within three years. Cato the Elder, a Roman senator of the second century BC, was among the faction particularly vicious in its desire to destroy Carthage. He never forgot the devastation of Hannibal's army in the north and he likely despised, as many did, the apparent mercantile genius of Carthage. Cato ended every speech he made in the Senate with a shout: "Carthage must be destroyed." Cato's invective delivered in the Senate just before the invasion of Carthage was instrumental in starting the third Punic War. In 124 BC, Rome and Carthage fought for the last time; this time it was over the trading port at Massilia. The clash put an end to Carthage and to the small remaining number of Etruscans, who had allied with those staunch enemies of Rome.

Among the spoils of war Romans found in Carthage was a book on agriculture that had been written by a man who shared the name of Hannibal's brother and military leader, Mago. But this Mago was a gentleman farmer and, although his book does not survive today, successive Roman agronomists and viticulturists studied and followed it. They put into practice his methods of planting, fertilizing, irrigating, and pruning vines.

Mago's instructions included an important section on the treatment of slaves on the farm as depreciable equipment. He also laid out a plan for efficient and quite intensive land use. Two hundred years following the discovery of Mago's book, during one of many periods of Roman vineyard expansion, the prominent agronomist, Columella, paid homage to Carthaginian viticulture, calling it the basis for all viticulture in the Mediterranean. In fact, the recipe that begins this chapter had been lifted by Columella from Mago's book on agriculture.

Cato the Elder was not only a Roman senator, he was also a gentleman farmer and prolific writer. He, too, published a farming manual that is today the earliest surviving text written in Latin. In *de Agri Cultura* (*Of Things Agricultural*), Cato, who despised Carthage so much, presents a beautiful irony in that he nearly mimics Mago's agricultural instructions. Like Mago, Cato's viticultural section includes detailed information regarding the nature of the vineyard, equipment needs and maintenance, the work calendar, propagation, grafting, transplanting and pruning, share-cropping, methods of vinification, recipes for different types of wine, how to market the vintage and, again, an extremely important message on how to handle vineyard slaves.

Cato instructs Roman farmers to provide slaves with at least seven amphorae of wine per year—about three hundred of today's standard 750-milliliter bottles. At first glance, it appears Cato is beneficent, if not modern, but his was practical advice for the time. Wine had become essential to Romans, not only for a healthy body but also for a healthy economy. Since much of the Roman economy was built on slavery, proper handling of slaves (as a depreciable asset) was also essential.

Following the Greek model, early Roman vineyards had been developed on small subsistence farms. If there were surplus grape crops on the family farms, an ever-expanding urban population soon evolved to absorb them. Recognizing that fact, Cato wrote a section in his agricultural book specifically on the profitable planting and care of vines near urban centers.

Rome was giving preference to cheap grain imported from its North African and Sicilian colonies, and that policy had hurt established mainland Roman grain farmers. Cato's book persuaded many of those farmers to switch to vineyards. Although vineyards were more expensive to operate than other kinds of farming, he assured the grain farmers who switched that their investment in vines would be profitable. He claimed that the overall profit from vines during the period would be the highest of any crop in the republic.

When Carthage fell, the average Roman vineyard size was about fifty acres. In just a few decades, with the help of Cato's instructions, that average had risen to one hundred acres; but the income realized from vineyards was not what Cato had promised. With the loss of value in their wheat and barley crops to the southern islands, small Roman farmers on the mainland had also lost their ability to raise capital. In spite of increased vineyard planting to meet growing demand, and in spite of rising wine prices, vineyards proved to be much more expensive to operate than either Cato had promised or anyone had imagined. Many family farms were finally seized by moneylenders, which placed them under the control of wealthy Roman bankers and politicians, consolidating small vineyards into larger properties. Wine was on its way toward becoming big business in Rome—bad news for the Greeks.

When the Roman Republic was emerging, 75 percent of Greek citizens of the period had been small farmers. Although its wine trade was widespread, the Greek model did not include large commercial farming. In Sparta, serfdom was the rule, and vineyards were part of a wealthy owner's vast holdings. In parts of Attica, tenant farming was practiced. So long as vineyards were kept in good order, leases to tenants were long and nearly unbreakable by law. But when a lease was within a few years of its legal end, landowners had the right to send their own experts into the vineyards to work and to ensure that they were in the best condition to offer to the next interested tenant.

This concentration of small vineyard farming persisted in Greece for centuries becoming a problem only after Rome established itself as a regional power. Although Greek wine remained in demand for about three hundred years after the Roman Republic was born, Greek family winegrowers systematically lost markets to Romans and their financial investments in viticulture. Soon, a viticultural breakthrough in Rome spelled the end for Greek wine dominance.

The year of Opimius, the Roman consul who built the Temple of Concord, was 121 BC. That year a few wealthy gentlemen farmers released to the market superior single-vineyard Roman wines from the once major Greek colonial holdings of Puglia, Lucania, and Campania.

From the Campanian hills, from one of the vineyards that had been trampled by Hannibal and his legions, came the most famous wines of 121 BC: Falernum.

Falernum comprised three vineyard sites: Caucinian, at the top of the hills; Faustian—considered the best—on the slopes of the hills; Falernian proper, resting at the foot of the hills. It began as a relatively small operation with limited expansion possibilities, and remained that way for quite some time. The price for Falernum wines soared. Only the wealthy, the noble and the well connected had access to these wines, but commoners were not left out of the new Roman wine explosion.

A great deal of other southern wines became famous at Pompeii and at Cumae. Pompeii became one of the most important wine centers of the period, with wineshops crowding its paved sidewalks. Archeologists digging among the volcanic ruins of Pompeii have uncovered and identified no fewer than two hundred taverns, some still showing wine prices posted on their walls. The wine was good at Pompeii; a lot of it could be had in the taverns in bulk form right out of the amphora.

As the Roman amphora came to a point at its bottom, the hole in the counter allowed for an amphora to fit into it so that it could be swiveled forward. When customers stepped up to the bar to order, bartenders would draw wine directly from an amphora by tilting the large storage container down to pour from it.

The Roman wine boom of 121 BC left the Greeks with the olive as their last source of economic strength, Over the next century the Italic peninsula and the islands to its immediate south produced the superior wines of the Mediterranean. In 70 AD Pliny wrote that there were about eighty wines worthy of note throughout the realm, and about sixty of them had been produced on the southern Italic peninsula and in Sicily. This was no small feat. By that time the empire had included wine producing regions from Egypt in North Africa, to Iberia, to southern Gaul, to the Aegean islands, and to Anatolia and farther east to Syria.

During this period, Romans popularized the screw press.

Based on the old foot press, the screw press included a large beam, a slab of stone and a screw. The beam stretched perhaps fifteen to twenty feet and had a hole cut out in its middle through which was fitted a large screw. The beam was hung with ropes above a large vat into which went tons of picked grapes. At the base of the beam was a large stone cut to fit the inner circumference of the vat. The vat likely was lined either with cloth or porous clay to act as a filter that held back pulp and pips. Controlled by ropes and pulleys, the beam and stone started out at the top of the press and was lowered in increments; it took from six to eight slaves to operate the press. Three or four of them on either side of the screw, with their arms spread out and over the beam, slowly walked in a clockwise rotation bringing the stone to bear on the grapes to press the juice out. The juice ran out the bottom of the vat into a trough and then settled in a smaller vat. Another set of slaves scooped the juice with pottery and then dumped it into large vessels to begin fermentation. The vessels were buried in the earth nearly to their tops in order to maintain a stable temperature.

"An objection sometimes made to vineyards is that their costs eat up the profit." This sentiment could have been written just weeks ago, but, according

> A replica of the Roman screw press exists today at Mas des Tourelles, a family winery located along the southern Rhône, five kilometers east of Beaucaire, between Languedoc and Provence, near some of the oldest viticultural sites in France. The winery offers "mulsum" taken from a recipe found in writings by Pliny.

to Unwin, it was written in 37 BC by Marcus Varro. The economy had inflated almost fourfold between 37 BC and the middle of the first century AD; therefore, the cost of production had become the hot topic in Roman viticulture.

Following Cato's more than one-hundred-year-old strict rules governing the sale of grape crops, subsistence and tenant farmers picked their crop, vinified and then stored their wine for however long it took to mature before putting it on the market. Holding a vintage for a few years in amphorae ensured that well-made wines were ready to drink when they reached the market, but it was quite an expensive practice. By Varro's time, the inflationary economy had started to squeeze small wine producers. Varro believed he knew how to help them. He felt that Roman viticulture had been too labor intensive and costly. He believed that the Iberian method of vine pruning was the most promising for small Roman winegrowers—this was of course the Carthaginian method that had been brought to Iberia.

Varro suggested that Romans train vines on the ground without supports other than maybe some sticks to hold the weight of developing fruit. Many farmers who followed his advice saw cost savings. They spread the word and soon Varro enjoyed a good reputation, which gave him the confidence to make further suggestions. He was not keen on the common practice of growing various grapes under the same conditions. He believed that individual grapes truly required individual treatment. As proof, he singled out the vineyards of

Falernum: nearly one hundred years after their rise to prominence, according to Varro, Falernian wines could be aged for complexity yet still offer finesse because the grapes grown at each site were given separate, individual, care. He recommended a system of vine selection based on a combination of climate, topography, and grape-growing techniques. Modern-day French winegrowers refer to this concept in one word: *terroir.* The word refers to the particular nature of a particular site, how the site's climate and micro climate, its setting, and its soil influence what a wine becomes.

Following Varro's lead, Columella published a twelve-book series on agriculture; he covered grapes and vineyards in books three, four, and five. Columella's book established his reputation as a vine consultant. In that role he supervised new grape vines and grape variety plantings across the empire. In one section of his third book he identified grape varieties whose performance in the vineyard he felt could be measured as a direct result of location. Although a shift toward large company vineyard holdings was in full sway, Columella stubbornly urged that small vineyard operations—about five acres—had the potential for producing wines in both large quantities and high quality. He also estimated that the potential return on investing in small viticulture could be as lofty as 33 percent or more. Quite often, Columella's idealism proved to be just that, yet he was still instrumental in viticultural improvements that decreased production costs in both small and large vineyards. While profits did improve, it was mainly a benefit found in large vineyards at the expense of wine quality.

What made Romans listen to Varro and Columella was the tremendous importance of wine as a daily food throughout the empire. It had become a considerable economic force and Romans believed it also improved their health. But the same inflation that was hurting small farmers in the first century had also begun to make wine too expensive for the general populace. When the average cost for a daily ration of wine exceeded that of a daily ration of bread in Pompeii riots ensued.

With small growers unable to lower their prices, wealthy financiers and large companies stepped in to appropriate vineyards and then change the way things were to be done. The financiers engaged in a practice that the Greeks at Thasos once considered an invitation to perpetrate fraud and to lower quality: Roman merchants made deals with contractors to buy crops that were still on the vine, and that had to be off the property by a set date. To live up their end of the bargain, contractors sent in crews at harvest time to pick and to ferment as quickly as they could. These investors had no patience for holding large inventories. Aging the wine was out of the question. They sold the wine quickly and profitably and without thought to its quality.

In Falernum the size of the overall vineyard plot became a drag on profits. Even though prices for the wines had reached wild heights, without more vines to increase production inflation threatened to outpace profits. Somehow, the most famous small vineyard of the empire managed to offer more and more of its wines. Unsuspecting Romans paid dearly for inferior wine that was being passed off as Falernian. The fraud even touched some government officials. When it reached Pliny the Elder and he referred to Falernian wine as merely second-class, a three-hundred-year run at the top had ended for Falernum.

Wine quality certainly fell, but inexpensive wine flooded the market. When the riots stopped, the government found so much excess in the market that it bought up wine to dole out to the general population in a kind of welfare program. This solution was similar to one developed earlier to handle problems with excess wheat from the south. When the government doled out wheat, the effect was to lessen its value and drive farmers out of business. The wine welfare program threatened to do the same thing to viticulture. The government, of course, did not pay market prices. Despite their vast production, large wine merchants were soon forced to search for ways to increase profits. Many of them looked to Gaul to solve their problems. The price of an amphora of wine in the province of Gaul at the time was much higher than it was in Rome. The perception of wine from the province had gained status in Rome. Roman merchants figured they stood to make a lot of money off their connections by exporting the better wines from Gaul, and that is what they did for a long time.

Then, Julius Caesar tinkered with the Roman caste system and, later, Emperor Augustus revamped laws to make freemen of slaves. Each time, a wave of emigrating Romans from rural farms filled towns and villages.

In the second century new citizens filled up urban centers and then spent lots of money on wine. The descendants of expatriate wine merchants who had earlier fled to Gaul to increase profits saw the shift in available disposable income as an opportunity to abandon Gaul for the Italic peninsula. Once again, the market for wine grew to great proportions. But within a generation Rome was faced with another serious wine shortage. To the horror of the Roman merchants, the shortage opened floodgates of wine from Iberia, Greece and—irony of ironies—from Gaul.

7.

Into Darkness

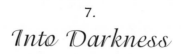

In the second century of the Christian era, the Empire of Rome comprehended the fairest part of the earth, and the most civilized portion of mankind.

—Edward Gibbon: *The Decline and Fall of the Roman Empire*

It is estimated that early Romans lost as much as 10 percent of their wine to the bacteria that causes wine to turn to vinegar. Over the centuries, agrarian experts like Cato, Columella and Varro found ways to improve the important product, but preservation methods were crude.

Wine was stored in thoroughly cleaned pottery amphorae with various additions of olive oil, resin, seawater, or plain salt to preserve it; the opening of the amphora was sealed either with wax or with rags. When the father of the famous ancient physician, Galen, discovered the preservative benefits of sulfur dioxide in the second century, the substance was used to preserve some wines, too, creating better longevity. For the first time, Rome could apply wine taxes on the basis of quality. Trained Roman wine tasters were sent into the field to make quality assessments and to assign taxes due: the higher the quality, the higher the taxes.

Wine taxes were sometimes paid in kind, which helped establish government reserves that went toward sustaining the wine welfare system. The government used some of the wine as gifts to allies and also as bribes to barbarians threatening along the borders.

Roman taxes were assessed in the provinces on separate districts, leaving it to the inhabitants to divvy up and send the money to Rome. This was during a time of growing political and social turmoil—civil wars threatened the entire realm. The Roman economy endured crisis after crisis, precipitating wide swings of under production and over production of wine. It became increasingly easy for a district to corrupt trained tasters sent into the field to assess taxes. Corruption created tax arrears, but the government found itself helpless and it certainly could not put a stop to the wine welfare system for fear of creating even more turmoil. And then there was the problem of Gaul.

From the time the Greeks had established vineyards at Marseille, Gallic wine had been considered mediocre. After Julius Caesar conquered the Celts in Gaul in the first century BC, communities established along the Rhône and Rhine rivers became depositories for large shipments of wine amphorae that regularly made their way to the region so that they could be traded mainly for wood and honey. The Celts, having come late to wine, saw it as a luxury item believing that—since elite Romans treasured wine—having it must reflect high social status.

Many local Celts, who had been given the job of tax collecting for Rome, offloaded the amphorae and had the wine emptied into their own wooden barrels for storage. The tax collectors became wine collectors so that they could boost their social standing. This is also the first sign that the Gauls preferred wooden barrels to amphorae for storage. Yet even before Caesar's victory viticulture had been established along the Rhône.

The Roman province and influential business center of Narbonne, at the mouth of the river, became an established viticultural site with a growing reputation for quality. From there, viticulture embarked on a slow but steady advance to the north, along the course of the river, with increasingly better wine quality. Some first-century Campanian wine merchants understood the potential threat from Gaul. To put a stop to Gallic wine imports they claimed to the government in Rome that vineyard plantings in the provinces led to neglect of grain production, which was true to some degree. Responding to the merchants, Emperor Domitian issued an edict in AD 92 ordering immediate reduction of vineyard acreage in the provinces: vineyards throughout the empire were to be uprooted and new plantings halted. To the Campanian merchants' delight, the first impact of the edict was to artificially increase the price of their wines; but to their dismay, the emperor's decree was only partially implemented. Gaul was still a threat.

Three large Italic merchant shipping associations formed to protect themselves against the turmoil of the times. Two of the shippers divided control of Adriatic and eastern Mediterranean ports. Figuring that if wine was going to be exported from Gaul they would at least be there to exert control over its flow, the third merchant association established itself north of the Rhône River. But when Rome came under increasing pressure from religious wars and barbarian invasions, Italic merchants at Lyon lost their grip. After they departed, Rhône winegrowers picked up the northern territory and rapidly advanced winegrowing into Burgundy.

In the year 212 the notoriously outrageous emperor Caracalla issued an edict that made citizens out of most freemen of the empire. With Rome again in financial trouble, and with its internal structure punctured, the emperor needed money. He thought that by creating so many new citizens he would increase the tax rolls. His action created further turmoil in the wine industry.

Vine cultivation had always been a privilege enjoyed only by Roman citizens. Caracalla's edict added scores of naturalized citizens who were free to establish vineyards, and many of them did. This new batch of winegrowers had bypassed cities, spreading themselves throughout the Italic peninsula. The situation caused yet another wine glut that helped to reduce both prices and quality. The glut had prevented Gallic wines from being exported to the Italic peninsula, but because Roman wine merchants no longer had investments in Gaul, local wine merchants of the Rhône and Burgundy gained free rein to operate on the empire's eastern borders.

In the early days of the republic, Rome flourished by building loyalty throughout its holdings. By the latter part of the third century, the disarray caused by overtaxation, increased corruption, and a series of strange emperors had created disloyalty throughout the Roman Empire. To some extent, the vagaries of the third century Roman wine industry foretold the fall of the Empire, even though that event was still a few hundred years away; in the meanwhile, Roman emperors continued to expand their realm.

The emperor Probus was neither economist nor businessman. He was mainly a warrior who made known to barbarians the consequences of crossing Roman borders. He was always hopeful that his severe methods would scare men into abandoning wars and armies and becoming loyal to Rome—he was often wrong. Probus also knew the value of viticulture to Rome, even if he did not know the best way to reap that harvest.

In the year 280 Probus issued an edict to expand viticulture. Like Caracalla before him, Probus created a wine glut. Prices plummeted again. It took a few decades for prices to rise and for merchants to feel safe enough to reinvest their money in wine. During that time, Probus went east, farther than any Roman had gone before, into the Teutonic territory of the Rhine and Danube regions. He set up a new capital city at Trier; he also opened a road that would one day be used against Rome.

The farther their armies traveled, the harder it was for the central government in Rome to maintain contact, and since Rome was experiencing major economic problems as well as military failures, many Roman armies in the field went unpaid for long periods of time. Fearful that they would be left stranded in barbarian lands, legions began to turn on their leaders. To keep his legions from entertaining mutiny, Probus put them to work planting and cultivating vines in the Moselle Valley.

During Emperor Probus's reign, viticulture in Gaul became more sophisticated and widespread. Vines flourished on Gaul's western border at Bordeaux and along the southern regions, including Languedoc, Narbonnes, and Marseille. The aggressive Burgundians also cultivated throughout the Rhône and Burgundy regions.

Gaul had positioned itself for a long run of wine dominance in Europe.

If it be possible, as far as in you lies, be at peace with all men.

—Romans 12:18

When the apostle spoke to the Romans, Christians were being persecuted in Rome. Although Christ's time on earth had been brief, the impact of his ministry grew steadily over the following centuries. By the fourth century Christianity had grown widely, following the Roman roads throughout Europe, Africa, and the Middle East; but there was no chance of peace between Christians and the Roman government.

Already weakened by civil disobedience and civil wars, Rome was dealt a serious blow by Constantine's Christian legions that he had based on the eastern fringes of the empire. Victorious, Constantine established himself in Anatolia, at the city of Byzantium, which was named in the seventh century BC by Greek colonists after their king Byzas.

Constantine changed the name of the city to Constantinople and from there he built a new Roman Empire. Although weak and but a shadow of its once powerful self, Rome coexisted with the new Eastern Holy Roman Empire until what remained of the original empire was overrun in the fifth century by barbarian invasions from the northeast, along those roads that Probus had opened to Rome.

Grade school teachers across the United States used to instruct children that the period following Rome's fall was the Dark Ages, a name that brings up images of gray, gloomy sadness—an apt description of Western Europe in that period. As cities and provinces lost the security that Rome had given them, the disarray created mass movements of people and wide sweeps of diseases and plagues.

From the eastern borders of Gaul to the western borders of Iberia separate warring kingdoms littered the land with the dead. All previous knowledge was threatened, too; economic instability created crippling poverty. The export markets that had been highly profitable under Roman rule had been obliterated. The once efficient Roman wine trade was dead. But the connection between wine and civilization was too old and too widespread for the fruit of the vine to simply fade into oblivion with an empire.

Written between AD 70 and 100, during a time of vineyard uprooting, the

New Testament certainly put forth a few strong cases for the vineyard and for wine. In the fourth book of the Gospels, the apostle John recounts the story of Christ's first miracle: changing water into wine to prolong the wedding feast at Cana. By so doing, Christ gave recognition to wine's sacred and celebratory status. The New Testament was originally written in the language of literature of the period—Greek. Perhaps that is why in chapter 15, the apostle John's account so closely relates to the mythology of Dionysus. John gives us Christ as "the True Vine," and his father as "the Vine-dresser." But there is no better example of the crucial connection between wine and Christianity than in the ritual reenactment of Christ's Last Supper: the faithful take bread as a symbol of his flesh and they drink wine as the symbol of his blood. This ritual alone made it imperative for priests and bishops of the early Christian church to secure a continuing flow of wine—and so Christians were employed in the service of wine.

Like the priests of ancient Mesopotamia, Christian monks became the main keepers of literature, farming, and general cultural activities during the so-called Dark Ages.

Viticulture was the main activity at the monastery founded in Gaza in the fourth century by an Egyptian Coptic monk named Hilarion. He had been exiled from Egypt and arrived in Gaza to serve the Christian empire. By the time of the fifth century, Gaza and Jerusalem had become the Christian Holy Land, where the faithful from Europe and from empire headquarters at Byzantium made pilgrimages. Some pilgrims carried back home with them wine produced from vineyards that had been planted by Hilarion and his monks. When the quality of that wine was recognized, the ancient eastern Mediterranean wine trade routes became active once again. Wine production was reestablished at what became the crossroads of Christianity: Greece, Turkey, Syria, and all of Palestine. Sweet Greek and Turkish wines, especially, were in overwhelming demand at central markets in Constantinople.

In the sixth century, a Roman ex-aristocrat—Flavius Cassiodorus—wound up serving a barbarian tribe on the northern Italic peninsula. When the Byzantines later arrived to push the barbarians out they found a territory that had been reduced to poverty. Anarchy had threatened all scientific knowledge so they also found little viticulture. Perhaps if Cassiodorus had stayed he might have helped rebuild the region. But he saw the period as a threat to science and to the mellifluous Latin language. He thought he could do something about it, but he did not want anyone to discover his Roman aristocratic roots. Cassiodorus went south to Squillace, where he established a Christian hermitage and monastery; then he took on the task of making it the center for the preservation of Roman literature and all its documented sciences, including viticulture.

Other descendants of the Roman aristocracy did not choose to live Cassiodorus's cloistered life. Many of them used this dark period to work themselves into new positions as petty rulers across Western Europe, in parts of the old empire. A great deal of this nascent royalty kept vineyards for personal consumption. They used wine to entertain their guests at elaborate castle feasts where they regularly formed and broke alliances. Some, when facing death after a life of warring over land borders, hoped for spiritual salvation, so they gave away parts of their vineyard properties to the monasteries that were being formed throughout Europe. Soon, control over the reborn wine trade had fallen into the hands of the monks. The great abbeys and monasteries of Christian orders were vital to whatever economic stability there was during the period.

Then, in the seventh century, a new religion exploded on the scene in the East.

Satan seeks to stir up enmity and hatred among you by means of wine and

> gambling, and to keep you from the remembrance of Allah and from your prayers. Will you not abstain from them?
>
> —*The Koran*, Sura 5:91

According to legend, Muhammad, while on a journey by foot, came upon a noisy, joyous Arab village. He asked a local man what it was that made the people so happy. The man told him that a wedding had taken place that day and now everyone was celebrating over some local wine. Muhammad made note of the joy that the wine had brought to the people, expecting that it might be a good idea to mention it to his followers.

On his way back, as he passed through the village where the wedding had taken place a few days before, Muhammad found the street littered with debris, injured men and perhaps a corpse or two. When he asked what it was that made this happy place come to such disaster he was told that the men over-indulged in wine, started to argue, and broke out fighting.

Muhammad supposedly decided on the spot that wine's power for mayhem outstripped its ability to create joy and he concluded that this is what he should let his followers know.

Legend notwithstanding, it is no accident that the English word *alcohol* comes from the Arabic *al kohl*. Drinking and gambling were strong diversions in the East. Muhammad knew that to command the attention of the faithful he had to reduce or eliminate those diversions. At the same time, Muhammad was a prophet who knew prevailing scriptures and so he must have known the value of the vine. That value was reflected numerous times throughout the Judaic Bible and the Christian texts of the Apostles and it is reflected in three separate passages of the Koran, as translated by N. J. Dawood. A most important one makes this promise to the faithful: *"This is the paradise which the righteous have been promised. There shall flow in it rivers of unpolluted water, and rivers of milk forever fresh; rivers of delectable wine and rivers of clearest honey."* (Sura XLVII. 15).

Some argue that the Koran does not ban alcohol use but merely attempts to discourage it. Indeed, wine has been prominent in the works of Islamic literary figures such as Omar Khayyam and Hafiz. Yet, as with all religions, interpretation is what matters. Contemporary interpretation of the Koran creates a general prohibition against the use of alcohol. And so the rise of Islam in the seventh century portended the death of the Middle Eastern wine trade, a trade that had been renewed only one hundred years before.

In its early religious wars, Islamic conquests included the whole Persian Empire and a great deal of the Byzantine Empire in the southern and eastern Mediterranean regions, which of course included Palestine. Caught in the middle, Constantinople was cut off from the West early on as it resisted numerous Muslim invasions. As battles between Christians and Muslims waged through succeeding centuries vineyards were often caught in the middle as well. Although the Koran did not prohibit grape growing, Muslim zealots often uprooted vineyards on their campaigns to prevent Christians from producing wine and to hurt them economically.

Through their conquests in North Africa, eighth-century Muslims entered Europe by way of southern Iberia. The Franks who inhabited the other side of the Pyrenees Mountains, and who kept the Christian traditions of winemaking alive, prevented Muslims from entering northern Europe. The prevailing wisdom is that viticulture and winemaking suffered in Iberia after the conquering Islamic Moors confined grape growing to the production of large, sweet table grapes, supposedly unsuitable for wine. There is evidence, however, that wine was produced under the Moors in Spain; the most potent evidence is the existence of *alembic distillation,* what we know today as brandy and for which the base product is wine. Historians have also noted an illicit wine trade between Muslims and Christians all the way into the Middle Ages, when Christian monks would send wine to Muslim Turkey labeling it "mineral water." At the same time, ships from Genoa sneaked wine from Crete into Muslim-dominated Egypt.

In a telling modern-day example of the hold on Islamic culture exerted by vineyards, Islamic cleric-controlled Iran at the end of the twentieth century was ranked sixth in world vineyard acreage, more than Germany, Portugal, Greece, Argentina, Chile, Hungary, or Australia. As to the use for Iran's estimated 667,000 acres of vines that year, we are left to speculate, but we should not forget King Jamsheed's decree at Persepolis!

Outside the Christian monastery walls, Western Europe was in chaos. Inside, it was not unusual to find a fine-tuned operation of multiple farms run by hundreds of monks. With no major European mercantile trading centers, orderly monasteries and abbeys became the center both for industry and for handicrafts. They existed in what today is Italy, France, Germany, Austria, Iberia, Switzerland, Britain, Ireland, and throughout parts of Central and Eastern Europe. Over time many monasteries developed into small cities.

> Peasants gave over their land and their labor for in-kind payments from the monks. This economic system helped to maintain needed stability in Europe between the sixth and twelfth centuries. Unfortunately, the system also laid the foundation for the system of feudalism that took root in the early Middle Ages.

In the ninth century, monasteries were on their way toward becoming the biggest landholders in Western Europe. They certainly were the biggest wine producers, and remained as such throughout the Middle Ages. Their legend lives in some of the most famous European wine appellations: Clos de Vougeot, Morey-St. Denis, Quincy, Lacrima Christi, Priorato, Steinberg, and hundreds more.

The abbeys required tremendous amounts of wine to service their growing populations and to service the numerous guests and travelers whom the monks hosted; until the very end of the Middle Ages monasteries offered the only lodging available to travelers.

One famous abbey, St.-Germain-des-Pres, in Paris, was reported to have produced an annual 11,000 gallons of wine to service hundreds of monks and probably thousands of pilgrims and travelers at communion and at dinner. This kind of operation was common even on the Île-de-France, where numerous vineyards were under the royal monastery at St.-Denis, just outside of Paris. In Germany and in Hungary a large part of tenth- and eleventh-century viticulture was under the control of Benedictine nuns.

In their role as the centers for commerce and as holy places, the abbeys offered peasants protection from the warring factions outside their walls. Although Islam had cut off the flow of wine from Byzantium to Gaza, Christian pilgrims still sought to visit the Holy Land. In the twelfth century, warrior monks known as Templars and Hospitallers took responsibility for the pilgrims; the former fought their battles for them, while the latter kept them warm and comfortable in lodges set up along the traveled routes. From those lodges came the concept of hospitality as well as the establishment of the hospice and the hospital.

Wine was also a kind of currency to the warrior monks. They sold wine they had produced to raise funds for war and they dispensed great amounts of wine provisions to their legions. If there were wine shortfalls, the monks extracted payments of wine from aristocrats and from sedentary monastic monks inside the monasteries that had been producing great wealth. In fact, the wealth in those monasteries reached such proportions that it spawned a new class of nobility; at the same time, it laid the foundation for the establishment of a Christian state religion across Europe.

PART IV

Northern Europe Seizes the Wine Trade

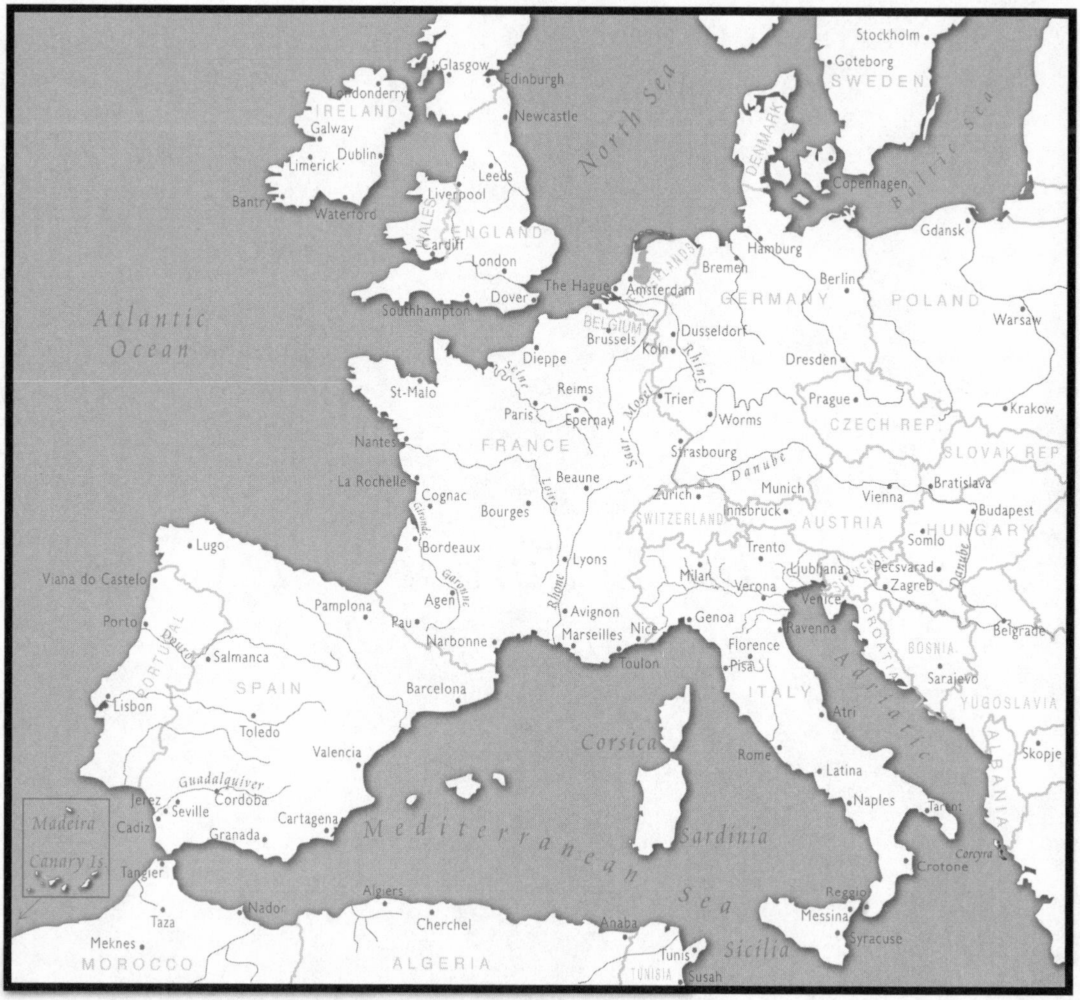

Northern Europe, circa AD 1400

8.

The French, Germans, and Hungarians

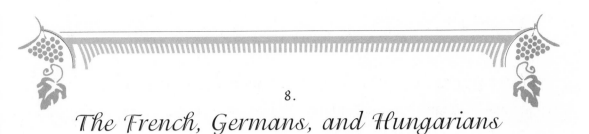

The result of economic stability seemed always to create conditions for an active wine trade.

—Edward Hyams, *Dionysus: A Social History of the Wine Vine*

During the waning days of its empire, the fiercely nationalistic Franks, Burgundians, and Normans had created a great deal of trouble for Rome. After Rome, the variety of European kingdoms that these groups had established throughout the continent were often better at fueling flames than at running national states. Economically, conditions were erratic at best. Trade and politics became regularly entangled with arrogance, greed, and the fire of nationalism, all of which played out for generations in interminable wars that culminated in the revolutions of the eighteenth century.

Despite the seemingly endless turmoil, there were periods of economic stability.

With monasteries at the center of commerce, trading in wine became a powerful economic force that led into the early Middle Ages. Despite the cooler, harsher climates of northern European abbeys, the talents of monks and northern nobility began to displace Mediterranean wine merchants. Vineyard plantings of the period far into northern Europe brought to fruition what Pliny had presumed about the region centuries earlier when he commented on the potential delicacy and finesse of northern wines; they were lower in alcohol, higher in acidity, and more refined than the forward, strong, alcoholic southern wines, which often had to be cut with water to be palatable. The northern wines were produced from vines that had been propagated to withstand cooler more erratic climates, the result of large-scale vine grafting at monasteries between the ninth and twelfth centuries.

Modern viticulturists know that large bodies of water act to moderate air temperature during seasonal transitions that might do damage either to budding vines in the spring or ripening fruit in the fall. Perhaps medieval traders were aware of the climatic benefit of being near bodies of water like the Rhône, Rhine, Gironde, and Garonne rivers, but they more likely chose those sites for reasons of transport. Overland transport was expensive and, considering the bands of marauders and myriad warring kingdoms during the period, overland transport was also dangerous.

Any transport of product took a lot of time, a situation that once created storage problems for the Roman province of Gaul. For centuries pottery had been the main vessel in which wine was stored and shipped. The Greek and Roman amphora provided as close to an impervious vessel as was possible, so long as the opening at its top was sealed tightly.

Abundant with dense northern forests, the Gauls preferred wooden vessels instead of pottery. Unfortunately, many long journeys of wine in barrels from Gaul to the Italic peninsula had been ruined in winter when wine froze and burst right through the barrels. The barrels weren't sealed well either, so as wine expanded in the summer heat, a lot of it leaked out. After the fall of Rome, the Franks of Gaul still had these problems with barrels, but the chaos of the period had created a shortage of pottery. The new France's wine merchants upgraded the design of barrel cooperage methods to make handling less cumbersome and, more important, to seal the barrels more tightly from the weather. As the French grew more and more important in the wine trade, wooden casks became more acceptable to all European wine merchants. Yet, the weather still posed problems so the French simply changed the way business was done: they held winter orders until spring and summer orders were shipped in the fall.

Meanwhile, Charlemagne, arguably one of the great kings of history, was generous in land grants to Christian monks of the ninth century. His land gifts became a driving force behind the wealth, power, and longevity of Teutonic monasteries. To help ensure the quality of German wines, Charlemagne produced a series of regulations to govern their production and distribution, and, of course, to ensure a tax revenue stream. Without a powerful Roman or Mediterranean wine trade as competition, the German wine trade might have been instrumental in setting the stage for economic stability. The German proximity to northern European markets was crucial, especially proximity to the British market; the few vineyards that Romans had earlier planted in Britain had been lost during the Empire's turmoil, but the British did not lose their thirst for wine.

As smart as he was, Charlemagne had not taken sufficient notice when the British expressed an interest in northwestern parts of Europe that were held by the French. Under Charlemagne's nose the French were about to make inroads in the wine trade with Britain, despite the fact that under Otto the Great, who succeeded Charlemagne by a hundred years, Germany would still be exporting wine to England. Over the long run, the French merchant infiltration into England won them preferential tax treatment and loosened trade restrictions, but not without a fight.

In the twelfth century, England's Henry II had gotten control of vineyards in Bordeaux and the Loire through marriage to Eleanor of Aquitaine, which of course helped solidify ties between Britain and the wines from both northwestern and southwestern France; tax abatements to the Bordelais were considerable. Nevertheless, Henry loved wines from the Moselle/Ruwer river region of Germany.

There is a record of a correspondence between Henry and German Emperor Frederick in which the British crown declares undivided closeness, not to mention safe trade, between the two nations. Henry administered an unexpected blow to the French when he saw to it that their German counterparts were protected from extensive taxation. He administered a further blow when he decreed that German wine merchants would receive the same favorable trade terms that had applied to the French at Bordeaux. Germany soon developed intense wine trading with England at the expense of the French. Among the special privileges given to German merchants in England was the right to their own trade guild—the Steelyard—in London and also in parts of the British countryside.

British merchants with ties to Bordeaux felt Henry had gone overboard in his treatment of German traders; uprisings and acts of sabotage against German shipments followed.

While German wine merchants dealt both with French displeasure and with British merchants tied to Bordeaux, a new threat to their wine trade had developed in Eastern Europe.

In Classical Greek mythology the Danube Valley is home to the son of Dionysus, but we know that it wasn't until Emperor Probus's third-century foray into the Balkans that large-scale commercial wine production made its way across the Danube region and into what is now Hungary. After defeating barbarians in Germany, Probus's restless, rebellious legions had done in Hungary what they had done earlier along the Rhine—plant vineyards. But by then the end for Rome was imminent. Probus's fears about his soldiers suffering neglect had become reality, and they staged mutinies. Once beloved by his army, Probus was murdered by soldiers in vineyards that some say were the very ones that later supplied the famous Tokaj wine region and its thick, sweet dessert wines. That the famous vineyards at Tokaj survived what has come to be known as the Great Migrations is a mystery; even Attila the Hun once established himself among the rolling hills of its vineyards.

The vacuum that mutinous Roman legions left was filled with massive movements of people across the Danube Valley. Wars and conquests plagued the Danube region and were catalysts for the growth of new settlements. Two particular migrant groups played a role in these wars and settlements and, by extension, in the expansion of viticulture across the Danube region.

Like the Huns who trampled and marauded, the Magyars were fierce and often victorious; they perpetrated raids throughout Byzantium, in the western Mediterranean, and as far as to the Swiss Alps.

In the wake of the Magyars, the Kaliz, a group of farmers and merchants, followed. They revived and cultivated the old Roman vineyards of Europe that the Magyars had neglected to trample. The industrious Kaliz settlements grew into important trade routes between Hungary and northern Europe.

After myriad Magyar raids and internal dynastic wars, Christianity finally took hold in Hungary. The Magyars converted to Christianity in the eleventh century.

The first Christian king of Hungary, Stephen, established an abbey at the small hillside location of Somlo near the western border. Wine production then flourished in Hungary as many of the monks arrived from Germany and some from Italy and France. Hungarian wines developed a stellar reputation among the ruling class: dukes were obliged to take at least one glass of wine from Somlo on their wedding night to ensure the production of a male heir. King Stephen had even set up a wine-producing Benedictine abbey at Pécsvárad in the south, in the valley of the Kaliz.

To the consternation of German wine merchants, a great deal of Hungarian wine began to make its way into the German market.

Surely some of the Roman nobility situated at the capital city of Trier had fled their homes along the Danube during the dying days of the empire, and some of them must have found their way into Hungary. The speculation is that the ones who possessed viticultural knowledge applied it to serve Christian monasteries and Hungarian kings. That is how the Roman recipe for the famous ancient Greek wine, Pramnian Essence, is believed to have made its way to Tokaj.

The Romans had produced the wine from overripe grapes that, instead of being pressed for juice, were allowed to rest in vats. The weight of the grapes was used as a natural press, allowing the juice to trickle freely to the bottom and into a vat. The resulting sweet wine produced from the juice became, and remains, one of the most sought-after dessert wines ever produced, and by the late Middle Ages it had given Hungary solid footing in the wine export trade.

The forgotten colony of Romania, located next door to Hungary, had also been planted to vineyards by Roman legions. After Hungary gained control over Romania in the eleventh century, King Stephen used it mainly as a buffer between the Christian West and Islam, a situation that has been blamed for keeping Romania from establishing an identity, which is perhaps true. It certainly is true that Hungarian dominance purposely kept the Romanian wine trade from flourishing.

By the twelfth century, the wine trades of France, Germany, and Hungary had become powerful and competitive economic forces. Germany gained an edge in the thirteenth century, when Tatar invasions from the east crippled the Hungarian wine trade along the Danube for centuries thereafter. Still cultivated—often secretly—by Christian holy orders and their subjects, Hungarian wines were for the most part consumed by Hungarians.

As Hungary began to reemerge in the fourteenth century it once again threatened to flood the German market, but it seemed unable to duplicate its earlier success. Germany was given another opportunity, in Britain, as the French trading relationship there was about to devolve into a series of skirmishes that would lead to war.

9.

The Middle Ages

The central and most sophisticated territory of the wine-vine seems always to correspond to the central and most sophisticated territory of Western civilization at any given time.

—Edward Hyams, *Dionysus: A Social History of the Wine Vine*

In Europe, "the central and most sophisticated territory" continues to change. But if today's wine merchants prove as resilient as their medieval counterparts they should be just fine.

The turmoil created by the medieval clash between Christianity and Islam gained new momentum when the Ottoman Empire emerged in the fourteenth century. Deep wounds had been cut into trade of all kinds by religious crusades yet, by the close of the Middle Ages, the wine trade may have been more vibrant than it had ever been, in part because of a near doubling of the European population between the ninth and eleventh centuries.

To meet the population growth, both agriculture and other commerce went into expansion. Commercial growth in England and in Flanders had produced a wealthy merchant class that was serviced by equally powerful and wealthy Genoese shippers and Florentine financiers, almost always tied to the rulers of individual states and often by family ties.

Manufacture and industrial companies that produced textile and other hard goods purposely set up trading centers close to populous cities. Soon enough money exchanges sprang up in the cities. Reasonably centrally located, Lombardy and Tuscany developed into two of the most successful trading cities, attracting wealthy and powerfully connected Flemish, French, German, and Baltic merchants.

Most northern European governments welcomed—embraced—the greater tax revenues that brisk trade provided. England, for instance, reaped a gold mine in taxes from Bordeaux through textile exports and wine imports. The wine trade with England produced many wealthy French merchants as well. When problems threatened the lucrative trade they were often caused by the monarchy of one or the other country, which was generally a reflection of dysfunctional family relations. For instance, the French monarch, Louis VII, was Eleanor of Aquitaine's first husband and, according to Eleanor, he was also a familial relative. He and subsequent French monarchs held a lasting grudge over the loss of Bordeaux and Gascony to England. The Bordeaux wine trade caused more and more French farmers to switch from grain to vineyards, threatening Gascony's food supply. Louis once antagonized both French and British wine merchants by directing Gascony merchants to reroute close to 40 percent of their wine to trade for grain in northern France and in Flanders.

Trade between Britain and Bordeaux was more like an elitist activity

> The British referred to the wines of Bordeaux as *claret,* some say because the wines were the clearest they had ever seen in Britain—but that may be conjecture. In reference to Bordeaux wines, claret made its appearance in England around the sixteenth century. The Bordelais, however, did not start clarifying their wines with the protein of egg white until the seventeenth century. When Britain gained the Bordeaux territory in the twelfth century, the Bordelais were producing a wine that they called *clairet,* which may very well be the source of the word *claret.*

between wealthy merchants. In most of the rest of Europe trade was built on the backs of peasants.

In the thirteenth century a mushrooming of noble wealth resulted in a new crop of lords and landlords who happily had on their hands an exploding population to exploit. Using as their guide the economic system that Christian monasteries had instituted, European nobles developed the system we know as feudalism, which was especially reliant on agriculture.

Land was the greatest of assets, transferable only by marriage or by conquest, not to mention chicanery. For peasants, feudalism was quite a barrier against moving up the economic ladder. For the privilege of working the lord's land, serfs at the bottom of the ladder turned over as much as half their crops, grapes for wine included. Wealthy landlords sold the virtually free wine in equally wealthy northern city markets, and they became not only wealthier for it but the valuable wine helped them to solidify and maintain political connections.

Peasants who barely could afford food certainly could not afford their own grape presses. After providing vineyard work and harvest labor, and then making and transporting the wine, tenant farmers were forced to pay rent to the landlord if they wanted to use the press to process their small share of the crop.

As a result, serfs hardly ever tasted the fruits of their labor in the vineyard. But serfs did consume alcohol—according to Fernand Braudel, in *The Structures of Everyday Life: Civilization* and *Capitalism, 15th–18th Century,* alcohol was one of the main sources of calories for the medieval poor; it was also a palliative against the drudgery of their condition. Peasants in the Alps and the Dolomites developed a way to use the pulp, *graspe,* that was left over after grape pressing and for which the landlord had no use. With some water and sweetener added, the *graspe* was fermented and then distilled to make the potent drink we know today as *grappa.*

Many peasants also drank beer that they had brewed at home, and the authorities sometimes allowed them to sell their surplus beer. In England, a law stated that ale could be sold from someone's home but only if a sign hung outside to call attention to the seller. Local officials sent tasters to try the ale and to guarantee its quality; they required that the ale be sealed in containers before issuing a license to sell it, and the license allowed the homeowner to sell ale only on the stoop in front of the house. As it was in the taverns of Babylon, a lot of medieval British ale sellers were women, and the ale regulations that were imposed by the authorities mirrored how British laws would later apply to wine sold in taverns.

Throughout much of history not only climate but also high, dense, impenetrable mountain ranges had been obstacles to trade in northern Europe. In medieval times, some mountain passes had been penetrated in an attempt to establish commercial links, and by the thirteenth century, it having been reasonably centrally located, the Champagne region had grown to host a series of commercial exchanges—trade fairs. To ensure the success of these "super markets," the nobility of major cities along the trade route to Champagne suspended tolls and taxes for merchants traveling to and from the fairs.

In the early fourteenth century, the north joined in trade with no fewer than five powerful industrial centers: England, Flanders, Germany, northern France, and northern Italy. Wine became a major economic stimulator, but its price indicated that it had become mostly a luxury item. As a result, peasants downed copious amounts of lowly grappa; craftspeople—one step up from peasants—drank home-brewed beer, and merchants, many of whom were in the nobility, displayed their social ranking by drinking wine and serving it to their guests; the higher their status, the more expensive the wine.

Still, the rich and powerful northern urban centers could not produce enough food to feed themselves. They were forced to rely on trade with the largely agrarian south, and since wine was food, the trade included lots of wine.

Transporting wine south to north was fraught with more dangers than traveling to the fairs; weather and other factors on long journeys ruined many shipments, and since the tolls that were relaxed during the Champagne fairs applied the rest of the time, the trip was expensive. In addition, there was always the risk of losing a shipment to road thieves. As the price of southern wines rose to meet the risks of trading with the north, northern nobles sought to produce more of their own wine.

In the south, wine technology had not advanced much from the days of Rome. In the north, despite their tough environment, merchants invested in vineyards and new wine technology. Although weather-related problems frequently diminished yields, making the expense of growing commercial grape crops in the north sometimes more costly than the price of finished wines from the south, the delicate, elegant northern wines that resulted compelled the nobility to continue.

Much of the trade at Champagne fell under a medieval barter system, but when the use of cash made inroads in the fourteenth century Italian merchants saw an opportunity to introduce a new brand of trade. Instead of producers lugging their wares to the Champagne fairs they sent manufacturers' representatives—traveling sales agents—who accepted cash or credit for goods. It took a lot of trust to buy goods sight unseen, but then, with trade being so centralized, a fraudulent trader could quickly be identified and ostracized. Sales agents began to bring only samples of their goods. After wine samples had been tasted and a deal was made, wine shipments traversed major waterways to their destinations under contract with Genoese and Venetian ships. Without the bustle of merchants and all their wares, the Champagne fairs petered out and local community fairs developed.

The new era of the traveling salesman created a generally good economy for wine traders. But political and social volatility still plagued Europe, making it common for wine routes of the period either to rise or to fall in importance as each new source of friction created a shifting alliance. The high risk of doing business helped wine prices to rise into the fifteenth century, in trade that alternately stabilized and destabilized. The weather also put pressure on prices. Wines for export had to be protected from losses during shipment in winter, especially when they were bound to the all-important, price-sensitive British. Although northern Spain had made inroads into the British market, shipping their wines along the coast of France to the famous port at La Rochelle, the British thirst for wine was quenched mainly by Gascony and Germany, the latter through Flemish merchants; those wines traversed northern portions of Europe where winters could be severe.

French and Flemish exporters put together annual wine-buying harvest festivals during late October and early November. They took orders at the festival and sent the young wines to English importers immediately. The importers either stored the wines, releasing them to market the following spring when they were ready to drink, or sold them to others in the trade who stored them until spring.

In the fourteenth century a schism developed in the Catholic Church, caused in part by the Crusades. Soon there were two popes, one in Rome and one in France, and further cause for conflicts. The popes often paid for allegiance and for battles from vast viticultural holdings. John XXII played his part from a summer home ten miles north of Avignon, calling it the New Château of the Pope, a place that lives on today as the famous Châteaneuf-du-Pape wine region.

Left out of the Champagne fairs because of lack of easy access, and being so far from the important British market, Burgundy wine merchants in the fifteenth century desperately needed markets. The Flemish came to their aid.

Northern Europeans had already learned that white grapes were better suited to withstand the cold; it is estimated that nearly fifty white grape varieties had been newly established by the thirteenth century. By the fifteenth century, technological advances in Burgundy had produced new success with red grape varieties such as gamay and pinot noir that resulted in elegant wines. Burgundian traders managed to get wine samples to one or more of the new local fairs where a few Flemish merchants got a taste of them, were impressed, and then introduced the wines to the Papal Court at Avignon. Finally, Burgundy wines had found a lucrative market and it was only just down the Rhône.

Despite their ties to the table wines of Gascony and Germany, the medieval British also nurtured a large appetite for sweet wine. The best sweet wines England imported were called Malvoise and Rumney. They had been produced in the Mediterranean for centuries—the former in the Pelopponesian town of Monemvasia, the latter in mainland Greece.

In its fourteenth-century prime, the Ottoman Empire took control of regions from the Caspian Sea to the Hungarian border with Austria, from the Persian Gulf to North Africa (Egypt, Carthage, and Algiers), and from Jerusalem and the western section of Arabia throughout the Mediterranean, with the exception of the Italic peninsula and some of the islands scattered about. Ottoman territory took in important wine trade routes between Europe and the East, trade routes that became unreliable. Malvoise and Rumney production was forced to shift to areas outside Ottoman control, to Crete and the Ionian Islands. The British had no commercial ties in these islands but the Venetians did.

During trade in Byzantium, Venetians had designed innovative ship galleys that could hold thousands of gallons of wine. In Constantinople they had been given major tax exemptions to take on the risky business of bringing sweet wine in from the islands. Venetian merchants were also given control over the taverns in Constantinople. The Venetians had it quite good and so they were distressed in 1453 when, after a long period of holding off the Ottomans, Constantinople fell and the lucrative market collapsed.

Venetian ships were capable of making it all the way to Europe, so Venetian shippers made a deal to bring sweet Malvoise and Rumney to England, plus some famous but illicit wines that were being produced in Damascus under Ottoman rule. The sweet wines arrived at British ports in summer, just in time

The British affectation for slurring—some would say mumbling—served to gradually change the names of Malvoise to Malmsey and Rumney to Romney. The heightened importance in the fourteenth-century British market of these wines brought with it stringent regulations. The regulations began at port, on the ship. Before the valuable Malmsey and Romney shipments were offloaded they were subject to local government tests.

to make up for the dwindling supply of German and French wines that had been released to market the previous spring.

The modern American wine export market is today a close second in importance to England. One of the conditions for penetrating the American market for wine is to play by stringent rules. Generally, by law, a producer must sell to a warehouse/distributor who must sell to a retailer/restaurateur who then sells to the consumer in what is known as a three-tier system. Unwin mentions a kind of three-tier system that operated in England during the Middle Ages, with British nobility reaping the best rewards, for they were at the top of the three levels. Political connections often allowed nobility to escape high customs duties and since they were able to buy direct at major trading centers the nobility could also circumvent having to pay the middle merchant while gaining access to the top highly prized wines.

The group that held the second rung of the system was made up of politically well-connected householders. They bought wine in bulk. They, too, avoided the middle merchant markup by grabbing up wine directly at ports of entry and in major markets. But members of this group were obliged to pay customs duties.

Tavern owners held onto the bottom rung of the British wine trade. The only avenue to buy that was open to tavern owners was through middle merchants. The taverns were also highly regulated. Each town was allowed a specified number of taverns, based on its size, population, and whatever value from political connections the tavern owners could muster. Taverns sold wine to people directly from the cask in gallons, quarts, or pints. But no tavern owner could sell wine until after it had passed a panel of experienced government tasters, who also fixed the wine prices. The mayor of most cities published wine prices annually.

The heavy customs duties imposed on tavern owners often meant that the wines they served were priced rather high. In other words, commoners paid dearly for the lowest value wines, the good stuff having already been gobbled up by the two top rungs of the trade. To assure that tavern customers did not pay more for wine than was within the law, inspectors marked the value of each cask at the front where buyers could see it. And to guard against wine adulteration, buyers had the right to stand in front of the cask so that they could see the wine being drawn from it.

Strict British regulations notwithstanding, with a large number of taverns throughout the country, and a sizable wine importing operation, it was near impossible to prevent adulteration and counterfeiting. The beloved Malmsey and Romney were particularly hard-hit by scandal and fraud. When the scope of the problem threatened the overall quality of these extremely important wines in Britain, something had to be done. H. Warner Allen uncovered a fifteenth-century proclamation by the mayor of London that speaks to "remnants of broken, sodden, reboiled, and unthrifty wine . . . offering . . . nothing in value."

In Babylon, perpetrators of such crimes would have been thrown into the Euphrates. London had the Thames nearby, but there seems to be no record of the river having been used as a repository for fraudulent merchants. Instead, the mayor threatened that those found to practice counterfeiting did so "on pain of pillory."

Many American politicians and trade unionists today see demons dancing between the lines of international trade agreements, placing American sovereignty and jobs at risk. Nations have fought over trade matters since the beginning of civilization—and wine was one of the catalysts for war. In the Middle Ages wine was involved in one of the longest war periods in Europe.

For those who had to pay them, British fourteenth-century import taxes were applied and levied right at ports of entry and paid directly to a representative of the crown. Tax payments generally included portions of the commodities onboard ships. The portion of wine paid for taxes could amount to one-tenth of the volume onboard. The king's representative selected at least half the volume of wine paid in taxes from behind the mast because that was the best spot on the ship for good storage. So as not to appear as if he represented an extortion ring, the king authorized a token payment for the wine. Yet, anyone found evading taxes lost the complete cargo, and evasion could, of course, be a matter of interpretation. And if you had the proper connections, you could avoid the whole affair on your ship.

Since Gascony provided England with a great volume of wine imports, French negotiators in the previous century had arranged a complicated customs system that applied exclusively to wine imports from Gascony. Many burgesses of Bordeaux were exempt, and many religious leaders in Bordeaux production zones paid lesser taxes on their extremely well regarded wines.

Once the wine was off-loaded, foreign merchants and sales representatives were told where they could lodge and how long they could remain in England, usually not much more than a month. Bordeaux merchants managed to receive dispensation that allowed them twice the amount of time to remain in the country.

Influence in the textile trade is what gave the Flemish access to the British market for German wine. But British importers with ties to Gascony were not impressed. They perpetrated acts of sabotage over the Steelyard trade guild. It was found that members of Parliament, many of whom were also wine merchants, had a hand in the turmoil.

The result of the turmoil was a charter that allowed safe passage for Gascons throughout the British realm while it restricted merchants of other countries, especially the Flemish. French merchants were allowed to openly trade wholesale and to lodge wherever they wished. What's more, on the arrival of the new vintage from Gascony, all remaining wines from the previous vintage were to be tested by merchants in the Gascony trade and destroyed if deemed to have deteriorated, giving them a free hand to create a ready market for their new wines. And while Flemish importers were forced to pay wine taxes based on quality, Gascon merchants got away with a flat tax based on volume. It was a serious blow to German wine trading in Britain but not the final one.

In the middle of the fourteenth century Edward III issued a monopoly grant to the Merchant Vintners of Gascony, a British-owned operation that was based in London. By doing so, the crown gave the British merchants the largest piece of the wine import trade. Flemish wine merchants had been officially relegated to second-class status. At the insistence of Flemish merchants, the monopoly was broken about a year later but damage had been done to their business. Over that one-year period London importers of French wines had locked their position, giving them near exclusivity as retailers of wines in England.

Thereafter, German wines were prohibited from being sold in taverns alongside French wines and the Merchant Vintners of Gascony secured the right

Flemish wine merchants also had some trouble in their northeastern European markets.

Refugees who had fled the expanding Ottoman Empire in the Balkans began to populate the Hungarian countryside. Hungary had developed in its southern region a system of egalitarian villages mixing all classes. From these villages, which were situated along several international trade routes, the Hungarian wine trade was renewed. Hungarian wine traveled the Danube and east through the Baltics, encroaching on the eastern and central European market for German wine and competing stiffly with the Flemish.

to inspect taverns throughout London and to destroy any wine that they considered faked or undrinkable—no questions asked.

In London, the patience of Flemish merchants had run out over the special treatment enjoyed by Gascon merchants. Violence erupted after the Merchant Vintners of Gascony instigated a number of cargo seizures. The king bowed—briefly—to the pressure. He leveled the playing field, extending to the Flemish and all alien merchants the same trading privileges as the Gascons; all imports were subject to a flat tax.

To bring the crown to its senses, some Gascon merchants left London to sell wines elsewhere. Their departure disturbed the king. The flat import tax was removed and the king renewed support for the privileges that had been granted only to Gascon merchants, but this time it was only his support, not a decree. In reality, it was too late for the Gascon merchants. During the turmoil, British merchants with ties to Flanders and to other importers had finally weakened Gascony's monopoly hold.

Bigger trouble soon erupted for the wine trade between Bordeaux and Britain.

Philip VI, and most principalities of central France, continued to despise the tie between England and western France. The French had tried for two centuries, since its loss to regain Aquitaine from England; to Philip, the turmoil between Gascon and Flemish merchants gave him an opening to try again. The French arrested some British merchants on trumped-up fraud charges—an act that was among the seeds for starting what we know today as the Hundred Years' War (1337–1453).

At the start of the conflict between England and France, Flemish nobility found themselves in a bind. They had been pro-French ever since an incident about a decade before, when the French monarch helped to crush a revolt of Flemish workers. But this new war between England and France was connected to the wine trade that Flemish merchants had worked so hard to secure and wanted so much to keep. In the end, Flemish royalty officially sided with the French, to the detriment of their trade relationship with Britain. (As an aside, the Flemish decision gave Spain new and lasting strength in the British wine market.)

The cost of shipping freight during the period had already been subject to weather conditions and various tollgates. During the war, transport costs between Gascony and England were at the mercy of shifting alliances, changing bureaucracies, and increased taxes at each port of call from the Gironde in Bordeaux to the Thames in London. Since British retailers priced wine based on expenses incurred relative to the distance from port of entry to point of sale, whatever French wine that got through was quite dear in England; the cost of wine tripled right at the start of hostilities and then it kept rising as vineyards were devastated during the conflict, and as shortages developed.

The French also suffered from fluctuations in wine prices and availability. Matters got so bad that high prices jeopardized the daily wine rations that French knights in the field demanded or at least expected. And since the Burgundians sided with England in the war, the flow of wine to French knights was placed in further jeopardy.

A brief first truce in the early stages of the conflict helped spur a rise in exports and a slight decrease in retail wine prices, but soon after the truce a more serious threat to trade than the war rampaged across Europe, killing more than one-third of the population—a disease that is believed to have come from Asia and to have wound up in an important Crimean trading city named Caffa, where Genoese merchants shipped cloth, caviar, timber, and wine—the plague, also known as the Black Death.

In 1347, Mongol soldiers who had died of the Black Death were thrown over the Caffa city walls in the hope that they would infect rivals, a tactic that worked all too well. Soon, Caffa citizens began to fall ill en masse. Genoese merchants fled, sailing along a variety of coasts to many Black Sea ports. The merchants were an efficient means of delivering the plague free of charge. They infected Bulgaria, Romania, and Greece; then the Levant and Egypt had outbreaks; then the Black Death arrived in Sicily; then, despite a decision by most European ports of call to turn back ships, it made its way from the Mediterranean Sea all across Europe. Disease increasingly diminished available labor, which in turn increased the cost of productivity, which of course weakened overall economic conditions.

In France, where the disease seemed to nestle in to cause the greatest havoc in Europe, the combination of war and disease caused vineyard acreage under cultivation to decrease dramatically, creating a pressing need for an increase in vine yield. Burgundians expanded plantings of the gamay grape, which yielded four times as much as the revered pinot noir grape. But Gascons did not follow suit; they stubbornly relied on what they already had in the ground even though the vines they had in the ground were shrinking in numbers. Both wholesale and retail prices of Gascon wines soared to unprecedented heights in England. Having been allies with the British, Burgundian dukes immediately gained financially from the situation, until Charles VII, crowned monarch in 1429 at Rheims in the Champagne region,

> As an unintended happy consequence, the sheer number of peasants and nobility who had died from the Black Death was so great that the disease also killed off the feudal system forever. When it was over, plague had offered Europeans a fresh start to reinvent their economies.

later signed a truce with the many dukes of Burgundy. Burgundy could no longer support the British.

The truce between France and Burgundy weakened the British war effort so much that the British surrendered Bordeaux in 1451. Charles took the opportunity to give English and Gascon wine merchants six months to get out of France. When they left, they took the vintage with them. Under Henry VI, the British took back Bordeaux in 1452 but they lost it for good the following year and the British crown also lost ownership of vineyards in France.

France instigated reprisals against England, beginning with Charles VII's high tax on wines from Bordeaux and, later, when Charles's son Louis XI expelled English merchants from Bordeaux. Over the long run, however, these moves backfired. It became apparent to the French crown that the French wine trade truly relied on the British market. Not long before his reign had ended, Louis XI once again allowed English wine merchants into Bordeaux, but not without a new set of rules, which included new French taxes on a revitalized and lucrative wine trade.

Flanders profited from its ties to Burgundy during and after the Hundred Years' War, except for a late fifteenth-century misunderstanding between England and Burgundy. Because Flemish merchants controlled the Burgundy wine trade at the time, Henry VII blocked them from trading with England. The problem lasted about two years and when it was over the Flemish merchants

At about this time Germany's Crown issued a decree to ensure that German wines were preserved with sulfur dioxide.The ruling gave German wines a slight edge because wines from France did not last as long as their counterparts.

The French didn't adopt the practice of using sulfur dioxide as a preservative until the eighteenth century.

quickly picked up where they had left off in the English market, pushing more and more German and Burgundian wines.

The relationship between the French monarch and the dukes of Burgundy remained tenuous until later in the century, after Louis XI defeated Philip the Good, who tried for his own kingdom located between Germany and France. With the victory came a wonderful tax resource from the financially successful Burgundians and their wealthy capital city, Beaune. But not all the money made its way to the crown.

Chancellor of the Exchequer to Burgundy, Nicolas Rolin spent the major part of his life serving the dukes as well as, some have noted, serving himself. His accumulated wealth gave rise to numerous accusations, but his flare for personal public relations appears to have helped keep him from being ruined by reputation. He was a charismatic fellow who used his charm to become close to Philip the Good. To Philip, Rolin was a friend and confidant and Philip showered his friend with gifts. At one point, under one of many clouds of financial scandal, Rolin offered to prove his loyalty and honesty by giving back to Philip all the gifts the duke had given him over the years. Philip was so taken by the offer that he considered Rolin's gesture a fine display and then he showered the Chancellor with even more gifts and a pardon for any and all potential misunderstandings. The records show that Rolin played a major role as advisor to Philip in the 1435 treaty with Charles VII.

Although it was still a wealthy city, Beaune did not escape the ravages of the Hundred Years' War. In 1443 Rolin redeemed his reputation with many people with a plan to build a hospice to serve the people of Beaune who were being adversely affected by the war. He persuaded Beaune merchants and politicians to finance construction of his dream. True to his allegiance to Rolin, Philip gave the venture a tax exemption. At Avignon, Pope Eugene IV issued a decree to protect the building from ecclesiastical intervention. Rolin's dream was called l'Hôtel-Dieu.

The first patient was admitted to l'Hôtel-Dieu soon after the war had ended. As part of his funding scheme, Rolin had gotten landowners to gift expensive vineyards to use to raise money for ongoing patient care. He devised and supervised everything connected to the success of l'Hôtel-Dieu, including winemaking from the vineyards that had been gifted—a job that remained in the Rolin family for a number of generations.

L'Hôtel-Dieu had lost its original name over time. It is known today as the Hospices de Beaune and it is the home of a major annual wine auction. Under the Rolin family, the first auction took place in 1820 to raise funds for the hospice. The auction occurs each November, attracting exporters and merchants from the world over. Since the hospice is no longer active and is, in fact, a museum, the auction serves as an indicator of the quality of past and future Burgundian vintages.

With the Hundred Years' War and the first major outbreak of disease behind them, northern Europeans set out to overhaul their economies. One way to do that was to rebuild trade; another way was to seek and find resources. The combination of limited natural resources and a sizable reduction in population quite possibly was the driving force behind what many European nations did next.

10.

Exploration

FALSTAFF: A good sherris-sack hath a two-fold operation in it. It ascends me into the brain; dries me there all the foolish and dull and cruddy vapors which environ it; makes it apprehensive, quick, forgetive, full of nimble fiery and delectable shapes; which, delivered o'er to the voice, the tongue, which is the birth, becomes excellent wit. The second property of your excellent sherris is the warming of the blood.

—William Shakespeare, *Henry IV*

As continents go, Europe is small and quite limited in natural resources, a situation exacerbated by a reduction in the labor force after the Black Death and succeeding plagues. In order to keep or to rebuild wealth, the nobility of the major European powers looked for resources abroad, using men who had a thirst for status and for adventure to chart the course.

The most forceful of the European powers were conveniently located close to the Atlantic Ocean. They had already established seaworthy fleets, so they set sail across the Atlantic to seek resources and riches. They usually thought they were going to Asia but they invariably wound up somewhere else. Eventually, the explorations came to mean a lot for the wine trade, even if they did not start out with that goal in mind.

With an earlier riff between England and Flanders having passed, sixteenth-century Flemish wine merchants restarted German wine imports into the British market by way of the Steelyard, the nearly four-hundred-year-old German guild. This time, however, the wines met with attack-dog British Francophiles in the medical profession. Doctors claimed, without offering proof, that the high acidity of German wines adversely affected internal organs. Back and forth attacks went on for some time until 1568, when the first known book about wine in the English language appeared—*A Book of Wine*.

In defense of German wines the book's author, William Turner, wrote: "Small white wines scour and drive out the uncleanliness of the body as much as it is possible to be done by them, and red and Claret wine stop and hold back and fill the body full of ill humors."

Turner's reference to ill humors was a reference to the medical belief that had been established in Classical Greece that sickness was caused by an imbalance of the four basic humors of the body: the two hot humors were blood (which represented air) and yellow bile (representing fire); the two cold humors were phlegm (which represented water) and black bile (representing earth). The practice of bleeding the ill—draining blood—was based on the belief that imbalanced humors were at the core of sickness. Sometimes wine was part of the cure for out-of-balance cold humors.

Turner had tapped into a growing segment of the British market, where lighter, more refined white wines had some appeal. In fourteenth-century Britain, German wines had been prohibited in taverns that sold Gascon wines; in the sixteenth century, the lighter and less expensive German wines became more readily available than ever in London. Yet, neither German white nor claret could do much to satisfy the also large British appetite for sweet alcoholic wines such as Malmsey, Romney, port, and sherry. Iberia became important in that wine trade.

Calling up the memory of Solon's sixth-century BC decree in Athens, in the fourteenth century Enrique III, King of Castille and rebuilder of Madrid, issued an edict that prevented either olive trees or grapevines from being destroyed on pain of a heavy fine. Where the Greek civil servant had managed only to delay ruin, the Iberian king had laid a foundation for success.

During their almost seven-hundred-year control of Spain, the Moors had oppressed neither Christians nor Jews, nor much of local culture for that matter. The ancient wine production in Andalusia continued—in fact, there is a record of the last Moorish king of Seville, Al-Motamid, praising wine both for the revenue and for the pleasure that it had provided him over his years in power. Much of Andalusian wine production was at Jerez, which had been one of the wealthiest Iberian cities under Moorish control. Just about all the Jerez wines for export went to England.

Christians took back Spain in the latter part of the fifteenth century; then, in 1491 they expelled the Jews and by 1492 they got rid of the last of the Moors. Foreigners from Italy, France, and Britain were called to fill the void, taking over much of the land and businesses that the Jews had left behind. British merchants put a tight grip on the wine trade at Jerez. At the time, much of the trade had been taking place along the River Gudaelete, not far from Jerez. This proved difficult and costly for British merchants, as the river's shoreline needed constant upkeep. That same year, seeking to lure the wine trade, the duke at San Lucar, a port city along the River Guadalquivir, removed export duties, which helped to concentrate British merchants on this new location for the production and export of what would soon become the world-famous sherry wine.

In the "Pardoner's Tale," Chaucer, whose father had produced wine, praised a white wine that he claimed was produced at Lepe and sent to San Lucar. The wine had been fortified with strong alcohol, which leads Julian Jeffs to state in his book, *Sherry,* that wine from Jerez was being fortified at least as far back as the fourteenth century and that the wine trade between Jerez and England may have begun as early as 1340.

Jeffs takes about a dozen pages of his book to explain the etymology of the word *sherry*. He says that, at first, the wine was called *sack,* a word that may have come from the Spanish verb *sacar,* which means to draw out or extract. Jeffs traced the word to a fifteenth-century town council meeting at Jerez, where wine was referred to as *sacas,* a word still used to identify drawing off sherry from its barrels. He believes that the word came into common usage in England because that was the common destination for most of the wine and, over time, the English changed *sacas* to *sack*.

Yet the word *sack* to refer to sherry could possibly have derived from the word *seco,* the Spanish word for dry. Early sherry was mostly on the sweet side, and that is what the general British population seemed to prefer. But there was a small market for *seco* sherry too, especially among the elite. They might have been the ones to have first applied the word *sack* when referring to the austere, dry version of the wine. Jeffs mentions this possibility to explain why a sixteenth-century sherry shipper might have selected a name for his product: the shipper blended immature wines that were quite dry, and then, in order to separate his wine from what most people thought sherry was—sweet—he named the product, redundantly, Dry Sack.

In any event, by the end of the seventeenth century, sack had faded from use (except for that Dry Sack, which is still marketed). Also at that time, Jerez had lost its place as the center of the sherry trade, it having shifted to nearby Sanlúcar de Barrameda and Puerto de Santa Maria. None of this information, of course, provides the definitive etymology of "sherry," but a wine that is produced like no other wine, at least deserves a brief, if simplified, explanation.

As grape skins everywhere normally provide an ample supply of the natural yeast that starts their fermentation, two European wine regions—the Jura in France and Andalusia in Spain—are naturally endowed with an abundance of a separate yeast cell known as *flor*. This yeast begins to do its work after the fermentable sugar has been used up during primary fermentation.

Flor cells thrive at the top surface of the wine while it rests in casks, forming a thick white film that creates a protective cover against spoilage bacteria, especially the vinegar bacteria, *mycoderma aceti*. Flor requires oxygen to do its work and so sherry barrels are never fully "topped up" with wine, a practice that is used to keep out oxygen. Flor also plays a role in providing organic compounds that help to build flavor intensity and complexity in the wine.

Sherry casks are stacked one upon another in the cellar. In the top casks go the youngest wines; the oldest wines are in the bottom casks. When wine in the bottom casks is bottled, some wine is purposely left in the casks. The bottom casks are then given an addition of wine from the casks stacked immediately above them; then those casks receive wine from the casks immediately above them. This process of drawing off (*sacar*) and refilling is repeated all the way up the stack until it reaches the young wines in the top casks, where the new, recently fermented wine is added. In this way, the ongoing *solera* is a blend of numerous vintages combined to create a consistent product. There are no vintage sherries.

Sherry starts out as a delicate still white wine and it ends up as a fairly strong fortified wine. While there is debate over why or when fortification began, it is believed that merchants discovered early on that fortification with distilled alcohol was necessary to kill off remaining yeast cells for stability on long journeys. Fortification was originally accomplished by adding distilled wine, which is another process and, because of its importance to a few wines, requires a brief explanation.

> It does not take much fortification to stabilize sherry, but since the British liked heavy, alcoholic wines, most early sherry sent to England, besides being sweet, was fortified in excess of 20 percent alcohol by volume. Delicate and delightful modern sherry is commonly fortified to between 15 and 17 percent alcohol by volume. Today, most fortification is accomplished with industrial distilled alcohol, usually produced from grain instead of wine.

Alcohol distillation may be as old in China as 1000 BC. Ancient Egyptians, Greeks, and Romans are also believed to have known about and applied distillation methods. The alcohol distilled by the ancients was mainly used as fuel for lighting, as a disinfectant, and for cosmetics.

In Europe, distilled fruit products, referred to as *aqua vitae* or *eau de vie* (water of life) were first produced to preserve dead matter for scientific and medical study. The products became the basis for medieval European medicines, into which herbs had been macerated. When it was discovered that distilled alcohol could be used as a cheap source of calories for the poor, and as a potent mixture to give to one's enemies who might have been withholding secrets, distillation found new markets. In seventeenth-century France, medicinal distillation was taken out of the control of scientists and put into the hands of commercial distillers, creating the earliest commercial and drinkable "water of life."

Distillation also took place under the Moors in Spain. Their important contribution to the practice was the alembic pot still method (from the Arabic, *alembik*). Like most other matter, wine is made up largely of water. The alcohol in wine generally accounts for anywhere from 8 to 14 percent of the volume. Alembic distillation concentrates the alcohol by separating it from the water as a vapor (the spirit).

Alcohol has a lower boiling point than water, so to collect condensed alcoholic vapors, wine is boiled in a highly conductive copper pot to release alcohol as steam. The steam is recaptured in a specially designed pot cover that channels impurities away from the steam. The steam "liquifies" and the alcohol is stored in a separate container. The remaining wine goes through more distillation cycles until all the alcohol has been drawn off. The end result is called *brandy,* a name—we learn from reading Gordon Brown's *Handbook of Fine Brandies*—that was not applied until the sixteenth century.

When war of independence freed the Netherlands from the control of Spain, shortages of distilled alcohol hit Holland, so Dutch wine merchants experimented with wine distillation on their own. They managed to create a successful commercial product that they called *brandewijn* (burnt wine). At first, *brandewijn* was shipped to northern European markets and to the East Indies. As the newly independent Dutch economy grew, merchants invested in more and more stills for their popular product.

During the time that the Dutch were developing brandy their ships had been carrying salt to France and then returning home with French wines. To keep down transportation costs, Dutch wine merchants set up brandy stills in the wine production regions where they already had an interest—in parts of Bordeaux and in the Loire.

Known mainly for its well-promoted wine industry, Bordeaux was a heavily industrialized region, as it remains today. Dutch distilleries first were installed along the coast of Bordeaux and then further inland. The Charente region, which lies between Bordeaux and the Loire, supplied the Dutch with the cheapest product for its stills, mainly from a grape named ugni blanc. Cognac is the name of an area in the Charente and that is where Dutch brandy production became centered.

Fine brandy is also produced south of the Charente, in an inland area called Armagnac, but Cognac became more widely known because it benefited from its waterway location. The original single pot distillation reigned in the Charente and elsewhere until the turn of the seventeenth century, when a more complex "continuous still" system was designed; this method dispenses with having to restart distillation for further runs for higher strength. Its efficiency also causes the continuous pot still method to produce a more neutral spirit. For that reason, producers in Armagnac prefer to stay with the single pot method, which they believe retains the fullness of the base wine's character. A taste of Cognac against Armagnac often points out the distillation difference: the former is cleaner, sometimes even smoother than the latter, which has a rustic charm all its own.

At first, brandy was produced and then quickly shipped to its customers. In the latter part of the seventeenth century, war between France and the Netherlands threatened Dutch brandy merchants. Much of the brandy had to be held for long periods of time while shippers scrambled, finagled, and begged to get the product transported. The brandy rested in oak casks. When the brandy finally made its way to market, merchants noticed that it seemed to have a mellowed character and that it had developed complex yet pleasant odors. Soon the oak aging practice became the preferred finishing method for fine brandy production, except for the portion of brandy that was used in wine fortification.

In Italy, Leonardo da Vinci designed his version of alembics in the late fifteenth century, but it remained strictly medicinal until about the eighteenth century; then, great quantities of Campanian wine were distilled in France to increase commercial brandy production.

Italic peasants in the mountain regions of the north enjoyed their version of distilled wine—grappa—which over time morphed from its rustic peasant roots to incorporate the pot still method.

Through British agents, Spain worked hard to solidify its wine trade relationship with England. Its Iberian rival, Portugal, was growing in power, too, and it had designs on the British wine market.

As in Spain, Celts had settled in Portugal hundreds of years before Christ. The group responsible for establishing wine production in each country, the Phoenicians, soon followed. Afterward, Portugal and Spain came under the Moors at the same time, but Portugal gained independence in the twelfth century, a couple of centuries before Spain.

Many successions of the throne took place in turbulent Iberia between the twelfth and fifteenth centuries. Within that period, Portugal and Britain engaged in nearly two dozen trade treaties, the result of which was to strengthen their ties, especially after the Castilian prince, John I, laid claim to the Portuguese throne through marriage and through Portugal's 1385 defeat of Castile. John led Portugal through about fifty years of colonial and mercantile expansion, a lot of it centered on a growing wine trade with England. The trade brought significant riches to Portugal and a great deal of new power.

Through the fourteenth and sixteenth centuries, as Portugal and Spain vied for favored treatment in trade with Britain, the two countries also competed for power in Iberia. The few trade disagreements that each country had with Britain during this period paled against the disagreements the Iberian neighbors had been having with each other. One of their biggest sticking points was exploration by way of the Atlantic, over which many fights had broken out. In time, however, the Iberians came to understand that the sea allowed room for both of them to explore.

In 1494 the budding Iberian powers signed a treaty to divide their interests across the Atlantic. The treaty cut roughly through Cape Verde—west of the cape went to Spain; east of it went to Portugal. Within about fifty years after the treaty, the Portuguese, who managed to get Brazil in the agreement, had made it to Africa (they had also made it all the way to Japan and into islands in the Pacific). The Spanish had conquered much of Central and South America.

Have some Madeira m'dear,
you really have nothing to fear;
I'm not trying to tempt you,
that wouldn't be right,
but you shouldn't drink spirits at this time of night.

—Anonymous

The Portuguese prince, Henry the Navigator, sponsored explorers to chart sea routes so that merchants could follow and establish trade routes. One of those journeys in 1418 took a Portuguese explorer named Zarco ("crooked eye") off course in a storm. He landed on a tiny island a few hundred miles west of Africa. From this island he saw in the distance another tiny island over which a dark cloud hovered. Zarco set out for the other island. When he landed on it he found it uninhabited and covered with trees. Taken by this seemingly undiscovered mountain-peaked island of hundreds of thousands of trees, Zarco named it Madeira, which meant "Isle of Wood," and vowed to return.

On his second trip to Madeira Zarco brought a contingent of Scots, Irish, and sundry nationalities to burn the trees and make way for agriculture. Legend has it that the fires raged for seven years. Perhaps, but when the fires did die out, sugar became the major crop of Madeira. During the island's development stages, sea merchants had brought vines to Madeira from Crete and so the locals began to produce a sweet wine from the vines mainly for their own consumption. When in the sixteenth century the price of sugar dropped as the Portuguese colony at Brazil produced it more cheaply, Madeira turned to its vineyards for economic relief.

At the time of Zarco's discovery of Madeira, Spain's Canary Islands had been producing Malmsey and Romney for export to England to make up for the loss of those wines from the East. The exporters continued to prosper, as the British capacity for the sweet wine seemed to have no end. The Canary Islands also became one of the stopover points for the extensive sea traffic of the period. By the sixteenth century, however, the seductive island of Madeira had been luring travelers as a stopover point. Ex-sugar merchants on the island, mainly Scots and Britons, began to sell to the explorers and their crews the sweet wines they produced from the vines that had been brought in from Crete. A lot of those travelers were on their way to what would soon be called the Americas.

When the Vikings arrived in North America around a thousand years ago their discoveries included what are now parts of Canada and the northeastern United States. They named much of the area Vineland for its abundant grapevines. The grapevines were wild, and there is no evidence that the natives produced wine from them. The Aztecs had at their disposal hallucinogenics to help them make contact with their spiritual nature, but neither is there a record of conquering Spaniards having found local wine in America.

Hernán Córtes came from noble stock, from the parched, harsh Estramadura region in Spain, the place that produced the rough, ambitious individualists known as conquistadors. Records show that Córtes had been arrested as a young man for "disobedience." Afterward, he flunked law studies at the university and then became a wanderer, showing up in Cadiz and in Seville. From Seville, Córtes joined an expedition to Santo Domingo in 1504. That experience gave him the ambition to become a conquistador and to join an exploration to Cuba under Vásquez, who already was a conquistador. But when Córtes left Cuba to explore Mexico he did so by defying his benefactor. Unhappy with the desertion, Vásquez had sent a contingent of soldiers to arrest Córtes. Córtes defeated the contingent and then converted to his side those who survived the fight.

When he arrived in Mexico in 1519 Córtes was after natural resources. As a representative of Catholic Spain, he also felt charged with converting the locals to Christianity. His offer to the Aztecs to convert them involved a decree that was read to them in Spanish, which Aztecs did not understand. Essentially, Córtes gave the Aztecs a choice either to convert or to suffer grave consequences (the decree included absolution for the Spaniards who were about to commit crimes against the Aztecs in the name of the Crown and of the Church). Within two years, Córtes had taken from the Aztecs what they had owned and inhabited for centuries, creating what he called New Spain; then he enslaved those his soldiers had not slaughtered.

Córtes also needed wine but there were no vineyards. Spain's wine industry at Andalusia was not enamored with the idea that the colonies would start their own wine industries, but it took so long to get wine across the seas as provisions that Córtes got himself grapevine cuttings anyway. The first European grapevines of the *Vitis vinifera* species went into Mexican soil around 1521. Córtes made vine cultivation mandatory. He demanded a thousand vines planted for each hundred Aztec slaves he gave to settlers. As the new vines began to grow, especially in the mountains, they proved unused to the region and failed. Córtes commanded a contingent of religious friars to apply their extensive viticultural knowledge in the mountains and then to teach the colonists. They succeeded in producing the first European-style wines in the New World, but Spain allowed none of it to be used for commercial reasons.

The same year that Córtes had set sail for Mexico, another Spaniard, Vasco Núñez de Balboa, became the first European to touch the eastern shores of the Pacific Ocean. He got there from his post as leader of an expedition to Panama. As was often the case with the jealousies aroused by explorers, Balboa was later accused of, and executed for, treason in Panama. One of his lieutenants, Francisco Pizarro, was with Balboa when Panama was established, and he was with him when they discovered the Pacific Ocean's eastern shores. Luckily for Pizarro, he was not with Balboa when the captain's head was chopped off. Like Córtes, Pizarro wanted to be a conquistador and so, after Balboa had been executed, Pizarro endeared himself to the new governor of Panama, all along nursing a desire to explore for riches in Peru. Pizarro must have had enormous charm, for the man who was a peasant in Spain grew to great wealth in Panama. In 1527, he used that wealth to finally set out for Peru. When he got there, he discovered plenty of gold and other mineral riches—but no vines.

Like Córtes in Mexico, Pizarro met with locals in Peru. Also like Córtes, Pizzaro subdued the natives. When an Inca ruler was killed it left the populace confused because, to them, the leader was a god. Those who killed a god were seen as gods themselves. When Pizzaro learned this about the Incas he set out to capture their ruler, Atahualpa. After succeeding in the capture he tricked the Incas into paying a hefty ransom for their leader's return, but instead of returning Atahualpa Pizarro took the ransom and then had the ruler killed.

From the introduction of grapevines into Mexico in 1521, and after Pizzaro's conquest of Peru, it took a total of only thirty years for a grape-growing tradition to develop all the way down the South American western coast. In 1556, plantings in Argentina completed the introduction of European vines to the continent. Since the mother country was interested in exploiting minerals from the New World and protecting its wine industry at home, early Spaniard colonial wine was confined to personal and religious consumption.

Spaniards arrived in South Carolina toward the end of the sixteenth century, at Parris Island, where they also planted vineyards. When their vineyards failed, the colonists might have thought to make do with wines produced from local wild grapes. If so, they would have been shocked by the results. In South Carolina, the native species *Vitis rotundifolia*—muscadine, for dark grapes, and scuppernong, for bronze ones—result in heady, overly grapey wines that bear no relationship to European wines. Yet in volume 1 of his *History of American Wine* series, Thomas Pinney found no evidence either of a harvested indigenous grape crop at Parris Island or of a small wine industry. He did find that earlier, in 1562, French Huguenots had produced wine from scuppernong grapes in Florida. Had the Huguenots the inclination to establish a commercial wine industry, no evidence of that exists, either. In fact, it took about a hundred years from Córtes's vineyard plantings in Mexico before wine was produced commercially in the New World, let alone as commercially successful.

Franciscan missionaries arrived from Spain in the northern portion of Mexico around 1626 in an area that included what is now New Mexico, southern California, and parts of Texas. Because the friars were missionaries, the grape they had planted took on the name of mission grape. The wine the friars produced had gone mainly to religious use, yet a small amount of it seems to have been traded to support the mission and that is the first record of wine commerce in the New World.

Mission grapevines soon became a regional mainstay that spread throughout the Southwest, but the Franciscans had been forced out of New Mexico by a contingent of indigenous people in 1680. The incident spelled the end of commercial possibilities for wine in the region for a long time to come.

Meanwhile, the thought of producing commercial wine in America had been gestating in England. Scots and Britons maintained strong financial interests in the Iberian wine trades, yet the British had grown weary of the monopoly Iberian governments held on that trade and of the many trade arguments and disagreements to which the monopoly gave rise. And despite the fact that Elizabeth I had resumed a relationship with the French, the crown remained perpetually unhappy with them and with the high tariffs they applied to the all-important wine trade. The queen responded in part to British wine merchants when she decided to finance a trip to the New World to establish a colony.

The earliest British journey across the Atlantic took Sir Walter Raleigh's expedition to the southern coast of North America in 1584. Pinney notes that Raleigh's records indicate the discovery of an abundance of wild grapes in North Carolina. Unfortunately, the Roanoke colony vanished without a trace three years later, leaving historians to wonder if their disappearance was the result of successful retaliation by North American indigenous people. Pinney's research brought up no wine, just the discovery of grapevines.

The British, of course, did not give up. By 1606, King James I, along with some wealthy investors, created and chartered a trading company to sail from England expressly to establish a commercial colony in the New World. Named after Elizabeth I, the Virgin Queen, the Virginia Company was listed on the London stock market. A total of 108 Britons representing the Virginia Company hit the banks of a river at the mouth of Chesapeake Bay in 1607. They named the location after the crown—Jamestown.

Pinney states that the Jamestown Virginia colonists were in awe of the grapes that "grew naturally," surrounding their settlement. But they would have been less surprised had they read the writings of an earlier visitor to the region, a Spanish Jesuit missionary named Father Juan de la Carrera, who hit the area about thirty-five years prior to the British. Carrera looked at that same coastline and noted, according to Pinney, vineyards that were "so beautiful and so well plotted as any in Spain." Whose vineyards were they? No mention was made.

Jamestown settlers were quickly given the task to produce wine for England; the first batch was sent to the crown within two years of the colony's establishment, produced of course from local grapes and with the same results as when other Europeans had tasted such wines. Dispirited, the Virginia Company could do nothing else but issue a call for European winemakers. The call proved fruitless. After ten years of trying to create a profitable wine industry from local grapevines that produced wine nobody seemed to like, the Virginia Company desperately lobbied Jamestown legislators for a law that would require every household to plant and to maintain European vines. Included in the law that finally passed was a mandate that settlers plant ten Europeans vines per year at the instruction of recognized European vignerons. The law is the first known record of a European attempt to transplant *Vitis vinifera* vines in the eastern part of North America. In addition, the Virginia Company petitioned the crown to impose price controls on wines from Spain and Portugal so that colonists would at least support the wines they produced locally.

The Jamestown wine experiment was a resounding failure. In London, prices of Virginia Company shares collapsed. Cash-needy Jamestown households put the thick viticultural manuals to use as fuel for the fireplace and then they

In 1619 eight vignerons from southern France arrived with vine cuttings at Jamestown. Within three years of that first delivery of vines tens of thousands had been planted and every family in the colony had become proud owners of a viticultural manual, printed and supplied by the Virginia Company. But in short order the European vines began to die without explanation. Some have speculated that the French vignerons had sabotaged the effort. The more likely reason for the failure is that the vines could not survive their new environment.

abandoned vines and turned their attention to tobacco. Over the next two decades, while most of those households wanted nothing to do with producing either grapes or wine, a few pressed on; they tried and failed, tried and failed again until, in 1658, Cromwell offered ten thousand pounds of free tobacco to the first Jamestown household to make two *tunne* of wine from its own vineyard. Pinney found no evidence that the prize had been claimed.

The Virginia Company's failure to successfully produce commercial European-style wine in the New World was no isolated incident. Each future seventeenth-century colony along the East Coast that tried to produce such wine—and most tried—had met with failure. Their knowledge of grafting, planting, and cultivating grapevines was not the issue. They were unaware that the combination of climate and various kinds of diseases in the New World would have a devastating effect on vines of the Old World. In other words, they did not understand that each grapevine species required its unique environment. Transplanted European vines survived in the North American Southwest and in the West, where the climate was conducive and disease was manageable. But the commercial center of the newly emerging colonies was in the South,

Southeast, and Northeast, closer to the Atlantic Ocean, and there the European vines simply could not survive. It took until into the nineteenth century for a viable commercial wine industry to develop in America. Meanwhile, the European wine trade was alive and well.

Following the seventeenth-century Religious Restoration, demand for alcohol, which had suffered during the religious turmoil, was growing again in England. Northern European merchants remained at the hub of the wine trade; they dealt in wines from France, Germany, Spain, Portugal, and the Atlantic Islands.

The varying interests of the dominant powers of course continued to create conflict. Conflict caused political power shifts, and each shift of power dictated which of the colonial powers would exert the most control over wine at any given time. For instance, when the colonies in Chile and Argentina began to expand and to consider exporting wine to mother Spain, the crown quashed colonists' dreams with two moves: a moratorium on vine planting in the colonies and inflated import fees. Dutch and British merchants, too, protected their respective wine trade by applying pressure on their governments for protectionist measures.

At the time, French and Portuguese wine traders were not considered alien, but Dutch merchants had been labeled as such, and aliens bringing wine into England were subjected to extremely heavy customs duties. England created the 1651 Navigation Act mainly to bar Dutch wine merchant imports. Sick of the British market struggles, many Dutch wine merchants, as they had in the past, abandoned the market, pulling back to Germany, the Balkans, a little into Spain and to parts of the Mediterranean, and then to South Africa. In South Africa's Cape district, Dutch commander Jan van Riebeeck set up shop under an East India Company charter. He produced the first wines of the region in 1659. The wines were sweet, alcoholic, and without much of a market. But others followed Riebeeck anyway and after two more decades, success was achieved.

Simon van der Stel planted vineyards at Groot Constantia on the Cape. He had access to labor from members of a large contingent of persecuted French Huguenots who had made their way to the Cape and who knew a thing or two about viticulture. The Huguenots eventually settled in the now famous wine regions of Paarl and Stellenbosch. Beginning in 1685, and over a period of about 20 years thereafter, the Huguenots' viticultural knowledge helped Stel's Groot Constantia dessert wines gain the world renown that it enjoys even today. After Groot Constantia's success, other Dutch merchants began to produce wine in South Africa, but with the exception of Constantia, East India Company officials were stingy in the prices paid to producers. Unable to afford viticultural experts, most South African producers had no choice but to turn to slave labor, which created a downward spiral. Slave labor meant poor output, which in turn meant low-quality grapes and wine, which in turn fed the East India Company's stinginess, which meant even lower prices paid, which meant no upgrading in labor, and so on.

Perceiving it as an inferior wine region, mainland Dutch merchants stopped investing in South Africa. Even if the colonial wines had been better, mainland merchants still would have had trouble justifying the cost of shipping from the Cape. It certainly was cheaper for them to import good Spanish and French wines on their own continent. When the East India Company finally gave up, the South African wine trade was forced to turn insular, and so it remained well into the twentieth century, after the demise of the apartheid system of government.

As the new century dawned, colonialism proved dangerous as local cultures became restless. The wine trades of the European mother countries, however, were about to experience some truly important innovations that managed to build more and more wealth.

11.
Innovations

I am drinking stars!

—Quote attributed to the Benedictine monk, Dom Pierre Pérignon

The earliest wine exported to Britain from the Portuguese mainland might have been a light, young country white wine, *vinho verde* (green wine), probably as early as the thirteenth century. By the latter part of the sixteenth century, led by Scots, a wine production and export center had been established in Portugal, at the town of Viana do Castelo, to focus on red wine for the British market. A British consulate was set up in the town to protect the commercial interest. To get the new red wine going, British agents promoted it as a prophylactic against plague. Shipments to Britain grew steadily.

Ties between Britain and Portugal were reinforced in the latter part of the seventeenth century by the marriage of England's Charles II to Portugual's Catherine of Braganza. The king made a royal pledge to assist Portugal in what had been, for a couple of centuries, an ongoing competition with Spain for trading markets and colonies.

The British king could do nothing to help the Portuguese when it was noticed that mainland wines did not travel well. The British market grew tired of the wines, even of the popular red wines of Viana. Another set of Scots shippers, located near the Douro River, had been making some headway in the British market with their red wines. When Viana wines fell out of favor, Douro reds were ready to fill the void.

The Douro received a break toward the latter part of the seventeenth century, when the British crown was once again feuding with the French; imports of wines from Bordeaux were banned and Douro wine merchants were asked to fill part of the gap. But the biggest break of all for the Douro merchants came in 1703, when Portugal and Britain signed the Methuen Treaty. The treaty created a market for British wool in Portugal in return for preferential tax treatment for Portuguese wine. British wine merchants in the Douro region began to see some nice profits and it stayed that way for them until the middle of the century—until the Marquês de Pombal, José de Carvhallo e Mello, known to some as Pombal, came home to the Douro from his post as Portuguese ambassador to London.

The marquês had been hailed for his organized relief work after a massive earthquake that had struck Lisbon. The Portuguese king at the time, José, also recognized the marquês for his work in restructuring a financial crisis that had struck Brazil. His status was rewarded with a crown-sanctioned free hand in the Douro region.

Once in power in the region, the marquês became quite aware of how profitable the wine trade with England had become. At a monastery in the mountains of the Douro it became the custom to arrest the ongoing fermentation of red wines by adding brandy. This created thick, sweet, high-alcohol red wines, the kind of wine that went over quite well in Britain. The marquês put his weight behind the monastery wines. Soon, exporters at Oporto, the largest city in Portugal, were shipping the "new" Douro wines to England in great quantity; and, thanks to brandy fortification, they traveled quite well.

The marquês carefully watched developments in 1755, when British merchants accused winegrowers in the Douro of dishonesty. The merchants refused to pay the listed wine prices for what they thought had been adulterated wine. When the Portuguese farmers appealed to the marquês, he discovered that the British merchants had good reason to be angry. A great many Douro shippers had indeed been adulterating with sugar, fruit juices—you name it—trying to pass their wine off as the original port wine. Marquês de Pombal, José de Carvhallo e Mello's solution to the problem was to take over the Douro wine trade by setting up his own company.

The marquês established the wine company and then he set up the first government controlled regional demarcation for wine production in Portugal. Under new regulations, specific vineyard areas were designated for quality and vineyard practices were spelled out more clearly to lower yield and to increase quality. Farmers were given better compensation for their efforts in order to prevent them from resorting to overproduction or reverting to adulterating wine. The marquês's company also cleared a gorge in the Douro River that was preventing easy traffic and then built a new road by raising export taxes.

Douro wines for export had always been stored in poorer-quality wooden casks; new regulations forced exporters to replace the cheap casks with premium well-coopered oak. With his changes in place, the marquês demanded that all transactions between the British merchants and the Douro producers be cleared through his government-controlled company.

Even if Pombal's intervention in the Portuguese wine trade had provided a benefit to merchants, to farmers, and to governments it could do nothing to stanch human greed and incompetence. The British export merchants certainly got the better wines that they had called for, but it was also true that the controls made it more expensive to produce and to ship Douro wines, especially when merchants dealing with corrupt government officials representing the company had to pay bribes to buy preferential treatment to smooth the way.

On the producer side, even though Pombal had come to their rescue, farmers and producers had grown tired of his stringent controls. When they turned against the marquês, he met their riots at Oporto with brutality, accelerating the deterioration of the relationship between his company and the producers. When the government wine company finally unraveled, the marquês managed to remain in power only because of his friendship with King Jose. He was forced to retire as soon as the king died, but he left the wine regulations

The spawning in Europe of the seventeenth- and eighteenth-century religious, philosophical, and social revolution known as the Enlightenment Movement also produced great turmoil. In the wine trade, turmoil often meant that the troubles of one wine merchant group became the fortunes of another. In bad times or in times of upheaval, wine producers, merchants, and governments quickly acted to bolster the wine economy, especially when change threatened the fortunes of the wealthy or the crown and its court. For instance, French wine merchants were quite happy over the protection wars between Britain and the Netherlands that led to the South African failure.

behind and somehow they managed not only to survive but also to become the inspiration behind French wine regulations two centuries into the future.

In his book, *The Wine Revolution in France,* Leo A. Loubère tells the story of how one French wine merchant and wine region had developed a renewed and stellar reputation as a direct result of England's seventeenth-century tax system to favor the French. Frenchman Arnaud de Pontac's combination restaurant and grocery opened in London around 1666. In the Médoc district of Bordeaux he produced the wine, known as Haut-Brion, that he served at the restaurant. His wine was being produced like no other wine imported into England at the time.

French viticultural practices of the period included combining grapes harvested from multiple vineyards under contract with producers. Arnaud de Pontac produced Haut-Brion the way Falernian wines of 121 BC had been produced in Rome, from old vines grown in a single vineyard. To sell his wines, de Pontac set his sights on the London elite who ate at his restaurant—Samuel Pepys, Jonathan Swift, and John Locke, to name a few. Upon receiving overwhelming endorsements from the luminaries for what they had referred to as "Ho Brian" wine, de Pontac soon was faced with resounding success. He engaged in a practice that can be traced to the ancient Phoenicians and Romans, yet he is credited as the first European to invest in expensive viticulture and production techniques. He produced not only superior wines, but also shaped demand in a specialized market and established a high price for what he made a sought-after product. Today we call the practice "niche marketing." According to Loubère, the daring de Pontac deserves credit both for establishing the reputation of the Médoc and for bringing great wealth to many small producers in Bordeaux who followed his lead.

Château-Margaux, La Tour, and La Fitte were owned by wealthy members of the Bordeaux parliament, so, after following de Pontac's lead, these properties were infused with capital and new ideas that ushered into the Médoc an unparalleled period of increased quality. New oak cooperage techniques had been developed to prevent leakage and oxidation, sulfur dioxide was employed to sterilize the porous wood of barrels, and a new method called "racking" came into being to remove dead yeast cells after fermentation.

Racking simply means moving wine from one vessel to another, leaving the dregs behind. Wines are racked a few times throughout the winemaking process. Each time they are racked, the wines become that much more free of the debris of yeast cells and other particles. Egg white had been discovered centuries before as a means to pull minute particles out of suspension, sending them to the bottom and thereby clarifying the wine—the Bordelais adopted egg white fining.

In the vineyard, the famous château owners dispensed with simple laborers, preferring instead to hire true farmers with superior skills. Most of all, single vineyard wine production in Bordeaux became a preferred calling card intended to impress British wine consumers who had access to lots of cash. When England turned against France in the latter part of the seventeenth century the rift was manifested in outrageously high taxes on French wine imports. The taxes had hurt, but the move did not kill the Bordeaux wine market in England. The connected few of the British upper class found ways to secure their share of the beloved "clarets." Still, the rift meant that a great deal of Bordeaux wines had been rerouted; the French appealed to their rival merchants in the Netherlands with only limited success, of course. To make up for losses in French wines, many British merchants called on the government to reduce customs duties on Portuguese wine imports; Madeira was among the first wine regions to benefit.

Madeira and the Canary Islands had vied for the attention of travelers to the New World since the sixteenth century. When, in 1580, Spain gained what amounted to sixty years of control over Portugal's shippers, the crown protected Jerez and Malmsey shippers in the Canary Islands, holding Madeira wine production back from exporting. But Malmsey production on the Canary Islands became one of the casualties of a war between Spain and England in 1588, which created an opening for Madeira.

During the period when Pombal had upgraded Douro wines, some British merchants had also recognized the potential for Malmsey in Madeira. Quality Malmsey production required a long growing season with warm daytime temperatures that were capped by cool nights, exactly what the island of Madeira offered along its sloping hillsides. Soon enough, ships from Europe, both to and from the New World, were being loaded with Malmsey and Romney with a Madeira appellation. And since brandy fortification was being applied to Malmsey production, it gave the wine more depth and more alcohol, something the British seemed always to desire. In addition, Madeira traveled better than any other wine.

Two versions of the same legend try to explain a particular production method that is employed in Madeira and is the reason for the wine's ability to travel and to age extremely well. In one legend, shipments of Madeira to colonies in the East Indies are implicated; in the other version, shipments to the British colonies in America are implicated. But it is the same story.

It seems that shipments of Madeira were usually accompanied by a document proclaiming not only the pedigree of the wine, but also a description of its attributes. Importers receiving the shipments sometimes were left to wonder over discrepancies between the wine and its description: the wines were often better than their descriptions. The problem was sorted out when an export shipment managed to get rerouted back to Madeira by mistake. The Madeira merchants had heard about the discrepancies between the wine and their descriptions and this time they had a chance to find out for themselves. They tasted and agreed. After some research, the shippers discovered that the source of the discrepancy was the heat of the ship galleys during long voyages. As the story goes, Madeira was subjected to so much heat during its voyage that it was being stabilized. (It was being pasteurized before Louis Pasteur had discovered the process.) In addition, the heat accelerated the aging process, creating depth and complexity. This particular legend is suspect simply because all wines must have been subjected to the heat of ship galleys, but the legend has another fact going against it.

There is evidence that Madeira vintners had learned right at home the special benefits of heat when applied to their wines. The term Vinho do Sol (wine of the sun) referred to early Madeira that had been treated by exposure to sunlight. Producers used glass roofs over casks filled with wine to create more heat from the sun. The heat was so intense that the wood of the casks could retain much of it after sunset and through the cool night. This method of production was being used well before Madeira's popularity had spread across the seas.

By the late eighteenth century, Madeira producers had fully developed a unique heating process known as "estufa" that continues today. Before export, the brandy-fortified Madeira wines are put into a storage lodge; there, they are exposed to temperatures as high as 104 degrees Fahrenheit for a few months; some remain in barrel storage and some are bottled beforehand. When the process is complete, Madeira wines are fully stabilized and can last in the bottle for decades (some claim centuries) even after having been opened and the contents of the bottle having been partly consumed. Madeira shipments grew steadily, eventually becoming the largest volume of wine imported in the British colonies in America—and then the wine gained preferential tax treatment there.

About a decade before the famous Boston Tea Party, British customs agents at Boston harbor had slapped a duty on a shipment of Madeira that arrived on a ship named *Liberty*. The townsfolk rioted in response. Within a few days the customs agents were forced to back down. The *Liberty* was a vessel owned by none other than John Hancock.

Shipping of Portuguese wine, and any other wine, was profitable but it was not without its problems, especially when it came to packaging.

Glass bottles had been in use since the Phoenicians, but mostly as ornamentals. The Romans used glass jars for wine, but only to move the wine from amphorae to serve into their guests' goblets. The first historical record of glass being used for wine storage is in the thirteenth century, at a Tatar headquarters where the leader entertained guests.

In the fifteenth century, innovative Venetian glass production finally led to fairly active use of glass wine bottles in northern Europe. As in Rome, the bottles were mostly used for transport of the wine from cask to bottle just before serving. Not until the seventeenth-century discovery of production methods to produce heavier glass was it possible to safely store and to age wine in bottles, let alone ship them on long journeys. When they were used for shipping, bottles were mostly capped with a layer of olive oil and wax, so they had to be stood upright, a situation that created a problem of its own.

In the latter years of the republic, some Romans had capped their amphorae with cork bungs produced from the *Quercus suber*, the cork oak tree that grew in their Iberian province, mainly in the area that is Portugal. But there is no indication that the practice became widespread. After the fall of Rome, cork gradually became the primary means for capping pharmaceuticals in Europe, but the wine industry stayed with the wax and olive oil method. At some point in the fifteenth century cork was used to cap some wine bottles, and then more and more until the seventeenth century, when it was brought into near widespread use for its ability to protect the wine in the bottle more than any other capping device. Being the primary producers of cork, the Portuguese profited greatly from its use. The new stopper also gave wine shippers the chance to increase prices to cover the new costs connected to packaging, thereby raising their profits through stealth. The new use of bottles and of cork certainly was a step in the right direction, but the packaging revolution needed some tweaking.

Bottles in use at the time were bulbous in shape. The only way they could be shipped was to stand them upright. On long journeys the corks could, and often did, dry out, causing losses and even ruining wines by spilling or letting too much oxygen in. Merchants addressed the dry cork problem by bottling wines right before shipping, a solution that worked, but inconsistently. In the eighteenth century, the Portuguese wine industry introduced an elongated wine bottle with a short neck and a shoulder. The new bottle design was better suited for stacking on its side, protecting the cork from drying out by keeping it in contact with moisture from the wine. As an added benefit, by stacking bottles on their sides shippers could fit more bottles—and more wine—into the same square footage of the ships' galleys that once held the upright bulbous bottles. Combined, the cork and shouldered bottle were so revolutionary they became industry standard without question.

Britain and France had become friends again in the early eighteenth century, and so Bordeaux shipments to England increased; the new wine bottles changed the way the wine trade between the two countries would operate. Many small Médoc producers had built good reputations by employing the single-vineyard concept. As part of their reputation, Médoc producers were known to hold wines in inventory until they were aged to perfection and ready to drink. The introduction of the shouldered bottle gave the producers an opportunity to shift the cost burden of aging wine from them to either the middle merchant or the consumer instead of holding large inventories of wine in casks, waiting for them to mature,

Médoc producers created a new system for buying wines. British merchants and consumers were invited to taste the vintage from the cask and then to lock in a price for it. Producers bottled the wine, collected their money for it, shipped it, and left the bulk of the aging process to take place in the already-paid-for bottles, either in the cellars of French agents or across the channel in the cellars of British importers or in the cellars of consumers. The cork and bottle certainly gave the Bordelais a new opportunity to increase profits by reducing costs. In another part of France, the cork and bottle essentially established a whole new wine production method.

Legend has it that a humble seventeenth-century Benedictine monk in a monastery stumbled upon a wine that had fermented in the bottle during storage. Upon opening the bottle, the monk, who was quite pleased with the wine's blast of bubbles, supposedly proclaimed to his compatriots, "I am drinking stars." And that was the discovery of Champagne.

Despite its lack of poetry, the real story of the discovery of sparkling wine in Champagne, as told by Desmond Seward in *Monks and Wine,* is no less interesting than the legend. (It is also interesting to note that in the south of France, in a wine district named Limoux, sparkling wine is believed to have been produced as early as 1535, a good century before Champagne and a matter best left to the French to sort out.)

Once the home of the great medieval merchant fairs, in the seventeenth century the Champagne region of northern France had achieved the status of a reasonably good wine district. Much of the wine production was under the control of monasteries; the most widely known today is the monastery of Hautvillers at Epernay, where a Benedictine cellar master named Dom Pierre Pérignon had produced his wines.

Dom Pérignon was keen to create a premium reputation for the wines of his abbey. The strict and direct vigneron was responsible for selecting grape varieties—he introduced pinot noir to the region—and he was always seeking ways to improve. He established new methods by which grapes were grown, harvested, and vinified at the abbey. His red grapes were being pressed without much skin contact, producing white wine or wine with just a faint color, known as *vin gris,* or gray wine. Even during his most innovative moments, however, Dom Pérignon was powerless either to control the weather or to protect his delicate vines and wines from it.

Champagne is in the north of France and as such it is subject to rather early, cold winter temperatures. The long, cool, natural fermentation of the wines that began in late fall was interrupted by early winter low temperatures. The abrupt—unplanned—cessation of fermentation would leave just enough unfermented sugar in the wines so that in spring, when temperatures warmed, yeast cells that had hibernated during winter awakened to a breakfast of sugar, and the wines of Champagne would re-ferment in their new bottles.

When yeast cells eat grape sugar they create not only alcohol but also carbon dioxide gas. Once capped inside the bottle, the carbon dioxide has nowhere to go so it is reabsorbed into the wine. The bubbling gas in suspension is released as soon as the wine is exposed to the elements (as soon as the bottle is open); this is what was happening to the early wines of Champagne. Yet, for whatever reason, these spring wines appealed to both the British and French courts.

Unfortunately, uncontrolled fermentation in the bottle can create wines that go seriously "off," or the carbon dioxide can be strong enough to break bottles. Dom Pérignon could not always avert the trouble but he tried, and as he searched for a solution he learned to control the effervescent wines; and then he figured out how to create even more powerful bubbles. A great deal of the new champagne was lost to bottle breakage from the increased pressure of built-up carbon dioxide. (Seward points out that in some instances more than 75 percent of the wine was lost to breakage.) In England, the process of introducing lead oxide in the manufacture of glass bottles was helping to create stronger bottles. After the monks successfully put that new glass technology to use at Hautvillers, their wines became more reliable and increasingly popular. By the end of the century the abbey became so wealthy that it financed excavation for a new cellar out of the earth to produce more and better Champagne.

According to another Champagne story, in the cellars of the widow Madame Cliquot, who had taken control of her dead husband's business, a worker grabbed one of Madame's tables, cut some holes in it and created the first "riddling" rack. Before then, champagne drinkers served the wine in dimpled glasses, presumably to hide the cloudiness caused by dead yeast cells floating in the wine. Riddling is the process used to get the dead yeast cells into the neck of the bottle by hanging the bottles in a rack through neck holes. After many quarter turns of the bottle over a period of time, more and more cells have fallen; the neck is dipped in a frozen brine; the cap is popped off; the carbon dioxide pushes the yeast cells out; the bottle is lifted quickly, and topped up with a formula secret to each Champagne producer; and it is recapped and wire-meshed shut.

England became the biggest market for Champagne, but the wine's popularity grew in France, too. After Champagne was embraced by the Duc d'Orleans in the early part of the eighteenth century, and later by Louis XV, its place in French wine history had been solidified. Because of the French Crown's favor, Champagne developed an image as an extravagant drink for the extravagant and for the intellectual. The wine likely sat at table to witness many new and unusual philosophical arguments of the Enlightenment period.

PART V

The Recent Past

North America

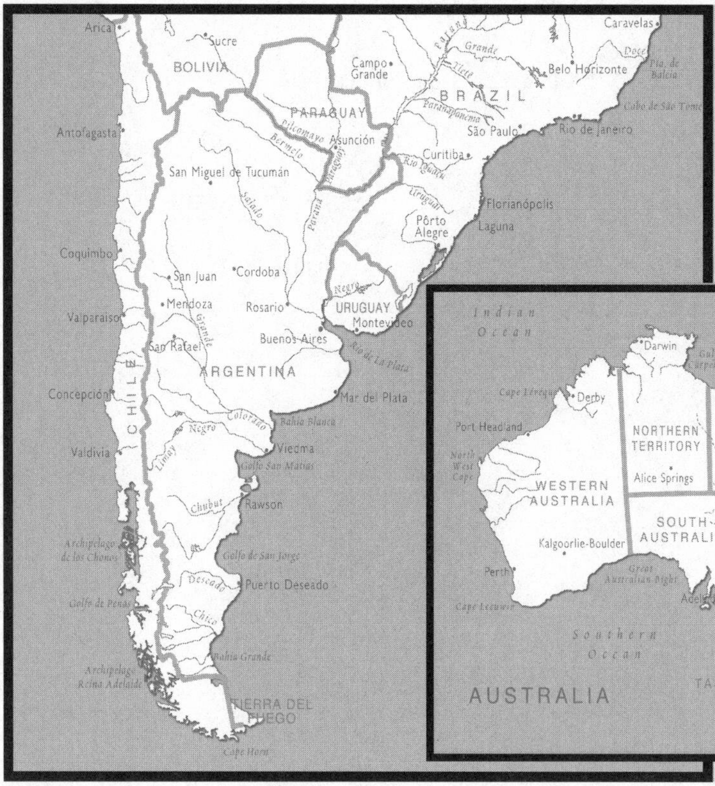

South America below the equator

Australia and New Zealand

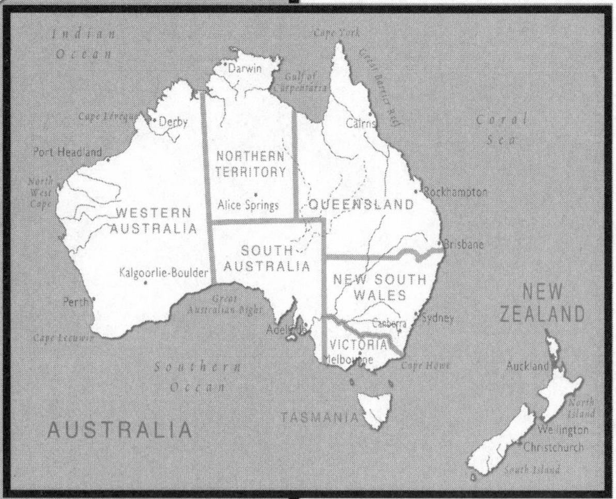

12.
Going Global

The culture of the vine is not desirable in lands capable of producing anything else. It is a species of gambling . . . wherein, whether you make much or nothing, you are equally ruined.

—Thomas Jefferson, 1787

When the French Revolution of 1789 failed to meet its egalitarian promises, the subsequent rise of Napoleon Bonaparte created renewed anti-British sentiment. Once again, ties between Bordeaux and England had been severed. France went on to vacillate nervously and impetuously through the nineteenth century between monarchy and republicanism, yet French wine merchants managed to survive. Some looked to a growing thirst for wine in the new Austro-Hungarian Empire, but since German and Eastern European wines also competed for that market, many French wine merchants sought opportunities elsewhere, in Spain and in the New World.

The Oja River region (Rioja) of Spain had produced wine under the Roman Empire but, beginning with the Moors' control of Spain, it had fallen on hard times. The only truly successful wine export from Spain was sherry and that, of course, went mostly to England. Around 1780 a few Bordeaux vintners had dabbled with vineyards in Rioja, planting their beloved French grape varieties among the local grape varieties. When Napoleon lost the British market, Britain would not deal with French merchants and some of them created a newly active wine industry in Rioja, but the industry remained confined to Spain for the most part.

Other European viticulturists were being lured to the possibilities across the Atlantic. Early attempts and failures at commercial winemaking in the American colonies that took place in the South did not dissuade Thomas Jefferson. In the latter part of the eighteenth century Jefferson arranged for a business associate, a Florentine named Filipo Mazzei, to plant vineyards at Monticello. Like Jefferson, Mazzei was a Renaissance man; the Italian was a surgeon, a merchant, a financer, and a horticulturist with a deep interest in the vine; at one point in his life, he worked as a wine merchant in London.

Mazzei got to Virginia and Jefferson's promised plot of land in 1773, and then he planted European vines that he had brought with him. His intention was for a wine company in the future, with Jefferson as a partner. But the following year Mazzei's vineyards met with a major American winter frost and the dream died. He and Jefferson continued their friendship, but their joint vineyard work was put on hold.

A little more than a decade later, Jefferson learned well the quality and importance of wine to the French culture and economy. Being a devout agrarian, he felt the potential power of viticulture could avert the eighteenth-century

French Revolution. Putting aside his understanding of the risks involved in viticulture, during his time as minister to France in 1787, Jefferson wrote to a friend that perhaps putting people to work in the vineyards would be a way to alleviate the rampant poverty of French commoners and maybe divert the revolution that was on the horizon. During his commission in France, Jefferson had traveled the country's major wine regions. And when his tour as minister was over in 1789, he traveled into the important Rhine Valley to get a handle on its wines, and also made a stop in Italy. His travels reawakened his interest in establishing commercial wine production in the new United States of America.

Back home from his tour of duty in France, Jefferson came close to becoming the official state wine consultant while serving as secretary of state under George Washington. He kept an association with European wine brokers, who in turn kept him in good supply of wine, allowing him to buy wine for Washington and other officials, and advising his associates on maintaining a wine cellar of good balance.

Meanwhile, various European viticulturists had arrived in America in the vain hope of creating a wine industry based on European-style wines. Like Mazzei before them, some had been friends who Jefferson had coaxed from Europe. They also, like Mazzei, failed. The only wine economy in America during the period remained in religious communities, but the situation was about to change in the latter part of the eighteenth century, thanks to a Frenchman named Legaux.

Legaux established a vineyard in 1793 about a dozen miles outside of Philadelphia. To get his Pennsylvania Vine Company into and off the ground, Legaux procured vines from Burgundy, Bordeaux, Champagne, and Constantia, at the Cape of Good Hope. He seems also to have been a controversial figure; he made grand claims that often ended up in litigation. The vines from Constantia turned out to be one of his claims that other viticulturists challenged.

Rather than originating in South Africa, the grape was believed to be one that James Alexander had discovered in 1740 and had named after himself; it was growing in vineyards that William Penn had owned in the previous century. (The Alexander vine is believed to have been a "field hybrid," created by nature from cross-pollination between the European *Vitis vinifera* species brought to America and the *Vitis labrusca* native species of the Northeast.) Whether it was South African or an American field hybrid, the Alexander grape was among the first to show great promise for commercial wine in America.

By 1802 Legaux was able to boast of a shareholders' roster for the Pennsylvania Vine Company that included Alexander Hamilton, Aaron Burr, and the person whose name now graces a treatment center for alcoholism in America, Benjamin Rush. Noticeably absent from the list: Rush's close friend and wine confidant, Thomas Jefferson. He probably was still smarting from having earlier wine investment losses, or maybe he just did not cotton to the flamboyant, litigious Legaux. Many subsequent years of financial and legal hassles had given Legaux quite a racy reputation; then, after numerous failures in the vineyard, he and his Pennsylvania Vine Company vanished.

In 1816 Joseph Bonaparte (Napoleon's brother) lived in exile in Bordentown in the southern reaches of New Jersey. Joseph's flight from France was accomplished with the help of some French army officers; they joined him and settled close to him, in Philadelphia. The officers formed an organization—without Joseph—with the express purpose of settling on the Ohio or Mississippi rivers to establish viticulture. Named the French Agricultural and Manufacturing Society, the group ultimately made its way to Mobile, Alabama, where the officers proceeded to produce a series of blunders and hardly any viticultural success.

In 1820 another Frenchman, named Loubat, attempted commercial plantings of European vines in New Utrecht (what is now a part of Brooklyn). Loubat's vines lived for a few years and then he lost them to whatever it was that the European species could not handle in America. According to Thomas Pinney, Loubat had produced no income at all from wine.

Prior to both Bonaparte's officers and Loubat, a Swiss-trained viticulturist, John DuFour, had failed in Kentucky with European vines. Records of his failures that Pinney uncovered include descriptions of grapevine diseases that had yet to be fully understood. Those who followed these early experiences of vignerons were forced to accept that the only way to build an American wine industry would be with grapevines that proved they could survive—the so-called native vines.

In 1824, two years prior to his death, Thomas Jefferson tasted, and liked, a wine called Tokay. The wine had been the product of John Adlum, of York, Pennsylvania. Adlum had already been hailed as the "Father of American Viticulture," and he had published his *Memoir on the Cultivation of the Vine in America,* in which he listed the numerous grape varieties being propagated at his nursery. Jefferson had unknowingly tasted what the soon-to-be American commercial wine industry would taste like.

Adlum's so-called Tokay was traced to Maryland, to the widow of a viticulturist. When she sold Adlum the cuttings, she told him the grape was the true Tokaj that her husband had brought in from Hungary. Adlum apparently did not know that the grape in Hungary responsible for Tokaj is named furmint. It turned out that the major grape the widow had sold to Adlum was catawba, a *Vitis labruscana* hybrid born in the Carolinas, as a spontaneous field cross between transplanted European vines that had survived their requisite few years in America and some native vines.

Despite Jefferson's proclamation that Adlum's Catawba wine was among the best he had ever tasted, the latter's attempt to build a commercial wine industry failed just like the efforts of those who had tried before him. Some claim that Adlum's failure had to do not with the vineyards but with the fact that he turned out to be a woefully deficient businessman. Perhaps, but there is proof that he had suffered major vineyard failures.

In any event, out of the wine business, Adlum went on to devote his work to tracking and documenting the various grape varieties available in the American Midwest and to influencing many other grape growers. Sadly, aside from two editions of his book, Adlum's legacy in viticulture seems to have died a few years before he did in 1836. The view today is that he might have been shortchanged. His true legacy is indeed in the Catawba wine that he had served to Jefferson, and that legacy was fostered by a wealthier man with more business savvy, a man who may have started the rumors about Adlum's business acumen.

A year prior to Adlum's introduction of Catawba wine, a millionaire lawyer and real estate and horticultural buff named Nicholas Longworth had started to produce wine. Records show that his was a white wine made from the red Alexander grape. Longworth's first experiment ended in failure, too, but rather than dissuading him, the experience encouraged him to continue.

Longworth disparaged Adlum and his Catawba wine, claiming that Adlum added inferior wild grapes both to increase his crop and to add sugar to the must. There was no mistaking, however, that the catawba grape offered the best promise thus far for those with commercial American wine aspirations. Within two years after Adlum's failure, Longworth had a successful Catawba wine on the market. Longworth possessed what Adlum did not—good business connections and a flair for self-promotion. By 1825, he was the proud owner of the first truly successful commercial wine production in the United States. The business was based at Cincinnati.

Longworth's run of success lasted for about twenty-three years, reaching its height in 1842 after his release of "Sparkling Catawba," which was the happy result of a winemaking mistake he had made. Unable to duplicate his sparkling wine success in subsequent years, Longworth took a French sparkling winemaker in to his employ; then he used his flair for self-promotion and his wealthy business connections to get his wines noticed not only in major American cities but also in Europe. His success naturally stirred others to produce commercial wine.

By 1852, about twelve hundred acres of vineyards had graced Ohio and at least three hundred separate producers or farmers had been enjoying a measure of success, thanks to Longworth's promotion. By 1859, with two thousand acres of vines and production of more than half a million gallons of wine, Ohio had become the most successful state in the union in commercial wine. In neighboring Missouri, German immigrants had also focused on the prolific catawba grape after they had been beaten fighting a few rounds with the inhospitable environment for European vines. Their efforts became particularly successful in a town named Hermann, the center of Missouri's wine industry even today.

Although successful at producing commercial wine, Missouri Germans were not becoming millionaires at it, so in 1849 many of them left Hermann and surrounding areas to join the search for gold out West. Like most everyone else who panned for gold, the German prospectors came up mostly with empty sifting pans. Many of them returned to Missouri, but some decided to stay in warm California. They settled in the Los Angeles Valley, where they soon established commercial winemaking at Anaheim.

Prior to the arrival of the Germans from Missouri, California vineyards had been hosting the mission grape for more than a century, the legacy of early Spanish settlers. Yet, when the soon to be successful firm of Kohler and Frohling began in the middle of the nineteenth century, the Germans recalled their failures in Missouri with *Vitis vinifera* vines, so they planted at Anaheim what had succeeded in Missouri: the catawba. In fact, much of the wine produced in early nineteenth-century America, commercial or otherwise, relied either on grapes native to North America or hybrid field crossings like catawba.

Over time, the urge for European-style wines overtook the German producers in California. They began to experiment with the mission grape and then they began to import European vines; to their delight, they found in California a hospitable environment for European grapevines. But in 1880 the Anaheim vineyards were wiped out by a disease that was not understood then, but is understood today as being caused by a bacterium that prevents water from getting to the vine—Pierce's disease, named after N. B. Pierce, California's first trained plant pathologist whose study led to understanding the disease.

The gold rush attracted French immigrants, too. Most had been farmers or producers in their native country. When they found no gold, they set out to work the California land. One of the most successful of these immigrants was Charles LeFranc, whose work in Santa Clara County lives on in California wine folklore. LeFranc is another of the early viticulturalists who wore the mantle "father of." In this case, he became the father of commercial wine in Santa Clara Valley, creating the first successful wine business there (Almaden) in 1856, not from the mission grape, but from grapes like cabernet sauvignon and pinot noir. Some twenty years later, a Burgundian, Paul Masson, joined LeFranc. Within five years Almaden had added the LeFranc-Masson label to its line, and Masson had married LeFranc's daughter. Toward the end of the century, after a runaway team and wagon had run over and killed LeFranc, his immediate family sold Almaden to a larger group, leaving Paul Masson to operate his own winery under his own name.

While LeFranc and Masson were busy establishing success, Agoston Haraszthy arrived in California by way of Wisconsin, where he had produced grapes and wine before the gold rush. Haraszthy was another character of the period with a keen talent for self-promotion and marketing; he was also a magnet for scandal. After establishing his credentials by writing the first California treatise on grapes and wine, Haraszthy was commissioned by the 1861 California legislature to work with and to improve grape growing in the state. With a legislative mandate in hand, he set out for Europe on a buying spree. When he returned to the now historic Buena Vista Winery in Sonoma County, Haraszthy planted hundreds of *Vitis vinifera* vines of many different grape varieties. When the wines showed up on the market a few years later they were an immediate success.

Folklore has it that Haraszthy established a hybrid *Vitis vinifera* known as the zinfandel grape that henceforth grew only in California. Pinney points to evidence that disproves Haraszthy had much to do with creating a hybrid zinfandel. More damning, however, is the latest DNA findings that identify the zinfandel grape as a direct relative of two grapes, one in Italy (primitivo) and one in Croatia (crljenak). The connection of zinfandel to Croatia, however, makes it likely that Haraszthy, who was Hungarian, brought the vine back with him from Europe and mistook it for a grape with a name similar to Zinfandel.

As flamboyant as he was successful, Haraszthy left all sorts of unanswered questions about his past, not the least of which was the reason he had to leave Wisconsin, which many people believed had to do with chicanery. In the latter part of the nineteenth century, the successful Hungarian vanished from Sonoma while under political pressure from some questionable business practices. He faded into oblivion, reportedly somewhere in the jungles of Nicaragua.

Despite disease and disavowed characters, by the middle of the nineteenth century America had finally established itself as a commercial wine-producing nation, with production centered in both California and in the Midwest; and then, things viticultrual began to happen on the East Coast.

In 1839, yet another Frenchman had established a winery in the United States. Jean Jacques built Blooming Grove Winery in Washingtonville, in the Hudson Valley region, using so-called local vines—cross-hybrids of European vines and vines native to America. It became the first successful commercial winery in New York State and it remained the only one for about two decades, after which a second winery—Brochton Wine Cellars—started up in the Lake Erie district. Brochton, too, grew "local" vines. For the next half dozen years Blooming Grove and Brochton wines sold well in and around New York State.

A couple of years after the Civil War, Thomas Harris, the leader of a spiritual group called the New Brotherhood of Life, had produced wine first in Duchess County and then at Brochton, New York, not far from the Brochton Wine Cellars. Perhaps tired of the native vines, Harris soon left for California. Upon his departure, he sold the Brotherhood of Life Winery to some New York wine merchants, who later took over Brochton Wine Cellars. Then in the 1870s, with Jean Jacques dead, the New York merchants acquired Blooming Grove Winery from Jacques's family. Owning all the commercial wineries in New York, the group of merchants merged the companies, moved everything into the Washingtonville location, and created the name Brotherhood Winery, which exists today as the oldest operating commercial winery in the state.

Table grapes had been grown in the Finger Lakes region of New York since 1830, after a minister named Bostwick established vineyards on the slopes around Keuka Lake, near a village called Hammondsport. Helped by the commercial success of the Erie Canal and then the railroad, Keuka's grape business was extremely successful and, as a result, vineyards were planted at nearby Canandaigua and Seneca Lakes.

It was a natural that the Finger Lakes region would enter the wine business, and it did in 1860, at the south end of Keuka Lake, in Hammondsport, where Charles Davenport Champlin and twelve local businessmen, with unusual promotional talent, started up the Pleasant Valley Wine Company. The company hired French vignerons, Jules and Joseph Masson, to produce commercial wines from local isabella and catawba grapes. The winery's true star rose in 1871, after Champlin sent some sparkling Catawba wine to a close friend and influential wine aficionado named Marshall Wilder. When Wilder dubbed the wine that "Great Champagne of the Western World," the first world-renowned American wine brand had been born and it immediately included a French place name as a means to promote it: Great Western "Champagne."

Unhappy with the cost of using the Erie Canal, Champlin and his investors built their own nine-mile railroad line for connecting to rails that went along the southern tier of New York all the way to New York City. The railroad became a secondary successful business for the wine merchants, trafficking wine on the way downstate and tourists on the way upstate.

> Right next door to the Pleasant Valley Wine Company, Greyton Taylor had established the Taylor Wine Company. By 1882 the two Finger Lakes wineries nearly eclipsed all American wineries in both size and name recognition, and they did it on the strength of local grape varieties—those so-called natives that included the hybrid catawba.

In the mid to late nineteenth century, the United States comprised thirty-two states, twenty-two of which had produced commercial wine. And while some of the wineries gained national and even international recognition, and some of the owners of the wineries became quite wealthy, the wine industry was by no means a major national economic force. Oddly, many of the American wines that had gained international recognition, at exhibitions in Paris and in Belgium for instance, had been produced from the grapes that did not appeal to Europeans earlier in America's wine history. Those grapevines would soon play a role in Europe that would be much greater than just winning awards for wine.

13.
Disaster

In the month of June 1863, I received from [the greenhouse in] Hammersmith a vine leaf covered with minute gall-like excrescences . . .

—Professor Westwood, botanist and entomologist, Oxford University

The poor relationship with Britain during Bonaparte's regime had become a big problem for French wine merchants. The emperor gave preferential tax treatment to French nobility at the same time that he applied a number of oppressive taxes on the wine trade. Vineyards were taxed and so was wine transportation, wine markets of more than four thousand in population were taxed, municipalities with a wine trade were taxed, and retailer may have paid the heaviest of all taxes.

When Louis-Philippe took the throne in 1830, he was shaken by the damage that had been done to the important wine economy. The crown precipitated the fall of general wine taxes by as much as 30 percent. Unfortunately for the producers, the single largest market for wine, Paris, maintained its oppressive tax structure, part of which was based on alcoholic content. Since wines were generally produced naturally, without much chemistry, lowering alcohol content to avoid taxes posed both a technical problem and a potential problem with stability and quality. The tax situation in Paris managed to produce a stagnant wine glut, which brought prices down for growers and for producers, as well as decreasing French and British wine merchant profits.

After having to endure Napoleon, British wine merchants, as they had in the seventeenth century, became sufficiently alarmed at their continuing reliance on imported wine. Their government responded by seeking a way to establish a wine trade through its colonies, specifically, through the old penal colony at New South Wales (Australia), and also the small landing Britain had established in New Zealand.

Before mining engineer John Busby arrived in Australia from England in 1824, three or four attempts had already been made to establish viticulture and winemaking in the colony. Busby was sent to build the water supply system for Sydney Township. His second son, James, who had studied viticulture, accompanied his father and by 1830 James had put out *"A Manual of Plain Directions for Planting and Cultivating Vineyards and for Making Wine in New South Wales."* For his efforts in Australia, James Busby was given a Hunter Valley land grant. Three years later he had planted vines from cuttings he had gotten on a trip to France and Spain. No records exist of wine imports into England from Busby's work. In fact, he sold his vineyards to his brother-in-law, William Kelman, and then he went off to New Zealand.

When the Australian gold rush struck in the 1850s, most of the immigrants from France, Italy, and Germany were unsuccessful at finding gold but they also hadn't much reason to return home. Many of them stayed put and many of them planted vines. From these vineyards the first Australian wine imports reached England nearly twenty-five years after Busby's plantings. But the wine industry stayed small until after World War I, possibly because of the distance between Australia and Europe. During the war, the Kelman family sold the original Busby vineyards to a C. F. Lindeman, ancestor to the family name that is behind one of the largest Australian wine success stories.

New Zealand had been discovered in the fifteenth century but had remained an isolated Polynesian culture until James Cook charted the island in the eighteenth century. In 1832, while James Busby was planting vineyards in Australia, the British were trying to beat the French in developing a colony in New Zealand. Famous for becoming the father of Australian viticulture, and for being the son of John Busby, James was given an assignment to become the "First British Resident" of New Zealand, making it a colony under New South Wales. He joined two thousand inhabitants of the North Island at Waitangi. In 1834 he wrote a New Zealand Declaration of Independence before the French could implement a plan to declare sovereignty over New Zealand.

There is evidence that vines had been planted at a Catholic mission in New Zealand in the early part of the nineteenth century, but no records of wine have been uncovered. Busby of course established vineyards and a winery right away in his new home. A second Catholic mission, plus a contingent of French families, got hold of some land on which they, too, established vineyards, and at the turn of the century Eastern European immigrants arrived in New Zealand to establish vineyards. It seemed that New Zealand was on its way in the wine trade, but, like Australia and possibly for the same reason, the New Zealand wine industry remained relatively small and mainly local into the twentieth century. Meanwhile, vine experimentation between Europe and America was heating up.

> In France, and in the regions where it is able to mature its fruits, only the vine has the ability to create wealth in poor and neglected soils: alone it can yield ten percent on the capital advanced, and alone it will be capable of maintaining great and rich estates.
>
> —Jules Guyot, 1860, Leo A. Loubère

Unpopular drink taxes in France popped up as a subject during an election campaign of the Second French Republic. The idea was to replace the drink taxes with an income tax. But the French again proved unsuitable to republicanism; Louis Napoleon (Napoleon III) became emperor in 1851. He was immediately embroiled in the lingering demands for tax relief from winegrowers and wine merchants. The emperor responded by reducing remaining entry taxes to half. He later reduced the retail tax substantially. The king also lowered duties on British goods and he lowered tariffs on exported wines. Bordeaux wines began again to flow toward England and money began to flow back to Bordeaux—French wine merchants seemed happy.

Tax relief aside, the friendliest gesture of Napoleon III toward the wine industry was his commission of Dr. Jules Guyot to study its industrial potential. At the time, the primary focus of European winegrowers and governments became the health of the vineyards and the return on investments that good health would allow. With money being made, wine had begun to suffer once more from greed. Merchants tended to leave winegrowers alone, as long as they delivered grapes, and so vineyards were being abused. Guyot felt that the best place to start to increase wine quality was to get peasant growers to upgrade their vine cultivation practices.

Believing it would give farmers an incentive to produce better crops, Guyot pushed to get rid of the wage labor system for sharecropping; then, he set out to teach landowners how to limit yield. After teaching them, Guyot demanded that landowners teach their growers his methods. This approach formed the foundation for what led to modern-day growing and producing regulations that govern conditions under which crops are produced in France.

Echoing Columella of the second century, Guyot proclaimed riches were to be found in the vineyard, and many that followed his advice were being rewarded, but nature had other plans for the vineyards.

Scientific discoveries of the period had been increasing the overall quality of viticulture and winemaking. America, England, and France were the focal points for most of the work; in America there lived a continued hope that European vines could survive other than on the West Coast; in Europe, scientists were curious about the American native vines that seemed to be producing award-winning wines; in England, horticulture and plant research had been a constant interest. The scientific experiments created vine traffic across the Atlantic, well before anyone ever thought of checking immigrant plants at customs for their potential to carry foreign diseases.

The first of two major vine diseases to strike France in the century arrived quietly in 1846 at just about the time wine prices had been on the rise under Louis Napoleon. The losses were minimal and confined to a few vineyards. By 1850, the sad sight of grapes bursting and then drying up became a widespread phenomenon known as powdery mildew.

The benefits of sulfur sprayed on grapevines had already been known, but peasant winegrowers did not cotton to chemicals and, even if they had, they could not afford to buy them. But when it was discovered in 1853 that the sulfured vines of a winegrower in the town of Beziers were surviving powdery mildew while the disease was devastating vineyards all around his vineyards, peasant farmers found the money to buy sulfur, as did most other French winegrowers. The holdouts were in Bordeaux at the great châteaux. The finicky wealthy winegrowers there were uneasy over sulfur's ability to cause hydrogen sulfide to settle on grapes and then perhaps give wine a rotten-egg smell. Since they enjoyed so much prestige, the Bordelais figured that shrinking crop losses could be made up in higher wine prices. By 1858, however, the disease became so threatening that the Bordelais gave in to using sulfur.

An Englishman of the period named Berkeley identified *Oidium tuckeri* (powdery mildew) on grapevines. He claimed the disease made its way to England by way of America and the disease then made its way to France. When powdery mildew struck, French wine producers turned to buying wine from Italians to make up the lost volume. Soon the disease spread to Italy and across Europe. The Portuguese Island of Madeira lost nearly 75 percent of its vineyards to the disease.

At the tail end of the powdery mildew blight, France's viticulture was given a break in the form of a string of spectacular vintages. Promotion of the run of fine vintages was kicked off in 1855 by Napoleon III's desire for a classification of what he considered to be France's "best" wines. The Médoc already had enjoyed status as the top red wine region of France, so at that year's International Exhibition in Paris, at the desire of the emperor, the now famous 1855 Médoc classification system came into being. Five tiers of classified growths (*crus*) wines were established and filled by dozens of producers, but only four made it to First

Growth (*Grand crus classe*): Château Lafite-Rothschild, Latour, Margaux, and Haut-Brion—the latter the only one produced outside the Médoc.

To the consternation of producers and merchants in the important wine departments of St. Emilion and Pomerol, the measuring stick for rankings back then was heavily weighted toward the price wines had commanded over the previous hundred years and, with the exception of Haut-Brion in Graves, the red wines of the Médoc commanded much higher prices than red wines produced anywhere else in Bordeaux. Some also claim that the political connections of the well-known producers had a lot to do with the classification. In any event, despite the progress made in winemaking technique and talent since 1855, not to mention the times some properties have changed hands over the centuries, the Médoc classification has been altered only once, after elevating one Second Growth producer—Château Mouton-Rothschild—to First Growth status in 1973.

Author Loubère calls the decade between 1860 and 1870 "the Golden Age of French Wine." The period began with a trade treaty between France and England in 1860 to lower and then to remove many tariffs that had been levied against international wine shipments. The treaty was later extended to many other European states. Steam power and the "iron horse" (railroad) had been stimulating international trade more and more, and winegrowers benefited from the faster and cheaper means of transportation. Steam-powered tractors increased vineyard efficiency at the same time that they helped to reduce labor costs. Faster and more efficient steam-powered winepresses also came on the market, lowering the cost of both labor and production, not to mention quality, since speed in pressing often helps the juice maintain stability. Profits grew and so did investments in new vineyards. Loubère estimates that in 1860 an incredible 7 to 10 percent of the total French population was either employed in the wine business or working in businesses that supported it or benefited from it.

With powdery mildew having come under control, good vintages seemed to come year after year, except for a small mysterious death of some vines in southern France in 1865. Having just come off one of the most devastating attacks on vines, French scientists certainly looked at the potentially new

> Before Louis Pasteur had gotten involved in midcentury, alcohol fermentation was largely a wonderful but mysterious act of nature. Pasteur's combination discovery of how fermentation worked and, later, how microorganisms play a role in the life of wine ushered in a new age of wine quality, including the establishment of the formal study of oenology. Coupled with great vintages, Pasteur's work helped producers release to market some of the best wines France had known. But his discoveries did not address the vineyard.

problem—but they were too slow to look. The disease that began silently and on a small scale in the Languedoc had edged its way into the Rhône Valley, and before anyone new what had happened, French vineyards had been lain waste by a new and seemingly more virulent pest.

After taking a look at the ravages of the new disease, how it seemed to cut the life juices out of the vine, drying out the leaves and fruit and then killing the vine completely, a French scientist, J. E. Planchon, named the disease *Phylloxera vastatrix* (a Greek/Latin construction that refers to dry leaves and devastation). Planchon had studied the disease and came up with the hypothesis that a microscopic insect was breeding and living on the vine roots and likely sucking the life out of the vines. But he seemed to have no advice for a cure and the disease picked up speed, ravaging across France.

Part of the reason for *phylloxera's* unbounded leap was infighting among winegrowers. Many did not believe Planchon and many others had not even heard of his theory. Without agreeing on the nature of the problem, finding a cure was impossible, so the French government's first move to solve the problem proved a disaster. It set up a commission comprising large vineyard owners and industrialists. The commission recommended pulling out infected vines. Never trusting either government or wealthy industrialists, French farmers disregarded the commission's inspector's orders to pull out infected vines. Twenty years after the outbreak of the disease a solution had yet been found; the French were nearly engaged in a civil war over it, represented by a riot and fight in the streets of Champagne between wine producers and local officials.

In 1869, Bordeaux winegrowers spread carbon bisulfide in deep furrows that they had dug in the vineyards. The practice worked only as a palliative by

> At one point during the search to cure *phylloxera,* the French government offered nearly half a million francs to anyone who could eradicate the disease. Numerous schemes poured in, from the use of toad venom to exorcism to either burning or flooding vineyards. One scheme to import a population of an insect from the United States that was known to eat *phylloxera* aphids failed when, after arriving from America, the insects refused to eat.

destroying living aphids yet allowing eggs to hatch. To be effective at all the procedure required an exact dose; excess carbon bisulfide could kill vines. Worse, mishandling the chemical could cause explosions, which it did in some vineyards. The foul-smelling chemical was also expensive and, since it was not really a cure, winegrowers continued to press for further research.

Meanwhile, *phylloxera* had crossed French borders and spread throughout Europe, wiping out thousands of hectares of vineyards and thousands of families who had relied on them. The virulent disease even crossed continents, spreading as far as Australia; by the latter part of the century, it had made its way back to the United States, to California, where European *Vitis vinifera* vines had been doing relatively well until then.

It had been known that with the exception of the West and parts of the Southwest European vines were unable to survive in America, but it had yet to be discovered why that was so. It was also known that Native American vines sent to Europe for experiments had less trouble surviving there than European vines had with survival in America. The answer to the *phylloxera* blight was hidden in those two facts.

Earlier in the century American scientists had shown that most North American vines were found to host the *phylloxera* aphid and its eggs, but the American vines did not seem bothered much by the insect. In 1881, in a conference at Bordeaux, scientists persuaded French officials to agree to an experiment with grafting French vines onto American rootstocks in the hope of creating European vines that would be resistant to the aphids and their eggs. It worked.

Between 1880 and 1910, T. V. Munson had traveled forty of the United States studying more than a thousand Native American vines. He spent three years on the first draft of a vine classification manual, which he submitted to viticulture study programs throughout the world. Munson not only studied grapes, he also collected and bred them in his quest to evaluate and select the most outstanding local vines. Munson's nursery was located in Denison, Texas; from there he sold grape cultivars throughout the South and the Southwest.

French scientists had known of Munson's work; he had sent them many cultivars on which they had experimented. Munson was asked to take on the job of moving American rootstock material to France for the cure to the disease. The vines he sent originated mainly from the Midwest, Northeast, and Southeast, and parts of Canada. They had to be pure Native American vines; *phylloxera* can affect field hybrids that have *Vitis vinifera* in their "bloodline." Over a four-month period, with the help of American laborers and farmers, Munson had filled about fifteen wagons of stem cuttings bound for France. He identified each lot by the species within it. It took three ships of root cuttings to fill the order. In France it took much trial and error before scientists struck the correct balance to maintain the integrity of *Vitis vinifera* vines after grafting them onto an American rootstock species that could survive the many different soils throughout Europe. In fact, later outbreaks of the disease, some occurring in California as recently as the end of the twentieth century, prove that there is no blanket cure, even after more than a hundred years of studying the disease.

Until the best cure had been found, the nineteenth-century *phylloxera* story produced mostly losers, with one major early-on exception. Wine merchants in the important British market were uninterested in sad stories; they wanted wine. French producers needed to come up with it. Since the prolific wine-producing Italic peninsula next door to France had at first been spared the blight, French wine merchants turned to their neighbor for help.

Between 1860 and 1866 most Italic states had joined Victor Emmanuel II of Sardinia to create a near unified kingdom. In 1866 Venice joined and then in 1870, when Rome was brought in, all of Italy had been unified under a constitutional monarchy. Nobles and industrialists in the north prospered after the new centralized government based in Rome developed policies that favored big industry. Large numbers of southern Italian peasants were brought north to work for a handful of rich nobles who held vast vineyard estates. Piedmont, Lombardy, and Tuscany produced wines that were light, subtle, and of decent quality—and expensive.

In the south, producers pumped out large quantities of ordinary, thick, high-alcohol wines from grapes grown almost as primitively as they had been grown when Rome was an empire. There was no single-crop agriculture. Instead, grapevines had been mixed in with various crops; it was common for grapevines to grow up the trunks of fruit trees. Since the south had little means to engage in international trade, farmers and wine producers could use any business that came their way. The blight had yet to reach Italy in 1870 so French wine merchants made deals to buy southern Italian wines, which the French blended into what little wine they had and labeled it as their own. Luckily for the French, a decade later, when the aphids had made it to Italy, grafting had already been decided upon as the cure. The Italians could no longer supply the volume of wine they had been supplying and the French would soon no longer need it.

In the process of serving the French wine industry, Italian winegrowers had learned single-crop farming. After they, too, had taken to using grafted vines to replant what had been lost during the blight, the new vines were set into their own special soils. Italian wines began to get better; but, still without good marketing, Italy had little access to export markets. It would take another hundred years before Italian wines would receive the international recognition that they were beginning to deserve.

A scant few wine industries had not been affected by the aphids that spread across the world. Some small portions of Spain's viticultural regions, especially in mountain areas, had been spared. And being situated where they are, with the Andes acting as a pristine (and cold) natural boundary, the two largest South American wine producers, Chile and Argentina, were said to have escaped *phylloxera*. Seeking a source for wine, many Europeans fled either to Rioja in Spain or to South America to produce or supervise its production. With the help of the new railroad to get grapes and wine moved efficiently to ports, exports of Chilean and Argentinian wines to Europe grew during the period.

When the vine scourge subsided it left behind a strong trade relationship between Europe and South America and an even stronger one between Rioja and Bordeaux. In the early part of the twentieth century Bordeaux wines slated for England were allowed to include at least 10 percent of volume from Rioja. British merchants were not overjoyed by the news but they swallowed it. Later, when wines from France's Algerian colony were included in the agreement, the British were not at all content and when it was uncovered that many wines supposedly from Bordeaux had, in fact, been 100 percent Algerian, the scandal shook up the French wine market in England.

Never having fully recovered from powdery mildew, by the end of the *phylloxera* blight Madeira's vineyards had been reduced to only 10 percent of what their acreage was at the beginning of the nineteenth century. Figures in the American market bear witness to the devastation to Madeira: toward the end of the eighteenth century 63,000 cases of Madeira had been shipped annually to America; by the end of the nineteenth century the annual shipments had dwindled to 7,500 cases.

14.
Modernization

No Nation is drunk where wine is cheap . . .

—Thomas Jefferson, 1802

The famous Dr. Benjamin Rush agreed with his friend Jefferson. Rush was no friend to alcohol spirits—he was the first in the medical profession to call alcoholism a disease—but he also strongly supported the moderate use of wine for health, and the federal government seems initially to have agreed with that position. In the early nineteenth century wine import taxes in America, with Jefferson's approval, had been reduced with the express hope that it would encourage "temperance" in a nation that seemed heading in the wrong direction.

The American wine industry enjoyed minimal government controls and intervention until 1920. Private citizens could traffic in wine without worrying about licenses or even taxes. While minister to France, Jefferson sent his American compatriots a large amount of shipments of wine, so much, in fact, that John Adams once begged him to slow down the shipments.

The year 1833 saw the rise of the domestic wine industry, but it was also the year for the rise of the American Temperance Movement (ATM) and the year of Rush's death. The ATM lasted a few decades but it ultimately factionalized and then, after the Civil War, disintegrated; out of its ashes rose the National Prohibition Party (NPP) in 1869; the Women's Christian Temperance Union (WCTU) formed in 1874 in the Lake Erie region of New York State. These two formations were in response to America's increasing thirst for beer and spirits after the Civil War. Generally being more costly to produce, domestic wine, which had been doing well before the war, wound up appealing mainly to people of means after the war; even the successful Madeira had lost its American market.

Much of the beer and spirits consumption during the nineteenth century had taken place in saloons, many of which were owned by breweries. One estimate has it that the nation hosted one saloon for every two hundred Americans—an obvious overstatement, but clear evidence that there were lots of saloons. To stay competitive, saloon owners added gambling and prostitution—a perfect target for a prohibition movement, especially one that was supported by women with husbands who spent time in saloons. Still, under its director, Frances Willard, WCTU sought first to gain women's suffrage. Only after realizing that to gain suffrage women needed first to gain a voice and some political clout did she direct her organization to ally with NPP.

The dictionary definition of the word temperance includes: *moderation, restraint and/or abstention.* The American "dry" movement put its emphasis on *abstention* through the establishment of the Anti-Saloon League, which had a mandate to use every measure necessary to achieve the goal of doing away with saloons.

Success for the Anti-Saloon League began in 1843, the year of the first recorded, so-called dry legislation in America, in Portland, Maine. By 1851 alcohol sales had been prohibited throughout the state of Maine; in the nine years to follow, eleven Northeastern and Midwestern states had passed similar prohibition laws, but with a variety of successful and unsuccessful enforcement attempts. Tired of spotty results, in 1876 the temperance movement came up with the idea for an amendment to the U.S. Constitution to prohibit the manufacture, traffic, and sale of alcoholic beverages. They made achieving that constitutional amendment their overarching goal. The first opening for an amendment to the U.S. Constitution arrived in 1880 when Kansas amended its state constitution to prohibit alcohol. Soon four states followed suit: the already pre-disposed state of Maine, Rhode Island, and both Dakotas.

Prohibition had gained momentum. The movement made use of Dr. Benjamin Rush's anti-spirits writings to promote their cause, and since he had died many years prior, he could not point out that he favored the moderate use of wine. Many who agreed with that position, certainly many in the wine industry, held out hope that wine would be spared the wrath of the movement. It took a total of eighty-five years for the anti-alcohol movement to reach its goal, which was met in 1919 with the introduction in Congress of the Volstead Act. Congress passed it as the Eighteenth Amendment to the U.S. Constitution one year later. Wine did not escape Prohibition.

The day before the Congress's errant prohibition went into effect, California, New York, Missouri, Ohio, and New Jersey hosted thriving and still growing wine industries; the day after, the American wine industry, which so many had worked so hard to build and which many of the country's founders had wanted to see flourish, was essentially dead. Only wine for vinegar, medicinal, and religious purposes could legally be produced, trafficked, and sold in the United States, and only a few wineries were able to convert.

Wineries could produce nonmedicinal and nonreligious wine during Prohibition. Most politicians behind the Eighteenth Amendment were concerned mainly with distribution and sales of intoxicating liquors, and so

> During Prohibition, grapes—and for a brief time just before its repeal, a grape concentrate called Vine-Glo—were sold to home winemakers who were allowed under the Constitution to produce as much as two hundred gallons of wine each year for personal consumption. Vineyard acreage and grape harvests in California doubled over the fourteen years of Prohibition just to meet the home winemaking market. Unfortunately, what was planted did not have to be, and was not, high-quality wine grapes.

there were ways to get around the law. Wineries could apply for a special permit to produce table wine but they had to promise to keep it in storage, which some did while waiting for Prohibition to come to an end. According to Pinney's research, on average more than 20 million gallons of wine was in storage in most years over the life of Prohibition. Ever diligent for their revenue, tax inspectors stayed on top of the wineries to ensure that those who would sell wine illegally would first pay the tax on it. Legal penalties were secondary.

It appears that Americans at first accepted the Volstead Act and then, two years into Prohibition, demand for alcohol began to grow and so did "bootlegging." This period in American history was quite agitated, as the new law eventually spawned a vast criminal empire, fed with soldiers to do the "bootleg-work," thanks to the Great Depression that followed Prohibition by nine years. (The word *bootleg* refers to early settlers carrying booze in their boots to deliver to local Native American tribes to induce drunkenness so they could exploit them.)

England had its women's movement, too, but it did ally with a powerful anti-alcohol movement as in the United States. England also had some good wine merchants to make sure that citizens were well stocked, merchants that were direct beneficiaries of Queen Elizabeth's sixteenth-century breakup of a monopoly that had been held by the Vinter's Company. Before Elizabeth stepped in, the company controlled nearly all alcohol traffic in England. The crown's action opened up alcohol licensing, especially in taverns, so that, in addition to serving consumers at the bar, taverns could sell wine by the bottle at retail, what we call today "off-premise sales." The advantage taverns gained from the change was later equalized by strong competition from a growing segment of retailing.

In the seventeenth century, after London society had discovered coffee, a wave of coffeeshops began to fill the city. Most shops sold coffee, tea, and other specialty items that often included wine or brandy. In 1698, from a tiny shop called the Coffee Mill, a widow named Bourne operated such a place at Three St. James Street. The Coffee Mill was at first wholesaler to the many coffee shops found in London during the period. The Coffee Mill's fortune, however, was built on its proximity to St. James's Palace, which had been converted from a hospital by Henry VIII for rendezvous with Ann Boleyn. Being in the neighborhood, the widow Bourne had the privilege of becoming a sometime supplier of goods to the crown and its court. The shop's location truly paid off in 1790, when George III made it an official supplier of goods to the Crown.

Being in coffee, tea, and spice wholesaling, the shop included a large scale for weighing commodities. Being also a period in British history of weight-conscious "dandies," it became a custom at the Coffee Mill for luminaries to have their weight recorded in the Coffee Mill's ledger. With such names as Beau Brummell, George III, Edward II, Napoleon III, Aga Khan, probably every member of the Rothschild family, and even Evelyn Waugh noted in the ledger over the centuries, the Coffee Mill and its later incarnation as a wine shop made great promotion of its celebrity.

No less than five families had something to do with the business at Three St. James Street. The widow Bourne's husband was a Pickering; later, a descendant named John Clarke entered the business; later still, a Mr. Browne was in the business, having married into a wine merchant family named Berry, a family with a connection to John Clarke. In 1803, Clarke's grandson, George Berry, began working at the Coffee Mill; within seven years he had gained control of the business. In the 1830s, after tea and coffee had lost the favor of London society, George Berry formed a relationship with Bass and Company, as agent for East India Pale Ale—but only for a while. At the time, England had finally entered into an anti-alcohol phase that was aimed mainly at gin and that seemed to be directed at the general population; wine, especially the named clarets, ports, and sherries, were the domain of the British elite, so it was left alone by the British dry movement.

In the middle of the nineteenth century, legislation to reduce wine duties, pushed in part by Gladstone, stirred George Berry to concentrate even more on retailing wine. In 1895, after George's son and some cousins had taken the reins and renamed the business, the last of its coffee, tea, and spice inventory had been sold off and the name was changed to Berry Brothers and Company; the business then dealt exclusively in wine retailing.

At midcentury, in Bristol, John Harvey II took over his uncle's wine importing business. By 1871, John and two sons operated John Harvey and Sons of Bristol, sherry and wine retailers. A decade later the firm became well known for its Bristol Cream Sherry, a sweet blended wine that was sold mainly to fill private orders; it became the company's "bread-and-butter" product.

The most troublesome competition to the Berry Brothers may have been William Hughes, who had built Victoria Wine, an expanding London retail outlet that boasted the lowest prices for wine, offering the middle and lower classes a chance to drink what the elite drank. But the competition proved weak. After Hughes died in 1886 the business was run by his widow until 1911, when she sold the business to a man who set it on a course that ended in its being gobbled up by the large distillery, Booth, in 1924. Berry Brothers and Company suffered no such fate.

Wine consumers of every social status looked to what Berry Brothers had proclaimed fit enough to offer for sale. When the Victorian era had given way to the Edwardian, Berry Brothers and Company made the news by buying up a major portion of the Queen's cellar in sherry. At the time, sherry had mysteriously fallen out of favor in England. News of the purchase of all that sherry by the country's premier wine merchants gave the wine a new life.

Berry Brothers and Company helped build and store private collections at the same time that it engaged in single bottle sales over the counter. To keep up that dichotomy, the Berries traveled the continent tasting and making deals for the known as well as the obscure. In 1918, the company furthered its reputation with the acquisition of a stash of various Burgundian vintages that had been hidden from the Germans in Belgium throughout World War I. As the story goes, in H. Warner Allen's book, *Number Three Saint James Street,* when the Germans were entering Belgium, a neighborhood of citizens had organized a wagon train to stop at homes to pick up the prized wines and take them to the local icehouse, through a trapdoor, and into a hidden cellar that the Germans had missed during inspection after inspection. The purchase of this stash added greatly to the renown of Berry Brothers and Company.

In 1920, new blood was introduced to the company; his name was Hugh R. Rudd. Rudd hailed from Norwich where his family was in both farming and wine, not an uncommon pairing in those days, as wool was often traded for wine. Rudd left Norwich in 1914 to serve in World War I and upon his return made his home in London. Having been an officer in the war, Rudd had traveled extensively. Having also been a wine merchant for the family, he made many friends and formed many alliances with producers, exporters, and general wine industry people. He spoke German fluently and he had become somewhat of a German wine expert; he wrote a book titled *Hocks and Moselles.*

Rudd joined Berry Brothers just as Prohibition took effect in the United States. By this time, Berry selections had been known throughout the world and no Prohibition was going to stop that. Francis Berry had created a relationship with merchants in the United States in 1909. When Prohibition threatened to sever those ties, a route for wine was found through the Bahamas. Francis visited the Bahamas in 1921, after which the Berry influence spread relatively unencumbered during Prohibition throughout the United States, usually by way of Canada.

In 1923, Francis Berry and Hugh Rudd created the first naturally colored blended Scotch whiskey brand—Cutty Sark (Gaelic for "short shirt," the name of a nineteenth-century tea clipper that obviously must have had a tie to the Coffee Mill). Charles Walter Berry had, in 1941, hired the wine writer and historian H. Warner Allen, who put in four years at Three St. James Street and who is responsible for recording the history of this venerable wine merchant company.

As Europe ushered in the so-called Industrial Revolution in the latter part of the nineteenth century, most of Europe's monarchical culture was about to unravel. Many European crowns fitted the heads of siblings, cousins and in-laws.

When relatives argue, bad things can happen, and the siblings had much about which to argue.

Since its rise, Ottoman power had emanated from the fact that its territories were situated at the crossroads of trade between East and West. By the beginning of the twentieth century, however, the relatively "fat" Ottoman autocracy had become complacent, and weak. In its relationship with the Ottoman Empire, Britain's powerful industrial machinery managed to exploit on a major scale. Happy to sell raw material to Britain and then buy it back in the form of finished goods, often at too high a price, the Ottoman Empire fell into serious debt and instability. Serbian nationalists read Ottoman decline as a sign for them to make their long awaited move against the ruthless Austro-Hungarian Empire, thinking that the caliph would not be in a position to take sides.

When the shots were fired in late June 1914 at Sarajevo, the assassination of Archduke Ferdinand ended a potential for federalism in the region and fed the beast of Balkan nationalism. The Balkans was one of the areas where European monarch rivalries had been interfering for some time. The trouble at Sarajevo gave many in power an excuse to start a war. When the war broke out, the Ottoman caliph did, in fact, align with the Austro-Hungarians, which Britain did not. Already heavily into Ottoman territory by way of the trade and market system, Britain made an early move, taking hold of Arabia and keeping a greedy eye on the Persian Gulf nearby for future exploitation.

Meanwhile, other Europeans were sucked into the conflict and the wine world was one of the losers. At the close of the nineteenth century, France and Italy combined had produced most of the wine in Europe. Italy had recently become a unified state, with most of its wealth concentrated in the north. The poverty of the southern region of the peninsula, including Sicily, created a large emigration. While northern wines, especially in the wealthy Tuscan region, managed to gain some respectability, technology had not reached southern

Italy; its wines either went to France for blending or they simply were consumed locally. Technology did make it to most French wine regions. Efficiency in the vineyard and quality in the bottle increased. Still, as the twentieth century unfolded, more changes were needed and more were scheduled to take place, but the war put a stop to it all.

When Kaiser Wilhelm II wrote in his memoir of 1914 that "Our entire diplomatic machine failed," Germany was at war on the side of Austro-Hungary. The kaiser mentioned in the same memoir that he felt betrayed by Czar Nicolas's collusion with England. The czar, however, was living up to a treaty he had made with Serbia. More important, Wilhelm was a close friend to the assassinated Archduke Ferdinand, and he certainly had interests in Prussia and in the Balkans.

The kaiser's mistake was to invade neutral Belgium, which brought—by treaties—France and England into war against Germany, and then, after first declaring neutrality, Italy went to war against its onetime allies, Germany and Austro-Hungary. From the start, World War I had diminished both financial resources and labor in the whole European wine industry. With their Balkan market in disarray and their British market turned against them, German wine traders were essentially put out of business.

That autumn the French government tried to help its wine industry by allowing harvest to complete before drafting workers, winegrowers, and their horses into the military. Maybe it helped get the vintage done, but with the economic upheaval in Europe, the move did little for the wine trade. England remained a wealthy power throughout the war, but much of its resources were put toward campaigns to grab territory (especially Ottoman territory) instead of to purchase expensive imports. Since France had declared war on Germany, the market for its wines there had vanished. French wine purchases were left largely to the government by way of the military, but much of those purchases had not been for wines of the great châteaux. Markets for expensive French wines had dwindled to close to nothing, and the profits of the great wine dynasties were further squeezed by increased taxes to pay for war. Worst of all, armies trampled vineyards. Some French wine regions suffered from bombings, the historic crossroad region of Champagne was among the most famous of them to have been pocked.

Even at war's end, not all wine traders had reason to rejoice. The loss of economic power in Germany made it difficult to rebuild the wine trade. But even if that obstacle could have been removed quickly, the fall of the Austro-Hungarian Empire and the rise of the Bolsheviks precipitated insularity in Central and Eastern Europe. A market for German wine simply did not exist either to its east or to its west, since Britain was not readily in the mood for fixing the trade relationship with Germany that had existed before the war.

Britain had benefited economically by gaining control over Palestine and the Arabian Peninsula, especially when oil had been discovered later on, but the decline of the Ottomans also gave rise to civil unrest in much of its territories. Britain had embarked on an expensive journey against Islamic nationalism, a force that has been historically bad for the flow of wine. It was left to Berry Brothers and Company exports to play one of the major roles in helping the British economy weather the tumultuous years between the first and second world wars.

With all its troubles, whatever wine trading that managed revival after World War I in Europe left France at its epicenter, with Italy a far, far distant second, just as it was before the war.

15.

New Rules and Wars

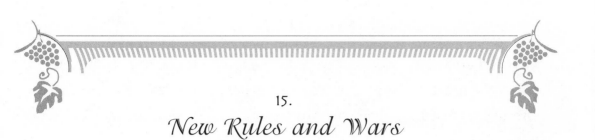

Americans had a complicated attitude toward the Europeans: a mixture of admiration for their past accomplishments . . . and a suspicion that, if the Americans were not careful, the wily Europeans would pull them into their toils again.

—Margaret MacMillan, *Paris 1919: Six Months that Changed the World*

According to Loubère, the end of World War I marked a wine revolution in France. He says that Frenchmen home from the front lines "were more sympathetic to novelty, more familiar with machines, and more mature in outlook." With better access to low-interest loans, rural farmers overcame their natural inclination to make do. Instead, they organized into cooperatives and then took advantage of the technological revolution by pooling resources; the wine crush and press were a cooperative effort, with facilities located centrally within a wine region.

A rebuilt and improved transportation infrastructure had also connected rural and urban populations like never before. All this joining together created new—and profitable—wine consumption patterns, and while the general pattern in the French wine industry was toward rapid redevelopment and speedy growth, some winegrowers still sought shortcuts.

> Cheaper and easier to produce, French-American hybrid grapes that had been developed by scientists in an effort to cure *phylloxera* created, in part, new emphasis on quantity at the expense of quality. Lacking solid regulations, the practice of adding hybrids, water, and sugar to stretch wine to grow profits became widespread in France. On top of that, some producers added dangerous lead oxide to preserve cheap wines.

Wine was in the top-five ranking in France's food economy. When producer associations organized earlier in the century to guaranty wine quality, the government was in agreement but it did little to help. Fraud and poor quality persisted. In 1905, with help from wine shippers, French grape growers finally instigated the first government-sponsored Appellation Controls (AC). But the creation of the new regulations got off to a bad start. Producers and consumers wanted falsified, flawed wines uncovered and removed from production. The government regulators placed emphasis on labeling laws. When wine producers balked, legislators did what legislators do: they formed a committee to study the two-hundred-year-old successful Portuguese wine production control system.

After adjustments and arguments spanning 1907 to 1912, French AC regulations were given a facelift.

The new regulations attempted to identify and control delimited areas and to keep tabs on specific wines. Considering the kind of fraud going on at the time, regulators saw fit to establish a definition of the word *wine*: a product exclusively produced from alcoholic fermentation of grapes or fresh grape juice. The definition presumably meant no additives were present.

In one of the biggest problem areas—the southern Midi region—it was not uncommon for wines to show up on the market masquerading as having been produced in Champagne or somewhere else, complete with flavor-enhancing additions to achieve a certain taste profile. This kind of fraud was not new to the region; in 1789 Thomas Jefferson made note of the southern French wine producers who promised to deliver any kind of wine that he desired.

The expansion of the AC was a good second step but the government wasn't there yet. The first signs of trouble for the revised regulations in fact showed up in the Champagne region right after World War I. Disagreements over restrictions placed in one locale and then lifted in another had created acrimony that developed into riots.

In 1919 the AC was revisited once again. This time the regulations provided producers with something that was not in the first two regulatory attempts but was necessary. Producers gained access to legal recourse against unfair practices of other producers or regions. Still, regulators had again missed a major point. The latest round of fixes had focused on areas of production or origin, which was all right so far as they went, but the biggest problems were in viticulture and winemaking practices. Many called for the regulations to include rigorous scientific wine analysis and to also provide trained tasting panelists.

The French government and wine producers continued to refine their AC rules. A 1927 law banned French-American hybrid grapes and established a requirement that each region produce its wines solely from those grape varieties

The loss of the American market to Prohibition helped to persuade European wine-producing nations to join together to prevent the movement from spreading. In October of 1927 Spain, France, Greece, Hungary, Italy, Luxembourg, Portugal, and Tunis formed the International Wine Office (IWO). Soon enough, membership expanded to twenty-five nations. The IWO mandate included spreading information favorable to wine drinking, to fighting fraud, and—important to all—to getting member nations to sign wine-friendly trade treaties.

that regulators identified as best suited to the region. The new regulations often prescribed the exact ratios for blending specified grapes. In 1935, the law, now known as Appellation of Origin Control (AOC), was expanded once more to prescribe minimal alcohol levels in wines and to clearly spell out regional viticultural and winemaking methods and, finally, in order to prove producers' claims wines underwent analysis and panel tastings before release to the market.

The quest to eliminate fraud and to increase quality was not solely left to the French. Getting back on more sound economic footing, Germany, too, became obsessed with regulations after World War I. Early controls were immediately aimed at assuring quality levels of the finished product. The main concern for German wines became added sugar. In mainly cool, German growing conditions, grapes often do not mature enough in order for sugar levels to ferment to alcohol levels that would ensure wine stability. Regulations became necessary to control how much sugar could be added, when, and in what form. (The preferred method became adding back juice, and in France beet sugar was added when needed.) All sugar additions in German wines had to be clearly identified on the label, and samples of all wines that fell under the regulations had to be analyzed and tasted.

In Spain and Portugal, where controls had already been applied for many years, government inspectors issued identification numbers on the label to prove that a wine lived up to regulatory standards. The Iberians had good reason for being careful and diligent. British wine merchants based in Iberia had for some time used place names indiscriminately, exporting to England such abominations as Spanish sauternes or Spanish champagne, hoping to capitalize on the general public's lack of knowledge.

Appellation control systems led to European producers and governments placing demands on the international community to honor the names of recognized regions such as Champagne, Burgundy, Port, and Rhine. In the 1920s and 1930s British wine merchants had been fined for using "sherry" on labels for wines that had not been produced in Spain's recognized district. Led by an association of Champagne producers, a case against Spanish champagne was brought before the British justice system as late as 1958. After losing the case in less than a week, the French brought it to a higher court in 1959 and prevailed, leading to a change that created the "Cava" classification for sparkling wines from Spain's Catalonia region that are produced in the Champagne method but could no longer be called champagne.

Most cases brought on this matter were based on a long-standing British legal ruling, the Merchandise and Marks Act of 1887 that had been established to protect brand names.

European wine producers had less luck in prosecuting name stealing across the Atlantic. In the early days of Californian and Australian wines, many producers used European place names indiscriminately, but because they were not part of the European collective the wine regions from which they stole names had little recourse.

Generally, European control systems worked, especially for producers blessed within certain delimited regions. As the regions became known, the producers became known not only for what they produced, but also for where they

John Harvey and Sons of Bristol had lost a good portion of its private customer orders, thanks to the post World War I economy. To rebuild sales, the family promoted in the opposite direction from using place names. Harvey developed an advertising campaign designed to get consumers to remember the brand name, Harvey's Bristol Cream, instead of the fact that the wine was a sherry. The campaign worked quite well and the product rebuilt its reputation and following as people remembered the name Harvey's.

had produced the wine. This type of monopoly on quality, whether perceived or real, created great wealth in the "ordained" regions of Bordeaux, Champagne, Burgundy, Moselle, Rheingau, and so on. Wine producers outside the elite monopoly suffered long-term secondary status, which of course reflected in the prices of their wines, yet their wines did improve under the system of controls.

AOC controls could unfortunately do little for Alsace, a region that before World War I was held in high regard in Britain and in Germany. Loubère noted that the average vineyard size had doubled in France in the decades between the First and Second World Wars, but this was not the case in Alsace. Before World War I the widely recognized centuries of superiority of wines from Alsace had given producers in that region ready access to a steady German market. After having been reabsorbed by the French at the end of the war, the cool, often difficult grape-growing region was in the position of having to compete with the hot, prolific grape-growing region of the Midi that everyone knew was flooding the market with cheap wine.

As postwar inflation kicked into high gear Alsace was under more price pressure and it could not compete in France. The region went into an economic slump. Then, the reannexation of Alsace by Germany during World War II hurt the region's winegrowers once more. The only customers available to Alsace were Germans, at prices that were set by German authorities and in competition with Moselle and other German wines. The suffering of the winegrowers of Alsace that began in 1914 remained until after the Second World War.

In America, in the years following World War I, the wine industry was in disarray from Prohibition. When legislators came to their senses in 1933, more than enough time had passed for the law to set back the nation's wine industry by about one hundred years. Just before the repeal of Prohibition a move to allow so-called light wine on the market (3.2 percent alcohol) was so laughable that it never went anywhere. No one was even sure that wine could be made at such a low alcohol by volume. To make matters worse, California vineyards were of such overall poor quality that any wine produced was sure to be cheap and nasty. To prove the point, one year after repeal 34 million gallons of California wine brought out of storage proved to be mostly low-quality dreck.

Also in 1934, the U.S. Department of Agriculture made failed attempts to civilize and integrate the wine industry into American culture, as well as to create regional appellation identity for wines along the lines of European control systems. In each case, Congress thwarted efforts by cutting off funds or by stalling.

Prohibition was dead but only on paper, as there were many legislators who sought to extend the reach of the Eighteenth Amendment even after it had become the first American constitutional amendment to be repealed. With repeal, legislators created an alcohol distribution system designed with taxation and repressive controls to punish those who would produce alcohol, as if they were criminals. Over the nine years that followed repeal many revitalized California wineries simply failed.

The most arguably damaging thing Congress did to the wine industry was to cede regulatory authority over alcohol to the states. Ironically, the move reversed Congress's attempt to punish criminals and wound up rewarding some of them, not to mention that it may have even created a few at the state level.

Congress gave the states the right to choose either to license and regulate commercial alcohol distribution and sales, to monopolize it as state controlled, or to forbid it completely. Many states opted to license and regulate in what is known as the three-tier system of alcohol distribution, meaning that all beverage alcohol had to go from producer or importer to a warehousing distributor and to a retailer before consumers could get their hands on it. The system served not only to inflate the cost of wine through taxes and guaranteed markups to merchants but also established separate state-mandated wine distribution monopolies across the country in a patchwork of confusion that defies human intelligence.

Many of the alcohol monopoly kingpins got their lucrative distributorships through political connections, and quite a few of the rest had run criminal enterprises during Prohibition.

Some states opted to create state-controlled monopolies, which is to say that the state buys the alcohol and distributes it to state stores where state workers sell it at retail. If that system wasn't open to corruption then, it certainly proved itself to be so over the subsequent decades. In one of those states, Pennsylvania, consumers are left with deplorable wine choices because small producers are largely locked out of the supply channel by government decree.

A few states decided to remain dry, but not for very long after they realized that other states had found a windfall tax opportunity by gaining control over alcohol distribution and sales.

Before Prohibition, a great deal of domestic wine was sold in America at retail right out of a bulk barrel or other large vessel. After repeal, with the exception of a brief period in California, this practice gave way to bottled wine. Bulk producers fought against the shift, claiming that the use of bottles would make production—and hence retail prices—rise. Many wineries, big and small, decided to sell their wines in bulk to those wineries that had installed a bottling line rather than investing in a bottling line themselves.

A lot of the arguments didn't much matter since, having very few standards and very little market, the majority of American wine produced at the time was truly awful and mostly fortified or sweet. To be sure, the government helped to quash attempts at bringing Americans to wine after repeal, but the bad wines released to the market might have done more to chase Americans away than any government agency could contrive.

The California Wine Institute was established in 1934 to help change both wine quality and the market for wine. In 1935 the institute had succeeded in gaining standards for wine production based in part on the European DOC standards but, according to Thomas Pinney, the new standards were decidedly tweaked to accommodate the special needs of California wine production. For instance, the standards did not properly address the issue of identifying American wines that had no relationship to the European place names used on the labels.

Soon after the standards had been set, the University of California, Davis Campus, under the influential professor, Maynard A. Amerine, developed grape-growing parameters that were based on climates within wine-growing regions of the state. The work of these agencies did a lot to upgrade California viticulture but then, just before World War II broke out, California experienced grape gluts. With not enough market and too much potential wine, the industry attempted to fix the situation with a marketing order that mandated that half the crop of a participating grower was to go toward distillation for brandy, to be paid for later. The order worked to remove wine from the market but it failed to help growers; some of the payments for the brandy did not arrive for a decade or more.

Pinney is particularly impressed by the Wine Advisory Board creation in 1939 of a cooperative national advertising to boost California's wine industry through print ads and radio. The ad campaign worked. For three consecutive years thereafter retail sales of California wines grew. It helped, too, that a British agent for the Wine and Food Society came to America to help create a branch of that club of connoisseurs in an attempt to make wine drinkers out of Americans. The wines produced by the few small California producers who had reinvigorated their vineyards with the premium grape varieties of Europe began to appeal to the connoisseurs.

Then, World War II began.

When World War II broke out in 1939, California and New York wine producers thought the shortages in Europe would create a market overseas for their wines, but things did not work out that way. Europeans had neither the money nor the inclination to drink their own wine, let alone American wine, and after America entered the war, exporting wine was not the country's priority. At home, the market for French and Italian wine was taken not by California or New York wine producers but by their Portuguese and Spanish counterparts.

Authors Don and Petie Kladstrup, in *Wine and War,: The French, the Nazis, and the Battle for France's Greatest Treasure* recount a speech given in 1932 by Monsieur Hubert de Mirepoix, president of the French Winegrowers Association. In the speech, he praised superior qualities of the French, which he said were given to them by wine and set them apart from beer drinkers. This was the year before Hitler became chancellor of Germany. Soon afterward, the powerful and prominent Bordeaux banker and wine producer, Baron Robert de Rothschild, a Jew who headed a synagogue in Paris, watched with increasing alarm as events began to unfold in Germany and Eastern Europe. The situation came to a monumental head in 1939, when the German army invaded Poland.

France tried unsuccessfully to stay out of World War II. In the spring of 1940, Germany invaded Belgium, the Netherlands, and then, through the Ardennes Forest, France, circumventing the so-called fortress structure known as the Maginot Line, named after a civil servant and member of the French parliament. Only recently having gotten back on its feet, the Champagne region was subjected once again to attack when the German army arrived in early June. Paris was next. Simultaneously other German units trampled Burgundy on their way south to the Pyrenees Mountains, and by the end of the month they were poised to take Bordeaux, among the most powerful of the European wine trade centers, plus one with a strong Jewish financial connection.

With Italy already in Germany's axis, and in disarray for that reason, the French formal surrender just two months following Germany's invasion brought the European wine industry to a halt. German winemaking had already suffered from having lost its export market and from the domestic monetary crisis that had preceded Hitler's rise.

The Kladstrups tell the fascinating story of how the top echelon of the German military revered not only Paris (the city had been saved from Hitler by Nazi generals) but also how they hoarded hundreds of thousands of bottles of French wine in a cave they had built at Eagle's Nest, a Nazi fortress situated at the top of a Bavarian mountain. The "nest" was accessed by an elevator that had been constructed to operate deep inside the rock formation. Hitler was known not to drink much, if any, alcohol; the wine definitely was there for the generals.

Maréchal Pétain became prime minister of France in mid-June. A small winegrower himself, Pétain had earlier praised the role wine had played in the First World War, very nearly calling it essential to victory. With him at the helm in the middle of the German invasion, winegrowers felt somewhat safe. Both winegrowers and Petain learned rather quickly the error of their ways. The first known seizure of wine by the Germans took place in Paris at about the same time Pétain took power. An avid lover of Château Lafite-Rothschild wine, German Field Marshall Göring walked off with thousands of bottles of the wine from the cellars of the famed restaurant La Tour d'Argent. One has to wonder about the irony of Göring's preference, since Rothschild was not only a Jewish family, but also one of the most powerful Jewish families in Europe.

The Germans demanded French surrender, which Pétain provided about one week after having taken office. It soon became clear to all of France that there was no working with Hitler and that his interests lay in a desire to strip the country of its riches—including its valuable wines. At the surrender, France signed onto a demarcation agreement that had given Germany control over a major portion of the country's top vineyards. Upon their arrival in Bordeaux German officers immediately began booting out the owners of some of the renowned châteaux to use as barracks, and if German soldiers weren't sleeping at a château, French refugees were. The famed Château Haut-Brion was converted into a rest home for German pilots.

> German soldiers apparently looted wine cellars throughout France. But when the Third Reich realized soldiers were looting goods bound for Germany, a command was issued to put a stop to it. The first example of the Reich's seriousness took place at Epernay, with the arrest of a couple of German soldiers who had been charged with breaking into the château of famed Champagne producer Perrier-Jouët. Perhaps it was fitting that this episode took place in Champagne; the region was filled with winegrowing families of German ancestry; the German foreign minister during the occupation, Ribbentrop, had once been a salesman in Germany for Mumm.

In Paris, Göring had devalued the franc, immediately increasing the value of the German mark. For Germans, everything French was cheap. For the French, life had become a bitter grind in poverty. For the wine industry, French merchants were forced to work under German wine merchants. Not trusting the French, the Nazis had sent German wine merchants to oversee production and export from the important French wine districts, but the move turned out in some cases to be a mistake. The Germans were not only brokers for French wines but also enjoyed long-standing friendships with many of the French producers. Some of the German wine brokers went so far as to help the French hide wine inventory behind cement walls for the day the war would end.

With the British, American, and Russian markets closed to them, French producers and merchants had no choice but to sell wine to the Germans. But when the war ended in 1945, stacks of unpaid bills for wines that had been shipped to Germany littered winegrowers' offices, a mirror image, perhaps, of the whole European economy.

PART VI

Post-World War II

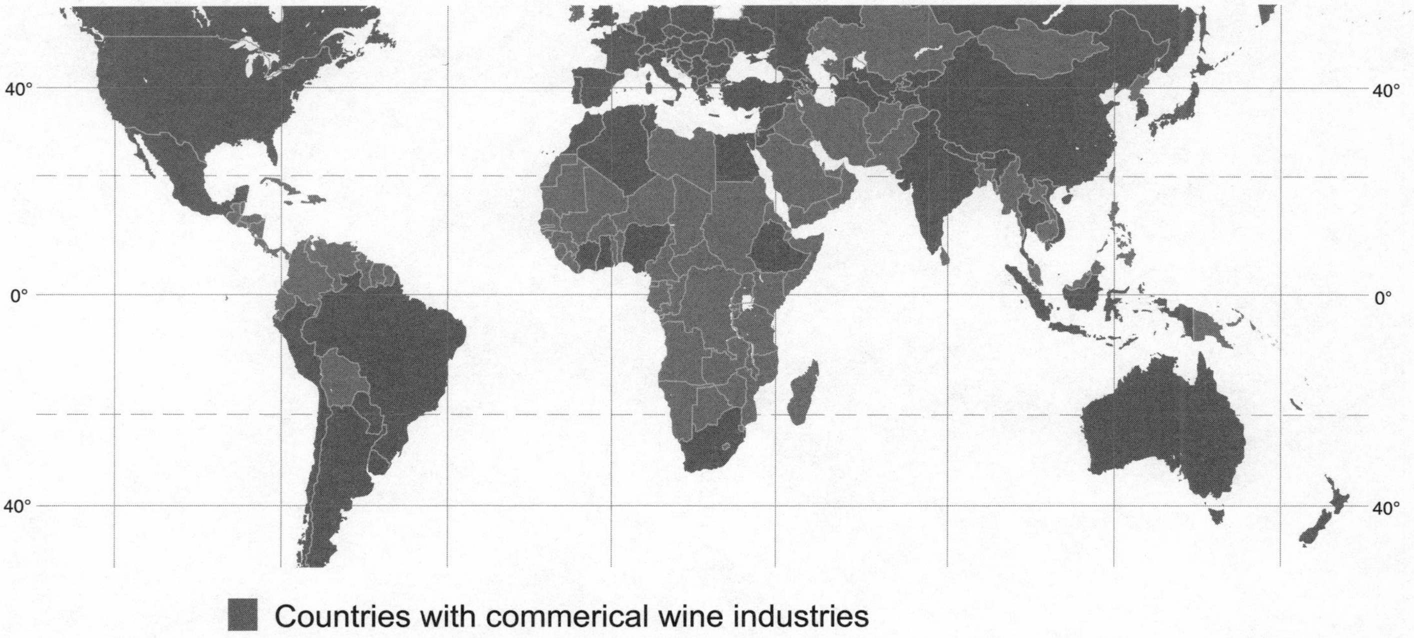
40°
0°
40°
40°
0°
40°
Countries with commerical wine industries

16.

The First Half

In this age of mechanization, man is returning to the wine of the soil, the drink of civilization.

—Alexis Lichine, *Encyclopedia of Wines and Spirits*

The American administration's Marshall Plan—to lend Europe money for reconstruction—provided winegrowers with a perfect moment to modernize once again and the French seized the opportunity. Modernization meant mechanization. To help small farms, the French government dispensed some of the Marshall Plan funds as subsidies. Subsidies notwithstanding, grape growing after World War II became an expensive occupation.

A majority of mature European vines had been set there on American rootstock in the previous century to prevent another *phylloxera* devastation. The revitalized vines were susceptible to other insect and plant diseases that had been unknown in Europe. The increased costs of insecticide and fungicide sprays became routine. Unlike the maxim of the old days—if it ain't broke, don't fix it; if it is broke, fix it yourself—post-World War II European farmers borrowed money to buy replacement equipment. Many went into serious debt to keep up with the rapid spread of mechanization. Their debt load brought the costs of grape growing to new heights. To be successful, farmers had to learn the ways of finance and business.

Mechanization also established a class of the rural unemployed. Unable to find work on the farm, the laborers flooded the cities. The wave of unemployed created social conditions that had to be quieted, which led to big social welfare programs—and then, in the 1950s, postwar inflation hit hard.

Mechanization and scientific advances gave grape growers in the overproducing French Midi region even more capability to overproduce. When inflation hit, the region was awash in wine inventories. Once again riots broke out in France over wine; at the start of the century, riots were the result of the Midi producing fraudulent champagne; this time, the riots broke out because the French economy had become too erratic for producers in the Midi to get rid of their wine profitably.

Severe vineyard restrictions and tough growing conditions made already expensive Burgundian wines even more costly, leaving producers vulnerable to cash flow problems as inventories built while new vintages came upon them. Strapped for cash, Burgundians in the lower Beaujolais region came up with a formula for raising it soon after the vintage finished fermenting. It was called Beaujolais Nouveau.

For the previous three generations, Beaujolais had been known for a class of young, clean refreshing wines, consumed mostly in bistros. The wines were never taken seriously; only for quaffing, they weren't even being bottled, just shipped in large containers soon after fermentation had completed, in mid November, to restaurants in Paris and other cities. The young wines were inexpensive, making them a perfect alternative during a time of inflation. Word got out and the wines became extremely popular. A few Beaujolais merchants saw a marketing opportunity. They ratcheted promotion with a publicity campaign built on the word *nouveau* (new).

The Beaujolais Nouveau campaign worked almost immediately in Paris and then the concept spread throughout northern France. November 15 became the traditional date when young Beaujolais wines would be shipped to bistros; soon, it became the "must-have-it-by" date; later it became the official date of the appellation; today, trucks line the district just before midnight on November 14, awaiting loading and delivery instructions. The cash that was raised with the Beaujolais Nouveau promotion allowed producers and middle merchants to finance their upper level wines.

The young wines were eventually exported to offshore markets where the concept also became, and remains but to a lesser extent, an annual wine event.

In the 1960s, French urbanites were rediscovering their land. As they laid down more and more francs to buy a slice of rural life, farmland values grew to unprecedented proportions. Once again the government stepped in, buying up land holdings and then breaking them into smaller parcels to sell as small farms. The government's program did not work, as a new bout with inflation broke out. Small vineyards that had been part of some government land deals were forced to sell out to larger landowners and wine producers. In addition, in premium districts such as Burgundy or Champagne, land purchases had historically been the pursuit of the wealthy. But by this time the so-called Napoleonic tradition of passing land to surviving blood relatives had created conditions for old parcels of premium vineyards to be split into smaller and smaller parcels. The small landholders who inherited valuable plots in this manner could then blackmail producers into either paying large sums for grape crops or buying the land itself at an inflated price.

With the exception of premium houses, French wine produced before World War II was generally sold in bulk to brokers called *négociants*. A négociant matured, blended, and bottled wines in his cellar and then found markets for it. Négociants also brokered and found markets for wines of the well-known top producers without having to blend, and they still perform that function, especially in Bordeaux. Cooperatives produced bulk wine that they had sold directly to retailers who sometimes blended or sold it—as is—drawn from the barrel. By the 1960s, French wine factories mirrored the large wine operations that had once developed in the Roman Empire. The French version called for the companies to hire a winemaker to supervise mass production of low-priced wines destined for large populations in the cities.

Despite the reputation of the top wine names in the country, most French citizens drank a lot of regular stuff and it was not always top quality. Some of the low-end wine in the 1960s entered France in great quantities from Algeria. Large companies blended the cheap Algerian wines with local wines for no reason other than to stretch mass-produced products to keep prices looking good and profits high. When France began to lose North African colonies, however, the flow dwindled.

Looking for a way to make up for the loss of cheap Algerian blending wine, the large cooperative companies turned to their old suppliers in southern Italy. Italy had not benefited yet either from the Marshall Plan or from any internal solutions to a bad economy. With no markets of their own and a lot of wine, the southern Italians could either take the money or let the inventory rot. The French managed to keep the Italian wine influence in their products a secret and the practice did nothing to better the Italian winegrowers' lot, since the French paid little for the wine. Premium French producers disliked the situation but got little satisfaction when they complained to the regulatory body; then, in 1970, when wine fell under the scrutiny of the European Economic Community, the practice was nearly sanctioned by EEC regulations in an attempt to skirt arguing about protectionism. It was a bad deal for consumers and an even worse deal for AOC producers; the public found it difficult to believe anybody about the quality of French wine.

Meanwhile, maligned and dispirited, Italy's wine industry remained in a postwar sleep. The rise of Mussolini had been the unfortunate result of two incidents: the loss to Germans in the battle at Caporetto and the unfulfilled promise of land at the treaty at Versailles after World War I. Each event made the Italian government appear weak. But Italy fared no better under fascism and, since Mussolini had entered the war on the side of Germany, at the end it the country was as poor as ever; as always, the southern part of the country was even worse off. What wealth there was remained in the north, and it was from there that Italian wines slowly regained footing. The American market gradually developed into the biggest export market for Italian wines, even though they weren't always the best Italians had to offer; much of the imported Italian wine in the United States was thin, acidic, less-than-top-quality Chianti—shipped in banjo-shaped bottles set inside straw baskets.

The Italians had mostly themselves to blame for their wine problems. Before World War II Italian wine producers adhered to hardly any regulations; after the war, they adhered to maybe one: no added sugar. Quality was a big problem.

Some wine industry people have made the argument that in the 1950s one television episode managed to marginalize any gains the Italians might have made. They refer to an unfortunate episode of Lucille Ball and Desi Arnaz's popular American television show, *I Love Lucy*. Lucy and Ricky Ricardo go off to Italy on vacation with their neighbors, Fred and Ethel; they mingle with the seemingly simpleton peasants, who kowtow to tourists. Lucy and her group wind up in a large vat stomping grapes and spreading an image across the United States of quaint, rustic Italians doing with their feet what no clean, middle-class American could imagine.

During the postwar period of the 1950s, by which time no adult Berry was alive at Berry Brothers and Company, Hugh Rudd had taken the reins until a new flock of Berries and Rudds could be trained. The company name was changed to Berry Brothers and Rudd, Ltd.

Right after the war there was little wine to be had in Europe. Harried as he was, Hugh Rudd was able to draw from the Berry Brothers' cellars to weather the period. The firm relied heavily on foreign customers of every social status who had heard of it, had visited it during their tours of war duties, and had come back to it when times grew quiet and prosperous once again. Many of those people were Americans who had been given the opportunity to familiarize themselves with some of the great wines of Europe. Some of them became instrumental in the soon-to-come overhaul of the wine industry in the United States.

When seen on a wine label, the words "Frank Schoonmaker Selection" once had great currency in America; in the postwar period, they represented the success of a true wine merchant.

With a writer father working at the U.S. State Department and a noted suffragette feminist mother, Schoonmaker certainly had been given the means to succeed when he was sent off to Princeton University after a primary education in arts and languages. Yet he dropped out of university life within two years, preferring instead to travel and to learn about life through first-hand experience. In 1925, at twenty years of age, he was off to Europe and the life of a vagabond—well, not exactly. Schoonmaker probably did not have to worry about supporting himself but, based on the notes he kept, he appears to have been aware of expenses. He turned his extensive notes into a series of guidebooks titled *Through Europe on $2 a Day* (which afterward inspired Arthur Frommer). From that small beginning, Schoonmaker created a number of in-depth travel guides that covered specific countries or regions. Many of those European regions produced wine, which appealed to him greatly. When he eventually realized that his travel writing would provide a limited income he decided to ground himself in the wine trade.

Many European wine merchants and producers had suffered greatly when they lost the American export market in 1920. On the hunch that Prohibition in the United States could not last—and that when it ended the need for an efficient representative in the American market would arise in Europe—Schoonmaker established a relationship with the leading wine reviewer in France at the time, Raymond Baudoin (who was also instrumental in the establishment of the 1935 AOC system). Trailing Baudoin through France, Schoonmaker met producers, especially in Burgundy, and kept copious notes.

At the time, unlike château bottling in the top Bordeaux houses, the top Burgundy producers sold their wines to négociant shippers, just like most other French producers. Such top Burgundy names as Drouhin, Jadot, Patriarch, and others were *négociant* families. They paid producers for raw material, blended, bottled, and put the names of the district and their companies on the finished wines, then shipped them to market from Beaune, a process that built no identity for the producers. But some of the Burgundy wines were a lot better than the everyday wines of France. Baudoin crusaded to change the system so that top Burgundy producers would get the recognition and the money they deserved for their premium wines. It all led to the concept of "estate bottling."

> Before the 1920s even some top houses in Bordeaux had not bottled their own single vineyard wines; after they started to do so, they enjoyed an increase in profits, which is what motivated the Burgundians to follow Baudoin's advice.

Two years after repeal Frank Schoonmaker Selections was in business in New York. To help build wine awareness in the United States, Schoonmaker coauthored *The Complete Wine Book* with a *New York Herald Tribune* columnist. He had great Burgundian contacts but his business was not the only one to start up in New York in the 1930s. When Schoonmaker faced competition, he was forced to realize that he might have been great at selecting wine but he was not so great on the sales end; and then he met Alexis Lichine.

Like Schoonmaker, Lichine was an impetuous young man who preferred experience rather than book learning; he, too, had dropped out of school (University of Pennsylvania); he, too, spent time traveling Europe; he, too, wrote while in Europe (the *Paris Herald Tribune*). Unlike Schoonmaker, who was born in the American Midwest, Lichine had been born in Russia and raised in Paris; he spoke a few languages and was so articulate he could self-promote with ease.

When the two met, Lichine was working in a New York wine shop where he had established a new concept to sign subscribers to a Wine-of-the-Month Club, sending along wines from producers he had become enthused over during his travels. Similarly, Schoonmaker had been selling wine to his list of buyers by way of a catalog—wines from the producers he had met and had established relationships with through his travels and through his connection with Baudoin.

The two men hit it off immediately and soon Lichine was on the payroll as national sales manager for Frank Schoonmaker Selections.

In 1939, with war breaking out in Europe, Lichine and Schoonmaker wondered how the shortages of European wines resulting from the war would be replenished; then they took a trip to California, where they found what they were looking for.

Along with the relatively large wineries of California that dealt in cheap bulk products, some small winegrowing families had managed to survive Prohibition. Like their French counterparts before World War II, the California farmers lacked technology and marketing and they were not accustomed to large capital investments. Yet, some of them—Louis Martini, the Wente brothers, Concannon, Martin Ray—had been producing fine wines and had persuaded bankers to finance them. Schoonmaker and Lichine met with these people in 1939 and persuaded them to plant more premium *Vitis vinifera* grape varieties and then to change how they marketed their wines by dispensing with European place names and instead labeling their premium wines after the name of the grape varieties that went into making

Both Schoonmaker and Lichine served in World War II, the former in Spain as a spy for the Office of Strategic Services—the forerunner to the Central Intelligence Agency—and the latter in Army Intelligence. Schoonmaker was instrumental in feeding information for the planned Normandy invasion. During his own tour of duty, Lichine was often responsible for procuring the wine that generals and political luminaries consumed during strategic meetings or dinners. At war's end the two men went their separate ways. In the 1950s, each embarked on a limited book-writing career that included Lichine's *Wines of France* (1951) and Schoonmaker's *Wines of Germany* (1956). In the following decade each produced his version of an encyclopedia of wine.

them. They called the idea "varietal labeling." When the producers took them up on the idea, they met with success, selling to a small number of Americans with a taste for premium wines. Schoonmaker Selections handled many of the wines in the East Coast market and prices for California wines rose during the war years.

The war also brought many European winemakers from France, Germany, and other countries to America. Some of these people became instrumental in upgrading American wines. Many made names in California: Kornell, Fromm, Sichel, and the Russian Tchelistcheff, who in 1938 began his ascension to king West Coast winemaker, his realm the Napa Valley, his throne Beaulieu Vineyards. Others made their way East: Charles Fournier went from Veuve Cliquot to Gold Seal in New York; Konstantin Frank went from the Ukraine to the Geneva Agricultural Experiment Station (as a janitor) and then to Keuka Lake, where he worked with Fournier attempting to produce viably commercial East Coast wines produced from *Vitis vinifera* grapes.

After his war duty, Lichine went to work for the wine divisions of United Distillers but, being unable to blend into corporate culture, he did not stay long. He soon made his way back to Europe, to Bordeaux, where he formed a shipping company in the village of Margaux. He broke into the Bordeaux export trade and became successful at it on the strength of his reputation. In Burgundy, however, he encountered great resistance and found that top producers had already been taken, some by Schoonmaker. The success of Burgundy in that period had been built on the export market, especially to the United States.

While he maintained interest in the export wine trade, Lichine ultimately became a gentleman farmer, first with his purchase of Château Prieuré—which he petitioned the Bordeaux Committee of Classified Growths to rename Château Prieuré-Lichine—and then as a partner in Château Lascombes with David Rockefeller and other wealthy shareholders. Until he died in 1989 at the age of seventy-six, Lichine fought to update the 1855 Médoc classification (without success) and to penetrate the wormy, legalistic, restrictive wine import and distribution rules in the United States (with a great deal of success).

Schoonmaker went back to New York to add a line of Bordeaux, German, and sherry wines to some of the top Burgundies that he was handling, but he also became national sales manager for Almaden. At Almaden he had created a successful rosé wine that was produced from a grape variety that most Americans had never heard of—grenache. Later he was forced by management to oversee the sales of bulk wines and to apply European place names on Almaden labels. On a hunch, Schoonmaker surmised that when Americans thought of the "Old Country" they likely conjured images of idyllic hillsides, so he came up with the Almaden "mountain" line of wines—Mountain Burgundy, Mountain Chablis, and so on—to great success.

Like many matters during post–World War II United States, the wine business was rapidly changing. When the war ended, nearly four dozen wine cooperatives and a few successful families from before Prohibition lorded over California wine, which by then had become the center for commercial wine in the USA. Beringer, Martini, Concannon, Masson, and others had made the relatively successful switch to "varietal" labeling. Gallo, another family name, retained the old ways of putting out lower-end wines for the mass market and reaped profits for its effort, especially after the Gallo brothers got around the restrictive post-Prohibition laws and created their own distribution network.

By the start of the 1950s the American wine industry was poised to become highly technological and extremely competitive; Italian Swiss Colony, Almaden, and Paul Masson began to show up with greater frequency on shelves across the country. As the big producers and cooperatives grew, many smaller wineries without the means to invest in technology and marketing were forced to sell out or fold up tent. The war years had seen a rise in interest in the California wine business from large spirits corporations. Along with other properties, Schenley gained control of California's onetime largest winery, Roma; National Distillers grabbed Italian Swiss Colony; and Seagram took over Paul Masson from Martin Ray, a savvy wine producer with an understanding of marketing and of making money (he had been a stockbroker), who bought the winery from Paul Masson in 1936. Under Ray, the Paul Masson Winery had commanded the highest prices of all premium California varietally labeled wines.

With corporate money flowing in, radio wine advertising soon filled American airwaves.

As fast as things had been changing and as much as postwar America was growing economically, the country's consumers had yet to embrace premium wine on a large scale. Most premium wine consumption in the United States was still concentrated in the industrial and financial centers of the country. The wine and grape market in America fluctuated wildly in the years after 1945. Yet by the end of the decade a small growth in mainstream consumption began to show on the map. The growth of California's wine industry in the 1940s continued into the 1950s. As small wineries sold out to larger ones and some larger ones sold out to conglomerates, new cooperatives started up, too. California wines serviced the new market either directly or indirectly with volumes of bulk wine. Reflecting the bulk status of the wines, larger bottles were introduced to the market. The California wine business was once again taken over by bulk wine producers. The premium varietal wines simply hadn't a large enough market.

Sales of bulk wine were helped along in the latter part of the decade and into the 1960s by the relatively powerful medium of television, which made it quicker and easier for large companies and cooperatives to establish national brand identity. Paul Masson, Almaden, and Gallo became household names in the homes of those who had recently discovered California wine. Italian Swiss Colony also became a household name, thanks to a man named Louis Petri, another in a long line of savvy promoters. Petri had founded a large cooperative, Allied Grape

Growers, and had created a company he called United Vintners. In 1953, United Vintners bought Italian Swiss Colony Winery from National Distillers, and then Petri set out to make it a major brand name. To illustrate Petri's promotional talents author Thomas Pinney recounts a 1957 incident. Petri commissioned a World War II tanker into serving as his floating wine ship. Capable of holding more than 2 million gallons of wine, the ship made ports of call in Texas and New Jersey. The bulk wine was offloaded and bottled at local facilities for distribution. The ship sank near the Golden Gate Bridge in 1960, but Italian Swiss Colony was still very much afloat. That was the same year the company's "Little Old Winemaker" TV ads made the biggest national splash in wine advertising.

For a time, money flowed into the coffers of the big California wine companies, but then the playing field got crowded.

Post–World War II France had gone into reconstruction, as had Italy, Germany, and all of Europe, for that matter. European wine producers had a problem similar to their U.S. counterparts: they could produce a lot of wine but, thanks to decimated economies, the home market was limited.

Recognizing that the United States was not sophisticated in its wine appreciation but seemed to love fortified wines, European producers exported all kinds of fortified wine products and liqueurs. Four imports to grow in the American market in the late 1950s—Cherry Kijafa, a sweet product from Denmark; Dubbonet, a sweet French wine-based aperitif; and some long-standing British products, including Dry Sack and Harvey's Bristol Cream sherries—got their positions at the top in large measure through television advertising. In the case of Harvey's, the advertising was an extension of what the company had earlier done in England to get consumers to remember the brand name rather than the fact that it was a sherry product. In the United States, in 1959, sales of this product surpassed sales in England. (Harvey's merged in 1960 with the larger Cockburn Smithes, a company that had been a supplier to the original Harvey and Sons of Bristol since the nineteenth century.) In the case of Cherry Kijafa, the advertising lure of this cloying cherry drink was far from subtle, with a beautiful woman intoning: "Put a little cherry in your life." It, too, was quite successful in the United States.

> While the global wine industry sought ways to convert more and more consumers with cheap, accessible, sweet wines, the baby-boom generation in the United States was maturing into what would become the largest group of the adult consuming market in the Western world.
>
> The effect this generation would have on wine consumption began to show itself in the 1970s.

In England, the wine merchant system that had been built on respectable family purveyors and shippers tied to French négociants and other northern European middlemen began to give way to corporate invasion. The move started in the beer industry: small pubs that dotted the landscape were being bought up and joined under large corporate roofs. Soon, wine and spirits melded into so-called beverage brands at major companies, often at some of the major breweries, but also at cosmetic or other consumer goods companies. (In 1968 Harvey and Sons became a cog in the wheel of the giant Allied Breweries Group.) In addition, large supermarket chains began to handle wine and, for the first time in British history, wine had entered the mass-market arena—with the promised low prices and a proliferation of fads.

For centuries England had been the largest export target for wine, but the real prize in the wine trade was becoming the United States. In the 1960s, a great many European home markets still hadn't been completely rebuilt from the ravages of war. The European Economic Union was eventually established, in part to pool resources to develop consumer markets across the continent, crossing what had always been national boundaries—and sometimes roadblocks—to trade. To tide them over, European wine exporters set their sights on the rich, powerful, and not so wine-savvy United States of America.

The world's wealthiest superpower still showed a dismally small per capita wine consumption, ranked at about 40 in the top 50 wine-consuming industrial nations. But with a couple hundred million adults and the money at their disposal, the potential was vast for creating new wine consumers in America to gobble up the excess.

With such names as Mateus, from Portugal; Blue Nun, from Germany; Egri Bikaver (Bull's Blood), from Hungary; Bolla, from Italy; Riunite, from Villa Banfi (an American company with an Italian connection); and many other lesser but no less successful producers, bulk products began to push into the American market in the mid-1960s, often at the expense of California jug producers. Since many European governments had been subsidizing the exports. By the 1970s a

By the late 1960s Schoonmaker was feeling—and showing—the strain of dealing with the restrictive American three-tier distribution system. The system allowed for severe markups along the supply chain, and when inflation kicked in Schoonmaker found that it was often the importer who had to eat the losses. When, in the early 1970s, Pillsbury offered a deal to bring his company into their fold, Schoonmaker took it. It did not take long for him to realize he had made a mistake. By 1975, Pillsbury had fallen victim to its failure to understand the wine industry, which is nothing like the food industry. Frank Schoonmaker Selections was sold along with the rest of what Pillsbury had called its wine portfolio.

A year later, just short of age seventy-one, Frank Schoonmaker died of heart failure. Some think it was more of a broken heart.

number of the large California cooperatives could no longer compete and started running into financial difficulty.

With the loss of merchants like Schoonmaker and Lichine to guide them and without an existing long-standing American wine merchant class like Berry Brothers of London to market them, the California wine industry (and the rest of America's wine industries, which were dwarfed by California just as they are today) seemed to be rudderless and adrift; it had become nothing like it had promised to become in the post–World War II period. In fact, it seemed to be sliding back to just a bit more than what it was during Prohibition and very much like what it had become right after repeal.

To California family wineries, the American wine market seemed stuck; with limited demand for their premium wines, their profits, if any, looked fixed.

Yet, corporate presidents thought they knew the power of the coming baby-boomer market. As the 1960s faded, major corporations began to buy into the American wine industry, just as their counterparts in the largest wine import country of England had done, where corporations had been buying up the distribution network.

In 1968, Heublein, the big liquor company, bought Petri's United Vintners, which included Inglenook and Italian Swiss Colony. In 1969, the venerable Beaulieu Vineyards, a premium house that had been established in 1900 by a Frenchman from Bordeaux named Georges de Latour, was sold to Heublein by de Latour's offspring. (Although it had become a cog in the corporate wheel its then president, Leigh Knowles, kept Beaulieu a signature expression of Napa Valley wine. The winery faltered after his death about two decades later.) Under Heublein, Inglenook and Italian Swiss Colony (which was renamed Colony) slid almost immediately toward nondescript but consistent bulk production. In 1971, Nestlé grabbed Beringer, a brand that had already been in decline. Nestlé managed to take the brand down a few more notches.

In the 1970s, America's retail shelves overflowed with cheap, nondescript, sweet, mass-produced wines from both domestic and imported sources. The retail market for top-tier premium wines, whether imported or domestic, stayed in the big cities where the sophisticates lived. The restaurant trade just about ignored domestic wine.

The French wine industry did not take part in the bulk export phenomenon at first. The French had an image to rebuild and to keep. Besides, French producers clung to the notion that their home wine consumption was large enough to keep the everyday wine within their borders. The majority of French exports to England and America were concentrated in the upper tier—the great châteaux, or at least their second labels.

The 1970s took French producers by surprise when overall domestic consumption of ordinary local wines dropped to less than half the economic value of French wines in the prior decade. The drop was due in part to economic instability (inflation and sharp rises in energy costs). The potential French baby-boomer market for wine was not becoming richer like its American counterpart market. Small French vineyards not attached to major châteaux and already flirting with extinction were hurt further when, in 1973, one of the oldest French family wine brokerage houses, Cruse, was implicated in and then tried in French court for fraud.

Cruse had bought some wine from a small-time négociant who had fixed the papers, switching documents that applied to some Appellation Control (AC) Bordeaux white wine with some cheap red wine he had gotten from the Midi; with the swirl of a pen, the *négociant* had created an AC-status red wine that commanded more money on the market. Since all the company had done was to buy something it thought was something else, Cruse was exonerated upon appeal, but that was two years after the scandal had broken and after it had caused one suicide in the family and the centuries-old Cruse business had come tumbling down.

The Cruse scandal did much toward weakening the French bulk wine market. French cooperatives and small wine companies found it difficult to compete. They began to sell out to chains with better resources to meet the need to go overseas, and it was the vast potential markets in the United States and England that the chains had targeted, wines handled by companies with names like Monsieur Henri Selection and Patriach. Soon, even the major châteaux needed a market boost to rid them of inventory; an example of their new marketing was Mouton-Cadet, a reasonable offering at a reasonable price from the famous Château Mouton-Rothschild.

Down under, Australian marketers had designed a new package that made mass marketing easier and that eventually became successful. The design included a bladder like bag filled with wine that was packaged inside a box. The box had a hole in one of its sides through which a plastic spigot connected to the plastic bag was pulled and turned to release the wine; as the wine emptied, the bag collapsed into a vacuum, allowing no air in to ruin the remaining volume of wine. The "bag-in-the-box" brought cheap wine to the public in an easy-to-carry, easy-to-open large package that, for Australian producers, increased volume sales. The first success of the packaging was in the home market. As that success multiplied it gave Australian producers the cash needed to invest in export markets.

England was, as it remains, Australia's largest export market, but in the

In parts of South America—Chile and Argentina especially—new private and government interest in economic stability began to take shape in the 1970s. The South Americans embarked on programs to upgrade viticulture and wine quality and then to move into the export market. Their success in the United States began to show in the 1980s.

latter part of the 1970s the Australian wine industry made moves toward the United States that ultimately paid off for them.

Despite the growing success of bulk cheap "pop" wines a small wine revolution had been taking place in the United States on both coasts. In New York State, in 1962, a partnership was formed between a Russian immigrant viticulturist, Doctor Konstantin Frank, and Charles Fournier, who was in charge of winemaking at Gold Seal Winery. The two released the first commercially successful *Vitis vinifera* wines of the Finger Lakes region: Riesling and Chardonnay.

With the release of the two wines, Dr. Frank had proved that, if carefully selected and nurtured, plantings of certain *Vitis vinifera* clones could survive the erratic, harsh, cool Finger Lakes climate and the resulting wines could compete with Europe. Since then, the wine world has recognized that Finger Lakes Riesling wines are on a par with the best that Germany has to offer. Yet, as important a development as it was, the New York Chardonnay and Riesling release was a small success that remained a small story in the domestic wine world for two more decades. The wine revolution that would truly shock the world was fermenting in California.

The flood of California bulk wine notwithstanding, some of the best California wines that had ever been released came on the market in the decade between 1965 and 1975. The wines mainly came from the older producer houses like Martini, Sebastiani, Concannon, and Beaulieu. These were top-notch varietally labeled products, albeit the market for them was confined to savvy wine aficionados. In the late 1960s new blood was making its way into the California wine scene. Many of their wines were in the same category as the premium varietals above. This new crop of producers included people with money (always important to expand in wine), vineyard owners with a vision, and transplants to the area with an unparalleled sense for wine marketing. Robert Mondavi was in that last category.

Around the time of Prohibition the Mondavi family had bought Charles

Krug, an established California winery that had been founded in 1861. For a couple of decades Krug went along with reasonable success, but nothing splashy enough for Robert Mondavi. After a trip abroad in the latter part of the 1950s, Robert was convinced that the family winery needed upgrading; his vision was to emulate Bordeaux winemaking practices and to put out top American wines with varietal labeling that anyone could buy. In a series of maneuvers that ended in a punching match between him and his brother, Peter, Robert became estranged from the family business.

Robert Mondavi had trained in the cellar and in winemaking, but he was truly a natural salesman and consummate merchant, which should come as no surprise. His father had operated a grocery business and then a saloon and had also supplied grapes to immigrant home winemakers in Virginia, Minnesota, before moving the family to Napa Valley when Robert was about six years old. In 1960, Robert got some money and some investors together, bought prime Napa Valley vineyard land and, on the strength of his charisma and vision, soon developed a maverick reputation and an overwhelmingly successful track record in building and growing the Robert Mondavi Winery.

The market for large bottles of cheap, "poplike" domestic wines from Almaden, Paul Masson, and Gallo that were distributed nationally was about to dry up. The maverick Mondavi knew their days were numbered and that the market for solid, premium California wine would grow. He fixed his eyes on that niche and then set out upgrading both winemaking and wine marketing in California. At his winery, he instituted programs in the cellar to use new French oak barrels for aging instead of large redwood or cement tanks; he created a line of varietal wines, but he also created proprietary product names to entice consumers. Then he got on the road to sell his show.

Robert Mondavi's success was proving a great influence. It helped, too, that land values in sleepy Napa and Sonoma were still reasonable. The region interested a new crop of investors who were every bit as determined as Mondavi to produce wines that would compete with the best Europe had to offer. In one estimate, between Mendocino in the north and San Francisco to the south of Napa and Sonoma, an average of 50,000 acres were planted to vines annually during this period. By 1973, many of these new wine producers had learned what they needed to know in order to compete; others had been taking notice.

Today Steven Spurrier is a well-respected wine expert with a global audience for his musings in *Decanter,* a major British wine magazine. In the 1970s he was a young wine merchant who had moved from England to Paris, where he and an American partner had established a specialty wine shop that was in need of promotion. In addition, the partners formed *L'Academie du Vin,* a wine school that was located close to the U.S. Embassy and not far from an IBM headquarters in Paris. The partners quickly had some American wine students on their hands. At the time, sales of top French wine had been growing in the East Coast American market in double digits, which meant that many of the American students at L'Academie du Vin knew a fair amount about French wines. Happily, Spurrier's specialty was French wine.

Yet Spurrier's partner had been talking about what was going on in Napa Valley. On a return trip from America, she brought some Napa wines to Paris for Spurrier to taste. He was impressed and then he got a promotional idea. In 1975 he went to California to pick up wines he would use for a blind tasting in Paris that he would sponsor, pitting California against Bordeaux and Burgundy. He planned the tasting for 1976, the year of the American bicentennial celebration. He figured the event was sure to appeal both to the French, who were certain that their wines would win, and to potential American students for his school.

In May 1976, at the Paris InterContinental Hotel, nine French judges evaluated six California Chardonnay wines against four top-tier white Burgundy wines, and six California Cabernet Sauvignon wines against four Grand Crus

Classé Bordeaux wines. The judges were of the top echelon of the French wine world—from the press and the restaurant trade, two of the top wine producers of France, and two officials representing two French wine-governing bodies. After the judges swirled, tasted, spit, huffed, puffed, and tried to make guesses—some with absolute certainty about what they thought they were tasting—six of the most highly rated wines were from California, and the two top rated wines of all were Stag's Leap 1973 Cabernet Sauvignon and Château Montelena 1973 Chardonnay, each from California.

Despite the several judges who refused to accept their own results and despite the fact that the French wine industry claimed the judging had been rigged, the California wine industry could not get better promotion if it had paid for it. Spurrier was as shocked as anyone. He knew the California wines were good and he figured they could hold their own, but the results were incredible. Years later he told a reporter that had he known any better he would not have arranged the tasting; after all, he sold mostly French wine at the store in Paris and his tasting made a lot French wine people angry with him.

Spurrier's event was so crucial to the California wine world that a complete book has been written about it: *Judgment of Paris: California vs. France and the 1976 Paris Tasting That Revolutionized Wine*, by George M. Taber.

While California premium wines exploited their new standing, on America's East Coast, Coca-Cola bought the venerable Taylor Wine Company in 1977. Coke's management knew that the new interest in California wine had produced a 79 percent increase in sales of domestic wine over the previous decade. They salivated over what seemed like a good marketing plan to couple the new interest in California wine with the recognized Taylor name by establishing a new line of low-end wines called Taylor California Cellars. But the statistics were unclear as to whether the increase in sales of domestic wine was the result of a major shift in wine consumption from European premium wines to

California products or if it was the result of a new crop of baby-boomer wine consumers who naturally leaned toward domestic products.

Coca-Cola's powerful marketing machine proved neither a match for the regulatory madness of alcohol controls nor for the fickleness of wine consumers. The company was used to paying grocery chains for up-front floor space so that the first thing that consumers saw as they entered a supermarket was Coca-Cola products stacked high. The alcohol regulations in many states outlaw such practices, a fact that the lawyers and marketers of that powerful worldwide corporation seemed to have overlooked before getting into the wine business. In addition, baby-boomers weren't just looking for the California name on brands; whether perceived or actual, they equated quality with premium varietal wines. Taylor California Cellars was a dismal failure.

Once a great name in domestic wine, the Taylor Wine Company passed from Coca-Cola to Seagram (where it was merged with Gold Seal), from Seagram to Vintner's International, on to the Canandaigua Wine Company (now Constellation Brands), and then into relative obscurity.

In California, with new interest in varietal wines, Almaden, Paul Masson, and others like them offering jug wines would suffer throughout the 1980s a fate similar to Taylor's. In 1982, RJR Tobacco bought Heublein and then closed Colony; in 1987, under a division at RJR, Heublein bought Almaden and then decimated it; Paul Masson wound up in the Vinter's International portfolio and it, too, fell apart. Corporate winery investments went into fad products like insipidly sweet, fizzy wine coolers intended mainly to get rid of a large volume of poor-quality grape crops, but also as a response to the theory that, since baby boomers had graduated from cheap fizzy wines to premium products, maybe the industry could establish new wine consumers with cheap fizzy introductory products. It proved an illusive if not erroneous goal. And then there is White Zinfandel.

The Trinchero name came into wine lore in 1948, when the family that had emigrated from Italy twenty years earlier remade Sutter Home Winery from its Prohibition-era ashes. For two dozen years Sutter Home was a small affair, one of those California wineries that produced wine on a family scale and sold it to a select group of Americans who appreciated the effort. In 1972, with Cabernet Sauvignon leading the red wine pack and with Zinfandel suffering from an image problem, the Trinchero family faced a glut of zinfandel grapes.

Second-generation Bob Trinchero came up with the idea for producing White Zinfandel, a wine that was produced mainly from red grapes but had most of the color bled out of it. With a touch of sweetness to the wine in order to appeal to a mass market, Trinchero's idea became a startling success in 1974; to novices, the product was close enough to premium wine for them to believe they had become drinkers of serious wine, which many ultimately did become. Sutter Home Winery went on to become one of the largest family-owned California wineries to offer medium- to low-priced so-called entry wines. White Zinfandel still sells well across the United States.

One other particular form of making money from the new wine boom in America was to form a wine club; in the early 1960s, a Washington, D.C., wine retailer had formed one of the most successful of them.

According to Elin McCoy, in *The Emperor of Wine: the Rise of Robert M. Parker, Jr. and the Reign of American Taste,* when he formed Les Amis du Vin (the Friends of Wine), Marvin Stirman got in the wine club business while wine sales in the United States were on the upswing. Yet most new wine consumers had very little product knowledge. Les Amis du Vin held wine lectures and tastings in hotels, restaurants, and other venues. Membership came with a subscription to *Wine,* a British magazine with some of that country's well-known wine writers as contributors. Stirman also created a newsletter, which he produced without advertising revenue and which came to club members as part of their subscription. The club was Eurocentric at first, but after the Paris tasting and as other wine retailers in major cities across the United States began to discover the profit potential of wine as opposed to liquor, they discovered Les Amis du Vin. The club went national, with control stemming from Washington, D.C.

Les Amis du Vin produced the results Stirman had intended: wine information led to wine sales increases. Importers and winery owners clamored to lecture and to present wine tastings at Les Amis du Vin chapters; Robert Mondavi used chapter meetings as an outlet for exposure of his new winery. By the end of the 1970s, Les Amis du Vin had crossed the Atlantic, with a chapter becoming established in Paris. Club members also began receiving a subscription of the club's own magazine, *Friends of Wine*. In fact, America would soon produce a number of periodicals devoted to wine.

Prior to the 1960s, in the two big markets—England and the United States—wine was a largely elitist affair. Les Amis du Vin, and other clubs like it, was the beginning of a general swing in the wine world toward servicing and raising the interest of the general consumer. The clubs instigated a wine newsletter industry; wine classes for the consumer began to flourish; traveling wine tastings became the norm; and, instead of relying on poets and philosophers to wax eloquent over wine, more in-depth wine writing and analysis began to develop.

Consumers discovered that learning about wine is not a linear exploit; it takes you down many winding paths and through myriad levels of understanding and appreciation. Newly educated consumers moved quickly to the next outlet, putting a strain on the "venerable" outlets. Les Amis du Vin folded up tent at the close of the 1980s. A few of the newsletters that had been formed a decade previously had closed up shop, too, but the gap they left would quickly be filled by a new crop of wine writers, some of whom offered definite opinions and a style that made them seem like gurus.

17.

The Second Half

This is a business that includes some wondrously rancorous family feuds and downright inept judging at wine competitions that allegedly set standards for wine quality.

—Jay Stuller and Glen Martin, *Through the Grapevine*

Wine writing began in Mesopotamia about four thousand years ago and continued throughout history, first as documentation and then as information. By the twentieth century, the tradition of wine writing in England had become a combination of information and self-promotion. Many of the British wine writers who rose to the top of their profession were often wine merchants: investors in vineyards, importers, exporters, employees of large producers, retailers, or some combination of one or more. In their role as writers, they had become the arbiters of wine taste and since their wine relationships were European their allegiances were, too. The fact that they knew the products so well was a plus for their self-promotion. When America began producing its soon-to-be famous wine writers in the early 1970s, wine writing began a subtle shift from informing to critiquing.

In her biography of wine critic Robert M. Parker, Elin McCoy offers a detailed look at the American wine writing hierarchy of the 1970s. Many of the writers were wine enthusiasts who had started up newsletters such as the *Connoisseur's Guide to California Wine,* or reporters who worked for newspapers, such as Frank Prial at the *New York Times,* or magazine writers, such as Alexis Bespaloff at *New York Magazine*. Bespaloff also did wine commentary on a local New York radio station, WNEW, and was one American writer who had come from the wine trade. But he apparently was not in it as deeply as, say, Gerald Asher, a Briton who worked at the American wine importing firm of Austin Nichols and who became wine columnist for the lofty *Gourmet* magazine. Among the writers who began during that period, Asher proved one of the most literary.

Unlike Britain, where wine writing had developed over centuries and was directed at a rather savvy market, the thrust of American wine writing was aimed at a new and growing American market for wine. Marvin Shanken's *Wine Spectator* is today one of the most successful and long lasting of the periodicals to serve that market. Under a previous owner, the *Spectator* had hit the stands as a tabloid in 1976. At the time, Shanken was a real estate and investment banker, talent that he eventually put to good use to forecast what was to come in the wine world. After buying *Wine Spectator* in 1979, Shanken quit Wall Street to focus on wine.

Although already enthusiastic over California wine, he quickly realized that his magazine needed to cover the whole wine world. He introduced to *Wine Spectator* a tasting panel that rated wines on the technical twenty-point scale that had been developed at America's top school for oenology, at the University of California. In 1980 Shanken's magazine may have had the wine ratings field (and maybe even American wine consumers) all to itself, small as the audience still was, and the magazine had hit a circulation upward of 70,000. But if Shanken's magazine had the market to itself, that situation would soon change.

Passion is often what separates people in the wine business from other businesses. In the 1970s anyone who knew him also knew that a young University of Maryland student, Robert M. Parker, was ravenously passionate about wine. Other students were out demonstrating, or maybe even studying, but the young law student was fixated on wine. He eventually put together a wine club that led him to lasting friendships with other wine enthusiasts over the years, as well as to publishing a wine newsletter.

Rumors exist about Robert M. Parker's innate ability not only to identify certain wines accurately, but also to remember those wines just as accurately years later when one of them appears in a glass before him. Perhaps, but what certainly turned out to be more than just rumor is that Parker could write compellingly about wine and he could influence others with his passion and talent. McCoy claims that Parker feels it is unethical for people to write about products in which they have a direct or indirect financial interest, which is of course the case with some British wine writers of authority. While Parker geared up in the wine world the British *Decanter* magazine was launched in 1975; by 1977 the respected wine industry insider, Michael Broadbent, wrote his first of many columns for the magazine. Over the years, other wine industry professionals began to write for *Decanter,* including Hugh Johnson and Steven Spurrier. Parker promised his writing to be outside prevailing tradition. His newsletter would be passionate yet impartial, educational yet critical, and he would be an advocate for the consumer. Hence, his newsletter would be called the *Wine Advocate*.

Parker was Franco-centric, with Bordeaux reds in the lead. McCoy mentions that he seemed unimpressed by the results of Spurrier's Paris tasting because he did not believe it was possible to compare Bordeaux to California cabernet sauvignon, the wines being in two separate classes: Bordeaux the elegant, California the brutish. Anyway, Parker was not interested in hyping wines to promote either a wine shop or a wine school. As he saw it, his job was to taste, to rate, and then to report with as much passion that a dispassionate advocate can impart. Parker's newsletter sold no advertising, he paid for his own wine trips, and he was affiliated with no one in the wine trade. At first, he seemed almost to go out of his way to avoid people in the trade.

By 1981 Parker was writing a wine column for the *Washington Post,* and then he began a freelance wine writing career. In his early years, Parker's wine writing was straightforward, clear prose, free of flowery descriptions and cryptic metaphors, and he accompanied his notes with a 100-point hedonistic wine scoring system that he had devised, but he reserved the point system only for his newsletter.

The combination of the *Post* being widely read outside of Washington and his freelance writing for national magazines helped gain newsletter subscribers for Parker that reached far beyond Maryland and Washington, D.C. In the spring of 1983, with a newsletter subscription rate of about seven thousand, Parker's opinion in the newsletter concerning the 1982 Bordeaux vintage would change his fortune and the fortunes of others in the wine trade.

To Parker, it was a spectacular vintage. He recommended that his subscribers grab the wines on futures. The news produced euphoria in Bordeaux, where the market for futures had been suffering from atrophy at the time. But Parker's opinion went contrary to other wine critics, especially one of the most important of them in the United States, Robert Finigan. To Finigan, the 1982 Bordeaux vintage lacked luster and certainly was not worth a financial investment. He was joined in that assessment by one or two other recognized American wine writers. (Gone unnoticed in America was that *Decanter* magazine's William Bolter happened to agree with Parker about the vintage, as did a couple of other European wine writers.)

In the end, Parker's call on the 1982 Bordeaux vintage was proved correct. It gave him enough credibility that he could eventually leave his law practice and devote all his time to wine. Today, the *Wine Advocate* reaches about 60,000 readers and has expanded to an online version.

The eventual rise of critics like Parker and others who write for wine magazines and newspapers brought a new power to the American wine trade and that made some wine merchants (and producers) nervous. Even before Parker, wine writers and critics had been gaining a measure of power over the American wine retail trade. McCoy points out that a major New York retailer complained that he had lost money on the prepurchases of the 1982 Bordeaux because some people who believed the critic Finigan had refused to buy the wines.

It took less than a decade for Parker's influence to overshadow just about all the other wine writers and critics. It gave him a kind of power that some producers, merchants, and consumers find arguably dangerous. Power like that can also be dangerous to the critic himself, who is bound to get into scrapes over it, which Parker has, most notably with *Decanter's* contributor, Jancis Robinson, in an ongoing argument that ostensibly pits Old World tradition against New World interventionist winemaking but really is only a matter of arguing over taste.

The strength of Parker's power seems even to have led to a change at

Wine Spectator: the technical 20-point wine rating system has been dropped and the magazine now mimics the 100-point Parker rating system. (*Decanter* uses a five-star rating system and the influential Italian magazine, *Gambero Rosso,* uses a three-wineglass rating system. All the wine raters, including Parker, rate hedonistically and, therefore, subjectively, which is one more reason for some wine merchants and some of their customers to complain.)

In contrast to the rise of wine writers and the complacency of many retailers who began to rely on ratings to sell wine, potent educator-promoters began to hit the wine market in the early 1980s. Edmund Osterland was one of the most dynamic of them.

Osterland was the first American to gain Master Sommelier status, which until then was a club of certified wine experts made up mainly of snobs. Osterland had a flare for self-promotion and theatrics, plus he had a talent for teaching without ceremony and pomposity. His aim was to educate both the consumer and the restaurant trade, which at the time was woefully deficient in wine knowledge.

Osterland studied wine in France under the respected Emile Peynaud and then he spent time in Hawaii as a wine distributor sales representative and part time sommelier in a restaurant. He was in the position at the restaurant to recommend to consumers the wines he sold to the restaurant for his company, which taught him the power of recommendation plus the need for educating the consumer. He soon started a wine school that he named The Grape Escape, and after immediate success with the school he discovered that he had saturated the island market—it was time for this big fish in a small pond to move on, to New York.

In New York, because he had tapped into a new wave, Osterland retained his big-fish status but the pond was quite larger. He teamed with the National Restaurant Association to create *Wine and the Bottom Line*, a book based on his restaurant training program, and he found a job.

A wine enthusiast named Al Hotchkin (with two partners) had started up The International Wine Center, which was located at the time on West 55th Street in Manhattan, across from City Center. The "Wine Center" was made up of a restaurant at street level, Tastings, and a wine education facility on the second floor. The center's director, Rory Callahan, hired Osterland to help him build upstairs what eventually became a nationally known wine training program.

Hotchkin introduced what at the time was an innovative concept for New York: one- and two-ounce sample wine pours at a wine bar that was part of the restaurant. The opened bottles of wines were connected to a system that fed nitrogen into the bottle to displace oxygen, thereby preserving the wines. Customers could sample the wines before buying them and they could buy them by the glass or by the bottle, whether or not they were high-end world-class wines or everyday drinkers.

Osterland's message to the wine world was simple. In restaurants wine is and should be treated as a major profit center; access to wine should be made easier and less expensive to customers; and consumers don't have to be experts to know what they like and to know what it is worth to pay for it, they just need some basic information and confidence. His was among a new breed of wine education programs that would soon sweep the country.

Hotchkin later went on to establish and operate in the Greenwich Village neighborhood of Manhattan a wine retail business that specialized in Burgundy. Callahan started his own wine and food consulting and promotion firm. The International Wine Center operates today under different ownership and its wine education programs are more formal.

In 1986, with a new baby, Osterland and his wife left New York City for La Jolla, California, where, over time, he established a new wine education business focusing on corporate chains and institutions. In his wine taste, he remains the Francophile that he was when he started out more than twenty-five years ago when it was good for a wine educator in New York to place emphasis on imports. The import wine market was in good shape.

Alongside the overwhelming developing interest in domestic products, wine importers in the United States got a boost both from a strong dollar and from severe European market conditions. With the exception of Britain, wine consumption in Europe was beginning to shrink, especially in the important wine producing countries of France, Italy, and Germany. South America, Australia, New Zealand, and, after the fall of the apartheid system in the late 1980s, South Africa would soon set their sights on both the British and American markets.

Exporters and importers alike viewed the low per capita wine consumption in America as a blessing; with a consistently developing interest in wine, the large American population still offered great opportunities for growth for producers who utilized good promotion. Some major European producers even began to buy into the United States, taking up vineyard land in California and in parts of the Pacific Northwest. Such products as Domaine Chandon and Piper Sonoma appeared on the market, produced in California by a subsidiary of the respective Champagne house in conjunction with an existing California producer. The well-known Burgundian négociant and wine producer, Joseph Drouhin, started operations in Oregon in 1987, where it was rumored that the pinot noir grape could be produced as well—or as problematically, depending upon one's perspective—as in Burgundy.

The Europeans developed the joint ventures not only to be close to the major American market but also to offset what was becoming a series of lost markets in Europe. For Californians, the joint ventures promised producers access to a European market that had never really been open to them.

Pinney points out that in 1970 exports of California wines were just about nil; a decade later they had reached 8 million gallons; by 2003, a total of 74 million gallons of California wines were exported to Britain, Canada, Japan, and Belgium. A particularly interesting piece of information is that a lot of the wine that travels from California overseas makes a stop in the Netherlands, where the Dutch play a role in smoothing the way for distribution just as they have in the past for German wines.

Despite the French wine investments, in the early 1980s Italian wine import sales in the United States surpassed their French counterparts for the first time ever. This situation was due in part to the Italian government's commitment through the Italian Trade Commission to increase promotion and marketing efforts.

In 1963, the Italians had come up with their version of appellation controls, but the regulations were weak. The new Italian Denomination of Origin Controls did not specify regions clearly and it did not create delimited regions with specified grape cultivars. In addition, the DOC made no provisions either for laboratory or for taste analysis. Wine industry people were left to wonder what it was that the regulations did cover. About a decade later, the DOC was revised and a stricter Denomination of Origin Guarantee (DOCG) came about. Stringent DOCG controls more closely resembled the French and German controls. But after some experience with the regulations, producers challenged them, not because they were weak but because they proved too restrictive. Leading the charge was the well-respected Antinori wine-producing family of Tuscany.

In the 1970s, Antinori crafted wines outside the DOCG regulations. They were bigger in structure, thick and chewy, and not nearly as acidic as many

Tuscan wines had been, in part, because of the grapes: Antinori added an outsider like cabernet sauvignon to local grapes like sangiovese to produce his new wines. The wines were also the result of Antinori's focus on winemaking technology and different ways of producing wine in Tuscany. The wines were not allowed a DOCG label, so it took good promotion, especially in the largest export market for Italian wine—America—for Antinori's new products to garner acclaim. But garner it they did. Soon others followed and the movement spread from Tuscany to Piedmont. Since they could not put a recognized DOCG zone on the labels of the new wines, producers either gave them proprietary names or used varietal labeling.

Germany's wine trade had hurt its reputation in America by exporting oceans of poor-quality, insipidly sweet wine in the 1970s. A decade later the Germans had gotten the message. Developing consumer savvy meant that they had to start exporting more of the dry wines they had been keeping to themselves. In the 1980s, a new crop of dry German wines made their way to America, but they simply were not right. The wines seemed over the top, too mouth challenging. While Americans seemed to prefer drier wines, they really were not ready for bone-dry, acidic white wines.

Never much in the American wine market, Austria sealed its fate in 1985 with a scandal that involved adding glycol (antifreeze) to sweeten their wines. It took until the twenty-first century for Austrian wines to gain small but growing recognition in the United States and in most of Europe.

Toward the end of the 1980s, Spain had begun to awaken to the American market through promotion firms based in the United States. Edmund Osterland's old boss at the International Wine Center, Rory Callahan, headed one of these firms.

Callahan was a trained winemaker who taught winemaking to consumers at the center. When the center was sold, he opted to get into wine promotion, especially to the restaurant trade. He landed contracts with people in Spain's wine exporting business. He had developed some good contacts in the restaurant business, which made him quite a catch for the exporters; a growth in interest in Spanish wines in the New York City market bore witness to that fact.

Spain's wine industry began to upgrade. Investments in new technology and new thinking began to show up on the market on a limited basis in the 1980s. To many, the new wines from Spain tasted similar to those from California or to the new Italian breed, but that worked out to be a good thing for Spain's producers, whose wines began to command prices that had been unheard of for Spanish wines.

Lagging behind the Europeans, Chile and Argentina invaded the American market with wines at prices so low that no one could believe it, not even the South American producers. The prices were often the result of fast-talking importers who visited South America, praised the wines, and promised entry into the vast United States market, but there was a catch. According to the importers, the wines had to sell cheaply, at rock-bottom prices, in America. The plan worked, despite the fact that, in many cases, the quality of the wines was weak. Instead of producers making the money, however, profits from the plan went mainly to importers and distributors. Worse, American consumers came to view South American wines as low-end introductory products, and once an identity is established, it is difficult to get consumers to change their perception. It took until the late 1990s—about fifteen years—before Chilean and Argentinian producers were able to get the prices their increasingly better-quality wine exports deserved.

In 1985, Australia's wine industry began a measured penetration for better representation in the British market and for new visibility in America. With a lot of practice in the British market, the new push by Australia worked well. In America, it took a little longer, but when the plan took off the Australian wine industry controlled its destiny in the U.S. market better than the South Americans had controlled theirs. Still, Australia's entry into the United States began mainly at the low end of the market, in part because it was an introduction and in part because Australia's capacity to produce massive volumes of wine threatened to drown producers if they didn't build demand for it. Only lately has Australia managed to put forward its high-priced "cult" wines on the American market, to great success.

In Europe the wine trade is a fairly large chunk of the economy. In the American economy the domestic wine industry is just better than a blip, which means little lobbying power in Washington. While producers from the world over clamored for the American wine consumer, and while California built a new and profitable wine image, antialcohol groups agitated.

The front-runner of the agitators was the Center for Science in the Public Interest, a so-called watchdog group whose leadership has expressed a decided antialcohol stance. The result of this group's efforts showed up in 1988 as federal government–mandated warning labels on wine, as well as a new tax on wine producers and wine merchants, called the Occupation Tax. The tax was in addition to the already existing federal and state excise taxes and fees required to produce wine.

Many in the American wine trade pointed out to whomever would listen—the press, consumers, local officials—that the mandated warning labels on alcoholic beverages seemed like a purposeful misinformation campaign. The warning makes three points: that alcohol impairs our ability to drive, that it may cause health problems, and that it may cause birth defects in pregnant women. In the first case, there is no mention of how much alcohol can do the job; in the second case, there are more than forty scientific studies to prove that moderate alcohol consumption may be beneficial to health; and in the third case, according to the U. S. Department of Health and Human Services' substance abuse Web site (www.fascenter.samhsa.gov/resource/tables.cfm), conflicting as the research studies are, most of them suggest the real danger to pregnant women is in drinking large quantities of alcohol at one sitting rather than drinking in moderate amounts over a long period of time.

The warning label was followed by a mandate that requires the words "Contains Sulfites" on wine labels. This, too, seemed to the wine trade to be another blatant attempt at scaring consumers rather than informing them. Wine had just about always contained sulfites (sulfur dioxide), since second-century Rome, and it is produced naturally as a by-product of fermentation in wine, cheese, bread, and the human stomach as it digests food. Baked goods, dried fruits, and wine receive additions of sulfites as preservative, but only wine comes with a warning label.

Seemingly overnight, the sulfite warning on wine produced consumers who claimed headaches from the ingredient, despite the fact that after twenty years of research no definitive scientific study correlates the sulfite levels in wine with headaches.

While the American wine industry contended with new prohibitionists, the television journalist, Morley Safer, of CBS's *Sixty Minutes,* reported on what he called "the French paradox." The paradox, according to the report, was that the French consumed large amounts of animal fats in their diet, yet suffered from fewer deaths from heart disease than Americans. The answer to the paradox, according to Harvard Medical School studies, was that the French drink more moderate amounts of red wine. Red wine, it appeared through research, provided the French with natural antioxidant benefits to the blood stream, thereby protecting the heart from certain diseases.

> Until the Morley Safer report, the largest-selling wine in America, next to White Zinfandel, was Chardonnay, a white wine. Within about a week after the television report, sales of red wine in America had skyrocketed.

Despite the warnings and despite the fact that consumers were confused, misinformed, and even scared away, overall wine consumption increased in America. At the end of the 1980s, the concern of the wine industry was not whether it would keep growing, but in which direction. Yet the thing that many merchants and producers had feared developed into a trend: the number ratings assigned to wine by critics increasingly carried more weight with a segment of consumers that spent the most dollars on wine.

Passionless merchants easily conceded. Instead of applying their own standards, they readily used the critics' scores and ratings to sell wine, fueling the notion that merchants could not be trusted, especially those who fudged the ratings by switching vintages or omitting important information from retail shelf talkers. In addition to ratings, wine magazines felt compelled to come up with a "best of" list in each issue culminating in a "best of year" in year-end editions.

To traditionalists, the critics and magazines were giving their love of wine the smell and flavor of a horse race rather than the sensual pursuit of aromatic and gastronomic pleasure.

At some point in his career, Parker developed a taste for the chewy California-style reds, and so, it seemed, did most of the rest of the American critical pack. As wines in that style began to gain high scores, wines from successive vintages seemed to get bigger, more chewy, higher in alcohol, and to receive even higher scores.

Around this time, wine consumers began chatting over the Internet through software provided by Prodigy, Compuserve, and AOL formats that today seem quaint. Nevertheless, the formats allowed for complaints online and the complaints were joined by letters to magazines that winemakers were "chasing Parker points," that is, they were creating wines to appeal to the star critic's palate at the expense of traditional "terroir" or plain elegance and finesse. While Parker denies the allegation by saying, "I don't think any quality-oriented winemaker would ever sell his soul and make a wine to please one critic," the history of human frailty certainly proves that belief to be naïve. The fact remains that more and more thick, chewy, alcoholic California wines show up regularly, and they gain high scores from wine critics.

In the late 1980s and into the '90s it seemed like new winemaker celebrities were born with the release of ratings in every magazine or newsletter issue. By the late 1990s a segment of the wine market had gained the status of "cult wines." The wines were generally big, "in-your-face," high in alcohol, and produced by the latest celebrity winemaker. Often one or more of the blockbuster wines were near impossible to find on the open retail market—a clear tactic for creating demand and profits through high prices.

The buyers for these wines did not seem to mind the manipulation.

At times, it seemed a contest was ongoing between Parker's newsletter (and its followers) and other magazines (and their followers). Parker would give one particular big, forward wine a 95, and *Wine Spectator* would rate the same wine an 82 (or the other way around). Although it also rates wines hedonistically, *Decanter* magazine's collective hedonism leans toward the so-called traditionalist style of wines. A couple of writers for *Decanter* have been quite vocal over the variance between their views and the views of other—read "American"—critics.

With the exception of their operations in the United States, the French at first appeared doggedly entrenched in the traditionalist mode. Then, in the mid-1990s the great Châteaux of Bordeaux were challenged by a small number of renegade winemakers that would become known as *garagistes*, a reference to their wine being produced out of barns and garages on their farms. To traditionalists, the wines are the French version of California cult wines and they exist merely to chase points. When one of the top Bordeaux houses—Château Pavie—came out with wine that traditionalists considered a point-chasing exercise, the *Decanter* magazine contributor, the respected Jancis Robinson, was herself exercised.

As the Internet became more and more sophisticated, so, too, did wine-specific bulletin boards. A few wine writers and critics, Parker included, became the center of attraction on Internet bulletin boards.

The bulk of visitors to the Web bulletin boards is made up of a new breed of wine consumers. They proudly refer to themselves as "wine geeks" (obviously forgetting or not understanding the role of a geek at the circus). These geeks have clout and almost mirror earlier merchant fears over the power of certain wine critics. It is estimated that American wine geeks, who generally are in high income brackets, account for sales of no more than 10 percent of all wine sold in the United States. But those sales are for the high-scoring, high-priced wines of the world. Many are also sold at auction.

Sadly, not enough wine retailers in the United States did or said much to persuade consumers against the developing trend. What's worse is that many retailers simply went along for the ride, using the critics' scores to sell wine in their establishments and by extension creating their own loss of integrity in the eyes of wine geeks. Many geeks use the retailer solely as a distribution point for what they already know they want to buy. On some of the wine-dedicated Web sites many geeks start threads to lambaste retailers for their lack of business and wine sense, of course providing one side of a usually sordid story about a wine deal gone sour.

For local wine producers of any country, getting into an overseas market usually means choosing either to engage in risky financing to try to build brand recognition or to sell out to a large international corporation with the resources to get them there. In France, as local wine sales plummeted in the 1990s, major wine names, some that went back centuries, sold out to or merged with international companies. Some of the companies that bought them had no beverage experience but great marketing clout; some were already large alcohol companies; some became a combination of the two.

A centuries-old family Champagne house merger illustrates what was happening in the market. Rumored to be the source of the development of one of the important processes in the hands-on Champagne method called riddling—to expel dead yeast cells from the bottle—Cliquot sold to the conglomerate partnership of Vuitton Luggage and the Hennessey Cognac brand. The conglomerate also includes two of Cliquot's competitors, Krug and Moët; the latter markets the Dom Pérginon Champagne brand.

It wasn't just France's wine trade that was in need of market expansion.

To secure markets for oceans of its wine, Australian wineries also coalesced into groups of conglomerates, some from inside Australia and some from outside. And ventures between Mondavi and South American producers took form so that each could have access to the other's home market. At the end of the 1990s, the Bronfman family of Canada would begin to sell off its giant alcohol firm, Seagram. Seagram had earlier bought out Heublein, a purchase that gained Seagram the prestigious Sterling and Beaulieu wineries of Napa, among other holdings; they had been placed under Seagram's Château and Estates division that already included a number of European wineries. In 2001, the giant British drinks conglomerate, Diageo, bought Château and Estates and all that it included.

In the United States, even some of the cult wines grew large enough to sell out to corporations and make their original owners quite wealthy, Ravenswood being one of the most recognizable of them.

The upshot of the formation of conglomerates in the two largest wine export markets—England and the United States—was inundation with wine, wine promotions, and wine critics.

> In the 1990s Gallo was the largest American wine producer, producing the largest volume of wine in the world. The privately owned company spread its tentacles, too, from California to Europe and beyond. (Gallo wound up with the venerable Louis Martini brand.) But no conglomerate in the wine business comes close to the American firm of Constellation Brands, Inc., which in the early part of the twenty-first century not only outdid the Gallo Winery, but dwarfed it.

Constellation Brands, Inc., began as Canandaigua Industries in 1945, founded by Marvin Sands in Canandaigua, New York, in the Finger Lakes region. Within three years Sands was showing his appetite; Canandaigua bought two North Carolina wine companies that produced scuppernong wines.

In 1951, under Sands's family, Richard's Wine Cellars started up in Virginia. In 1954 the company launched Richard's Wild Irish Rose, an oddly colored product with a label that included the words "grape wine." Along with Wild Irish Rose, Sands created a franchise system and established bottling plants throughout the United States to make shipment of the product cheaper and faster. By 1965, Canandaigua Industries was so successful with Wild Irish Rose it had the capital to buy a local South Carolina wine company and make a royalty deal to distribute an old established product called Virginia Dare. And then, between 1969 and 1972, the company bought out two old Finger Lakes sparkling wine companies.

The Canandaigua Wine Company went public in 1973; between then and 1990 the company went on a buying spree across the United States and as far away as Brazil. When the spree was over, it owned Colony, Widmer, Manischewitz, and other American brands.

In 1991 the company ate up Guild Wineries and Distilleries, a large California cooperative that produced and distributed a number of low-end, mass-marketed brands. By 1995, Barton Incorporated and Vintners International's Paul Masson and Taylor brands, the giant United Distillers, and the Almaden and Inglenook brands at Heublein became part of the Canandaigua Wine Company.

The company continued its march, entering Britain in 1998 with an acquisition of a leading wine, cider, and water distributor, sweeping up a few Canadian whiskey brands in 1999, and taking a few more California wineries that weren't so big on their own.

In 2000 the Canandaigua Wine Company changed its name to reflect what the company's flow chart resembles: Constellation Brands, Inc. Today the company also owns the Robert Mondavi brand, the Hardy's Australian brand that was established in 1853, and a 40 percent interest in Ruffino.

Constellation Brands continues to feed its voracious appetite for brands from California to Scotland to Italy to Australia to New Zealand to . . .

When conglomerates control the playing field consumers often suffer, not always from lack of choice but sometimes from too much choice. While the high-end premium cult wines remain in short supply and their prices continue to rise, a lot of the products on the middle to low end of the market are bottled and sold almost in fad fashion, with catchy labels, slick marketing schemes, and low to moderate prices. The wines are often manipulated to appeal to the lowest common denominator of taste, which often means sweet or oaky or both.

Large conglomerates feed volumes of information to general consumers through promotion, yet they manage to keep them in the dark, if not about the pedigree of their wines certainly about the real value of the wines they are consuming.

In the late 1990s a few retailers in major American markets on the coasts grew tired of the situation. As a test case, Joshua Wesson is a great example of those merchants.

In November 1996 Joshua Wesson and a business partner, Richard Marmet, opened a retail wine shop in Manhattan named Best Cellars. The opening happened to coincide with the nouveau craze but aside from that accidental promotion vehicle, the partners' overall retailing theory was based in part on the fact that far more novice wine consumers walked the earth than did wine geeks, and that in the future a lot more of the former would be out there.

Wesson had a background in the restaurant trade as an award winning sommelier. He subsequently became a wine and food author and consultant. In his experience, he discovered that the majority of people he met sought simple guidance—they wanted to know what to expect from the taste of a wine.

As a sommelier, Wesson knew there were many unknown wines in the world that were of good quality and reasonably priced. As he saw his job at Best Cellars, he was to give everyday people understandable access to wine that they could enjoy every day at everyday prices. He also knew that neither wine magazines and newsletters nor small wine producers were speaking to the novices. Certainly, retail merchants who stuck shelf talkers and rating scores on the shelves to sell wines were not speaking to them, either. Wesson not only set out to speak to these consumers but also to invent a language for them so that they could know what a wine would taste like before they bought it.

At the time, the overwhelming majority of New York retail alcohol outlets were liquor stores selling distilled spirits, lots of it, and some wine. Best Cellars applied for the somewhat cheaper wine-only retail license for its small store location on the Upper East Side's heavily trafficked Lexington Avenue.

The design of Best Cellars was slick and as upscale-looking as the neighborhood commanded. The store was not littered with stacked boxes, nor was it crowded and stale with the smell of cardboard and smoke, the way many older liquor stores were. The wines sold at Wesson's store were out of sight, stored in the back; only a representative bottle of each wine in supply stood on the clean shelves. The wines on the shelves were not identifiable brand names backed by big promotion budgets. Further, below each wine on the shelves the consumer saw no point scores to recommend them, but only words.

Most American consumers are not familiar with the great wine regions of the world and how they work, nor do consumers know as much about the grape varieties from which wine is produced as they are led to believe. Instead of organizing his shelves based on wine regions or wine grape names, Wesson organized by the wine's character; he used terms like juicy, fizzy, smooth, fresh, etc., to characterize the wines, terms he knew would appeal to everyday consumers more than the special language wine geeks used and that turned most general consumers off.

To further appeal to the consumer, the price of wines sold at Best Cellars topped out at $10 a bottle.

Best Cellars was an almost immediate success.

Wesson has since expanded to six locations in New York, New England, Washington, D.C., Virginia, and Texas. The top bottle price has been raised to keep up with inflation and the devaluing of the dollar, but the average price for wine at Best Cellars stores remains far below what wine geeks pay.

Wesson's successful concept helped spawn hundreds of retail shops in New York and across the United States. Some shops go so far as to specialize in wines of one country or of one region. Most of the shops specialize in wines that are not rated by critics; in some shops, they simply stop carrying wines if they are eventually rated.

The success of magazines, critics, conglomerates, and new-style retailers notwithstanding, from the end of the 1990s to the present day the world has generally been awash in wine. To handle its wine glut, Australia exports oceans of syrupy, sweet, manipulated wines at low prices. California gets rid of its glut similarly. In Britain and the United States a lot of these wines show up in supermarkets (some under myriad separate labels and at a wide range of prices for the same products).

French winegrowers handle their glut by blaming the government for their problems and perpetrating riots. The fact is that the French wine industry has been relying too long on its complicated past history and too little on effective information programs in the two biggest export markets. Generations of wine consumers or potential wine consumers have neither time nor desire to learn the intricate nature of the French wine classifications; French wine regulations, labels, and marketing all need updating.

The wine glut always has the potential to be a boon for consumers, but gluts are never much good for merchants. Comes an anomalous vintage, like the long hot summer of 2003 in Europe, and both an added glut and a potential low wine quality create even bigger problems for the wine trade. Couple that with a falling dollar against the euro and you've got looming disaster for American wine merchant profits. Still, the future for wine and for wine merchants is salvageable.

Epilogue:
The Future

> The idea that wine not only can be but should be inexpensive, plentiful, and good rather than costly, rare, and indescribably complex seems in danger of disappearing . . . and this when the supply of inexpensive, plentiful, and good wine is greater than ever before in the history of wine.
>
> —Thomas Pinney, *A History of Wine in America: From Prohibition to the Present*

As an agricultural product wine has been an outstanding leading economic indicator in most cultures that have embraced it. Throughout its history the wine trade has vacillated between small and big business. Today it is rather big, and big business likes to take surveys, to understand the market and, if possible, to control it.

Analysis of a combination of statistics put out in 2005 by A.C. Nielson, the Wine Institute, and the Adams Beverage Group, points out that retail wine sales in the United States increased by about 57 percent in the ten-year period between 1994 and 2004. Assuming an average wine price of $100 for a case of twelve bottles, the retail sales figures in the United States for 2004 represented $27 billion.

Wine is, indeed, fairly big business. You can read it in the press releases of Constellation Brands of the United States, Diageo of Britain, Pernod of France, and Andres of Canada; each holds a stable of wine companies from the world over and each seems to like to shout about the number of cases of wine moved. And it is apparent that the strategy of exporters to target the United States market has merit.

According to Marvin Shanken's *The Global Drinks Market: Impact Databank Review and Forecast,* per capita wine consumption worldwide had declined in 2004 by 1 percent from its 2003 figures, yet by 2010 the United States is estimated to surpass Italy's per capita wine consumption, which is in second place behind France. (France and Italy combined account for 26 percent of world per capita wine consumption and it is the decline in consumption in these two countries that led the overall decline in 2004.)

It would be a monumental feat for the United States to take second place in per capita consumption by 2010, since in 2003 the country ranked thirty-fifth in consumption among industrial nations while it was also ranked fourth in the global wine-producing nations. The potential for wine consumption growth in the U.S. market remains staggering.

Large as it is, the U.S. potential for wine consumer growth is tiny compared to the sleeping Asian giant, China. According to the trade association, Interwine China, in the year ending 2004, bottled wine exported to China increased by nearly 54 percent; in 2005 China reduced its import wine tariffs from 43 percent of value to 14 percent. While Chinese interest in wine grows, by the middle of the twenty-first century the country's population is expected to reach 1.6 billion.

Changes are also afoot in the British market. Once the repository for oceans of European wine, according to an A.C. Nielsen report German wine sales fell in Britain in 2004 by 11 percent and sales of Argentinian wines rose by 44 percent at the expense of the two largest wine exporter nations, France and Italy.

In the past, to call the wine trade global was to see it generally through Western eyes. That is no longer the case. The fall of the Soviet sphere has opened the gates for Eastern European wines once again to travel trade routes; England is developing a commercial wine production industry; Canada and the United States have, inside of thirty years, developed truly competitive wine industries (a commercial wine industry now survives in every one of the fifty states); North and South Africa are joined in wine production by coastal African countries; in Palestine, Israel and its neighbor, Lebanon, enjoy new status as premier wine regions; from India to China the historical Asian indifference to wine has given way to a deeper interest and even some wine production; the Japanese produce a small amount of wine but their consumption of highly prized, quite expensive wine has swept through their affluent culture; even in Indonesia, or in islands of the Pacific, wine is the subject addressed by many citizens who sign onto Internet bulletin boards.

In Europe, as boundaries to trade have eroded, wine trade has benefited. Still the largest market for European and Australian wines, Britain has opted out of the common European money system, the Euro, but it has acquiesced to opening its borders to the wine trade. On weekends Britons can make a journey across the Channel to pick up their favorite French wines and take them back home duty-free. (Perhaps the French will return the favor after the few British wineries that have begun operating one day gain acclaim.)

Border crossings are now common throughout Europe, sans passports, and wine seems to be one of the most important passengers in the trunks of European cars. Europeans have also agreed on a series of wine regulations in an effort to halt practices in one country that might help the local wine industry at the expense of the wine industry of a neighboring country.

Surely the Internet promises to be one of the biggest changes to hit the global wine market, if it isn't already.

In the first few years of the twenty-first century, magazines, newsletters, and wine gurus remained the information medium of choice. But by 2005, more than a dozen wine-related Web sites from blogs to bulletin boards could be found on the Internet. The majority of sites—including the consumer "talk" portions of magazine sites—are cluttered with redundant arguments over traditional as opposed to point-chasing winemakers, the benefits of terroir over the so-called international style of wine, and whether or not the subjective nature of taste can be measured by a rating system. These arguments are largely exercises of the ego, and the discourse all too often sinks ever so readily into name-calling. Yet, amidst the clatter, information gets through and wine merchants have caught on. The past six years has witnessed a proliferation of wine merchant Web sites with increasingly sophisticated marketing.

Today, many consumers read the gurus and then can choose to shop either in a bricks-and-mortar wine retail outlet or online to find the best deal. In England, the online system works rather well, since there are no shipping restrictions. (There aren't even restrictions on consumers buying direct from producers.)

In the United States, Internet wine merchants and consumers are up against that patchwork of alcohol controls that vary from state to state. Shipping wine is often more difficult than shipping guns.

American wine merchants and small wine-producing companies have hung

> One of the more successful British online wine merchants happens to be called Best Cellars, unrelated to Wesson's United States merchant business of the same name. Britons can even shop online at the old merchant house of Berry Brothers and Rudd, Ltd. Of course, Best Cellars in the United States operates a Web site, as do a few other wine retailing operations, but they are hampered by regulations.

their hopes on a 2005 Supreme Court decision. The case brought to the court was a challenge to legislation in Michigan and New York that barred interstate wine commerce; wineries within each state were allowed to ship wine direct to resident consumers but wineries from other states could not have direct access to those same consumers.

The court's decision said that if a state allows its wine industry direct access to consumers, it must allow wineries from other states the same access. Since the states have the right to regulate alcohol sales within their borders, the Supreme Court decision gave the states a choice either to allow all American wineries direct shipping access to its residents or to allow no wineries that access. (At this writing, fifteen states ban shipping alcohol directly to consumers; after the decision of the court, New York and Michigan have opted to open up wine shipping, but with fees and restrictions that are sure to keep the debate alive.)

Strong criticism over the direct-shipping issue should be aimed at one particular segment of American wine merchants—wholesaler-distributors. These merchants view any changes in alcohol controls as a threat to their government-sanctioned monopoly under the three-tier system.

In their arguments against direct-shipping legislation, wholesaler-distributors exploit the state government addiction to growing, uninterrupted tax revenue. A major part of the wholesalers' claim against direct wine shipping to consumers is that it will open up wine sales over the Internet and that Internet wine merchants could avoid paying taxes. Since state excise taxes are applied at the points of production and distribution, the wholesalers' claim is specious at best. And if their claim applies to the separate state sales taxes, that argument can be made for every product that is sold over the Internet.

The recent Supreme Court decision will likely prove insufficient, and further challenges will be made against the present restrictive system. The challenge that needs to be made is one based on Article 1, Section 8, of the U.S. Constitution's Commerce Clause, where states are prohibited from hindering the free flow of commerce across their borders.

In past Supreme Court decisions under Justice Brandeis, the court shot down numerous challenges to the conflict between the Commerce Clause and the Twenty-first Amendment to the Constitution, and they did so not so much through cogent argument as through displaying deference to Congress. In the 2005 Supreme Court decision, when Justice Kennedy spoke for the court, he specifically mentioned that the Twenty-first Amendment is an exception to the Commerce Clause, but again he offered no compelling reason for that situation except to say that alcohol is different from any other commodity.

Shipping restrictions or not, wine will one day be sold in America extensively on the Internet, just like everything else. That is not to say that the old-fashioned retailing model—a storefront—will fade away. The two markets are likely to coexist quite nicely, for if passionate wine people are anything they are social animals. Many prefer forming and keeping a relationship with a warm-blooded, reputable wine merchant. (Besides, many state laws require a bricks-and-mortar location for licensing.) If the wine market continues to grow as predicted, there will be plenty of American wine consumers to keep those two retail markets alive and well. The wine industry is tracking what that market might look like.

In first-century Rome, in an attempt to prevent wine from Gaul from encroaching on their market, Roman wine merchants sought government protection.

In twenty-first century America, the wholesaling merchants are doing the same thing.

In one of the states that brought the recent shipping case to the Supreme Court, Michigan, local newspaper reports brought to light that the Michigan Beer and Wine Wholesalers Association sent about $50,000 in campaign contributions to the Michigan governor and some lawmakers in the six months following the Supreme Court's 2005 decision.

In the fall of 2005, the giant Constellation Brands, Inc., issued the results of a study it funded, which was named the Project Genome. The study was intended to identify and classify who buys wine and why. One hundred questions were asked of participants who, in order to qualify to take part in the study, had to have bought at least one five-dollar bottle of wine within thirty days of the study, which was not exactly a stringent requirement. Still, as such studies go, the thirty-five hundred consumers who took part represented a large enough number for marketers to consider the results seriously.

The study reveals that the wine buying public can be sliced into six segments:

(1) Twelve percent of wine consumers are passionate about the product. They research and they taste. The study identifies them as Enthusiasts.

(2) Twenty percent of wine consumers make buying decisions that

reflect the sophistication of labels and brand-name marketing. They are identified as Image Seekers.

(3) Fifteen percent of wine consumers enjoy shopping for wine. They seek good quality-price ratios. The study refers to them as Savvy Shoppers.

(4) Sixteen percent of wine consumers trust only well-known, long-standing wine regions and producers when they make their buying decisions. They are viewed as Traditionalists.

(5) Fourteen percent of wine consumers seek sensible wines (whatever that means) that they can serve to dinner guests and friends. (That kind of response may mean that this group doesn't drink wine as regularly as, say, the Savvy Shoppers.) This is the Satisfied Sipper group.

(6) Twenty-three percent, the largest group of wine consumers, find shopping for wine too complex and stressful. They rely heavily on the shelf talkers on retail shelves to help them make buying decisions. The study identifies this group as the Overwhelmed.

It is clear what Constellation and other giant corporations will take away from the survey data: the last two segments represent 37 percent of consumers and they are not comfortable buying wine; the study also seems to show that not many consumers take the time to learn about wine and that a large percentage buy wine as a statement of status. Knowing those things about the consumer is sure to result in a bombardment of advertising and promotion schemes aimed at one or more of the market segments.

Glaringly missing from Constellations' survey, however, are the wine geeks. Perhaps geeks don't engage in surveys. Or perhaps large corporations don't view the geeks as a worthwhile market. If so, that should keep wine gurus solvent in America for a long time to come, as they will have the eyes, ears, nose, mouths, and throats of wine "geekdom" all to themselves.

> I often wonder what the vintners buy
> One half so precious as the goods they sell.
> —Omar Khayyam, *The Ruba'iyat*

When Frank Schoonmaker and Alexis Lichine recommended more than sixty years ago that California wine producers give their wines varietal names instead of European place names, the two probably had no idea how influential that advice would be. The concept of varietal labeling certainly was not new—it already had been going on in parts of Italy, Germany, Alsace, and southern France—but in the New World it was the beginning of a conversion that led wine producers out of an identity crisis.

With the strength behind New World marketing, the concept of varietal labeling has even affected long-standing wine regions like Tuscany, Rioja, and Burgundy. In fact, many believe that the move toward varietal labeling threatens to weaken centuries-old established European regional identity and will cause venerable place names to lose currency. Many Internet bulletin board threads are eaten up by this argument.

Segments of the European wine trade as well as traditionalist consumers argue that, as wine's place of origin loses importance, more wines produced in a variety of countries and regions are beginning to taste alike. Many wine geeks counter the complaint by blaming the industry for having placed so much emphasis in the past on place at the expense of quality; they have no compunction about also blaming wine merchants for allowing it to happen. Traditionalists counter argue that it is not just about quality but also about the refined concepts of taste and culture, especially food culture (one particularly strident wine geek posted on the Parker-affiliated Internet bulletin board that you cannot taste culture). The other side counter argues and, as the saying goes, "the beat goes on."

So long as at least 90 percent of the general wine-consuming public drinks most of what is sold at retail, and drinks it right away, the traditionalists have a good chance at losing the argument. To wine consumers, it is easier to remember the taste of their favorite wine than to have to study the subtleties of wines from certain regions; it is easier to remember the name of a grape variety than to have to remember a wine's location on the map.

For some, it will be a sad day when place names and the quality controls that helped to establish their identities lose out to single grape variety and celebrity winemaker marketing. But the global wine industry has to do whatever it takes to keep the market happy.

For the past 8,000 years the wine trade has sometimes followed and often led the way and has even gone its separate way, yet it has always traveled right beside the course of civilization. Today the wine trade is in another of its states of change and, provided global climate change does not result in catastrophe for agriculture, it certainly has a future. Whether that future means wine will be labeled by grape variety or by region, or transported in a container on a ship or in the belly of an airplane, or found on the shelves of retail shops or sold over the Internet, or shipped to your door or picked up at a store, it is certain wine will not make its way from point A (producer) to point B (importer-distributor) to point C (the consumer) without the help of the wine merchant and without whom there really would be no point.

Bibliography

Allen, H. Warner. *A History of Wine*. New York: Horizon Press, 1961.

———*Number Three Saint James's Street*. London: Chatto and Windus, 1950.

Ambrosi, Hans. *Where the Great German Wines Grow*. New York: Hastings House, 1976.

Amerine, Maynard A., and Singleton, Vernon L. *Wine: An Introduction*. Berkeley: University of California Press, 1965.

Bakalinsky, A.T. *Sulfites, Wine and Health, Wine in Context: Nutrition, Physiology, Policy.* Edited by A. L. Waterhouse and R. M. Rantz, 2005.

Bainton, Roland H. *Christendom—A Short History of Christianity and Its Impact on Western Civilization.* Vol. 2, *From the Reformation to the Present*. New York: Harper Torchbooks, 1966.

Barun, Stephen. *Buzz: The Science and Love of Alcohol and Caffeine*. New York: Penguin Books, 1996.

Bespaloff, Alexis. *The Fireside Book of Wine*. New York: Simon and Schuster, 1977.

Braudel, Fernand. *Civilization and Capitalism, 15th–18th Century.* Vol. 1, *The Structure of Everyday Life.* New York: Harper and Row, 1981.

———*Civilization & Capitalism, 15th–18th Century.* Vol. 2, *The Wheels of Commerce*. New York: Harper & Row, 1982.

———*Civilization & Capitalism, 15th–18th Century,* Vol. 3, *The Perspective of the World.* New York: Harper & Row, 1984.

———*The Mediterraneans and the Mediterranean World in the Age of Philip II.* Vol. 1. New York: Harper & Row, 1972.

Brillat-Savarin, Jean Anthelme. *The Physiology of Taste.* Translated by M. F. K. Fisher. New York: Heritage Press, 1949.

Brown, Gordon: *Handbook of Fine Brandies: The Definitive Taster's Guide to the World's Best Brandies*. New York: Macmillan, 1990.

Cantor, Norman F. *The Medieval Reader*. New York: HarperCollins, 1994.

Chadwick, John. *The Mycenaean World*. London: Cambridge University Press, 1976.

Clark, Kenneth. *Civilisation: A Personal View*. New York: Harper & Row, 1969.

Clark, Peter. *The English Alehouse: A Social History, 1200–1830*. London: Longman, 1983.

Cousineau, Phil. *Once and Future Myths: The Power of Ancient Stories in Modern Times*. Berkeley: Conari Press, 2001.

Croft-Cooke, Rupert. *Madeira*. London: Putnam, 1961.

———*Port*. London: Putnam, 1957.

———*Sherry*. London: Putnam, 1955.

Crosby, Everett. *The Vintage Years: The Story of Hi Tor Vineyards*. New York: Harper & Row, 1973.

Dallas, Philip. *The Great Wines of Italy*. New York: Doubelday, 1974.

Dawood, N. J., trans. *The Koran:* 7th ed. Edited by Thomas Wyatt. Harmondsworth: Penguin, 1991.

Diamond, Jared. *Guns, Germs and Steel: the Fates of Human Societies*. New York: W. W. Norton, 1997.

Dickenson, Patric. *The Aeneid: Virgil's Great Epic Poem Concerning the Adventures of the Trojan Hero Aeneas*. New York: Mentor Books, New American Library, 1961.

Fernadez-Armesto, Felipe. *Near a Thousand Tables: A History of Food*. New York: The Free Press, 2002.

Field, S. S. *The American Drink Book*. Kingsport, TN: Kingsport Press, 1953.

Fieldman, Christopher. *Is This the Wine You Ordered, Sir?—the Dark Side of the Wine Trade*. London: Christopher Helm, 1989.

Fisher, M. F. K. *The Art of Eating*. New York: World Publishing, 1954.

———*With Bold Knife and Fork*: New York: G. P. Putnam, 1968.

Flandrin, Jean-Louis, et al, ed. *Food: A Culinary History*. New York: Columbia University Press, 1999.

Freeman, Charles. *The Closing of the Western Mind: The Rise of Faith and the Fall of Reason*. New York: Alfred A. Knopf, 2002.

Gabler, James M. *Passions: Wines and Travels of Thomas Jefferson*. Baltimore: Bacchus, 1995.

———*Wine Into Words: A History and Bibliography of Wine Books in the English Language*. Baltimore: Bacchus, 1985.

Gibbon, Edward. *The Decline and Fall of the Roman Empire,* Vols. 1, II, III. Edited by Smeaton Oliphant. New York: Random House Modern Library, Everyman's Library, 1950.

Green, Peter. *Alexander of Macedon*. Middlesex, England: Penguin, 1974.

Halasz, Zoltan. *Hungarian Wine Through the Ages*. Budapest: Corvina, 1962.

Hamilton, Edith: *Mythology—Timeless Tales of Gods and Heroes*. New York: Little, Brown & Co., 1940.

Harrison, Babs. *The Art of Wine*. Philadelphia: Courage Books, 2001.

Heintz, William F. *Wine Country: A History of Napa Valley, 1828–1920*. Santa Barbara: Capra Press, 1990.

Hines, Richard Davenport. *The Pursuit of Oblivion: A Global History of Narcotics*. New York: W. W. Norton, 2001.

Hyams, Edward. *Dionysus: A Social History of the Wine Vine*. New York: MacMillan, 1965.

Jagendorf, M. A. *Folk Wines: Cordials and Brandies*. New York: Vanguard Press, 1963.

James, Kenneth. *Escoffier: the King of Chefs*. London: Hambledon and London, 2002.

Jeffs, Julian. *Sherry*. London: Faber and Faber, 1961.

Johnson, Hugh. *Wine*. New York: Simon and Schuster, 1966.

Khayyam, Omar. *The Ruba'iyat of Omar Khayyam*. Translated by Peter Avery and John Heath-Stubbs. Hammondsworth: Penguin Classics, 1981.

Kelly, Amy: *Eleanor of Aquitaine and the Four Kings*. Cambridge: Harvard University Press, 1950.

Kennedy, Paul. *The Rise and Fall of the Great Powers*. New York: Random House, 1987.

Kenyon, J. P., ed. *Pepys's Diary*. New York: Macmillan, 1963.

Kladstrup, Don and Petie. *Wine and War: The French, the Nazis and the Battle for France's Greatest Treasure*. New York: Broadway Books, 2001.

Kramer, Samuel Noah. *History Begins at Sumer*. Philadelphia: University of Pennsylvania Press, 1956.

Lesko, Leonard H. *King Tut's Wine Cellar*. Berkeley: University of California Press, 1977.

Lichine, Alexis. *Encyclopedia of Wines and Spirits*. New York: Knopf, 1967.

———*Guide to the Wines and Vineyards of France*. New York: Knopf, 1979.

Loewen, James W. *Lies My Teacher Told Me: Everything Your American History Textbook Got Wrong*. New York: New Press, 1995.

Loftus, Simon. *Anatomy of the Wine Trade*. New York: Harper & Row, 1985.

Loubère. Leo A. *The Red and the White: the History of Wine in France and Italy in the Nineteenth Century*. Albany: State University of New York, 1978.

———*The Wine Revolution in France: the Twentieth Century*. Princeton: Princeton University Press, 1990.

Lutz, H. F. *Viticulture and Brewing in the Ancient Orient*. Leipzig: Hinrich, 1922.

Macdonough, Giles. *Brilliat Savarin: The Judge and His Stomach*. London: John Murray, 1992.

Macmillan, Margaret. *Paris 1919: Six Months That Changed the World*. New York: Random House, 2001.

Mariani, John. *The Dictionary of Italian Food and Drink*. New York: Broadway Books, 1998.

Matlock, Jessie M. *Greek and Roman Mythology*. New York: The Century Company, 1917.

McCoy, Elin. *The Emperor of Wine: The Rise of Robert M. Parker Jr. and the Reign of American Taste*. New York: Random House, 2005.

McGovern, Patrick E. *Ancient Wine: The Search for the Origins of Viniculture*. Princeton: Princeton University Press, 2003.

McNutt, Joni G. *In Praise of Wine: An Offering of Hearty Toasts, Quotations, Witticisms, Proverbs, and Poetry throughout History*. Santa Barbara: Capra Press, 1993.

Miller, Mark. *Wine—A Gentleman's Game*. New York: Harper & Row, 1984.

Mondavi, Robert. *Harvests of Joy: How the Good Life Became Great Business*. Orlando: Harcourt Inc., 1998.

Murray, Gilbert, trans. *Euripides: The Bacchœ*, vol. 8, part 8. Edited by Charles Eliot. New York: Harvard Classics, P. F. Collier & Son, 1909–14.

Ordish, George. *The Great Wine Blight*. London: Sidgwick and Jackson, 1987.

Osborne, Lawrence. *The Accidental Connoisseur: An Irreverent Journey Through the Wine World*. New York: North Point Press, 2004.

Osterland, Edmund. *Wine and the Bottom Line*. Washington, D.C.: National Restaurant Association, 1980.

Picard, Liza. *Dr. Johnson's London: Coffee-houses and Climbing Boys, Medicine, Toothpaste, and Gin, Poverty and Press-Gangs, Freak Shows and Female Education*. New York: Saint Martin's Press, 2000.

Pellechia, Thomas. *Garlic, Wine and Olive Oil: Historical Anecdotes and Recipes*. Santa Barbara: Capra Press, 2000.

Pinney, Thomas. *A History of Wine in America: From the Beginnings to Prohibition*; Berkeley: University of California Press, 1989.

———*A History of Wine in America: From Prohibition to the Present*. Berkeley: University of California Press, 2005.

Pray Bober, Phyllis. *Art, Culture and Cuisine: Ancient and Medieval Gastronomy*. Chicago: University of Chicago Press, 1999.

Prial, Frank. *Wine Talk*. New York: Times Books, 1978.

Robinson, Jancis, ed. *The Oxford Companion to Wine.* Oxford: Oxford University Press, 1999.

Robinson, Herbert Spencer, and Knox Wilson. *Myths and Legends of All Nations*. New York: Bantam Reference Library, 1961.

Root, Waverly. *Food*. New York: Simon & Schuster, 1980.

Rosengarten, David, and Joshua Wesson. *Red Wine with Fish: The New Art of Matching Wine with Food*. New York: Simon & Schuster, 1989.

Sacks, David. *Language Visible: Unraveling the Mystery of the Alphabet from A to Z*. New York: Broadway Books, 2003.

Saintsbury, George. *Notes on a Cellar Book*. New York: Macmillan, 1933.

Sayers, Dorothy, trans. *The Song of Roland*. Middlesex: Penguin, 1968.

Schaeffer, Dennis. *Vintage Talk: Conversations with California's New Winemakers*. Santa Barbara: Capra Press, 1995.

Seward, Desmond. *Monks and Wine*. New York: Crown, 1979.

Simkin, C. G. F. *The Traditional Trade of Asia*. London: Oxford, 1968.

Simon, Andre. *Encyclopedia of Wines*. New York: Quadrangle, 1973.

Stark, Freya. *Alexander's Path*. New York: Harcourt, Brace & World, 1958.

Stuller, Jay, and Glen Martin. *Through the Grapevine: The Real Story Behind America's 8 Billion Dollar Wine Industry*. New York: HarperCollins, 1994.

Tannerhill, Reay. *Food in History*. New York: Stein and Day, 1973.

Tomalin, Claire. *Samuel Pepys: The Unequalled Self*. New York: Vintage Books, 2002.

Tousaint-Samat, Maguelonne. *A History of Food*. Cambridge: Blackwell Publishers, 1992.

Treber, Grace. *World Wine Almanac and Atlas: Complete Wine Buying Guide and Catalogue of Wine Labels*. New York: International Wine Society, 1976.

Tuchman, Barbara W. *A Distant Mirror: The Calamitous 14th Century*: New York, Knopf; 1978.

———*The March of Folly*: New York: Knopf, 1984.

———*The First Salute: a View of the American Revolution*. New York: Knopf, 1988.

Unwin, Tim. *Wine and the Vine*. London: Routledge, 1991.

Veyne, Paul, et al. *A History of Private Life: From Pagan Rome to Byzantium*; Cambridge: Harvard University Press, 1987.

Wagner, Philip M. *A Winegrower's Guide*. New York: Knopf, 1945.

———*Grapes Into Wine*. New York: Knopf, 1982.

Waldo, Myra. *The Pleasures of Wine: a Guide to the Wines of the World*. New York: Gramercy, 1963.

Yourcenar, Marguerite. *Memoirs of Hadrian*. Translated by Grace Flick. New York: Farrar, Straus and Giroux, 2000.

Index

Note: page numbers in *italics* refer to illustrations

Out of the Frying Pan

OUT OF THE FRYING PAN

Seven women who changed the course of postwar cookery

HAZEL CASTELL
and
KATHLEEN GRIFFIN

BBC BOOKS

Published by BBC Books,
a division of BBC Enterprises Limited,
Woodlands, 80 Wood Lane
London W12 0TT

First Published 1993

ISBN 0 563 36481 5

Designed by David Robinson
Set in Bembo by BP Integraphics, Bath
Printed and bound in Great Britain by Clays Ltd, St Ives Plc
Jacket print by Belmont Press Ltd, Northampton

BBC Books would like to thank the following for providing photographs and for permission to reproduce copyright material. While every effort has been made to trace and acknowledge all copyright holders, we would like to apologise should there have been any errors or omissions.

Camera Press front cover (centre) and page 38; **Express Newspapers** front cover (top left) and page 60; **Neil Farrin for BBC** front cover (bottom left) and page 140; **John Freeman** front cover (bottom right) and page 86; **Prue Leith** front cover (top) and page 110; **Marguerite Patten** front cover (bottom) and page 8; **Radio Times** front cover (top right) and page 162.

Contents

Introduction

We were in a restaurant – where else? – discussing our plans for this *Woman's Hour* book marking the achievement of seven women in transforming food in postwar Britain, when our conversation was overheard by a fellow diner. He remarked – not originally it must be said – 'It would be a short book then'. On the contrary, a substantial book emerged thanks to the contributions of the cooks and food writers featured in the following pages. Marguerite Patten was the first cook to appear on the newly established *Woman's Hour* in 1946, after coming to prominence during the war giving advice on rationed foods and dried eggs. The food writer, Elizabeth David who sadly died before being able to take part in this book, brought the flavours, sights and smells of the Mediterranean to postwar Britain. We are very grateful to her publisher and friend, Jill Norman, for writing a tribute to her. Sophie, the daughter of the food writer Jane Grigson explains how her mother came to write seminal books on English fruit, vegetable and pork cookery. Claudia Roden has brought to life the neglected cultures of the Mediterranean basin, and Madhur Jaffrey has inspired millions to tackle the complexities of Indian cuisine. With her school and restaurant, Prue Leith has set new standards for catering and improved food sold on trains and in parks. Josceline Dimbleby's inventive approach has produced unusual combinations of flavours and her puddings have given satisfaction to millions of chocaholics. Delia Smith, who has helped so many new generations of cooks, was unfortunately unable to take part in the book because of other commitments.

These women have two qualities in common; a love of good food, and hard work, and we hope that you will enjoy, literally, the fruits of their labour. At the end of each chapter is a selection of recipes. The last recipe in each chapter – excepting Elizabeth David and Jane Grigson – is a new one specially created for this book.

Hazel Castell
Kathleen Griffin

Marguerite Patten

The Kitchen Front

'You take your life in your hands, but I absolutely love it – I love an audience.'

In the 1950s and 1960s, Marguerite Patten was a Variety star, demonstrating her consummate professional skills to capacity audiences at London's Palladium. She was the top billing in shows that included artists such as Cyril Fletcher, Bill Pertwee, Pearl Carr, Charlie Chester and Dicky Murdoch. But the real performers the audience had come to witness were the Swiss rolls that never cracked, the sponges that always rose, and the roast beef that was always perfectly cooked, in front of their eyes, on stage.

The visitor sitting in Marguerite's Brighton home today, looking at a beautiful garden containing her pride and joy, a huge, pale-purple clematis overwhelming a large walnut tree, might be forgiven for imagining – just for a second – that she had retired to home and garden since those heady Variety days. Before us is spread a quintessentially English home-made tea of tiny, square, salmon sandwiches, brown bread rolls with asparagus, scones with whipped cream and jam, cookies and cakes. But the idea of retirement has simply not yet crossed her mind. Making teas was the subject of her 156th book, published three years ago, and she is often working on the next books at 4.00 in the morning.

Marguerite has always had boundless energy and is able easily to recall her experiences fifty years ago when her clear voice was first heard broadcasting on the BBC's *Kitchen Front* during the Second World War. These radio broadcasts made her into a household name and after the war she continued to advise on erratic food supplies, giving a tasty recipe for whale stew on an early edition of *Woman's Hour* in 1946.

As food stocks improved, she helped the nation's cooking skills and palate recover and became one of the pioneers of television cookery shows. These programmes, unlike today's, proved to be excellent training for the London Palladium as they were broadcast live.

Her speech is peppered with the vocabulary from those times using words such as 'uppish', 'rotten' and 'by Jove', and she loves to mimic the voices of her friends and colleagues on stage and screen. In fact, her first love was not cooking but the stage. 'There was no question about it, I was going to be an actress, and preferably a Shakespearean one.' Her interest in cooking was minimal until her teenage years. 'People often imagine that if cookery is your profession you had a burning desire to cook as a very small child, but I hadn't. I have no recollection of helping mother or doing anything in the kitchen until I was about thirteen. And then it really began by accident.' Marguerite's father had died when she was twelve and one day she decided to help her mother by cooking the planned lunch – a rabbit pie. 'I knew nothing about cooking. I remember showing off to a schoolfriend who had come to watch – the demonstrating instinct was always there – I was balancing the pie on one hand to cut round the edge and my friend thought 'how ridiculous', gave my hand a shove, and down on the floor went the rabbit pie. Hygienically, of course, it should have been gathered up and discarded but that wasn't possible; we had to have lunch. I can't tell you what it tasted like, but after that I began to do some cooking and found I liked it very much.'

When she was about to leave school, her mother tried to persuade her to go into teaching, a family tradition. 'Everyone said I should be a domestic science teacher but I thought this was a rotten idea. My dream was to become an actress.' She took the entrance exam into the Royal Academy of Dramatic Art and was accepted. 'But in my era there were no grants for frivolous things like acting, you had to be something very worthy, but at least I knew that I had a certain amount of ability.'

Her mother suggested a short training course in cookery with a view to becoming a home economist in either the gas or electricity industries. That, to the aspiring young thespian, sounded a rather better prospect – the carrot being that she could stand on the platform and perform.

A job with the electricity industry followed but Marguerite was soon to get the chance to join the professional stage as an actress rather than a cook. In her spare time, she performed with amateurs and young professionals at Hampstead's Everyman Theatre and when one of the young actresses was offered two jobs in repertory at the same time, she suggested Marguerite should take one of them. Nine happy months at the Oldham Rep. followed. 'It was a wonderful help and, if I think of all the various things I've learnt in my life, I will put that very high up. They're very outspoken in Lancashire and, if they couldn't hear you, you'd hear a shout from the gallery, "Come on love, speak up". So I had a little bit of extra voice production.'

That experience was invaluable in helping her get her next job as a senior home economist in the refrigerator industry when the acting work finished. 'At the interview they did a terrible thing for most people, they made us give a demonstration, but without a refrigerator, or a cooker or a table. After rehearsing in rep I was used to performing with non-existent props so I launched forth pretending I'd got the refrigerator. I really shouldn't have had that job, I wasn't experienced enough, but it's like everything in life, if you get something you very speedily get the experience to meet the challenge.'

In less than two years Marguerite would be giving advice on how to eke out and use substitutes for rations of meat, sugar and dairy products. But before the war began she was dealing with food at the other extreme – two pints of double cream were part of her standard shopping list to demonstrate 'cold cookery' in the shape of ice-creams, sorbets and salmon cream.

The dishes were designed to show off the latest new appliance – the refrigerator – and this was the first of many new gadgets that Marguerite has had to test and evaluate. 'I've always been very appliance-minded, but I'm no good at mending anything!' She wrote the first ground-breaking manuals for pressure cookers and for food mixers, and has advised on how to use food processors, washing machines and microwaves. 'I came across an old manual from those days which I helped prepare, and believe it or not there's a phrase which says "do not switch off your refrigerator in winter". Can you imagine anybody doing that? But there must have been some who were, for the warning to be there.'

As war became imminent she could see that no one was going to bother with the peacetime luxuries of ice-creams and sorbets so she rejoined the electricity industry as a senior home economist. She was working in Lincolnshire when rationing came in 1940 with its strict limitations on fat and sugar. As a farming community, the local people were relatively well off; they had rabbit, they could shoot game in season and probably kept chickens for eggs; most people had stocks of foods that they were eking out. But, as rationing continued, it became obvious to Marguerite that she would join either the services or go to the Ministry of Food. By this time she had met her husband who was in the RAF at Lincoln, and she hoped to be able to stay in the city. But with no vacancies in the area, she joined the Ministry in Cambridge, where it had part of its headquarters, as a Senior Home Economist.

'By 1942 the whole scene had changed enormously. Mothers were working, they were also probably the only parent as the father was in the forces, it really was becoming very, very tough for everybody.' School dinners began as a wartime measure, to make sure children had an adequate main meal, and Marguerite, together with a scientist, was asked to check the vitamin C content of that universally loathed dinner dish, school cabbage. 'I shall always see that school cabbage, you didn't need a scientist to tell you it hadn't an ounce of vitamins in it, and it was absolutely ghastly to eat.' The canteen staff were volunteers and had never cooked such large quantities before, but there was an additional problem. 'As a race, our vegetables were awful. We believed in drowning them, in cooking them with plenty of water so they swam around, we believed in a pinch of bicarbonate of soda which might by some lucky chance put back some of the colour we'd taken out.'

It was during the war period that Marguerite believes the nation learnt to cook vegetables properly and to appreciate them raw. She was part of a network of Ministry of Food Advisers that demonstrated across the nation, in hospitals, canteens, village greens and in market squares. Wherever the Advice Centre was, the message was always the same. 'Before you started to demonstrate, your number one priority was a great big platter of a raw vegetable salad. You would have been shot at dawn if somebody from headquarters had come and watched you and that salad wasn't there. It was absolutely imperative that we got used to eating raw cabbage, carrots, swedes and parsnips because that was where we were going to get our vitamins.' Any scarce supplies of oranges, or imported orange juice, were reserved for children and expectant mothers. 'We used to spend an enormous amount of time trying to get people interested. I can still see those salads – they were so pretty with the reds and golds. I don't know if people ever got to like them – this was departing very much from tradition.'

During her childhood, Marguerite had tasted salads that very much broke with traditional notions. In spite of her mother's lack of interest in cooking, she was a very keen gardener. 'People would say, "Oh, what a funny salad" – as she'd put in strawberries and blackcurrants, things that nobody else in Britain ever did. As a child I was quite ashamed of them and I used to wish she would make an ordinary, dreary salad.'

After the wartime starter of raw vegetable salad, Marguerite and the other home economists had the challenge of persuading the public to eke out meat with what were known as 'second-class proteins'. These were foods such as split peas or lentils as at that time it was believed that meat, fish and poultry, followed by eggs and cheese were first-class proteins. The second-class vegetable proteins, which Marguerite refers to in some of her early books, were considered a poor substitute. 'You see, the motto then nutritionally was "You can't have too much protein, pack in the protein, as much protein as you can possibly eat". We've done a complete roundabout on that now but we didn't know that then, and the public latched on to the word protein. So we often said to people, "You'll add protein if you add some rolled oats to a dish," to which they'd ask, "Are you sure dear?", and we'd say, "Yes, you really will."'

The advice they gave was dictated by what was available. The key factor was home-grown food, with thousands of land-girls working to get the most out of terra firma. One of those foods was potatoes, and the advice was to have potatoes not only for lunch, dinner and supper, but also for breakfast and tea. There were recipes for two types of potato scones – drop or coffee – and grated raw and mashed potato was also used in pastry to help compensate for the reduction in fat.

Making the most of home-grown fruit became a national effort in the summer of 1942. Fruit was no longer being imported and, to meet the preserve ration of a pound every two months, anyone who could was asked to help make jam. As Women's Institutes gathered their forces, Marguerite was sent by the Ministry to a farming area to head jam making sessions. Sugar, already rationed to half a pound per person a week, was supplied by the Ministry. 'It was a ghastly experience, I was quite young at the time, and there were all these terrifying women. I'd tell them how to make jam to the Ministry's specifications, and they'd say, "We were making jam before you were born, young woman." I was very glad when the fruit season was over.'

Such was Marguerite's importance to the war effort that the Ministry of Food went to great lengths to get her back to work after the birth of her daughter Judith. It was a particularly anxious time, with her husband serving in the RAF, completing well over eighty missions during the war, and surviving three crashes. She had gone home to her mother in London and was keen to get working again. A trained nanny was found, and Marguerite began large demonstrations all over London. But the bombing was getting worrying and she was anxious about leaving her daughter at night-time. So in late 1943 she took charge of the Ministry of Food Advice Bureau in Harrods.

It was at this time that Marguerite first began creating her own recipes. Until then she was following traditional, British, standard recipes. Before the war, when she worked in the electricity industry, the recipes were a means to an end. 'We weren't teaching cooking, that was a by-product, we were demonstrating the appliances. The acme of perfection in those days was a Victoria sandwich and everyone wanted to make a perfect one. So the two halves that came out of the oven had to be like two peas in a pod. If you demonstrated and weren't a good cook it rebounded on the appliances you were using.'

Her previous work with the Ministry of Food had been a means to an end; to get the message of healthy eating across to as many people as quickly as possible. 'You tried to be creative and clever with the garnishes but you didn't have to think out anything new. You followed the Ministry's recipe leaflets.'

At Harrods, that was precisely what Marguerite had to do. She was set up with a cooker and refrigerator in the famous food hall, giving demonstrations of four or five new recipes twice a day. She was allowed a demonstration ration and, although the Ministry of Food supplied many recipes, she simply had to begin creating her own to cope with the volume of demonstrations. 'There'd be masses of people standing around, and that's where the Oldham "speak up luv" came in so useful.'

She not only created recipes, she collected them. 'Harrods was an interesting place to be, with refugees from various countries like Czechoslovakia regularly coming in to watch. They'd often offer me recipes.' Limited rations meant she was unable to make them at that time, but wrote them down for use in later years once rationing had ended. 'It was my Harrods years that taught me. You might say that was a finishing school for me.'

Like everyone else at that time, Marguerite was following the advice to bottle fruit. 'I used to come home, feed the baby, and then my mother and I would go out into the garden and pick and pick and pick. And then we'd bottle and jam and jam and bottle. Have you any idea how long it takes to pick a pound of blackcurrants? They're the worst of them all because you have to pick them singly. So I don't grow anything useful now except herbs. I swore I'd never grow potatoes, cabbage, onions or radishes.' She adores gardening now, using it to relax from work and, although her garden is packed with clematis, camellias, begonias and fuchsias, no vegetables are in sight.

During the war, she was regularly asked for advice on bottling vegetables but was unable to help. 'They were terribly dangerous, I remember the word botulism hung over us like some terrible menace – almost like Hitler's bombs.' But there were other options for preserving vegetables – like salting beans.

Many of the dishes dreamt up by wartime food advisers were substitutes for foods no longer available; Jerusalem artichokes were used to make mock oyster soup, and mock duck was made with cooking apples and sausagemeat. 'I'm not sure looking back that we were right to be so nostalgic – we kept talking about these "mock" dishes, which brought back all the lovely memories of things we hadn't got any more.'

But, in spite of all the restrictions, Marguerite feels a sense of pride in many of the recipes produced during the war. 'I think we were very successful in our use of oatmeal. (See recipe for Oatmeal Sausages at end of chapter.) I'm very fond of oatmeal, rolled oats and oatmeal sausages. Of course, the oatmeal sausages, which had double the quantity of oatmeal to meat, aren't like real sausages but they're very pleasant.'

The recipes can still come in useful today, particularly the eggless fruit cake which she considers one of the best. Containing 3 oz (75 g) each of sugar, dried fruit and fat and 10 oz (275 g) of self-raising flour, moisture was provided by the addition of ½ pint (300 ml) of weak tea. 'I've got a whole lot of recipes for eggless cakes and puddings, which I give out now if someone who's allergic to eggs writes to me.'

Many dishes made the most of the nation's traditional love of spices, a result of contact with the colonies. Herbs were less important but ingredients such as curry and mustard powder were used to liven up corned beef or tinned sausages; nutmeg and vinegar were added to savoury dishes; and cinnamon and mixed spice used in cakes and puddings. 'Of course, we knew that many of these ingredients were better if they were freshly ground but we had to put up with them being a bit stale.'

Marguerite laughs as she fondly remembers the new ingredient introduced in 1942. 'If Queen Mary has Calais engraved on her heart – I've got dried egg on mine!' Fresh eggs were rationed to one per person a week at best, often reduced to one per fortnight. This was supplemented by a monthly packet of dried egg which could be made up to the equivalent of twelve fresh eggs. At first, Marguerite's experiments with the new substance were unsuccessful. 'Then we learnt that it had to be measured almost scientifically – *exactly* one level tablespoon to two of water. We got very clever with those dried eggs and could do an awful amount with them. In the end I could make soufflés!'

The health of the nation was surprisingly good during the war, despite the many hardships. Infant mortality declined and the average age of death from natural causes increased. Part of the reason may have been the advantages of the imposed diet; large quantities of vegetables were eaten, often raw; 'second-class proteins' such as lentils and dried peas were used that are now so highly regarded; and sugar and fat intake was compulsorily restricted. But, in Marguerite's view, it was not the only reason for the nation's good health. 'We hadn't time to feel under the weather. We were fighting a war and I'm sure it was the feeling that was in Britain at the time that helped to keep us healthy.'

Advice on how to keep the nation healthy was broadcast daily on the BBC's *Kitchen Front* at 8.15 in the morning. The radio doctor, Charles Hill (later Lord Hill), appeared weekly, advising on health and nutrition. There were gardening spots, sketches by the Buggins family, and Marguerite began to make regular broadcasts based on her demonstration work. When she appeared on *Woman's Hour* again recently, the interview was recorded by chance in the same studio as her wartime broadcasts: a large studio in the sub-basement of Broadcasting House. 'It was very lonely and terrifying. We were just left in a studio with "Get on with it dear" – no friendly producer in those days!' But she soon began to enjoy making the live broadcasts. 'We were all so tremendously cheerful and bracing. I remember making an eggless fruit cake and saying to the listeners, "No, you haven't made a mistake, there isn't an egg in it and it's beautiful!" I always thought that Joyce Grenfell, with her impersonations of games mistresses, missed a golden opportunity to parody the equally bracing Ministry of Food Advisers.'

The talks may have been relentlessly cheerful but she believes today's food advisers could learn something from them. 'All too often the advice given today is about what you should not do. Do not eat too much fat – cut down on sugar – eat less meat – less animal fat. Often the recommendations seem negative with nothing constructive offered. Every nutritionist who gives a talk on the right diet to follow should include some absolutely super recipes afterwards. That's the way we worked in the wartime years. We didn't shake our heads in gloom, we tried to "lure" people to do the very best with what was available.'

Whale meat was one of the new foods that Marguerite had to 'lure' people to use after the war, as many foods, including meat, were still rationed. In her first appearance on the newly established *Woman's Hour* in 1946 she gave a recipe for whale stew complete with onions, vegetables and tomato. 'I remember preparing whale meat and the smell was pretty awful; a cross between liver and rather strong meat, with a very fishy and oily smell as well. People must be shivering with horror today at the thought of those beautiful creatures being eaten.'

Rationing for some foods became even worse and in 1946 the combined effects of the years of war and droughts caused wheat crops to fail. The worldwide shortage resulted in bread rationing being introduced in Britain for the first time. 'I remember talking about cobs on *Woman's Hour* as a way of eking out the bread. A tiny bit of fat, which was still rationed, was rubbed into self-raising flour with a pinch of salt and milk to bind, to make a soft dough; then rolled into balls and put into a very hot oven for ten minutes. If you ate them straight from the oven they were jolly good. But kept a day, they were like hard miniature footballs.'

Preserving fruits and vegetables was just as important after the war as it had been during the war. Marguerite teamed up with Mrs Arthur Webb, who was an expert on preserving and country recipes. 'She was everybody's picture of a countrywoman; small with white hair and rosy cheeks. I admired her wonderful knowledge which had been passed down through generations of country cooks.' (A recipe from Mrs Arthur Webb – for apply jelly – is included in the collection at the end of this chapter.)

Woman's Hour, the first programme of its kind, was soon inundated with letters from listeners wanting advice from Marguerite; including a request from a naval cook for help in making a good egg-custard with dried egg. A letter from a more typical listener at that time was this: 'I'm newly married and my husband is very fond of steak and kidney pie. I'd like to know how thick the pastry should be and whether I should use plain or self-raising flour for flaky pastry.'

Marguerite gave out recipes and tips that became famous for their step-by-step approach – a necessity, she believes, after seven long years of rationing. 'Girls were coming out of the services, getting married and having families, and were beginning from scratch in the kitchen almost as a child would.'

As a result of her radio work, Marguerite was invited to do a cookery demonstration in 1947 on the new television programme *Mainly for Women*, also known as *Designed for Women*. The television service was still in its infancy, with only one BBC channel and no ITV. The set at Alexandra Palace in north London was equally rudimentary; a table with a boiling plate on it. She was set the task of demonstrating 'something for tea', using only rationed ingredients, and came up with yeastless doughnuts that used the invaluable dried egg. 'Because of the shortage of fat, the doughnuts were shallow-fried and they turned out rather flat, not unlike fritters. Even so, I am happy to report that my "eight-minute doughnuts" became popular.'

Marguerite was eventually given an old cooker from the BBC to widen the variety of dishes she could produce. Unlike most of today's television cooks, she had to perform live. 'Once I was showing how to make light sponges and a Swiss roll but, as I went to place them in the oven, I discovered that I had forgotten to preheat. As it was live, I had to tell the viewers but fortunately had one that I had made earlier! For years people would remind me of that terrible event – they never recalled the countless times when everything had gone as planned.'

During the 1950s rationing was gradually phased out and now Marguerite had a chance to do more of the traditional prewar dishes. She believes there were three distinct groups of people that accounted for the phenomenal interest in her cookery shows. 'The middle-aged wanted to return to what life was like before the war and were keen for their children to taste steak and a proper joint of roast beef. Then there were the young people who wanted to gain some knowledge of cookery. The third group was the women and men who had served overseas and had experience of other cuisines. It's always been said that scampi became famous in this country because of the men in the Eighth Army in Italy who had tasted it, liked it, and wanted to have it again at home.'

Marguerite made a point of buying fruit, vegetables and other ingredients not seen in Britain since before the war, and showing them to viewers before they were cooked. By this time she had begun to work with another pioneer of cookery on television, Philip Harben, who was a trained chef from a theatrical family, and they became good friends. Cookery programmes were often used to alleviate problems with food supplies, although one year this was an excess of produce rather than the more usual shortage. 'There was a plague of woodpigeons destroying farmers' crops and so I was asked to show various ways of cooking them, in order to encourage people to buy them.'

Food rationing continued until 1954 but each year it became a little easier. At Christmas in 1952 the Ministry of Food released special rations so everyone could make prewar Christmas cakes and puddings. 'I demonstrated my favourite recipes and I still remember that "reckless" feeling as I used four fresh eggs for one cake.' (A recipe for that Christmas cake appears in the collection at the end of this chapter.) The Christmas recipes were so popular that they were repeated in 1953 and 1954. She demonstrated the cake on one programme, marzipanned it on the next, and on the final programme, iced it in various ways. 'The best complaint I ever had came from a viewer who had followed the series. The letter simply said "the cake was delicious, but the icing was burnt to a cinder"!'

Her television kitchen was given a face-lift when transmission moved to the Lime Grove Studios. The old cooker was replaced by a modern one, which was just as well as Marguerite was beginning an ambitious project involving viewers. She had become President of the BBC Cookery Club, and each month held a competition for viewers to send in recipes. These were produced in a monthly fact sheet and the winners were invited to take part in her programmes to demonstrate their winning entries.

This forerunner to today's *Masterchef* had one vital difference; it was broadcast live. 'It was always my job to bring the programme out on time, jolly tiring that was I can assure you. The family always said, "Be a bit careful how you tread tonight, she's a bit dodgy" when I was doing a show.' All of Marguerite's pioneering work – her *Kitchen Front* broadcasts, her talks on *Woman's Hour*, her black and white television shows – will never be seen or heard again. Live programmes were simply never recorded. 'I hope the judgement on those early programmes would be that we tried to help viewers to solve cooking problems and instil in them a love of food and good cooking.'

In spite of the lack of archives, one of Marguerite's broadcasts has gone down in television history. She arrived home one day in 1956 after finishing a programme about bread-making to be greeted by her husband with some exciting news. The BBC had rung to say that pictures of Marguerite had been received in America. This was in the days before satellite transmission, and the broadcast had been caused by freak weather conditions. 'The BBC received a call from America saying, "Have you a dame making a pud?" It was my bread! What excitement that caused; that I was the very first person on British television to be received in America earned me far more publicity than all of my previous hard work put together!'

The style of cookery shows began to change in the 1960s with the advent of Fanny and Johnnie Craddock. The afternoon programme ended and the emphasis shifted to the evening and to entertainment. 'The BBC decided, quite rightly in my opinion, that women had had enough of "make do and mend" cooking. The Craddocks were bon viveurs, more glamorous than anything seen before and often wore evening dress. They were treated like Variety stars. I was considered more straightlaced.'

She laughs as she says this; ironically she was already becoming a Variety star. Since leaving the Food Bureau at Harrods in the early 1950s, she had been asked to demonstrate cooking in large halls and theatres that held up to 2,000 people. Producers and manufacturers who wanted an outside home economist to evaluate their products wanted her to test food and appliances. For years, Marguerite travelled to theatres and city halls to perform for an hour in a two-hour programme. The shows, usually free, began with a band, followed by Marguerite's first spot, then top singers such as Pearl Carr and Teddy Johnson would perform. They were followed by

Marguerite teaching comedians like Dicky Murdoch, Bill Pertwee and Cyril Fletcher to ice a cake or make a trifle. 'I remember doing a series of shows with Charlie Chester and he said, "Ooh, you can deal with the laughs all right." He wanted to know where I was working the next week and when I told him I didn't have a show he said it was a pity as I was really quite good.'

A family-run flour firm decided they wanted even more of a Variety feel to Marguerite's cookery demonstrations. The Palace Theatre in Manchester was booked for a week and the audience had to save two flour-packet tops to be admitted. They were to be entertained by a full orchestra, a top comedian, and dancers drilled by Lionel Blair. On stage were three cookers and three home economists standing by. Marguerite's act was to be the creation of a successful sponge. 'I was doing an entirely different thing from my usual demonstrations, I had to turn it into Variety. I talked it over with my husband, and decided that the best trick would be to select men in the audience to cook. When I selected the men from the audience, I learnt not to pick those who considered themselves to be a scream but to choose a solemn little man and he'd be a winner. The interesting thing was that we never had a bad sponge; they used to hold them high with pride when they put the jam in.'

The show was so original and successful that the *Financial Times* devoted a whole column to it. 'Pearl Carr once said to me, "You wait for the London Palladium," and I replied quite seriously, "Pearl, the London Palladium doesn't mean the same to me as it does to you."'

In fact, she was soon to fill the London Palladium twelve times for her cookery demonstrations. They were grand affairs with Marguerite on a revolving stage with all her cookery equipment around her. 'When the stage came round, I suddenly thought, "What on earth am I doing here? Heaven help me!" But by then I'd almost become a Variety performer and knew I wanted the audience with me. So I always, always, did something they had to time, telling them to remind me when the eight minutes was up, for say, a Swiss roll. Do you know, nobody could time anything. At the end of *three* minutes, someone from the audience would shout out "Swiss roll, Swiss roll." But it was a way of involving them. Think of the size of the London Palladium, and what a soufflé would look like on stage. I didn't have the advantage of those enormous television screens, so I had to be like a conjuress. I had to make people imagine they saw that soufflé.'

The shows were extremely expensive and funded by a number of food producers, usually producers of generic food such as British bacon, eggs, flour, cheese. 'You had to get your plugs in but I never minded that much. I'd make a mention about bacon and looking for quality but I don't call that a commercial, I call that a good selection of ingredients. Teaching people to shop and choosing the right ingredients is part of good cooking.'

As with all home economists and cooks using commercial products, they have to be professionally convinced of the value of the product they are using. 'I think people are very foolish if they let their name be used too much because I don't think the public believes what they say. And they'd be equally foolish to let their name be used for something which they don't think is good. Once I was asked to do a presentation for a mixer, and had some doubt about its performance. The company told me they would put it right after the demonstration but I was adamant I wouldn't go ahead with it. I can't let myself down.'

By this time, Marguerite was already putting her expertise as a home economist into print; book number six was for 'Bachelors and Bachelor Girls'. In 1960, once postwar shortages had ended, she had a chance to celebrate on a grand scale the joys of good food and cooking with her *Cookery in Colour* encyclopedia. It was a huge volume containing over 1000 recipes that demonstrated the 1960s fascination with colour. Not only were there whole-page colour photographs but also the recipes were set on brightly coloured paper – pink, orange, red, blue and green. Colour television was just beginning to be introduced and, to mark this expanding leisure 'activity', Marguerite introduced a new section of television snacks and sandwiches into the traditional cookbook mix of pastry, pies and puddings. These snacks included spaghetti Bolognese, soufflés, a bacon and baked bean sandwich and in a throwback to the war years, corned beef tart.

But the main meat of the book was the huge selection of recipes for breakfast, lunch, tea, dinner and supper, as well as guides for picnics, barbecues, dinner parties and children's parties. The book was a great success, selling over two million copies in spite of coming out at the same time as the new *Mrs Beeton*, to which Marguerite also contributed. 'I'm always very proud when people say, "I learnt to cook from *Cookery in Colour.*" I feel I had a great advantage when I came to writing it. I've never stopped demonstrating and so have had to show audiences new recipes and new foods, like avocados or aubergines. I always remember selling the idea of a risotto to an audience by telling them it was the Italian woman's shepherd's pie, all the odd bits.'

Many of the recipes used ingredients new to many British people, often with wine and cream; others included canned fruit or meat, and packet or canned soup. 'I wasn't afraid to use canned or packet ingredients because they were sometimes the only form you could get. We hadn't freezers so many of the fresh foods, particularly from abroad, were expensive for the average person. Canned foods were cheap.'

She was approached by a senior editor at Paul Hamlyn's publishing house to write the book, and it was the beginning of a long partnership that still exists. 'I am one of the most prolific writers and I suppose it's because I had and still have a prolific publisher. I've enormous admiration for Paul as a friend and employer who wanted things done not tomorrow but yesterday please.' Many more books followed, including the 500 series; inexpensive, soft-covered books containing 500 recipes for main meals, or for fish dishes, or for suppers and snacks. The series includes two books that forecast a general trend in cookbooks: a collection for slimmers, published in 1962, and for working wives (as she was herself) in 1970. 'The 500 recipe books were the ones that took the hard work but nobody thought so because they were in paperback. At one time I had three full-time secretaries – I could create the ideas, but I needed people to type them correctly and help me check the proofs that seemed to arrive non-stop.'

Her home has always been Marguerite's workplace, with every recipe created tested in her kitchen, and the experience of running a home was put to good use when she produced *Home Making in Colour* in 1966 to accompany her *Cookery in Colour*. In the introduction, she explained the rationale for the book. 'Today many housewives do two jobs – they run a home and they have an outside career – and it is, therefore, vitally important that their home-making should be as easy as possible.' To this end, she included a cleaning routine for the career woman and a chapter on making washday easier.

Marguerite's long career has been aimed at helping those cooking at home. 'In the 1930s when I began my training, if a girl was interested in cooking she would study domestic science or become a home economist, whereas a boy would automatically become a chef.' But she has no regrets about this lack of opportunity and has never wanted to have a restaurant. When she did run a guest house in Hove for a short time, her husband described it as 'the best philanthropic institution on the south coast' as it was costing so much money. But surely she would have enjoyed the showmanship and the individualism of today's high-profile chefs? 'Of course I would, but chefs have changed their roles since then. When I began, chefs were the people you never saw, now you see them all the time.'

Marguerite believes the difference in training between the sexes accounts for why women have dominated the food writing industry since the Second World War. A home economist's training simply involved far more writing than a chef's. She particularly admires the writing of her contemporary, Elizabeth David. 'She was very special and made you think "Oh – you can tell people about the place as well as the dish." I would quite like to do more of that kind of writing but I suppose I'm associated with practicalities and publishers do tend to put you in pigeon-holes, but maybe that's right because we each have our place. I'm basically not a person who writes a lot about recipes but I admire people who write very well and Elizabeth was the first to do this.'

As well as becoming food writers, many women are becoming chefs, and home economists now take degrees. 'I think it's terribly exciting. There was a time when the attitude towards domestic science was that it was for nice girls who weren't very bright. I'm delighted home economists now have a degree, although it does knock out good craftswomen and potential good teachers of Home Economics who are less academic.' Over the last decade, competitions such as television's *Masterchef* and Sainsbury's *Young Cooks* have demonstrated the high level of creative cooking in the general population. 'I'm sure that *Masterchef* does a lot more good for the British diet than all this finger-wagging about the right and wrong things to eat. The competitors often use cheap ingredients and make them into a pleasure to look at and to eat.'

Her only concern about the ever-increasing interest in new foods and recipes is that traditional British food is overlooked. 'Some of the regional English food, in particular, is extraordinarily good and imaginative, like the meat concoctions of the Midlands – the galantines, the brawns, as well as pigs' trotters and chitterlings. The Welsh, for example, have a soup almost identical to classic French vichyssoise.' She is also interested in the effect of the close link between France and Scotland, from the time of Mary, Queen of Scots. 'The Scots have a very similar recipe to the classic French dessert, Floating Islands. The Scottish version, Snow Eggs, isn't exactly the same but it's the same idea – a creamy, custardy base and meringue – and funnily enough it's more interesting.'

Marguerite was writing in the decades when French food was held up as a shining example in comparison with British food. 'We generalize far too much about countries, including our own. Some French cooking is lovely, some is bad. I've had worse food in Provence than I have had anywhere else in the world.' The emphasis in French food has turned away from *nouvelle cuisine* to *cuisine grandmère*, and she is anxious there should be a similar movement in Britain to preserve traditional recipes before they disappear.

A country's cuisine, though, should never be static but influenced by other foods and methods so that new traditions eventually develop. 'One Christmas I thought I'd try the latest new vegetable – sweet potatoes – with the turkey. Everyone liked them and now I'd be soundly reproached if they didn't appear, and that's how traditions start.' She enjoys Chinese and Indian food but her special affinity is with Arabic food. 'My favourite country is Morocco because it's so cosmopolitan, there are any number of influences on the food produced.' Her more recent books have included dishes such as Chicken Biryani, an Indonesian fish dish Otak-Otak, sweet and sour and stir-fried dishes.

Undoubtedly, her experience in the war, experimenting with dwindling food supplies in an effort to make tasty and nutritious meals, left her with a desire to explore new recipes and techniques constantly. In 1991 she was awarded an OBE for 'services to the art of cookery', and she is a member of many professional organizations including the Royal Society of Medicine's Forum on Food. 'I've had a wonderful life but if somebody said you could only ever do one thing, I would choose to do demonstrations. That's my real love and is terribly important to me.' She was recently due to appear on a television programme about the Second World War when the train was delayed. 'I was going to ring in and go home but then I thought of my two Victory sponges I'd made and my parsley honey, and I thought, blow that, I'll carry on. And the second I got into that studio I loved it.' For Marguerite, much of the joy of demonstrating throughout her long career has been the audiences, and their attitude towards cooking. 'It makes me extremely angry when British cooks are compared unfavourably with cooks in other countries. I had and have enormous admiration for people who run a home. And during the years of rationing, if people hadn't been clever, the children wouldn't have grown up strong and healthy. It was the women who did the cooking – the mums, the aunts, the grandmothers – they were the experts at that time.'

OATMEAL SAUSAGES

SERVES 4

During the war, oatmeal and rolled oats were unrationed foods and we used them as part of the ingredients in pastry, biscuits and other dishes. The flavour compensated for the lack of fat.

2 tablespoons chopped onion or leek
*15 g (½ oz) cooking fat or dripping**
100 g (4 oz) oatmeal or rolled oats
300 ml (½ pint) water
*2 teaspoons salt***
¼ teaspoon pepper
50 g (2 oz) meat or sausages or bacon, chopped
browned breadcrumbs

Fry the onion or leek in the fat or dripping until lightly browned. Work in the oatmeal or rolled oats, add the water gradually and bring to the boil, stirring all the time. Cook for 10–15 minutes, stirring frequently. Add the seasoning and chopped meat or sausage or bacon, mix well and spread on a plate to cool. Divide into 8 portions and roll into sausage shapes. (These may be prepared the previous day.) Coat with browned breadcrumbs and either fry in a little hot fat or grill.

* We saved dripping from cooking any meat or bacon.
** This is a high amount of salt but there were no warnings about the effects of the high intake in those days. I think we probably used an excessive amount of seasoning and spices in our cooking to try to counteract the lack of flavour of the bland food.

Christmas Cake

At the beginning of the 1950s, as rationing became less stringent and finally ended in 1954, it was my pleasant task to talk on *Woman's Hour* and on BBC television to give recipes for proper Christmas cakes and puddings.

350 g (12 oz) plain flour
1 teaspoon ground cinnamon
1 teaspoon allspice
a pinch of salt
100 g (4 oz) candied peel, chopped
100 g (4 oz) glacé cherries, quartered
50–100 g (2–4 oz) almonds, blanched and chopped
900 g (2 lb) mixed dried fruit – preferably
450 g (1lb) currants, 225 g (8 oz) sultanas
225 g (8 oz) seedless raisins
4 large eggs
4 tablespoons milk or sherry or brandy or rum
finely grated rind (zest) of 1 lemon
finely grated rind (zest) of 1 orange, optional
225 g (8 oz) butter or best quality margarine
225 g (8 oz) sugar – preferably dark moist brown sugar
1 tablespoon black treacle or golden syrup

Preheat the oven to 160°C, 325°F or Gas Mark 3.

Sift together into a bowl all the dry ingredients. Mix the peel, cherries, almonds and dried fruit. If the cherries are slightly sticky, flour lightly using flour from the recipe, not extra flour. Blend the eggs with the milk or sherry or brandy or rum. Cream together the lemon and orange rinds (zest), butter or margarine, sugar and treacle or golden syrup until soft. Do not over beat, as this type of cake does not need as much beating as light cakes. Gradually blend in the beaten egg mixture and the sifted dry ingredients. Stir in all the fruit.

Prepare the tin carefully: line the bottom of a 23 cm (9 in) round or 20 cm (8 in) square tin with a double round of brown paper and cover this with a double thickness of lightly greased greaseproof paper. Line the sides of the tin with greased greaseproof paper. I know many people say this is unnecessary with modern tins, but I believe it keeps the cake moist.

Put the cake mixture into the tin, smoothing this quite flat on top. Press the mixture with damp, but not over-wet knuckles, as this helps to give a moist topping.

Tie a double band of brown paper round the outside of the tin.

Put into the centre of a very moderate oven, 325°F, 160°C or Gas Mark 3. Bake at this temperature for 1½ hours, then lower the temperature to 140–150°C, 275–300°F, or Gas Mark 1–2 and cook for another 1¾–2 hours. Baking times for rich fruit cakes vary considerably according to your particular oven.

To test the cake: first press firmly on top – it should feel firm, then check to see if the cake has shrunk away from the sides of the tin. If it has, remove from the oven and listen very carefully. A rich fruit cake that is not quite cooked gives a definite humming noise, in which case return the cake to the oven until cooked.

Cool the cake in the baking tin, then turn it out carefully and wrap in foil, if wished, and store in an airtight tin. Leave the greaseproof paper on the cake until moistening it with sherry, etc. and covering it with marzipan and icing.

Golden Christmas Cake

If you prefer a lighter coloured but still rich cake, then follow the proportions and method of making the Christmas Cake on page 22 with the following adaptations.

1. *Omit the spices, add an extra teaspoon of finely grated lemon rind.*
2. *Increase the amount of peel and glacé cherries to 175 g (6 oz) of each.*
3. *Use only 450 g (1 lb) light sultanas and omit the darker raisins and currants*
4. *Add 225 g (8 oz) chopped crystallized pineapple.*
5. *Use milk or light sherry and not the darker alcohol to mix the cake.*
6. *Use caster sugar and not brown sugar.*
7. *Use golden syrup and not black treacle.*

Apple Jelly

Mrs Arthur Webb was an incredibly interesting lady. She broadcast about many traditional foods and was an acknowledged expert on preserving. She looked the perfect country housewife with her lovely rosy complexion and clear eyes. I loved talking to her and learning from her.

cooking apples or crab apples, unpeeled
water – allow 600 ml (1 pint) to each 900 g (2 lb) fruit
sugar, see method

Wash the fruit in cold water, drain well. Chop large apples into small pieces, retain the peel and cores. Put the fruit into a preserving pan, cover with the water. Simmer until a thick pulp is formed.

Strain the pulp through thick muslin or a jelly bag. Do not press the fruit or squeeze the jelly bag for this gives a cloudy jelly.

Measure the juice. Allow 450 g (1 lb) sugar to each 600 ml (1 pint) juice. Heat the juice in the preserving pan. Stir in the sugar and when dissolved boil rapidly until setting point is reached.

Fill heated jam jars while the jelly is still very hot, so there is no chance of it beginning to set in the pan. Cover and store.

APPLE AND GERANIUM JELLY

Follow the recipe and method for Apple Jelly but allow 2–3 fragrant geranium leaves to each 450 g (1 lb) apples.

STUFFED MUSSELS

SERVES 4

During the 1960s many people began to travel abroad. I was one of them for I enjoyed holidays in other countries and also had the opportunity to work right across Australia on television, radio and giving cookery demonstrations to large audiences.

Although the tradition of cooking in that country at that period was largely based upon British fare, this was adapted in many ways.

The shellfish of Australia were wonderful and as a fish addict I enjoyed many delicious dishes with their scallops, oysters and mussels. This is one I liked particularly.

1 kg ($2\frac{1}{4}$ lb) large mussels
1 onion, sliced
1 sprig of parsley
300 ml ($\frac{1}{2}$ pint) dry white wine
salt and freshly ground black pepper

FOR THE FILLING:

100 g (4 oz) butter
2 garlic cloves, peeled and finely chopped
3 tablespoons finely chopped spring onions or fennel root
50 g (2 oz) soft breadcrumbs
2 tablespoons finely chopped parsley
1 teaspoon finely chopped fennel leaves

Scrub the mussels in cold water, discard any that are not closed, or do not shut when sharply tapped. Remove the beards. Put into a large saucepan with the onion, parsley, wine and a little salt and pepper.

Heat for 2 or 3 minutes until the mussels open. Strain the mussels, but keep the liquid. Discard one of the shells and leave the mussels on the remaining shells.

Cream 75 g (3 oz) of the butter and add to the garlic and other ingredients for the filling, season well. Press over the mussels, covering them completely. Melt the remaining butter, sprinkle over the top of the filling. Place the mussels under a preheated grill and cook for 4–5 minutes, or until piping hot and lightly browned.

The heated wine from opening the mussels can be spooned around each portion of shellfish.

CHICKEN AND MUSHROOM PILAFF

new recipe

SERVES 4–6

Today's recommendations that we include plenty of pasta and wine in our diet pleases me a great deal, for I enjoy dishes based upon both these foods.

Now that the real Italian (arborio) rice is readily available, it means we can make good risottos and a pilaff, such as the recipe below.

4 chicken breast portions
225 g (8 oz) chicken livers, fresh or frozen
225 g (8 oz) mushrooms, preferably a mixture of various kinds
50 g (2 oz) butter
2 tablespoons olive oil
2 onions, finely chopped
225 g (8 oz) arborio rice
900 ml (1½ pints) chicken stock
salt and freshly ground black pepper
2 tomatoes, skinned and chopped
½ teaspoon finely chopped thyme
2 fresh bay leaves
chopped parsley, to garnish
Parmesan cheese, to garnish

Bone the chicken breasts and cut into small portions. Defrost the chicken livers, if these are frozen, and drain well. Cut liver portions in half. Wipe and thickly slice the mushrooms.

Heat half the butter and oil in a large pan, add the chicken pieces and the livers and cook until the chicken is lightly browned. Remove from the pan with a fish slice or slotted spoon.

Heat the remaining butter and oil in the same pan, add the onions and mushrooms and cook for 5 minutes, stirring well, so the onions do not brown. Put in the rice and mix with the onions and mushrooms, making sure the grains are well coated with the butter and oil.

Heat the stock, add half to the rice pan, stir well then add salt and pepper to taste with the tomatoes and herbs.

Cover the pan, cook steadily for 10 minutes, then add more hot stock. Continue cooking for another 10 minutes then add the reserved chicken and chicken livers. Continue cooking for another 5–10 minutes, or until the rice and chicken are tender, adding stock as required. The mixture should be pleasantly moist.

Spoon into a heated dish, remove the bay leaves and top with the chopped parsley and a generous sprinkling of Parmesan cheese.

ELIZABETH DAVID

Elizabeth David died before being able to take part in this book. Jill Norman, her publisher and friend, has written this tribute to her.

South Wind in the Kitchen

The cooking of the Mediterranean shores, endowed with all the natural resources, the colour and flavour of the South, is a blend of tradition and brilliant improvisation. The Latin genius flashes from the kitchen pans.

It is honest cooking, too; none of the sham Grande Cuisine of the International Palace Hotel.

"It is not really an exaggeration," wrote Marcel Boulestin, "to say that peace and happiness begin, geographically, where garlic is used in cooking." From Gibraltar to the Bosphorus, down the Rhone Valley, through the great seaports of Marseilles, Barcelona and Genoa, across to Tunis and Alexandria, embracing all the Mediterranean islands, Corsica, Sicily, Sardinia, Crete, the Cyclades, Cyprus (where the Byzantine influence begins to be felt), to the mainland of Greece and the much-disputed territories of Syria, the Lebanon, Constantinople and Smyrna, stretches the influence of Mediterranean cooking, conditioned naturally by variations in climate and soil and the relative industry or indolence of the inhabitants.

The ever recurring elements in the food throughout these countries are the oil, the saffron, the garlic, the pungent local wines; the aromatic perfume of rosemary, wild marjoram and basil drying in the kitchens; the brilliance of the market stalls piled high with pimentos, aubergines, tomatoes, olives, melons, figs and limes; the great heaps of shiny fish, silver, vermilion or tiger-striped, and those long needle fish whose bones so mysteriously turn out to be green. There are, too, all manner of unfamiliar cheeses made from sheep or goat's milk; the butchers' stalls are festooned with every imaginable portion of the inside of every edible animal (anyone who has lived for long in Greece will be familiar with the sound of air gruesomely whistling through sheep's lungs frying in oil).

There are endless varieties of currants and raisins, figs from Smyrna on long strings, dates, almonds, pistachios and pine kernel nuts, dried melon seeds and sheets of apricot paste which is dissolved in water to make a cooling drink ... With this selection (it does not claim to be more) of Mediterranean dishes, I hope to give some idea of the lovely cookery of those regions to people who do not already know them, and to stir the memories of those who have eaten this food on its native shores, and who would like sometimes to bring a flavour of those blessed lands of sun and sea and olive trees into their English kitchens.'

This splendidly evocative passage comes from the introduction to *A Book of Mediterranean Food*, Elizabeth David's first book, published in 1950. Her writing career began in the winter of 1946–7, in a hotel in Ross-on-Wye. She had just returned to the deprivations of postwar Britain after several years of relative plenty, living in the Middle East, and briefly in India. Although the hotel was at least warm, and the staff kindly, the food she described as unpardonable and 'produced with a kind of bleak triumph which amounted almost to a hatred of humanity and humanity's needs'.

She revolted against the hotel meals by writing descriptions of Middle Eastern and Mediterranean cooking. Those notes eventually became part of her first book, although at the time she had no thought of publishing; she was writing for herself as a refuge from the cheerless reality of rationing and food shortages.

'Well, at least I could put my memories on to paper,' she wrote, 'so that I would not forget about the bright vegetables, the basil, the lemons, the apricots, the rice with lamb and currants and pine nuts, the ripe green figs, the white ewes' milk cheeses of Greece, the thick aromatic Turkish coffee, the herb-scented kebabs, the honey and yoghurt for breakfast, the rose petal jam, the evening ices eaten on an Athenian café terrace in sight of the Parthenon . . . ' (from the introduction to the 1988 edition).

In 1949 a friend in the literary world offered to show her 'ragged' collection of recipes to publishers. Most of them thought the idea of a cookery book mad at a time when there was no food to cook, but John Lehmann liked the material and agreed to publish. Years later his reader, Julia Strachey, confided to Elizabeth that she had been beguiled by the recipe for 'Turkish stuffing for a whole roast sheep', when the meat ration was only a few ounces a week. Lehmann also commissioned John Minton to illustrate the book and design the striking jacket – a bright blue Mediterranean bay, and in the foreground tables holding fruits, a lobster, bowls of food, pitchers and bottles of wine.

The recipes were all authentic, collected in Provence, Italy, Corsica, Malta and in Greece, where Elizabeth was living on the island of Syra until the Germans overran Greece. She was evacuated via Crete to Alexandria, where she worked for the Admiralty, and then moved to Cairo to run a reference library for the Ministry of Information. In Cairo she met and married Anthony David, an officer in the Indian army, and at the end of 1945 went to join him in New Delhi. In India she became ill – the climate did not suit her – and after some months she returned to Britain.

Even though scarcely any of the ingredients used in her recipes were available at that time, Elizabeth did not compromise or adapt her dishes. Courgettes, fennel, aubergines were barely known, garlic and fresh herbs impossible to get. The book was published to great critical acclaim as a serious work on the food of the Mediterranean, with reviewers expressing their belief that once the shortages in Britain were lifted the book would be of practical as well as inspirational use.

The first Penguin edition, published in 1955 at 2/6d, brought the book to a very wide audience. Rationing had ended in 1954, and imports of olive oil, tahina, salami, pine nuts, chick peas and the like were starting to trickle in. Many of Elizabeth's dishes were quite unknown in the Britain of the fifties, but over the years food like paella, moussaka, ratatouille, hummus and gazpacho have become familiar in home kitchens, restaurants and supermarkets throughout the country.

Already in this first book, Elizabeth was thorough in her descriptions of foods and their regional differences. *Pissaladière*, a bread dough topped with cooked onions, black olives and anchovies, 'is one of the delights of Marseilles, Toulon and the Var country, where it is sold in the market places and the bakeries in the early morning, and can be bought, piping hot, by the slice, off big iron trays. . . . Further along the coast, across the Italian border, these dishes baked on bread dough are called *pizza*, which simply means a pie, and there are many variations of them, the best known being the Neapolitan *pizza* spread with skinned chopped tomatoes cooked in olive oil, plus anchovies and mozzarella cheese'.

The success of *A Book of Mediterranean Food* was followed in 1951 by *French Country Cooking*, another small book, consisting largely of French recipes that had not been appropriate for the first book. In her introduction she dispels the myth, still occasionally encountered, that all French families eat grand, rich meals. 'A certain amount of nonsense is talked about the richness of the food to be found in all French homes. It is true that the standard is much higher than that of most English households, but it will not, I hope, be taken as an ungracious criticism to say that the chances are that a food-conscious foreigner staying for any length of time with a French middle-class family would find the proportion of rather tough entrecôtes, rolled and stuffed roast veal and sautéed chicken exasperatingly high. For parties and festivals there would be more elaborately cooked fish and poultry, separate vegetable courses and wonderful open fruit tarts; but he would not find many dishes cooked in cream, wine and garlic – it is bad for the *foie*, he would very likely be told. Those who care to look for it, however, will find the justification of France's culinary reputation in the provinces, at the riverside inns, in unknown cafés along the banks of the Burgundy canal, . . . in the hospitable farmhouses of the Loire and the Dordogne, of Normandy and the Auvergne, in sea-port bistros, . . . and nowadays also in *cafés routiers* . . . it is in the heart of the country that one may become acquainted with the infinite variety of *charcuterie*, the sausages, pickled pork and bacon, smoked hams, terrines, preserved goose, pâtés, *rillettes*, and *andouillettes*, the cheeses and creams, the fruits preserved in potent local liqueurs, the fresh garden vegetables, pulled up before they are faded and grown old, and served shining with farmhouse butter, the *galettes* and pancakes made from country flour, the mushrooms, *cèpes, morilles* and *truffes* gathered in the forest . . . '

Enticing descriptions like this one and the vivid pictures of the provinces in *French Provincial Cooking* (1960) drew many English enthusiasts to France to explore the foods of the countryside (what is now called *cuisine du terroir*). Pâtés and terrines, satisfying vegetable soups enriched with bacon and garlic, meat and poultry stews simmered in wine, and open tarts both savoury and sweet found their way into the repertoire of enterprising and creative British cooks. In the sixties many an enthusiastic amateur opened a small restaurant with little more than his or her well-used copies of Elizabeth David, the necessary minimum of equipment and the will to succeed. And many of them did. In those days, more often than not, dinner parties, whether cheap and cheerful or stylish and sophisticated, were drawn from her books.

While *French Country Cooking* covered rustic, peasant cooking, the more substantial, classic work on French provincial cooking dealt with 'sober, well-balanced, middle-class French cookery, carried out with care and skill, with due regard to the quality of the materials, but without extravagance or pretension'. In *French Provincial Cooking* we hear about the Robertot family who were responsible for introducing her to good French food. 'Torn, most willingly, from an English boarding school at the age of sixteen, to live with a middle class French family in Passy, it was only some time later that I tumbled to the fact that even for a Parisian family who owned a small farm in Normandy, the Robertots were both exceptionally greedy and exceptionally well fed. . . . It was only later, after I had come home to England, that I realized in what way the family had fulfilled their task of instilling French culture into at least one of their British charges. Forgotten were the Sorbonne professors and the yards of Racine learnt by heart, the ground plans of cathedrals I had never seen, and the saga of Napoleon's last days on St Helena. What had stuck was the taste for a kind of food quite ideally unlike anything I had known before.'

Elizabeth was born in 1913, one of four daughters of Rupert Gwynne, conservative MP for Eastbourne; her mother was the daughter of the first Viscount Ridley. She had a conventional middle class upbringing, with a nanny and governess, and later went to a girls' school where the food was decidedly inferior. 'My sisters and I had a nanny who used to make these (mushrooms in cream) for us over the nursery fire, with mushrooms which we had gathered ourselves in the early morning. I don't suppose they will ever taste quite the same, for the sensations of childhood food elude us in later years – but as a recompense nothing will surely ever taste so hateful as nursery tapioca, or the appalling boiled cod of schooldays.' (*French Country Cooking*.)

After her 18 months in Paris, Elizabeth spent some time in Munich, then returned to London to work briefly as a *vendeuse* at Worth. She then had a spell at the Oxford Rep. before a brief acting career at the Open Air Theatre in Regent's Park. In the late 1930s she went off to Italy and met the writer Norman Douglas on Capri; the two became great friends in spite of the disparity in their ages, and Norman Douglas had a great influence on Elizabeth as a writer and through his own approach to life.

At the beginning of the fifties she returned to live in Italy for a year, researching and collecting material for *Italian Food*, which came out in 1954. This was still a difficult time for getting the right ingredients, but she urged her readers to try those recipes needing only everyday ingredients and not to attempt others until imports from Italy were more frequent. 'The difficulties of reproducing Italian cooking abroad are much the same as the difficulties attendant upon any good cooking outside its country of origin, and usually they can be overcome. Italians, unlike the thrifty French, are very extravagant with raw materials. Butter, cheese, oil, the best cuts of meat, chicken and turkey breast, eggs, chicken and meat broth, raw and cooked ham are used, not so much with reckless abandon as with a precise awareness of what good quality does for the cooking. . . . Since the war Italian cooks have had to learn to make a little go a long way. Their methods of tackling this problem are notably different from ours. When an Italian has not the wherewithal to cook one of the traditional extravagant dishes, she doesn't attempt to produce an imitation. No amount of propaganda could persuade her to see the point of making a steak and kidney pudding with tinned beef and no kidneys, neither would she bother to make a ravioli stuffing [with "fragments of the cold joint"] because the results would not at all resemble the dish as it should be, and would therefore be valueless. So her method would be to produce some attractive and nourishing little dish out of two ounces of cheese and a slice of ham, or a pound of spinach and a couple of eggs. A hefty pizza made of bread dough and baked in the oven with tomatoes, cheese and herbs costs very little and is comforting, savoury food.'

Elizabeth was one of the first writers to point out the importance of regional differences in Italian food. The country was not unified until the latter part of the 19th century, so to an Italian there was, and is, no such thing as Italian food; 'there is Florentine cooking, Venetian cooking, there are the dishes of Genoa, Piedmont, Romagna; of Rome, Naples and the Abruzzi; of

Sardinia and Sicily; of Lombardy, Umbria and the Adriatric coast'. These provincial differences in food in Italy are clear to every discerning traveller, but it has taken a long time for the message to be received here, because until recently few of our Italian restaurants showed any regional characteristics but merely served up the spaghetti, veal and chicken dishes that the British had come to regard as Italian food. In the introduction to the 1963 Penguin edition of *Italian Food* Elizabeth criticised other British cookery writers for spreading misconceptions about Italian food. 'As I write this, I have just come across, in a respected monthly magazine, a recipe for a risotto made with twice-cooked Patna rice and a tin of tomato soup. What way is that of enlarging our knowledge and arousing our interest? Minestrone, that hefty, rough-and-ready, but nutritionally sound traditional midday soup of Northern Italian agricultural and manual workers, features frequently in such publications. Often the readers are told that it can be made with some such ingredients as a bouillon cube, a tin of chicken noodle soup, and a few frozen french beans. A crumpet or a made-up scone mix spread with tomato purée and a slice of processed cheese turns up regularly as a Neapolitan *pizza*. I can't help wondering how we should feel if Italian cookery writers were to retaliate by asserting that a Welsh Rabbit is made with polenta cake and Gorgonzola, or steak and kidney pudding with veal and tomatoes and a covering of macaroni.'

Once *Italian Food* was delivered to her publishers Elizabeth started work on *Summer Cooking*, a smaller and less demanding book. It is a delightful collection of recipes for simple summer meals, cold buffets, picnics and holidays, drawn from old English dishes as well as the countries she had travelled in. She concentrates on herbs, fruits and vegetables in season: tiny broad beans, new peas, marrow flowers, cherries, blackcurrants; on light dishes of poultry and game, or fish combined with the vegetables and fruits (*Filets de sole véronique*: 'Wait until the muscat grapes come into season in August to make this dish. No other grapes will really do.').

By 1964 all five books were available in paperback and finding an immense new audience, especially among the young. During the years of writing the books, Elizabeth also contributed regularly to a variety of newspapers and journals, having first been commissioned by Anne Scott James to write a piece entitled 'Rice Again' for *Harper's Bazaar* in 1949. At different times she was a regular contributor to *Vogue, House and Garden, The Sunday Times, Wine and Food, The Spectator* and *Nova*. Writing for *The Spectator* pleased Elizabeth most for there she was allowed to write a column about food, getting away from the usual formula of an introductory paragraph and a clutch of recipes. Her subjects were usually topical and wide-ranging, from describing the pleasures of a modest restaurant to reviews of eccentric books or 'harmless fun at the expense of restaurant guides and the baiting of public relations persons who made imbecile suggestions to the effect that two tins of tomato juice packed in a basket tied with red ribbons would make a nice neighbourly Christmas gift' (*An Omelette and a Glass of Wine*). Essentially, the columns were about the pleasures and benefits of good food, good wine, good cookery books, expressed in generous and lively terms.

'What on earth comes over wine waiters when they take the orders of a woman entertaining another woman in a restaurant? Twice in one week recently I have dined in different restaurants and with different women friends, on one occasion as the hostess and on the other as the guest. On both occasions, after the regulation lapse of twenty minutes, the wine waiter brought a half-bottle of the wine ordered instead of a whole one. Please don't think I have anything against half-bottles; on the contrary I find they have a special charm of their own. There are occasions when a half is what one wants, a half and nothing else, in which case I really don't believe one has to be a master-woman to be capable of specifying one's wishes in the matter. I suppose the assumption on the part of wine waiters that women are too frail to consume or too stingy to pay for a whole bottle must be based on some sort of experience, but instead of having to go back to change the order (ten minutes the second time, one is getting edgy by then, and well into the second course; if they held up the food to synchronize with the wine one mightn't mind so much) he could inquire in the first place, in a discreet way. Or even in an indiscreet way, like the steward on the Edinburgh–London express a few years ago who yelled at me across the rattling crockery and two other bemused passengers, "A bottle, madam? A *whole* bottle? Do you know how large a whole bottle is?"' (*The Spectator*, 13 July 1962.)

With the launching of her kitchen shop in 1965 Elizabeth's writing came to an end temporarily, but through the shop her influence on Britain's cooks continued. In *French Country Cooking* she wrote 'Some sensible person once remarked that you spend the whole of your life in your bed or your shoes. Having done the best you can by shoes and bed, devote all the time and resources at your disposal to the building up of a fine kitchen. It will be, as it should be, the most comforting and comfortable room in the house.'

She scoured Britain and the continent for the best in knives, earthenware, stoneware, cast-iron, soup pots, omelette pans, pepper mills, bread tins, plain white dishes. In *French Country Cooking* and *French Provincial Cooking* she had written at length about the need for the right tools, and here they all were. Restaurateurs like Michel and Albert Roux who had just opened their first restaurant nearby shopped there for equipment that hitherto had had to come from France. Elizabeth's own stylishness and impeccable taste were in evidence in the design of the shop and in every item stocked. 'Look at the friendly browns and warm terracottas, the ivories and greys and the pebbles-on-the-beach colours of old English earthenware and stoneware,' she had written in *House and Garden* in 1958. 'You see that utterly plain unadorned long white fish dish? On that dish a whole pink and silver salmon trout is unimaginably elegant and lovely.'

Within a few months of the shop opening kitchen shops sprang up everywhere. Thanks to Elizabeth's early initiative we can now buy good cooking equipment and the right tools for the job in department stores and specialist shops all over the country. Unhappily in 1973 she felt obliged to sever her connections with her business; she felt her standards were being compromised by her partners, who continued to run the business, using her name.

During the years at the shop she had written and privately published a few pamphlets on English cooking – potted meats and fish pastes, bread making, syllabubs and fools. Although she is often thought of primarily as the writer who awoke British cooks to the pleasures of French and Mediterranean food, she had always had a passionate interest in English cooking, and a fine collection of early English cookery books which she read avidly.

From this enthusiasm came the idea for a series of books which we perhaps grandiosely called *English Cooking, Ancient and Modern*, and of which the first title was *Spices, Salt and Aromatics in the English Kitchen*, published in 1971. Drawing on her favourite authors, Eliza Acton, Marcel Boulestin, Mrs Leyel, and earlier writers about Anglo-Indian food like Col. Kenney-Herbert, and on her own experiences in India and the Middle East, she compiled a fine collection of English spiced and aromatic dishes, reviving for us old treats such as salt duck and spiced beef. Scholarliness is always present in Elizabeth's work, and in the English books it came to the fore. *Spices, Salt and Aromatics* contains a lot of fascinating history, exploring the English relationship with the East, the trade cycles which led to the importing of oriental foods and the early attempts at recreating oriental dishes, pickles and chutneys.

English Bread and Yeast Cookery, intended as the second title, took five years to write and outgrew the series. It is and will remain the definitive book on English baking, and at the time of publication it had an immense influence. Eighty per cent of the bread sold in Britain came from factories, soft, white and sliced. The milling monopolies controlling the bread industry supplied the characterless flour used to make most of the rest. The awfulness of English bread was nothing new. Eliza Acton noted in her *Bread Book* (1857) that our bread 'was noted both at home and abroad for its want of genuineness, and the faulty mode of its preparation', and in *Practical Bread-*

making (1897) Frederick Vine wrote 'To describe some of the tackle sold as bread in London as anything else than batter would be to stretch a point in its favour.' In the 1970s a revolt against the blandness and sogginess of industrial bread was gathering momentum and people were starting to bake their own bread. They seized the bread book in their thousands, created a demand for flour from small millers and for supplies of yeast and good bread tins. Today the industrial loaf is still with us, but look at the wide variety of other breads on sale in supermarkets, delicatessens and bakers. For this we can thank Elizabeth David.

During the last ten years or so of her life Elizabeth became increasingly frail, suffering broken limbs, having difficulty in getting about and in standing and therefore being able to cook – a source of great chagrin to her. She went on working on her book on the use of ice and the making of ices (due to be published next year), doing painstaking research in a wide variety of books and journals. When she was well she worked at the kitchen table, always piled high with books. Later on she worked in bed, surrounded by precarious heaps of books and papers.

Writing was never easy for her. Her polished and elegant style came from writing and rewriting, always by hand, until she was satisfied with the result. She was constantly curious, marking pieces of useful information with slips of paper, a stickler for accuracy and the full acknowledgment of sources. In conversation as well as in writing Elizabeth could be wickedly funny and witty, mocking and critical. The wittiest pieces are also very informative, like the passage in the introduction to the booklet on Syllabubs and Fruit Fools (reprinted in *An Omelette and a Glass of Wine*) where she describes the demise of the syllabub and the rise of the trifle.

'Already for nearly a century the syllabub had been keeping company with the trifle, and in due course the trifle came to reign in the syllabub's stead; and before long the party pudding of the English was not any more the fragile whip of cream contained in a little glass, concealing within its innocent white froth a powerful alcoholic punch, but a built-up confection of sponge fingers and ratafias soaked in wine and brandy, spread with jam, clothed in an egg-and-cream custard, topped with a syllabub and strewn with little coloured comfits. Came 1846, the year that Mr Alfred Bird brought forth custard powder; and Mr Bird's brainchild grew and grew until all the land was covered with custard made with custard powder and the Trifle had become custard's favourite resting place. The wine and lemon-flavoured cream whip or syllabub which had crowned the Trifle had begun to disappear. Sponge cake left over from millions of nursery teas usurped the place of sponge fingers and the little bitter almond macaroons called ratafias. Kitchen sherry replaced Rhenish and Madeira and Lisbon wines. Brandy was banished. The little coloured comfits – sugar-coated coriander seeds and caraways – bright as tiny tiddlywinks, went into a decline and in their stead reigned candied angelica and nicely varnished glacé cherries.'

Elizabeth could have written on many other subjects; we are fortunate that she chose food. Literature, travel and social history all feature extensively in her work; she had an unfailing knack of finding apposite passages to quote. The depth and breadth of her knowledge combined with her own literate and literary style ensure that in future her own work will be similarly used by others.

She was honoured with prizes, made *Chevalier de l'Ordre du Mérite Agricole* by the French and awarded the OBE in 1977. She received the Order from the Queen who asked what she did. 'Write cookery books Ma'am', said Elizabeth. 'That must be very useful' replied Elizabeth II. In 1986 she received the CBE from the Prince of Wales who confessed that his wife liked Italian food. Honorary doctorates were conferred on her by the universities of Essex and Bristol. In 1982 she was elected Fellow of the Royal Society of Literature, an honour which perhaps pleased her most.

When Elizabeth died on May 22 last year, the obituaries were fulsome and extensive from California to Greece. This woman, who shunned publicity, who only once or twice diffidently broadcast, had a memorial service on September 10 which crowded St Martin-in-the-Fields with friends, cooks, colleagues and readers. The tributes were profound, generous, funny and stylish, as was Elizabeth. Afterwards, a group of young London chefs offered a picnic lunch prepared from her books: cornmeal and rosemary bread, *bocconcini* with basil, marinated lentil and goat cheese salad, spinach and gruyère tart, baby beetroot and chives, spiced aubergine salad, Piedmontese peppers, grilled tuna with red onions and beans, accompanied by fresh young wines and followed by fruit and marzipan *pan forte*. It was what Elizabeth called 'rational, right and proper food'; she would have enjoyed it.

LE CASSOULET DE CASTELNAUDARY

'Je veux vous amener chez Clémence, une petite taverne de la rue Vavin, où l'on ne fait qu'un plat, mais un plat prodigieux. On sait que pour avoir toutes ses qualités le cassoulet doit cuire doucement sur un feu bas. Le cassoulet de la mère Clémence cuit depuis vingt ans. Elle ajoute de temps en temps, dans la marmite, de l'oie, ou du lard, parfois un morceau de saucisson ou quelques haricots, mais c'est toujours le même cassoulet. La base demeure, et c'est cette antique et précieuse base qui donne au plat une qualité comparable à ces tons ambrés si particulier qui caractèrisent les chairs dans les oeuvres des vieux maîtres vénitiens.'

So wrote Anatole France of the *Cassoulet*, wonderful dish of south-western France, which through the years has been raised from the status of a humble peasant dish to one of the glories of French cooking. Toulouse, Carcassonne, Périgord, Castelnaudary, Gascony, Castannau, all have their very own versions of the *Cassoulet*. The ingredients vary from fresh pork and mutton to smoked sausages, garlic sausages, bacon, smoked ham, preserved goose or pork, duck, calves' feet, the rind of pork and pigs' cheek. The essentials are good white haricot beans and a capacious earthenware pot (the name *Cassoulet* comes from Cassol d'Issel, the original clay cooking utensil from the little town of Issel, near Castelnaudary).

SERVES 6–8

750 g–1 kg (1½–2 lb) medium-sized white haricot beans
a wing and a leg of preserved goose or half a fresh goose
a coarse pork sausage of about 450 g (1lb) or several small ones
225 g (½ lb) bacon
3 onions
4 or 5 cloves of garlic
2 tomatoes, and, if possible, 2 pints of meat stock

Put the beans to soak overnight; next day put them into fresh water and cook for about 2½ hours, keeping them just on the boil, until they are three-quarters cooked, then strain them.

In the meantime prepare the stock in which they are to finish cooking. Slice the onions and cut the bacon into squares and melt them together in a pan, add the crushed garlic, the tomatoes, seasoning and herbs, and pour over the stock and let it simmer for 20 minutes. Take the pieces of goose out of their pot with the good lard adhering to them. (If you are using fresh goose, it must be half roasted; have some good pork or goose dripping as well.)

Put the goose, the dripping, the sausage, and the bacon from the stock, at the bottom of the earthenware pot, which has been well rubbed with garlic, and the beans on the top. Add the prepared stock. Bring the *Cassoulet* slowly to the boil, then spread a layer of breadcrumbs on the top and put the pot into a slow oven and leave it until the beans are cooked. This will take about 1 hour, during which time most of the stock will be absorbed and a crust will have formed on the top of the beans.

Serve exactly as it is; a good young red wine should be drunk with this dish; a salad and a country cheese of some kind to finish will be all you need afterwards.

Duck can be used instead of goose, and at Christmas the legs or wings of a turkey go very well into the *Cassoulet.*

MULET AUX OLIVES ET AU VIN BLANC

Grey mullet with olives and white wine

A very simple and effective recipe which can be applied to many sorts of fish, including red mullet, sea-bream, sea-bass, whiting and mackerel; I have chosen grey mullet as an example because for some reason it is sold in this country at prices far below its true value, and represents something of a bargain.

For 2 medium-sized fish, each weighing approximately 450 g (1 lb) gross weight, the other ingredients are:

a coffee-cupful (after-dinner size) of olive oil
a little piece of fennel (or a sprig of thyme or a bayleaf)
salt and pepper
2 or 3 tablespoons of white wine
a dozen stoned black olives
some slices of orange or lemon

Put the cleaned fish into a shallow oval fireproof dish, pour the oil over them, add your herbs, a sprinkling of salt and pepper and the white wine. Bake, uncovered, for 15–20 minutes in a medium oven, 350°F (180°C, Gas Mark 4).

Now add the stoned black olives and cook another 5 minutes. The mullet can be served in the dish in which they have cooked, or be transferred to a flat serving dish, in either case with their own juice and slices of orange or lemon arranged along each fish. May be served hot or cold.

Aubergine Dolmas

A Turkish and Middle Eastern dish

a cupful of cooked rice
salt and pepper
100 g ($\frac{1}{4}$lb) of minced mutton (either raw or cooked)
onions
2 tomatoes
herbs
a few pine nuts or walnuts
8 small round aubergines (or 4 large ones)
olive oil
lemon juice

Mix the cooked rice with the well-seasoned meat, a chopped fried onion or two, the chopped tomatoes, some marjoram, mint, or basil, and a few pine nuts or chopped walnuts.

Cut about an inch off the thin end of the aubergines, and with a small spoon scoop out most of the flesh. Cut this into dice and mix it with the prepared stuffing. Fill the aubergines with the stuffing (not too full), put the tops in, inverted, so that they fit like corks, lay them in a pan with a little olive oil; let this get hot and then pour hot water over them to come half-way up. Simmer for 30 minutes, add the juice of a lemon, and cook very slowly another 30 minutes. There should be only a very little sauce left by the time they are ready. If there is any stuffing over, use it to fill tomatoes, which can be baked and served with the aubergines.

TORTA DI ALBICOCCHE

Apricot Tart

FOR THE PASTRY:

200 g (7 oz) of flour
100 g (3½ oz) of butter
100 g (3½ oz) of vanilla sugar
the yolks of 2 eggs
the grated peel of a small lemon
½ teacupful of water

FOR THE FILLING:

1 kg (2 lb) Apricots
a little sugar

Knead the pastry very lightly and roll it out as little as possible.

Spread it on flat buttered pie tins. Two 15 cm (6 in) tins are about right. Or use 150 g (5 oz) flour to 75 g (2½ oz) of butter, and about 450 g (1 lb) of apricots, to fill one 20 cm (8 in tin).

On top of the pastry arrange 1 kg (2 lb) of apricots which have been cooked with a little sugar, cut into halves, and stoned. There should not be too much juice or the pastry will be sodden.

Cook for 25 minutes – the first 15 minutes in a hot oven (420°F, 210°C, Gas Mark 7), and the last 10 with the heat diminished. Serve cold.

A most delicious sweet. The vanilla sugar is important to the flavour.

Sweet–Sour Melon Pickle

Made with honeydew melon, this is a most delicious and unusual pickle to serve with all the cold meats and poultry of the Christmas season, and is also excellent with curry.

For an average size honeydew melon weighing about 1.75 kg (4 lb) when bought, about 1.5 kg (3 lb) when skin and pips have been removed, the other ingredients are:

300 ml (½ pint) of mild wine vinegar or Orleans vinegar
750 g (1½ lb) of preserving or other white sugar
a couple of teaspoons of pickling spice tied in a twist of muslin

Pare the melon thinly. Cut in half, throw away the seeds, slice the fruit, then cut it in cubes roughly 4 cm (1½ in) wide by 1 cm (½ in) thick. Bring a large wide pan of water to the boil, throw in the melon, and as soon as the water comes to a full boil again, remove the fruit with a perforated spoon to a colander to drain, then plunge it all into a bowl of cold water. When it has cooled, bring the vinegar to a full boil. Put in the strained melon, and cook it in the vinegar for 2 minutes after the vinegar has come back to the boil. Then pour all into a large china or glazed stoneware bowl, cover when cold, and leave for 48 hours. At this stage, the melon takes on a somewhat sinister aspect. It looks dull and jammy. During the second cooking it will clear, and all will be well. Strain off the vinegar, bring it to the boil with the sugar and the little bag of spices, and simmer 15 minutes removing the scum as it rises. Put in the melon, boil 3 minutes, and then take out the melon with a perforated spoon and pack it into preserving jars. Extract the bag of spices. Give the syrup a final boil and a skim. When cool pour it over the fruit, filling the jars quite full. Screw or clip down the lids when cold.

Leave for at least a fortnight before broaching the jars. This pickle keeps exceptionally well, even after a jar has been opened.

Jane Grigson

A Companionable Presence in the Kitchen

'Jane Grigson left to the English-speaking world a legacy of fine writing on food and cookery for which no exact parallel exists . . . She won to herself this wide audience because she was above all a friendly writer . . . However much more she knew about this or that than do the rest of us, she never seemed to be talking down to anyone. On the contrary, she is the most companiable presence in the kitchen; often catching the imagination with a deft fragment of history or poetry, but never failing to explain the "why" as well as the "how" of cookery.'

When Jane Grigson died in March 1990, Alan Davidson's obituary in the *Independent* summed up the feeling of her many readers in Britain. Jane Grigson, almost singlehandedly, had grabbed the declining standards in British food by the scruff of the neck and shaken them. She was a modest, unpretentious woman who was genuinely surprised at her enormous influence and success; her daughter, food writer Sophie Grigson, said she would probably have hooted with laughter at all the ballyhoo after her death.

Sitting in my kitchen – where more fitting place to talk about Jane Grigson than around a kitchen table? – Sophie speaks of her mother with affection and pride. 'You should have seen the letters we got after she died, from readers who had never met her or people who had just met her once very briefly, saying that they felt in some ways they had lost a friend but on the other hand the great thing was they had the books.'

Jane Grigson was born in Gloucester and raised in the north-east, in Sunderland, where there was always good food in the house. After she studied at Cambridge she became a translator from Italian, winning the John Florio prize in 1964 for her translation of an eighteenth-century classic, *Of Crimes and Punishment* by Cesare Beccaria.

Her long and happy relationship with the poet and critic Geoffrey Grigson lasted for thirty years until his death in 1985. Jane became his assistant, secretary, organizer and banker, 'he was hopeless with money' says Sophie, and they began collaborating on a series of books for children about painting and the stories told by paintings.

They divided their time between Broad Town in Wiltshire and a small French village called Trôo in the Loire valley. Sophie spent much of her childhood there and believes it had a fundamental influence on her mother's work.

The conditions in the house in Trôo, for a budding foodwriter, let alone a woman with a family to feed, were primitive, to say the least. Sophie laughs when she remembers the early years there. Her parents had bought the house in the early 1960s with £500 given to Jane by her parents, who were 'horrified that she spent it on some hole in the rock in France!'. The house had no running water, drains or electricity, 'the loo had a proper pedestal loo seat but when you opened the lid, there was a saucepan inside, it was that kind of place!'

'The huge fireplace was roomy enough to become the entire kitchen – with no electricity or running water, sink and fridge were impossible luxuries. They made do with a two-ring gas stove which ran off bottled gas and a tin oven which sat on top of the rings. Water came from rainbutts and the local well. We got electricity before we got running water, but for a good ten years we had to do without either. Despite the limited circumstances, Jane conjured up wonderful meals.'

The cooking facilities might have been primitive but the village atmosphere could not have been more conducive for someone with Jane's interest in food. Like most of France, this was a place where food was taken seriously. Indeed it was often the main subject of conversation and they were able to get very good-quality ingredients in the markets and shops. 'Both my parents became very intrigued by the charcuterie shops, and the range of cooked pork products that were available even in our very small village, let alone the nearby town. She had always liked cooking but had no intention of becoming a foodwriter.'

Jane's career as a foodwriter was a happy accident. Adey Horton, a friend who lived in the village, had been asked by a publisher to write a book. Sophie remembers, 'She set up a deal whereby she would research the book on charcuterie and he would write it'. In the end he was unable to write it and Jane wrote the book on her own.

The book, *Charcuterie and French Pork Cookery*, published in 1967, announced a new approach to food writing. It is clear from the first paragraph that a new voice in cookery was emerging – one that took the subject seriously.

'It could be said that European civilization – and Chinese civilization too – has been founded on the pig. Easily domesticated, omnivorous household and village scavenger, clearer of scrub and undergrowth, devourer of forest acorns, yet content with a sty – and delightful when cooked or cured, from his snout to his tail.' Jane then proceeded to tell the reader what to do with everything from the snout to the tail.

Jane managed to combine her serious academic side with a genuine enthusiasm for food. As Sophie says, 'Sitting and reading Jane's books is like sitting over coffee after a meal with your elbows on the table with a friend who is very knowledgeable, but is not a pain in the butt about being knowledgeable, who actually just wants to share this fascinating information with you.'

Her style and thoroughness were there from the first book: not only does it contain all you could ever possibly want to know about the pig, inside and out, but she also holds your attention throughout the book with a wealth of historical detail and anecdote. And, like all the very best food writers, you find yourself reading more and further than intended. One thing leads to another and suddenly you're consulting recipes on making not just a huge variety of sausages but also brawn, pressed tongue and trotters and thinking that, with Jane holding your hand, you might actually make these dishes!

It is a measure of the seriousness and thoroughness of her work that it not only remains the definitive book on pork cookery but has also been translated into French.

On Jane's death, Elizabeth David wrote that the first time she encountered Jane Grigson was when she was sent the typescript of the charcuterie book by Michael Joseph, who were her own publishers. She saw it as a welcome novelty, 'Now that the book has long since passed into the realm of kitchen classics we take it for granted but, for British readers and cooks in the late 1960s, its content, the clarity of the writing, and the confident knowledge of its subject and its history displayed by this young author were new treats for all of us.'

Elizabeth David recognized new talent when she saw it and when the *Observer* rang her to ask her to do its food column she declined but suggested Jane. So began a relationship with the *Observer* which was to last until Jane's death. Elizabeth David spotted Jane's particular talent that had given her such a loyal and faithful readership over the years. 'There was a writer who could combine a delightful quote from Chaucer on the subject of a pike galantine with a careful recipe for a modern chicken and pork version of the same ancient dish, and who could do so without pedantry or a hint of precociousness. Jane was always entertaining as well as informative.'

In many ways Jane was a natural successor to Elizabeth David who had herself, with her books on France and the Mediterranean, opened up food writing with a new enthusiasm. Jane's contribution was to put food in a wider cultural context, showing that food was at the very heart of life, so it was natural that literature, history and poetry should be included alongside recipes. Jane wanted to get our intellectual tastebuds going again.

The idea of applying the same intellectual rigour to food as to any other important subject in life seems obvious now, but in the 1960s it was still shockingly new. Cookery was still seen as the poor relation of *haute cuisine*, a distinction Jane herself had no time for. In her opinion there were only good ingredients, well-prepared.

There was also a gender difference: cookery was something women did but *haute cuisine* was food prepared by male chefs in expensive restaurants. Jane Grigson and, later, Claudia Roden changed that view of cookery writers.

It is also significant that in Jane Grigson's obituary Elizabeth David remembered Jane's practical side. Describing the time Jane had come to lunch to find water gushing through the ceiling and a flustered Elizabeth David panicking about her books, rugs and furniture, she remembers Jane efficiently fetching bowls, and moving furniture and generally restoring calm.

'We shared many tastes and convictions, so it was hardly surprising that we soon became firm friends, conducting long Sunday morning conversations, corresponding on subjects of mutual interest – anything from medieval English bread laws to eighteenth-century French ice-creams and every now and again meeting for a lunch or a dinner in London.'

When the job offer from the *Observer* came in 1968, Jane was surprised and not a little anxious at the thought of producing articles on a weekly basis. But she sat down with her husband Geoffrey and decided to apply the same technique that she had used with the charcuterie book. Sophie grins, 'All she knew about was pork at that point, and I can remember her saying she was suddenly faced with writing her first article. She and my father sat down and said, "My god, what do we do?" And they decided to approach the article from the point of view of putting strawberries within a cultural context, in a context of art, literature, historical importance and development, and that was really the basis for all her writing.'

That first article on strawberries, which was to be the beginning of more than twenty years of writing for the *Observer*, set a standard that she was to follow during her whole time there.

First she filled in the historical background, mentioning that 'bulgy modern strawberries would hardly have been recognized by a medieval miniature painter who ran hautboys – or wood strawberries – round the margins of his *Book of Hours*.' Then she traced the development of the strawberry we know today across the Americas and through France at the end of the eighteenth century.

Jane then contrasted a picture of real strawberry picking with a literary scene in Jane Austen's *Emma*, demonstrating that the strawberry pickers in *Emma* could hardly have been taking it seriously, as they were only there for half an hour – nothing like the backbreaking work of real picking – although she acknowledged that it was certainly a good backdrop scene for a love story. The idea of the lover's knot then takes her back to Hieronymus Bosch and his painting, the 'Garden of Delights'. And then the reader is given several recipes, with advice on how to get the best strawberries and what to do with them. Recipes for Strawberry Brulée, *Coeurs à la Crème* and *Barquettes aux Fraises*, a little strawberry tart, follow.

Many of her books were based on the series she had written for the *Observer*. *Good Things*, published in 1971, seemed the perfect title to sum up Jane's philosophy. 'This is not a manual of cookery, but a book about enjoying food . . . Anyone who likes to eat can soon cook well.'

The book is divided into sections: fish, meat and game, vegetables, fruit and dessert, and fruit liqueurs. Once again there is the mix of history (as in the opening sentence on apple and quince, 'we have rather betrayed the apple') with a desire to rehabilitate produce that has been ignored, forgotten or given a bad reputation.

Jane even manages to make prunes sound interesting, 'One must ignore what modern puritans of the last century or two have done to prunes, the dreadful alliances they have made between prunes and rice, or prunes and custard . . . ' Jane then returns to the medieval tradition of mixing sweet and savoury with a mouthwatering description: '. . . in such things as genuine mincemeat (ox-tongue, beef or mutton with suet and dried fruits); or plum (i.e., prune) porridge, the original of the plum pudding, which was made with tongue, raisins, prunes, spices, wine, meat stock and breadcrumbs.'

The book also contained one of her own personal favourites which she had invented, curried parsnip soup, '. . . one doesn't immediately recognize the parsnip taste, but no other root vegetable can produce such an excellent result.'

In her introduction to the section on parsnips she suspected that the general neglect of parsnips by European cooks is due to the fact that it is one of the few vegetables of British origin. Another reason given is that it became associated with Lenten cod and fasting. 'Certainly the English have been eating parsnips from the Middle Ages or earlier. A raw parsnip round your neck kept off adders or reduced swelling in the testicles. Cooked parsnips gave men an "appetyt for wymen".'

In her *Observer* column, Jane's sense of humour is always present between the lines. She was not afraid to tell a story against herself, as when describing a conversation with Anton Mosimann about the English menu he had put on at the Dorchester.

'"Please no bread and butter pudding, Anton." Clatter and crash, that was a real brick. "I am giving you bread and butter pudding for lunch, Jane and you'll be asking for a second helping." And he was right. By using good bread and cream in the custard and cutting down the sultanas, he had transformed the hated school pudding. I looked up his recipe in his *Cuisine à la Carte* and converted the family the following Sunday.'

The family wasn't always quite so enthusiastic however. A good cookery writer needs to test her recipes again and again to ensure reliable accuracy. The recipes generally get tested on nearest and dearest which is why there is always that heartfelt thanks to the family in the acknowledgements section of any food book.

Sophie was generally quite happy in her role as guinea pig but remembers one book, *The Mushroom Feast*, with dislike. 'I especially remember that book because I happened to be loathing mushrooms at that particular time!'

The next large subject Jane tackled in book form was fish. *Fish Cookery*, published in 1973, lamented the fact that, despite being an island race, only ever about sixty miles from the sea, it was often impossible to buy really fresh fish in Britain. This led to the familiar circle of ignorance and fear: ignorance of what to buy, other than cod or haddock; and fear of cooking any unfamiliar fish.

Comparisons with France – in her village she was 150 miles from the sea – showed that things didn't have to be as bad as they were in Britain. But improvement depended on re-establishing good relations between consumers and sources of supply. Finding a good fishmonger, asking his advice and gradually building demand for better and fresher products would take time. After seeing how well that relationship between market trader and shopper worked in France, Jane was optimistic that things could be changed in Britain. And it is in great part due to her determination and enthusiasm that the British shopper has become more demanding and that, for example, wet fish stalls are reappearing in the major supermarkets across the country.

Jane wistfully compares the service and quality she gets even from her small local market in France with the English equivalent. Madame Soarès, the fishmonger, is keen to introduce her to new fish, give advice on preparation and cooking. "Here's some parsley for you. Have a lemon too. And why not a handful of shrimps – they'll make a finish to the sauce! *Extra*!"

It was that delightfully enthusiastic '*extra*', roughly translated as a mixture between 'great' and 'yum yum', that Jane tried to put across in her books and articles.

Fish Cookery takes us through the stages of choosing, cleaning and preparing fish, including chapters on court bouillons, sauces and butter, shellfish and crustaceans (which includes RSPCA guidelines on the best method of killing a lobster humanely), and cured and preserved fish.

She was not hugely enthusiastic about the British favourite, cod. 'You can do a number of things with fresh cod, it just depends whether it is worth it.' Much better to try a fish such as turbot. Standing in the market in France one Wednesday afternoon, they look at a beautiful turbot that was too big for their largest pan. But Madame Soarès promises to cut them a fillet and give them a recipe.

'In Madame Soarès' hands we are as spineless as squid; she treats us like gentle barbarians who need to be shown the light, and to be pushed a little for their own good. We watched her remove a large section from the majestic creature, then shape two pieces from it of exactly the right size. "Now," she said, leaning forward earnestly, "this is what you do."'

To encourage her readers to experiment, the back of the book contains a glossary of fish names with regional or unfamiliar alternatives. Jane was determined that her readers should feel her own enthusiasm for fish beyond the everyday cod and fish fingers.

In 1974 Jane decided to tackle English food. European cookery was fast becoming fashionable but home-grown food and recipes were still not taken seriously. Jane changed all that and won the Glenfiddich Cookery Writer of the Year award for her book, *English Food*.

She was very keen on keeping up traditional skills and championing the small producer. Indeed, another of her books, *The Observer Guide to British Cookery*, is a panoramic tour of Britain, complete with lists and photographs of what the best products are from each region and where they can be bought.

Jane was not just a traditionalist, looking back to some imaginary golden past: although she was certainly fascinated by the history and pedigree of food, she was grateful for modern gadgets as Sophie recalls, 'She was not somebody who said you must pound your paste in a pestle and mortar because that's the way it has always been done, she loved her processor. It was not the sort of blinkered, "You must do the traditional thing", or that it's a sin to adapt something for modern tastes. I think in the last few years of her life she was enchanted by new ideas and always longing to learn about modern things without losing sight of what is good from our past.'

In her later years she had become enthusiastic about the possibilities of the microwave, rather than dismissing it as vulgar, as many foodwriters had done. 'Her intellectual approach does not mean that you produce something that's dry and tedious and out of reach of people', Sophie explains. 'Intellectualism is not about élitism.' She also hated things being reduced to their lowest common denominator, especially the modern notion of quick and easy cookery, '. . . which is not to say she did not realize people have jobs and that they cannot spend all day, every day, cooking, but she did not see why quick and easy had to exclude anything else.'

Jane revised *English Food* just before her death, for the edition published in 1992. In a previous revision in 1979, Jane considered the changes over the five years that had elapsed and came to a pessimistic conclusion. In the feverishly obsessive hunt for recipes and keys to instant success, she felt we had lost sight of the importance of prime ingredients.

'The English like the Americans, are always demanding "recipes". And cookery writers like myself provide them. I am lucky in working mainly for a paper that allows me enough space to hint at the fact that words such as apple, cheese, bread are meaningless: that for good food one needs to understand that a Cox's Orange Pippin in a pie will give you a quite different result from a Bramley; that for a good cheese sauce Parmesan must be used because English hard cheeses will put too much fat into the sauce before they can achieve the same intensity of flavour; that sliced bread and frozen poultry are not worth buying – ever.'

Sophie Grigson believes that although Jane had to be more precise in her recipes than she might have wanted to be in an ideal world, 'she falls somewhere between that camp of the very loose recipes which belong to a slightly earlier time in this century of food writing and the modern-day camp where recipes have to be spelt out to the last grain of salt, which is not what cooking is really about.'

Although precise in her recipes, Jane did not believe that cooking is like mathematics, that the exact following of a recipe will produce a perfect dish. Food is much too important to be quantified in that way, it's much more of an art. One point that is striking in Jane's writing, both in her historical anecdotes and in her recipes, is her willingness to credit her sources. She will always say this is so and so's recipe, unlike too many foodwriters who skate over the fact that they have borrowed the recipe from elsewhere.

The reason her column and books were so successful is that she managed to convey the feeling that the reader was having a real conversation with her about food, and that she had picked up this nugget of information that she thought one might find interesting. In her book *The Mushroom Feast*, for example, published in 1975, she considered the question of aphrodisiacs with particular reference to truffles.

'It could quite reasonably be argued that any finely prepared meal, well-chosen dishes, beautifully cooked, discreetly served, with the right wines and so on, has a softening effect. Certainly I would expect the provider of truffles to gain his point more rapidly – all other things being equal – than the provider of panhaggerty or shepherd's pie. Or of haggis and bashed neeps, however abundant the whisky. More than that cannot be claimed, I think, for any food. But if you wish to make the experiment here are some of Monsieur Oliver's suggestions . . . '

When Jane became an established writer, she developed a routine of work. As Geoffrey Grigson, who was more than twenty years her senior, got older and his health began to fail, he needed more looking after. She tended to get up early in the morning and try to get a good bit of writing out of the way before he surfaced. After breakfast with him she would go back to her room. Sophie remembers, 'she was disciplined as a writer but as a family we always stopped for lunch, we always stopped for supper, and somehow she always managed to get lunch and supper on the table.'

A look at Jane Grigson's bibliography – and there are eleven books published – shows that she was not afraid to tackle the larger subjects. But she does them with a fresh tone that makes the reader feel she or he has never read about vegetables or fish before. The combination of serious academic work with a zest and enthusiasm for the subject shows that Jane is taking the subject and the reader seriously. None of her books has the thrown-together appearance of so many modern cookery books, which seem to have been produced by committee.

In 1978 she published one of her great classics, *Jane Grigson's Vegetable Book*, which won her the Glenfiddich Writer of the Year Award and the André Simon Memorial Fund Book Award. In the introduction Jane paid tribute to Elizabeth David, '. . . who championed vegetables in their own right, not just as adjuncts to meat'. But she then goes on to lament the fact that while we can now buy exotic vegetables freely, native vegetables like seakale or even fresh spinach remain difficult to find. The solution, she says, is to grow our own. Every house could have a selection of vegetables grown for flavour and interest.

'Marmande and plum tomatoes in pots, herbs in window boxes, courgettes and squashes trailed round the doors. Inside, there could be aubergine, pepper, chilli and basil plants on the windowsill, jars of sprouting seeds, dishes of mustard and cress, with mushroom buckets and blanching chicory in the dark of broom and airing cupboards. In my most optimistic moments, I see every town ringed again with small gardens, nurseries, allotments, greenhouses, orchards, as it was in the past, as assertion of delight and human scale.'

Sophie remembers her mother's first culinary encounter with an artichoke. Jane's own mother had come down to visit when she was in her twenties and first living in London. They had come across some artichokes and they bought some and took them home.

'They worked out that you probably had to boil it, so they boiled it, and prodded it and it seemed to be done, and then they had to work out how to eat it. And I can remember my mother saying my grandmother and she were choking on bits of the choke because they hadn't realized you had to take them out!'

That natural curiosity which she seemed to get from her own mother became one of her guiding principles. 'If you see something on a menu you've never eaten, eat it; if you see something in a shop you've never seen before, buy it.'

Jane loved doing the research for her books and was fascinated by historical figures. When she wrote her book *Food with the Famous*, published in 1979, those two interests came together, giving her a chance to re-read authors that she loved, to really examine them, to try to get to know them better as human beings and to understand them through food. The book was one of her favourites and had come about as a result of a reader's inquiry about the white soup in Jane Austen's *Pride and Prejudice*.

Food with the Famous reads like a conversation down the centuries with some of the great writers on food from Parson Woodford, Thomas Jefferson to Proust and Zola. Sophie explains: 'What was important to her is that food is part of social exchange. All those people saw food as the stuff that brings together people in the most natural of ways, that a table full of people sitting around and eating together is perhaps one of the best things in life.'

In her foreword to the book, Claudia Roden wrote, 'For myself and other cookery writers she represents an inspiration, a spur to excel, a standard to aim at. She elevated the profession and made it worth being in. It is a joy to catch a glimpse of Dumas cooking bare-chested and singing with Courbet . . . and to hear bits of gossip – the novelist Daudet comparing a hazel hen he had eaten at Zola's with "the scented flesh of an old tart marinaded in a bidet"; the false rumours that Dumas was all talk, all eat and could not boil an egg.'

Having tackled vegetables, the logical sequel was fruit. *Jane Grigson's Fruit Book*, published in 1982, again won her both the Glenfiddich Writer of the Year Award and the André Simon Memorial Fund Book Award. 'This special feeling towards fruit, its glory and abundance, is I would say universal.'

In the introduction Jane explains that during her childhood in Sunderland there were only apples, oranges and bananas in the shops and that this is why she has a special feeling for later glorious fruit memories, '... an orchard in Gloucester where old trees bent into tunnels and tresses of plums, a huge basket of strawberries that an uncle produced one day when we were visiting him in Worcestershire ...'

The index to this book shows Jane's usual comprehensive approach, running from A for Aam malai, indian mango with cream, to Z for Emile Zola, taking in the exotic and the ordinary along the way.

In the appendix she invites readers to compare the fruit availability in Britain with that in France. Having made a trip to the exclusive Fauchon on the Boulevard de la Madeleine in Paris, she was stunned by the varieties and quality available. To bring the point home she made a list dated 7 August 1979 which includes five varieties of grape, exotic fruit, wood strawberries and red bananas. 'I recommend anyone who is on holiday there to go and study what a food shop can be.'

On another visit Sophie recalls laughing with her mother at the sight of a very rich, chauffered Parisienne being driven to the doors of Fauchon, only to emerge with several tins of Bird's Eye Custard!

Jane was very clear when she felt a new dish in a restaurant did not work. In the introduction to the fruit book she describes eating in a smart restaurant in France. 'I tried a salad of lobster and white peaches: it looked pretty – yellowish-white and pink on a bed of deep, bright-green summer spinach – but tasted pointless. It was evident that lobster and peaches have little to say to each other.'

When her husband died in 1985, Jane was devastated, and Sophie says that her work was something that helped to keep her going. 'I think, for Jane, work was one of those really important supports in life, the thing that she could turn to and lose herself in time and time again.'

Later, as she was approaching her sixtieth birthday, she rang her daughter to say that although she had no intention of retiring she was not going to take on any more work that she didn't really enjoy, 'No more duties from now on, I'm just going to do what I really like doing, which is writing about things that fascinate me.'

It was a great joy to her that her daughter Sophie became a food writer too, despite having taken a degree in mathematics and never intending to write, especially about food. Long conversations on the telephone followed, 'She was tremendous, we used to talk for hours about what we were both writing and we would both bounce ideas off each other for articles.'

In the last years of Jane's life it seemed that her influence was finally bearing fruit. Britain appeared to be waking up to the fact that it had some of the best ingredients and traditions in the world and was in danger of losing them. Jane had always championed the small producer and suddenly they became fashionable and began to flourish. Successive health scares about chickens, milk and eggs made her very angry.

During the salmonella crisis in 1988 Jane made a speech at a meeting of the Guild of Food Writers that left a deep impression on everyone who witnessed it. Sophie remembers, 'It was one of the most phenomenal speeches because she found a passion rise in her, she suddenly realized that food was becoming something that one could actually change, after years of frustration.'

Colin Spencer remembered the speech in his tribute to her in the *Guardian*. 'Many of us will never forget her passionate denunciation of Government policy to the former Minister, John McGregor, over allowing salmonella into eggs. "I advise action, not just another research committee. You may get away with allowing agribusiness to poison our drinking water, it cannot get away with eggs." We would have marched behind her to the barricades.'

Jane later wrote of her anger and this new political role in the Guild magazine. 'I never thought that I would end up being forced into polemical food journalism as I have been during the last six months. It was one thing to crack away at the producers of watery tomatoes. Being frightened about what one can safely give a child to eat is something else. Having to avoid mayonnaise, scrambled eggs and omelettes, having to remove the peel of apples and potatoes when a young family comes to stay is appalling. There one has to take a stand. Knowing what we know, how can we be silent?'

Jane championed quality throughout her working life and did not see why we should not all have the best ingredients. 'Whenever I buy nuts these days they have little taste and look old and fatty, except for the occasional lucky find of young fresh walnuts. What has happened? Have growers taken to poor-tasting, high-yield varieties? Are nuts badly stored? Over-dried?' And then, characteristically, she goes on to make the reader's mouth water with a culinary memory of how nuts should taste. 'It seems to me that the last decent hazelnut I tasted was at Avellino, behind Vesuvius, many years ago; we had large, plump hazelnuts patiently toasted right through until they were a pale brown.' She not only knew how food should taste, she knew how to make the reader feel *she* or *he* knew how it should taste too.

Sophie recalls, 'Her attitude was you have to eat, so make it as much fun as you can. It seems a very fundamental and logical attitude to make your life just that much more pleasant.'

Reading the tributes after her death, it is striking that it is Jane Grigson the person, as well as the food writer of enormous influence, that shines through.

Paul Bailey in the *Daily Telegraph* recalled her famous laugh. 'Her laugh, like everything about her, was unique. It was like a hoot, starting low and getting higher and higher. It signified her delight in the living world, which never quite left her, even in those terrible months after her beloved husband Geoffrey had died.'

After her death, her daughter Sophie and a group of colleagues and friends set up the Jane Grigson Trust to create a lasting memorial to her in the form of a cookery library. Jane's own collection of cookery books forms the core of the library, which will eventually be built up to become the first and most comprehensive cookery library in the country. It seems a fitting tribute to someone who loved both books and food. Two sentences from *Good Things* seem to sum up her philosophy. 'I think food, its quality, its origins, its preparation, is something to be studied and thought about in the same way as any other aspect of existence . . . Somehow I can never quite suppress a manic optimism.'

CURRIED PARSNIP SOUP

SERVES 6–8

This is a wonderful soup, delicately flavoured yet satisfying. One doesn't immediately recognize the parsnip taste but no other root vegetable can produce such an excellent result.

1 large parsnip
100 g (4 oz) chopped onion
1 clove garlic, crushed
75 g (3 oz) butter
1 tablespoon flour
1 rounded teaspoon curry powder
1.2 litres (2 pints) hot beef stock
salt and pepper
150 ml (¼ pint) single cream
chives

Peel and slice the parsnip. Put the onion, parsnip and garlic into a heavy pan with the butter and cook for 10 minutes slowly with the lid on the pan. The vegetables must not brown, but gently absorb the butter. Add the flour and curry powder to take up the fat, and gradually incorporate the hot beef stock. Simmer until the parsnip is cooked.

Liquidise or push through a *mouli-légumes*. Return to the pan, correct seasoning with salt, pepper and a little more curry powder if liked (but be cautious: keep the flavour mild). Add the cream and a sprinkling of chopped chives. Serve with croûtons of bread fried in butter and oil.

Note: liquidised soup may need the further dilution of some extra stock, or some creamy milk.

White soup

Serves 6–8

We know that this was a popular soup of country-house entertaining not only from Jane Austen, but also from Eliza Acton who published her *Modern Cookery* in 1845. One of the two recipes she gives is headed *Westerfield white soup*, and at the end she adds this note: 'We have given this receipt without any variation from the original, as the soup made by it – of which we have often partaken – seemed always much approved by the guests of the hospitable country gentleman from whose family it was derived, and at whose well-arranged table it was very commonly served.'

Miss Acton grew up in Ipswich – she was born in 1799, which makes her a generation younger than Jane Austen – and seems to have shared in the kind of country society described in *Emma* or *Pride and Prejudice*. Westerfield is to the north of Ipswich, and Westerfield Hall, built in the seventeenth century, is still standing – perhaps this is the house where everyone enjoyed the white soup.

White soup goes back to the Middle Ages when many dishes were thickened with almonds or made with almond milk. Few people make it now, and I wondered why, until I read this sentence in Mrs Beeton, at the end of her recipe: 'A more economical version may be made by using common veal stock, and thickening with rice, flour and milk.' Horrible. The decline in English food through meanness is summed up in that remark.

100 g (4 oz) lean gammon, or a small bacon hock
meaty veal knuckle bone, chopped in three
onion and carrot, quartered
4 large stalks celery, sliced
1 teaspoon lightly crushed peppercorns
2 blades mace
2 level tablespoons salt
60 g (2 oz) blanched almonds

30 g (1 oz) white breadcrumbs
1 egg yolk
300 ml (10 fl oz) double or whipping cream
lemon juice
cayenne pepper

First make the basic veal stock by putting the bacon and veal bone into a large pan, and covering them with at least 2 litres of cold water (3¾ pt). Bring to the boil, skim, add a ladle of cold water, then skim again until clear. Add the vegetables, pepper, mace and 2 level tablespoons of salt. Keep the pan at a bare simmer for 4 hours. Strain, chill overnight and remove any fat from the jellied stock (the soup debris can be boiled up again with more water for a secondary stock for other dishes).

Heat the first stock, and boil it down to 1½ litres (2½ pt). Put almonds and bread into a blender, adding some of the stock, so that you can liquidise them to a smooth paste. Strain into the remaining stock, pushing through as much as you can – this is quite easy after liquidising the almonds and bread, but it helps to make the soup smoother. Beat the egg yolk with the cream and add that to the soup. If possible leave for 2–3 hours, as the flavour develops better with a rest of this kind. Reheat, keeping the soup well below boiling point. Add lemon and cayenne to enhance the flavour.

Serve with small croûtons of bread fried in butter. Or with 30 g (1 oz) blanched almonds cut into strips – this was the garnish of Miss Acton's Westerfield soup, but writing twenty-five years later she added that almond spikes could be suppressed, as they were 'unsuited to the preparation, and also to the taste of the present day'.

Boiled vermicelli or macaroni was also added on occasion, but this I think is unsuited to our modern tastes. We should prefer almonds or croûtons.

TOMATO AND OATMEAL TART

SERVES 4–6

Savoury tarts, so-called '*quiches*' that would make a chef from Lorraine pallid with outrage, have become a cliché of institutional catering. This recipe makes no claims at all to being a *quiche*. I was trying out oatmeal pastry and wanted to work out a good filling that would be complemented by its rough crispness. The secret is to make a good thick reduction of the tomatoes and onion, with a fiery seasoning to give the whole thing lightness.

FOR THE PASTRY:

125 g (4 oz) plain flour
125 g (4 oz) rolled oats
a good pinch salt
125 g (4 oz) butter or lard, or both mixed
1 large egg, beaten

FOR THE FILLING:

1 medium to large onion, chopped
1 large clove garlic, chopped
50 g (2 oz) butter
1 medium tin (400 g/14 oz) tomatoes
1 large egg
single or whipping cream
1 heaped tablespoon grated Parmesan cheese
1 teaspoon harissa, or chilli sauce, or 1 small seeded chilli, or cayenne pepper
60 g (2 oz) Cheddar cheese, grated

Make the pastry in the usual way and use it to line a 20–30 cm (8–9 in) tart tin with a removable base. Put it in the larder or fridge to rest while you make the filling.

Cook the onion and garlic until soft in the butter, without browning them. Tip in the tomatoes with their juice (and the small chilli, if used: chop it first). Boil hard until fairly thick and not at all watery. Meanwhile break the egg into a measuring jug and bring it up to 150 ml ($\frac{1}{4}$ pt) with the cream, mixing them thoroughly together. At this point switch on the oven to 190°C, 375°F or Gas Mark 5 and put a baking sheet on to the centre shelf to heat up at the same time.

When the tomato mixture is nicely thick, remove it from the heat. Stir in the cheeses, then the egg and cream. If you have not used a chilli, stir in the harissa (which I think is best) or chilli sauce or cayenne pepper; do this gradually, to taste. Add more if you think the mixture could be hotter, and a little salt.

When the oven is at the right heat, turn the tomato mixture into the pastry case and use the trimmings of pastry to make a simple lattice. Or sprinkle the top with some grated Cheddar cheese and breadcrumbs. Put the tart on to the heated baking sheet and leave for 30 minutes, or a little longer. Serve straight from the oven, or warm, with a green salad.

TURBOT AU POIVRE

SERVES 6

Although *steak au poivre* has now become a national dish, in England at least, we have not yet followed the French in cooking fish by the same method. It also works extremely well for firm steaks of halibut, cod, tunny or monkfish. Surprisingly the strong pepperiness does not overwhelm the delicate flavour of fish.

6 × 2½ cm (1 in) turbot steaks
salt
2 heaped tablespoons peppercorns
1 rounded tablespoon flour
1 tablespoon oil
100 g (4 oz) unsalted butter
50 g (2 oz) brandy
50 ml (2 fl oz) port
150 ml (¼ pt) light beef or veal stock
150 ml (¼ pt) double cream

Salt the fish steaks. Crush the peppercorns coarsely, and mix with the flour (more pepper can be used, if you like). Coat the fish with this mixture. Brown it lightly in oil plus 50 g (2 oz) of the butter, then lower the heat until the fish is almost cooked and just beginning to part from the bone. Flame with brandy, deglaze with port. Pour in the stock. Remove the fish to a hot serving plate when it is *just* cooked.

Boil the pan juices down slightly, stir in the cream and continue to boil until the sauce is rich and thick. Correct the seasoning, stir in remaining butter and pour round the fish. Serve very hot with boiled potatoes.

One of the best fish recipes.

STRAWBERRY FRITTERS

Beignets aux fraises

One evening in Paris, we went to the Escargot restaurant in the rue Montorgeuil, in search of snails of course, and of Montreuil peaches. I did not expect to find anything special about the strawberry fritters which I chose out of curiosity for dessert. It had been a good meal, in black and red surroundings of past elegance, with a close friend. Those fritters were to be the fault, the way Chinese and Japanese potters deliberately put a fault into their vases to make them human. But I was not allowed my fault after all. The fritters were perfection, the batter crisp, the strawberry inside firm but meltingly delicious. Even the *crème anglaise* was right.

What an original idea, strawberry fritters! But is there ever an original idea in cookery? Eight months later, I came across a recipe for them in an 1810 translation into French of an English cookery book, *Le Cuisinier Anglais Universel ou le Nec plus Ultra de la Gourmandise*, by F. Collingwood and J. Woollams.

The Escargot fritters, half a dozen, were served in the centre of a large plate with a thin custard covering the base. A good combination, so long as you make the custard of eggs and milk, or milk and cream. Pour it on to each plate and leave in a cool place.

Sort out and hull six fine strawberries for each person. Make a batter with:

125 g (4 oz) flour
¼ teaspoon salt
grated peel of half a lemon
1 tablespoon white wine
2 egg yolks
enough water to make a single cream consistency

Just before cooking the fritters, stir in a tablespoon of oil and 2 egg whites stiffly beaten.

Spear the hulled strawberries, one by one, with a skewer, or two-pronged fork, dip into the batter and then into deep-frying clean oil, preheated to 385°F (195°C). Cook about six at a time. You can keep them warm in the oven, but it is better to serve people straight from the pan even if they do have to eat seriatim. That way, the batter stays crisp.

CLAUDIA RODEN

Sheep's Eyes and Testicles

When Claudia Roden first came to Britain to go to boarding school, she got the shock of her life. 'It was just the most terrible culture clash. I came from an extended and close family which was very warm and lively and somehow to come to an English public school where most of the girls were riding and being presented to the Queen, it was as though I was on another planet.'

That other planet eventually became her home and the base from which she has written books on Middle Eastern food that have transformed Western attitudes to the cuisines of the Middle East. In 1992 she won the prestigious Glenfiddich Food Writer of the Year Award.

Claudia Roden's approach to food is more one of a cultural anthropologist than of a straightforward food writer. As a child in Egypt she was surrounded by the sights and smells of mixed cultures and this cultural interest has remained. Born into a Jewish family in Egypt, she considers her heart, or at least her style of cooking, to belong in a great part to a place that she has never seen, Aleppo in Syria.

'My father's side and my grandfather on my mother's side came from Aleppo and although my father, who is now 94, was born in Egypt, he was conceived in Syria. Despite that, he and I identify as Aleppo Jews: even though we have never been there our food habits come from Aleppo. It is so funny that in a way Jews think of their food as identity, and actually their identity has come from what has been their enemy now for many years!'

Claudia did not cook in her childhood, there were cooks to do that, but she observed and absorbed a cultural attitude to food that has remained with her ever since. Food was an important part of life from an early stage. 'We were a community that was very hospitable and people spent a long time looking for things that tasted good. Most of our pleasures were visiting – visiting relatives, visiting friends – and food, of course, was a major thing because hospitality was part of the traditions.'

Claudia's comfortable home in north London reflects those traditions. Life is centred round the open-plan kitchen and dining room with long tables and lots of chairs – clearly a place where large groups gather regularly. As she makes us a pot of strong, black coffee, we chat and exchange gossip about the food world. She is the sort of person you feel you have always known and conversation flows easily.

In many ways her upbringing was the very traditional one of the Middle Eastern educated woman. She was sent to boarding school in England, which she hated so much that she threatened to throw herself in the river if her parents did not take her away! She was then sent to the Lycée Héleñe Boucher in Paris which she remembers with affection.

At the *lycée*, like children everywhere, girls would dare each other to concoct and eat the most revolting mixtures of food, such as jam and mustard. But it was also taken for granted that meals were taken seriously. 'We would get a three-course meal. It started with something like radishes or some salami. There was style and ceremony and we were made to feel that it was all worthwhile and we would enjoy eating. We would get wine, watered down, and beer in the evening.'

After the *lycée*, Claudia studied art at St Martin's School of Art in London and became a painter. She married and settled in London and had three children. 'I had very much been brought up to feel I should be a mother and a good mother was what I wanted to be most of all in the world. Because, like a lot of Middle Eastern women, the idea is that you are there as a person who gives pleasure, to give joy to others and you are supposed to be the sunshine of the home.'

Claudia started writing about food as a way of holding on to a lost heritage. Her world had disappeared when her family and the whole Jewish community left Egypt after the Suez crisis in 1956. As they dispersed throughout Europe and the Americas, relatives and friends often stopped off at her parents' house in London. At those get togethers food took on the symbolic importance of the lost homeland. 'After asking how everybody was in the different countries and hearing all the gossip, people would start saying, "I found this recipe," and recipes came to seem almost the most important thing that we had lost.'

The loss of the homeland and the knowledge that they could never return involved much pain. Talking about the old days and the great meals somehow eased the nostalgia. The natural impulse to record the community's existence seemed to have found its expression in food. But the traditions of food had been handed down orally, no one ever wrote a recipe down, and so Claudia realized that a part of her people's culture would soon be lost. Collecting the recipes became a means of combating the pain of exile, not only for herself but for her whole community.

Claudia began to research the subject, collecting recipes from relatives passing through London and writing off to fellow exiles all over the world. The word quickly spread and she began to receive letters with detailed instructions for particular recipes.

'The search itself was part of the excitement for me – to find the woman who did the best whatever – and I had masses and masses of letters. People would write to tell me how to salt smoked cod roe and to dry it and they would write a three-page letter saying, "I put it on this shelf and then I put it on another shelf." I would never have been able to gather recipes in

Egypt because everyone there guarded their recipes jealously. Women were very competitive.'

The recipes had become a code for the exiles, a way of checking on their past and re-living it in the present. Strangers would meet, discover they came from the same part of the world, and exchange anecdotes about food. 'Somebody would say, "I was in the queue in the cinema in Paris and I met the man who owns the restaurant in Helipolis and he told me how to make this ice-cream," and so the recipes became like the most precious gift to pass on.'

With three young children it had become difficult for Claudia to continue to paint and the idea of publishing the recipes gradually came to her. An unknown mentor intervened – Elizabeth David.

'I didn't know anybody who used Elizabeth David's books, but I was enthralled by her. I think she gave us so much when we came, her books were the only places where we found recipes we wanted to cook, in the sense that it was the familiar things we hankered for.'

In fact, it was a phrase in one of Elizabeth David's books that persuaded Claudia Roden to publish all the recipes she had been collecting: 'In one of the editions of her Mediterranean book she gave a lot of Middle Eastern recipes and she said, "This is the tip of the iceberg, somebody has got to go on and look." And that phrase made me decide that was what I had to do.'

Food was not fashionable in those days and her English friends were horrified that she should give up painting to write a cookbook, especially a Middle Eastern cookbook. 'There was so much contempt about what people ate in that part of the world. It sounded disgusting to so many people – "Isn't it all sheep's eyes and testicles?"'

'So I felt, well, we have got to do a bit more than just write the recipe. We have to tell them the context because then they might be persuaded to try it. For example there is a dish of beans we adored which was *the* national dish eaten for breakfast. It was said to be as old as the Pharaohs. Street vendors put the beans in large copper pots with thin necks to cook overnight in the ashes of the fires used to heat the waters of public baths. To tell their stories was a way of making the recipes appealing.'

Claudia's need to gather the culinary traditions of her dispersed community developed into a wish to discover the cooking of other Middle Eastern countries. It is this necessity to get the details right and to encompass the whole subject that informs all Claudia Roden's writing. It is surprising that she ever finishes a book, she seems to be determined to write the definitive edition of whatever new culinary topic she is tackling. So whether her subject is coffee, picnics or Middle Eastern food, her books can be read as a comprehensive guide to the subject, not just consulted for recipes. When you go to look up one thing, you find yourself drawn to something else quite different on the page and then on to another page.

A Book of Middle Eastern Food was first published in 1968 and is an extraordinary introduction to that part of the world. It is packed full of proverbs and anecdotes as well as recipes and you feel you can smell the coriander in the markets, and hear the bustle of life. It contains many stories, like this one in the liver section.

'One day the Khoja bought some liver, and as he was carrying it away a friend met him and asked how he meant to cook it. "Oh as usual," answered he. "No!" said his friend, "there is a very nice way of doing it. Let me describe it to you."

'He did so but the Khoja said, "I cannot remember all these details. Write down the recipe on a piece of paper and I will cook the liver accordingly."

'His friend wrote it down and handed it to him. He was proceeding home deep in thought when a hawk pounced down, took the liver out of his hand and flew off with it. The Khoja, however, did not seem to mind, for he held out the recipe and called to the hawk, "What is the use of your doing that? You cannot enjoy it, because I have got the recipe here."'

It is a huge book with a historical introduction, advice on etiquette and technique, and hundreds of recipes from all across the Middle East. Astonishingly, in the original edition a great part of the recipes had never been published before.

One of the most unexpected elements of the book is the savoury pastries section, with its seemingly infinite number and range of different shapes and parcels. Claudia maintains that she has included just a small fraction of the number of possible pastries. Turkey is one of the most sophisticated pie and pastry countries where they have a specialist tradition with guilds of pie makers. When she visited Turkey with a Turkish food writer they went to a special pie maker in one of the suburbs around the Bosporus. 'My companion said I must listen to him and the way he cut the pie. He made a song by chopping and he had his special tune. This was the tune of that particular pie.'

Middle Eastern food is indeed not just sheep's eyes and testicles. Claudia Roden shows us all the delicate flavours of the region's specialities. She describes Middle Eastern food as 'elaborate but easy . . . every vegetable is stuffed, everything is wrapped up in leaves and there is a long slow cooking – in those societies where women did not work, they spent a lot of time cooking together and enjoying the company – but there are also many simple, quick and easy things and there aren't the French sauces or the trickiness of a soufflé. You can't fail.'

The food of the Middle East has been an influential one since ancient times and it is appropriate that, through her book on the Middle East, Claudia Roden should have continued those traditions of influence and change.

It was during the establishment of the great Persian Empire of *c.* 500 BC that the character and style of Middle Eastern food was born. 'It is in the Persia of the Sassanid period (third to seventh century AD) that it blossomed. The rich and sophisticated cuisines of the different empires, Persian, Ottoman and Islamic, influenced the development of European cuisine. (The Arabs, for example, spent 700 years in Spain.) Although we in the West have only recently rediscovered them, these are societies well-known for the importance they attached to the pleasures of the table.'

It is hard to imagine now that when the book was published in 1968 it was still difficult to find simple ingredients such as peppers and aubergines in Britain. The increasing availability of more exotic ingredients and the explosion in the cheap package holiday market has made people more adventurous in their cookery and more willing to try out recipes at home that they have tasted abroad. But this was not always the case.

When Claudia Roden was a young housewife thirty years ago, the subject of food in Britain was almost taboo and she found herself caught between two cultures. On the one hand her mother would phone her every day to discuss the planning of their meals and to talk in detail about the best way to cook a fish or some lentils. On the other hand her British neighbours had a very different approach. 'I would ask my neighbours every day, "What are you making tonight?", and they would look in horror as though I was talking about sex and money. I mean they were absolutely horrified and sometimes people would say, "Oh, I shall just give them bangers and mash, they're not getting anything else." They did not want to appear that they cared what their family was going to eat.'

In the 1960s and early 1970s food was not a fashionable subject in Britain. To someone raised in Middle Eastern traditions of hospitality and enjoyment of food, the British approach seemed immensely strange. What is more, the attitude to food seemed to permeate the whole society.

'There was this furtiveness about eating, I remember. We would go on a train and people would come out with this little box of sandwiches and then they would put their hand in front of their mouth and bring the sandwich up and eat it, so that no one could see what they were eating. And you wondered what was in their sandwich! But I think now there has been a complete change.'

That change is certainly partly due to food writers such as Claudia

Roden who by their infectious enthusiasm have encouraged their readers to re-evaluate their feelings about food.

Collecting recipes for the book on Middle Eastern food involved translating the informality and expertise of the East to the more rigid structures of the West. 'Most of these people explained in the minutest detail the washing and handling of ingredients, the feel, the smell and the colour of the food – but usually omitted quantities, weights and cooking times.'

'I learnt that to some "leave it a minute" meant an hour, that "five spoonfuls" was in order to make a round figure or because five was for them a lucky number and that a pinch could be anything from an eighth of a teaspoon to a heaped tablespoon. People did not have watches or weights – I never ever saw anybody weigh an ingredient – and I think in some ways it is more correct not to be precise.'

The close understanding of food made recipes superfluous, it was all about look and smell and touch. The cook would be so close to her ingredients and the way the final product should look that a formal recipe just was not appropriate.

'They would say, for instance, when you make this dough, put as much flour as it takes and then they would tell you what the finished product should feel like. It would be either like grains of wet sand or else it would be, "If you touch the lobe of your ear with your finger while touching the dough, that's how it should feel, that kind of softness."'

Claudia herself believes that, when working with dough, no two lots of flour are the same, even from the same field in different years, because the weather and other variables will make each harvest different. But, of course, if you are writing a book of recipes for people unfamiliar with those culinary traditions, precise and accurate recipes are vital. Stroking your earlobe is not quite precise enough for the British obsession with detail!

Claudia Roden has tried to instil the students in her cookery classes with Middle Eastern attitudes. She gets them to trust their own taste and feelings about food rather than relying too heavily on recipes and authority.

So when students ask how much of a particular ingredient to put in she simply tells *them* to decide for themselves and nearly always the final product is very close to the original recipe. But when she shows them the recipe afterwards, they are invariably taken aback by quite how close they had been to the original, just by trusting their own judgement.

But when it comes to writing Claudia has an almost fanatical attention to detail and gives all the possible information so that nothing can go wrong. She is concerned with authenticity and approaches each book as a scholarly enterprise. This seems to be partly compensation for the university education she never had as it was not considered appropriate for girls of her background to study too much.

'I have always liked to see what is behind things, to have a social look at things, even politically there is always a reason why food has come into a country, which can be to do with a peasant's life or people migrating, and I want to find the secret, it becomes a bit of a thriller.'

Claudia Roden sits back and sips at the strong, black coffee that she has made, a big pot that gradually empties as we talk. She laughs at her own tendency to overdo the research, and the impatience of publishers who have to restrain her enthusiasm in order to prevent the books becoming lifetime works. In many ways she is a food detective, following up clues after a chance overheard remark, tracking down the truth, cataloguing the important anecdotes, wanting to find out the whole story. She is a natural talker, the sort of person people tell their life story to on buses – and she will probably prise out their favourite recipe from them too.

Her family do not always get as much fun out of it as she does though. 'In New York I tracked down one of the few restaurateurs of Cairo who is a Syrian Jew who came to Egypt and did things in Egypt in a Syrian manner. He was in Brooklyn and I went there with my daughter and I was enthralled, in a state of exaltation. And my daughter just thought, "Oh God, what a bore, we have come all this way, it took us two hours to get here, it is only another baklava,'' but for me I had always heard about Mansoura and there he was, Mansoura in Brooklyn, to find him again!'

A Book of Middle Eastern Food has become an important part of Claudia's life, it has been translated into many different languages and can be found throughout the Middle East. Indeed it is so successful that there are pirate copies throughout the Arab world. It has also been translated into Hebrew and is used by the Israeli army and kibbutzes. It gives her tremendous pleasure that the book is a bridge between communities which are traditionally hostile.

'I meet people who are Palestinians and Saudis and they feel immediately they can come and talk to me because they have used my book. It certainly is a very big bridge that you have been known to do something as intimate as that, you are writing about something that is very personal and that has become part of their everyday life. But I think there is also a downside, which is that it makes you a prisoner when you go to parties, that's all people want to talk about!'

The language of food is an international language which crosses cultural and religious barriers. These days there is much talk of Europe but women such as Claudia Roden show there are wider geographical loyalties. If she belongs anywhere it is to the Mediterranean basin. But then she is a typical product of the Middle East, a Jew brought up in Egypt with French as her first language, having a Yugoslavian nanny who spoke native Italian. Claudia was educated in Britain and France. It is often difficult for the British, obsessed with the idea of nationality, cut off by geographical boundaries, to understand someone with such diverse cross-cultural roots. Yet it is the very fact of having affinities with several countries and cultures without really belonging to any, that gives Claudia her particular insight and allows her to cross cultural divides.

When the BBC director Claire Brigstock approached Claudia to work on a new television series about cooking in seven Mediterranean countries she was worried that Claudia was too associated with the Middle East.

She laughs, 'I felt it was very strange because my home language was French and I was Italian-speaking, because of my nanny and also going to Italy a lot and then I am partly Spanish-speaking because Ladino [the ancient Spanish dialect of Sephardic Jews], was part of my background. How could I be more Mediterranean?'

Claudia persuaded the powers that be that she was the perfect person for what became the series *Mediterranean Cookery with Claudia Roden* (1987) and that it should be filmed abroad in the houses of ordinary people. Although not as clinically perfect as film in a studio, it had all the thrill and fascination of the real thing.

'I think the producer and director were a bit worried at first that people would be disgusted by the kitchens looking dirty or primitive, or they would not want to cook the food, but on the contrary the most primitive ones, it seems, were the most popular. Though I did get one or two people saying, "My God, that woman who was doing the *pastilla*, which was a big pigeon pie in Morocco, she was using a dustbin lid," and I said no, it was a lid, but not a dustbin lid.'

The series also taught viewers some valuable lessons about equipment and the simplicity of the great Mediterranean cuisines.

'Utensils were old and chipped and kitchens were small and simple. Even a grand Turkish lady had a most primitive kitchen. In a way it made it very intimate and it made people feel you don't really need to have every utensil and every labour-saving device. It can be as easy with just a spoon, a knife and one saucepan.'

Etiquette is very important in the Middle East. Tradition and strict rules govern the behaviour of both guest and host. The position of each person in the family is important and there are many niceties to observe which mingle tradition with superstition.

As a guest one is supposed to eat very little while the host is supposed to provide a huge amount of food. Showing ravenous hunger is considered impolite.

'It often ends up in a sort of fight, with the host trying to make you eat and you trying not to eat! So people eat before they go to a party, to stave off the hunger, so they will not appear too hungry when they get there.'

In contrast the traditional British buffet seems quite a scrum! 'It is a big shock when people from the Middle East come to England and go to a buffet and see everyone fighting to get to the food.'

The notion of the evil eye is also important, 'If you are hungry people are afraid you will put the evil eye on the food because you are so desperate to eat it! Women are also thought to have the evil eye more than men and they are often asked to eat first so that they do not put the evil eye on to the food.'

Although she thought the Middle Eastern book would be her last, Claudia found she was hooked on writing about food. 'It was my first book and I intended it to be the last, it was just a total labour of love. I felt the last thing I wanted to be was a professional cookery writer. But in the end two things happened. I got totally addicted to food, in a gastronomic way and also to what it can tell us about life and people. I am still fascinated.'

She also divorced and found herself bringing up her three children on her own. Working from home seemed a good way of combining the mothering that her culture considers so important with her blossoming food writing career.

Her next book, *Coffee*, was first published in 1977. It is written in the now familiar style, part historical study, part anecdote, part recipe, so that you close the book with the smells and tastes of coffee from different parts of the world lingering in the air. She describes in the introduction, her own coffee ritual as a child with her parents.

'Maria, our Yugoslav nanny and housekeeper, brought in a large brass tray ornately engraved in praise of Allah, on which were placed five small cups in delicate bone china with gold arabesques near the rim. A glass of water held a piece of ice chipped from the block in the ice box, and was scented with a drop of orange flower water. A small plate carried a pile of oriental *petits fours* filled with dates, pistachios or ground almonds. My father poured out the coffee from two small copper kanakas with much ceremony, carefully shaking his hand so as to drop a little of the much prized froth in each cup. We passed the water round, then drank the syrupy black brew in little sips and with much reverence.'

In 1981 she published *Picnic: the Complete Guide to Outdoor Food*, which takes us from the simple sandwich to instructions on how to build a successful campfire. Claudia stresses the practical approach and is also keen to show us traditions from other parts of the world.

Here Claudia recognizes another important influence in her work, Jane Grigson. 'It was her high literary standards and also her kindness. Everybody was involved with Jane, she helped us all. When I rang her to ask her advice about the picnic book she sent me a huge letter, with all sorts of pointers and trails to follow. Actually she was the one who talked to me about Chinese picnics and the Japanese – she said that was something to look into.'

Those pointers turned into an unusual chapter about graveyard banqueting in China. 'Feasting at the graveside is the happiest part of ancestor worship in China . . . Whole pigs are brought already boiled, or roasted and glazed to a beautiful brown, and when the family clan is a thousand people strong there may be as many as seventeen pigs, as well as cooked chickens and ducks, squid, duck eggs and green-yolked "hundred year eggs" preserved in ashes and lime.'

The television series on the Mediterranean led to a commission from the *Sunday Times Magazine* to write a series, 'The Taste of Italy' which in turn led to another book, *The Food of Italy*, published in 1989. She travelled throughout Italy from region to region and from town to town *à l'aventure*. Everyone she met, chefs, food professionals, people on buses and trains, were hugely enthusiastic about her project. 'You can feel the love of food which is a kind of *joie de vivre*.' They were also extremely proud of their own regions and often scathing about other regions, suggesting that it was not really worth her while to visit anywhere else in the country!

'People were immensely helpful, they would invite me to go eating with their friends. And they would ask where I was going next, I would say I would be in the next region in two weeks and they would come and join me by train. There was this great wish to show me their food which, for me, was just wonderful and out of this world with happiness.'

She found that the Italians were very conscious of the danger of losing their food heritage because everything is changing so fast. But authentic regional foods are still hard to find in restaurants. One reason is that young people do not want to go out to restaurants to pay for food their grandmother still makes, so food fashions such as smoked salmon ravioli and seafood pasta with curry take over.

But now, with the death of a generation of grandmothers, and with younger women of the next generation keener to work than spend long hours in the kitchen, Italy is changing again. In Bologna, in northern Italy, there are special groups of enthusiasts who have banded together to preserve the quality and perfection of one dish, 'They go round in a big crowd of twenty or more, say, eating tortellini everywhere and saying no, this isn't right, this is how you make real tortellini.'

Claudia also believes that our attitudes to food in Britain have changed in the years she has been here. 'I think this thing of enjoying company, enjoying good food, enjoying wine, is not lost. I think possibly people now in the cities which are very fraught, like London, are feeling, "Look, we have lost too much", and food is a way of getting back some of the balance. People say that when they have come back from a heavy day in the office, the best relaxation is to start chopping an onion.'

Claudia's latest book on Jewish food is a selection of recipes from Jewish communities all over the world – a typically small and unambitious project! She has been working on it for many years, collecting, collating and amassing recipes, anecdotes and historical information. 'It is almost unending, it is really a lifetime's work: the more I do, the more I say I have to give up and not do any more because it's unending.'

The Jewish communities of the world each have their own very clear style which is defined not only by religious and ethnic differences but by geographical ones too – in India alone there are four different types of Jewish communities, each with their own separate and particular attitudes to food.

The particular mix of culture and food, a sort of gastronomic anthropology, suits Claudia Roden's style best. With her book of Jewish food she is also out to challenge our assumptions again. It is not all lox and bagels – although she has found a bakery in New York that makes forty different types of bagels, including ones with chocolate and cinnamon.

When Claudia, herself a Sephardic Jew, first came to England she did not think much of Ashkenazi Jewish food. While the Sephardic Jews are from Spain, Africa and the Middle East, Ashkenazi Jewish food is broadly the cooking of Eastern European Jews and probably the one with which most people in the West are familiar. It is also largely the type of food that was transported to America as the vast majority of Jewish immigrants to the United States were Ashkenazi Jews fleeing the successive pogroms and then the Holocaust.

'Ashkenazi food is actually very limited compared to the very wide range of Sephardic cooking. For historical reasons, what the Ashkenazi Jews call Jewish food is the same everywhere; whereas in Sephardic cooking, because people have only just left the homelands (and one of the reasons being they weren't persecuted in the same way and were not in ghettoes and were therefore more assimilated), their food is regional, totally different even town by town. I researched what the life of the Ashkenazi Jews was in the ninth and tenth centuries because that is when their food started crystallising.' No wonder her publishers were begging her to stop!

Claudia feels that in the West we need to understand that the most interesting cuisine comes from areas of the world which have a mix of cultures that have cross-fertilized one another over centuries.

Claudia finds herself an interpreter of the rich Middle Eastern mix where the pull of two communities, Arabic and Jewish, is perceived in a different way in the West. When Claudia Roden was interviewed by someone from a Jewish American magazine about her Middle Eastern book the journalist said, 'I cannot believe that Jews ate Arab food!' Claudia Roden laughs at the complete misunderstanding such a remark indicates, 'I said, look, it was our food just as much.'

When Claudia Roden met an orthodox Jew from the Hassidic community in New York, she found another strange mix of influences. They ate every type of food, Chinese, Thai, Japanese, prepared according to the kosher laws. 'She said we are spiritually Jewish, we are not gastronomic Jews, we do not care what the Poles ate in the eighteenth century, we cook anything because we are Jews through and through.'

Claudia laughs at the contrast with her own community, '. . . and there we are, eating Aleppo Syrian food out of identity as Jews, and with the Syrians at war with Israel!'

She sees food writing as a new and developing field. 'You can tie it to all types of disciplines, anthropologists to anthropology, sociologists to sociology, even to architecture. What kind of tables? What kind of professionals? I do feel unbelievably lucky but I pay for it in all the hard work. For instance, I hate working alone, spending a lot of time in front of the computer or working out recipes.'

While her approach to research and writing is detailed and methodical, Claudia's natural inclination when it comes to recipes is that of her past.

'I would much rather just cook and not weigh or anything but I have never sent in a recipe I have not tried and recorded myself. I have a perfectionist view of the recipe: if they do not work you have to re-try, and there is an enormous amount of finicky work which is not joy. I mean eating is joy and cooking is joy but measuring is not and certainly writing it all up is horribly boring but it has to be done!'

MOROCCAN CIGARS

These are called *briouats* in Morocco, where they are made with paper-thin pancakes called *ouarka*, but *fila* makes an easy and perfect substitute. They are elegant party fare that you can make by the hundred (perhaps with the help of your children) and keep uncooked in the freezer. In Morocco they are fried but it is much easier and just as good to bake them.

One of my favourite fillings is meat. For 500 g (1 lb), prepare the following minced meat filling:

1 medium onion, finely chopped
4 tablespoons oil
750 g (1½ lb) lean minced beef or lamb
2 teaspoons cinnamon
½ teaspoon allspice
¼ teaspoon ginger
salt and pepper
pinch of cayenne pepper or, more optionally, a bunch of parsley, finely chopped, or a bunch of fresh coriander, finely chopped (or both)
5 eggs
180 g (6 oz) butter, melted

Soften the onion in the oil. Add the meat and crush it with a fork. Add seasonings and spices and cook, stirring with a wooden spoon for 10 to 15 minutes until the meat is done. Add the herbs. Lightly beat the eggs in a bowl and pour them over the meat. Cook gently, stirring all the time, for a minute or so until the eggs have set to a creamy consistency. Let the filling cool. Add more spices and pepper if you like.

To roll the cigars: cut each sheet of *fila* into three rectangles and put them together in a pile so that they do not dry out. Brush very lightly with melted butter.

Put a tablespoon of filling along one of the short edges, roll the *fila* over it, tuck the ends in to stop the filling falling out, then continue to roll up like a cigar. Place side by side on a greased tray, brush with melted butter and bake in a preheated slow oven (150°C/300°F/Mark 2) for 30 minutes or until golden. Serve very hot.

PESCE ALLA MARINARA

Fish in tomato sauce

SERVES 4

I like this one because it is so simple.

2 cloves garlic, chopped
4 tablespoons olive oil
4 medium tomatoes, peeled, seeded and chopped
salt and pepper
a bunch of parsley, finely chopped
1 kg (2 lb) fish (use small sea bass or other white fish such as monkfish, hake, halibut, skate and cod, whole or cut into steaks)

Heat the garlic in the oil in a large pan. Add the tomatoes, salt and pepper and cook for 10 minutes until the sauce is reduced. Add 300 ml ($\frac{1}{2}$ pint) of water and the parsley and cook 5 minutes longer.

Put the fish in and simmer gently with a lid on until it is done – from 4 minutes for fish steak to about 15 minutes for monkfish tails. The flesh should just begin to flake from the bone.

FERAKH MAAMER

Poussin with Couscous Stuffing

SERVES 4

The glittering Moroccan dynasties of the Almoravides, the Almohades and the Merenides, whose realm stretched over North Africa and a great part of Spain for centuries, produced a prestigious cuisine. Young spring chickens (poussins) stuffed with almondy couscous cooked in a honeyed sauce are one of the great delicacies of Morocco. They are served at feasts and celebrations presented on great platters around a mountain of extra stuffing. If you want to make it easier for yourself, do not stuff the birds but prepare and serve the stuffing separately. It will be just as spectacular and just as delicious, and, since the only couscous available here is pre-cooked, nothing could be easier.

The stuffing is sweet, characteristic of the cooking of Fez which boasts the dominant and most refined cuisine of the country. This recipe uses less sugar than they do in Fez where it is added by the glassful. You can leave it out altogether if you prefer but I recommend you try it.

4 poussins
3 tablespoons butter or sunflower oil
1–2 large onions, grated
2 garlic cloves, crushed
2 teaspoons cinnamon
¼ teaspoon ginger
½ teaspoon saffron-coloured powder
salt
2 tablespoons honey

For the stuffing:

500 g (1 lb) pre-cooked couscous
salt
1–2 tablespoons caster sugar
3 tablespoons sunflower oil
1½ teaspoons cinnamon
2 tablespoons orange blossom water
3 tablespoons raisins, soaked in warm water for 10 minutes
125 g (4 oz) blanched almonds

To prepare the stuffing, moisten the couscous with a little less than its volume of salted water – about 600 ml (1 pint). Stir well so that it is evenly absorbed. After about 5 minutes, stir in the sugar, 2 tablespoons of the oil, the cinnamon and the orange blossom water. Drain the raisins and add them. Fry the almonds in the remaining oil, coarsely chop them and stir them into the stuffing.

Fill each poussin with about 3 tablespoons of stuffing. They should not be too tightly packed or the stuffing may burst out. Sew up the skin at both ends using cotton thread (or use cocktail sticks) so that it overlaps the openings. Reserve the remaining stuffing.

In a wide and heavy saucepan put the butter or oil, the onions, garlic, cinnamon, ginger, saffron and salt. Add 300 ml (10 fl oz) water and the stuffed poussins.

Simmer gently, covered, for about 30 minutes or until the birds are tender, adding more water if necessary. Turn them over at least once, ending up breast down, so that they are well impregnated with the sauce and its flavours. Lift one out (to make a little room) and stir in the honey, then return the poussin to the pan and continue to cook until the flesh is at 'melting tenderness' and can be easily pulled off the bone.

Heat up the reserved stuffing in a saucepan, adding a little water if necessary until the grain is plump and tender. Be careful that it does not stick. Alternatively, heat it up in a covered dish in the oven.

To serve, make a little mountain of the stuffing on a platter and place the birds around it.

Variations

* Add 3 tablespoons coarsely chopped pistachios, a pinch each of ground cloves, allspice and nutmeg to the stuffing
* At the Hotel Merinides in Fez they stuff 1 large chicken and steam it in the top part of a couscousier, making the sauce separately.
* Baby pigeons (like the French *pigeonneaux*) are the traditional and favourite birds for this dish. Our own wood pigeons will not do.

FRÜCHTEPUDDING

Fruit pudding

SERVES 8

175 g (6 oz) white bread, crusts removed
600 ml (1 pint) milk
65 g (2½ oz) butter, softened
3 large eggs
65 g (2½ oz) almonds, finely chopped
100 g (4 oz) sugar
1 teaspoon cinnamon
zest of 2 lemons
2 lb (1 kg) fruit such as apple, pear, seedless grapes, cherries, peaches, apricots and plums, cubed

Break up the bread in a bowl and pour in the milk, working it in with your hands and crumbling the bread.

Beat the butter with the egg yolks then add the sugar, cinnamon and lemon zest and beat into the soaked bread. Beat the egg whites until stiff and fold them into the mixture. Then fold in the fruit (apples and pears should be peeled).

Pour into a wide oven dish and bake at 180°C, 350°F or Gas Mark 4 for over an hour, until firm and golden on top.

Serve hot or cold. The plums give a beautiful red colour where they touch the surface.

A PLATTER OF ROAST VEGETABLES

new recipe

SERVES 4

This recipe makes use of different kinds of vegetables besides the usual aubergines, peppers and onions. It is more a way of cooking by roasting in the oven than a recipe and it gives the vegetables a more intense flavour.

2 aubergines
4 red peppers
4 medium onions
salt
olive oil
450 g (1 lb) asparagus
a bunch of spring onions
250 g (8 oz) sugar snap peas
a large bunch of mixed herbs such as parsley, basil, coriander, dill

Put the aubergines, peppers and onions on a tray and roast in the hottest possible oven for about 30 minutes. Turn the peppers once so as to brown them all over and take them out when they are soft and browned and the skins blister. (They are usually done before the other vegetables.) Put them in a heavy-duty polythene bag and twist to close it tight. This helps to loosen the skins. Roast the aubergines and onions until they are very soft.

Peel the aubergines, peppers and onions while they are still warm and cut into ribbons, removing the seeds from the peppers first. Keep and strain the juices from the peppers to add to the dressing. Dress with salt and oil.

Trim the asparagus and spring onions and top and string the sugar snaps. Put them in another tray, sprinkle with oil and salt and roast for 10 minutes or until tender when you pierce them with a pointed knife.

Arrange all the vegetables together on a platter and sprinkle with the chopped herbs. Serve cold with bread.

PRUE LEITH

The Food Business

Dressed in full chef's whites complete with hat and checked trousers, Prue Leith gets down to business – tasting twenty-four identical three course meals in ninety minutes. Advanced students at her School of Food and Wine in Kensington have been toiling for the last four and a half hours for this, their final examination. As Prue inspects the first course, a diamond shaped puff pastry *feuilleté* filled with a mixture of scallops, prawns, plaice and scampi with spinach and *beurre blanc*, she exchanges remarks with Alex Floyd her fellow judge and chef at Leith's restaurant. With students safely out of earshot, her assessment of food and presentation is candid: 'horrid' describes the look of one set of lamb cutlets, although this is tempered by a 'very good' for the taste, and for the sauce made from bone stock. Then on to the vegetables, cooked to the students' own specifications, which range from thin slivers and slices of potato, carrot and courgette, to a 'delicious oniony carroty concoction' formed into an uneven but nicely textured round. For dessert, they dip the backs of teaspoons into the *crème anglaise* surrounding the coffee *bavarois* testing the consistency, and the rectangular *brioche* is sliced, sniffed and sampled. As the pair work their way around the tables, marking each individual component of each course, their comments are noted by one of the school's principals. The crucial test of this examination which students must pass to get their certificate, is whether the food is of saleable quality.

There is probably no one better able to judge food saleability than Prue Leith. Graduates from her school have been hired by top restaurants such as the Roux brothers' Le Gavroche, and Mosimann's, as well as Leith's restaurant itself. It opened in a blaze of publicity nearly twenty-five years ago, when Prue was something of a rarity – a female restaurateur. She well remembers meeting a top chef a couple of years later who informed her that women were banned from his kitchen as 'at a certain time of the month, they curdle the mayonnaise'. Now, over eighty per cent of her graduates are women, joining the increasing number of female chefs and restaurateurs in Britain.

Providing up-market food is only one element of an extraordinary success story which won her Businesswoman of the Year two years ago and an OBE in 1989. Committed to mass catering, she was responsible for introducing the brown bread sandwich to British Rail, and in London's Hyde Park, she provides not only three-course meals by the Serpentine but also ice-cream trolleys, snacks and sandwiches.

Sheer hard work combined with energy, enthusiasm and initiative has undoubtedly got Prue Leith where she is today. We talked early one morning in her small office above Leith's restaurant, lined with the most recent and the most classic cookery books. As usual, she was working to a deadline, knowing her afternoon would be spent judging at her school. Immediately after our interview she was dashing off to Hampton Court Palace where in the flower beds and formal gardens, her catering organization provides traditional English teas with scones, jams and clotted cream.

Food combined with beautiful surroundings has long been one of her great pleasures in life, since spending her childhood in South Africa in the 1950s. 'I was a greedy child and I can remember sitting on the beach thinking "I wonder if my brother's going to get the last Marie biscuit with butter on it,'' and I'd get anxious about whether my father would let us have a double Coke with ice-cream in it, called a Brown Cow, or whether we'd only be allowed a single one.' The whole family was extremely interested in food and food came to be associated with pleasurable occasions. 'My mother was pretty greedy too, and if she gave a party outside, or picnic, the food was always wonderful. I always associated good food with a good time, and I still do.' Her father was a director of a large chemical company and, as a treat, in her early teenage years she used to be taken out to dinner with him, without her mother and brothers. 'We used to go to a little downtown restaurant which seemed so sophisticated. They did Chicken in the Basket, which was delicious. I can remember pulling the chicken to bits and it seemed such a treat. When he introduced me to snails, I thought they were the most wonderful thing in the world.'

She was part of the privileged white middle class in South Africa employing black cooks, and never had any ambition to go into the kitchen. 'It just wasn't a career that jumped into the forefront of your mind. As my mother was an actress, I thought I'd be one too, it seemed glamorous.' She began training at Theatre School, then Art School, and then started a BA at university in Cape Town. 'I kept swopping and couldn't decide what I wanted to do. I was having a good time and not doing any work, so I kept saying this isn't the career for me. I now think that I could probably have done any of them if I'd really put myself into it.'

She became interested in French and persuaded her parents that, in order to do well at her latest subject, she needed to be immersed in the real thing not the second-hand French in Cape Town. Before beginning at the Sorbonne, she became an *au pair* for some first-hand experience of the language and stumbled across what was to be her real vocation. 'That was that. My employer just took so much trouble about meals. Every day was a treat, it wasn't just parties where food was special.' The two children aged six years and eighteen months had marvellous meals and ate the same as the adults but Prue was denied access to the kitchen. 'I wasn't even allowed to mix the dressing because the very fact that I spoke English guaranteed I would produce horrible food. She was absolutely right, of course. I didn't know anything.' But after six weeks with the family in Bayonne, Prue became hooked on the local ham, and *gâteau basque*, and the way the French approached the buying and preparation of food. 'My employer shopped in that really French way of cheese from one shop, meat from another, local specialities from another. She took a lot of trouble over very simple food.'

By the time Prue began her studies at the Sorbonne, she was already hankering after another change in direction and wanted to go to cookery school. Once again she approached her father, who suggested a holiday course first of all to make sure it was what she really wanted to do. She persuaded a friend from England to join her and they went to the Cordon Bleu school to enquire about the month-long course in July. All the arrangements were made in French and, after managing to say 'Combien?', Prue understood the course amounted to £80, which seemed a huge amount. 'I wrote to my father and after a great deal of battle he agreed. So Angela and I turned up on the first day with our knives and our little mop caps and aprons, only to discover that the £80 was only the deposit! So we couldn't do the course, as we couldn't have got the money.'

Being nineteen and in Paris with or without a cookery course was never going to be too much of a disaster and she laughs as she remembers how the pair soon found new interests. 'We were sitting in a café afterwards, and two fellas who were about the same age came and sat down with us. We became "enormously good friends" and so spent a month pretending to our parents we were at the Cordon Bleu while we were actually bumming around Paris!'

After spending some time as a waitress in a Parisian restaurant, she decided to pursue her cooking career in England and completed a six-week intensive course at the Cordon Bleu before applying for their advanced course. 'I thought that by now, having helped cook in family houses in France, having been an *au pair*, having got very interested and started reading books, that I was up to doing the advanced course. Over-confidence has ever been my problem!' The school required advanced students to have completed the previous Cordon Bleu courses, or to have worked in a restaurant. 'Of course, I said that I had worked in one in Paris, and they never asked me what I did there – which was washing up and carrying plates! So I did the advanced course and it was wonderful, they were such terrific teachers.'

Now with her own cookery school, Prue finds herself echoing the words of one of her teachers, Mrs Proctor, who originally trained at Joe Lyons. 'She knew how to do things like turning the ends of tomatoes – that had been cut off for sandwiches – into tomato paste. And she'd say things to me like, "What do you think you've got there, a hedge?" because I wouldn't chop the parsley quite fine enough. And I find myself saying to my own students now, "What's that, a hedge? Chop it finely, chop it finely".'

Ever confident, Prue and a friend leapt at the opportunity to cook professionally for a dinner party for the first time. The school had been rung up at short notice and as no teachers were available suggested two keen students might be interested, adding that the school took no responsibility for the results. So the two of them decided on a menu of egg mousse, roast pheasant, and hazelnut meringue cake with raspberries. 'I remember the meal very well, because it took us two days to cook, and we didn't even have to pluck the pheasants! We thought we'd done it absolutely brilliantly, and were so tired decided to take a taxi home.' But the journey from Hampstead cost 10 shillings, which left them with a net profit of two shillings and six pence for two solid days of work each – not a lot of money even in the 1960s. 'But it was a very good thing to have done, as it made me much more sympathetic to new people on their first day with us now. I always try to drill that into chefs now, trying to get them to remember their first day, how tired they were, how their legs ached. You're so anxious, you don't sleep the night before, and so you're tired before you arrive. You have to be sympathetic to the young.'

She persevered with other dinner party engagements, and, after finishing at the Cordon Bleu, took a job as a cook for a firm of solicitors in Whitehall. This was just the right size of job for a beginner; Prue had to cook lunch for three partners, three times a week. 'I started with the Cordon Bleu bible, a big pink book called the *Constance Spry Cookery Book*, and cooked my way from page one to the end.' Her employers were sympathetic to her efforts, even though the order of the book dictated what would be served up for lunch. 'I was very selfish, and busy educating myself, and I remember hitting the suet pudding chapter in the middle of summer. Eventually one of the directors said that, although they loved suet pudding, it was August and how about some strawberries and cream?'

Her employers though did get the benefit of her steady progress through the bible. Soon Prue was providing the catering for their daughters' weddings and for cocktail parties, eventually employing an assistant to help. Two years later, with a dozen partners in the firm, she decided to leave as cooking lunches had become a full-time job. She now had enough work to become self-employed and began her catering company, Leith's Good Food, from an Earls Court bedsit. Luckily, her landlady had no sense of smell but the game was up when she discovered a bath full of live lobsters.

The fledgling catering company took a giant step forwards when Prue moved from her bedsit to a small mews cottage in Paddington. With a proper kitchen she was able to cook food on her own premises instead of going to her clients' houses and she employed an assistant who theoretically could deliver lunch to offices while she cooked. 'When she arrived we had practically no work, so we used to make lampshades and I can remember painting the garage with her, which became the larder. And we played tennis a lot.' She makes it sound a haphazard existence but the company was steadily growing and in 1969 moved to her newly opened restaurant, Leith's.

'I thought this was very clever, since we were only going to open the restaurant at night, and so the kitchens could be used all day for outside catering. But I made a great mistake and it was absolute hell because the restaurant chef and the head cook of the catering company couldn't agree about who wasted the cream. Or the restaurant would suddenly be blitzed with customers, and the chefs would help themselves to the puddings that were for Madame's dinner party tomorrow. The arrangements only lasted six months.'

Opening the restaurant had been Prue's long-term goal since her days as a washer-up and waitress. 'The problem with outside catering is that you have to adapt your ideas to what the customer likes. He's paying the bill – it's his daughter's wedding and she'll have her own ideas on the food. So in a sense you're interpreting somebody else's dream. In a restaurant it's your dream. You cook what you like and just hope that enough of the public want to come and eat it.'

For nearly twenty-five years, the public has wanted to come and eat at her restaurant, situated on the ground floor of a house in Notting Hill in London. Inside, mirrored window frames on walls give a sense of light and space to the restaurant, simply decorated with pale painted walls. The style is very different from her original dreams inspired in Paris. 'I used to go to these wonderful bistros in basements with checked tablecloths, with Juliet Greco singing in the corner, and serving marvellous bean soups and pasta dishes which were completely new at the time. I thought I would love to have a restaurant where I was Mother Earth doling out these peasant soups, with rough bread and wine in a carafe. There'd be unknown painters on the wall who would make their fortune because somebody would declare they were the new Picasso.'

But by the time Leith's finally opened, Prue's ideas on the style of her restaurant had changed completely. 'I wanted something which was quiet and profitable. I got an American architect who did this rather minimalist work, and we had a bare bar, nicely lit with white walls.' This new style of restaurant failed to appeal to all her staff. Her Spanish barman decided to liven up the decorations when Prue was in Germany for the weekend looking at wines. 'When I came back he was so proud of himself because the bar was festooned like a taverna with Chianti bottles and plastic grapes. Of course, I couldn't have that, you have to hang on to your style, and you have to hang on to it like crazy.'

A women restaurateur was something of a rarity in 1969 and attracted public attention. 'At that time Madame Prunier was running a restaurant in London and she was the great female restaurateur, in fact one of the great restaurateurs of all time. She was getting on a bit, and was tremendously respected so I got a lot of publicity along the lines of the first serious female restaurateur since Madame Prunier. It was very good for me because it linked me to her. Most other women had rather short-lived bistros.'

Reviewers who came to see this unusual restaurant included the great cookery writer Margaret Costa, who complimented Prue for her 'wonderful parsnip sticks'. 'People raved about our veg. We didn't have a freezer, mainly because I couldn't afford one but also because I didn't want any frozen food. At the time, smart veg was frozen broccoli or tinned celery hearts. Or people ate frozen peas and asparagus thinking this was terribly posh. I used a lot of cheap veg as I was trying to keep the cost down. We'd do cabbage with caraway seeds or honey-roast parsnips. These were very simple vegetable dishes that had gone out of fashion with the arrival of frozen food.'

The style of food at Leith's today has naturally changed since she first opened. A starter today could be a courgette flower filled with mousseline of chicken containing salmon caviar, with a light curry sauce and diamond-shaped slivers of tomato and courgette; or a tartlet of aubergine soufflé with a ratatouille vinaigrette and pine nuts. Main courses range from a noisette of salmon with celeriac and horseradish gratin, to a pot-roasted baby guinea fowl with leeks, Jersey potatoes and sherry vinegar sauce. One main course that has lasted the course is Leith's Duckling. 'I invented this in my mews kitchen when I started up the catering business. I tried two ways of doing it: one with carrots and fennel; and the other with almonds and orange, with the almonds on top. That's the one we decided on and it is still on the restaurant menu.'

The ginger syllabub on the trolley has also been a constant factor, although other sweets change daily. On offer might be an individual three-layered strawberry shortcake, a white and dark chocolate terrine with pears, or a hot dessert that could be a variation on an English classic such as warm rhubarb tart with cinnamon ice-cream.

Although the style of cooking has changed, the restaurant still has the same pricing system, with a two-course, three-course and four-course fixed price. 'We've always felt we have to give people enough – we cater for people who want to eat a huge amount, and want second helpings. For example, it says the roast duck is for two but if you really want to eat the whole duck then nobody would charge you anymore. That's the point about a fixed price.'

In the beginning there was just one price for three courses, and portions became known for their generosity. 'When I first opened, people used to say they wouldn't eat lunch because they were coming to Leith's in the evening. I think we did overfeed people.' This conclusion followed a visit from a fellow restaurateur Albert Roux, who spent the evening standing by the dustbins in the kitchen, watching what came out of the dining room. 'After a few minutes he came into my office and said, "You're either serving filthy food or you're giving them far too much because your profits are going into the dustbin." I was extremely indignant about this and told him that, as we charged a lot, we had to give a lot. He took me out to the bin and started pulling all these ducks out, saying "Look at the flesh on there! You want your customers hungry enough to lick every piece of meat off," and suggested I buy three and a half pound ducks instead of five pounders. He pulled an apple out of the bin in the chef's end, and asked what was the matter with it. I replied that it was bad, and he then said only a third of it was bad, took a knife and cut out the bad bit.' The next discarded items to come out of his rummage in the bin were watercress stalks, which he advised Prue to use to make soup. He also suggested she buy cream in half pint rather than gallon pots. The bigger one might be cheaper but chefs carefully ration themselves if the cream is in a small pot, making sure they get the last bit out of the bottom.

This kind of useful, practical advice was invaluable to Prue when she first started as a restaurateur. 'I was twenty-nine, which doesn't sound very young, but I was certainly a complete greenhorn. I knew nobody in the restaurant business and I just made it up.' She hired a chef by advertising and then auditioning the applicants and chose a young head chef in charge of huge banquets at one of London's top venues. 'I made him cook a spinach quiche and a soufflé and it was absolutely remarkable. I'd never seen anybody kick an oven door shut or slam about in that very male chef's way. I was so impressed by this performance that I hired him.'

The restaurant appeared regularly in the press, it was fashionable, packed and expensive, but Prue was losing money fast. She met up with another restaurateur, Joseph Berkmann of the *Jardin Des Gourmets* restaurant who told her that as Leith's was 'packed and overpriced' she must be making a fortune. When she told him the truth he offered to help. 'He looked at our books and said "Your chef is robbing you blind." And I said, to my undying shame, "He can't be, he's English." And Joe said to me in his charming Austrian manner, "Even the English can be thieves."'

Following his advice, Prue hired another chef and the restaurant began to be a financial as well as a critical success. 'There's a real brotherhood among restaurateurs. We'll always rescue each other with ice or ingredients. My closest rival, Sally Clarke up the road, who I suppose should be my deadly enemy, is a good friend and I would do everything I could to help her.' The Roux brothers have continued to give advice and support her throughout her restaurant career and she admires them enormously. 'They've been at it longer than I have and their standards are better than ours. They just never give up, and that's the most important thing in any business – the dogged ability to keep going and to get back on track after every setback. That's what I admire about them, their stickability, and I hope that I have some of that.'

One of the problems that tested her 'stickability' was the problem of recruiting staff for her new restaurant. 'I began to feel that we were spending a lot of time teaching people how to cook, and paying them at the same time. If I started a cookery school, they would pay us to teach them to cook.' She discussed the idea with Caroline Waldegrave who was then head cook of Prue's catering company. Like Prue, she had trained at Cordon Bleu and had worked her way up from junior to head cook. 'I was conscious that she was re-training people all the time. She always seemed to have her arm around some weeping newcomer, very firmly telling them how it was done, but at the same time being very nice to them as a friend and mentor.' By the time Prue had decided to go ahead with the school, Caroline was working in America. 'I wrote to her and said, "If you come back and be Principal I'll open a cookery school." She was about twenty-three at the time, and we had to keep terribly quiet about how young she was because it didn't seem respectable.' Prue was a similar age herself when she began her catering company, and the head chef she employs today at Leith's restaurant is only twenty-four. She and Caroline then began building up the school and a formidable business partnership. They regularly produce general cookery books together based on the school's methods and recipes.

In their first joint publishing venture, a three-part series for basic, intermediate and advanced cooks, published in 1980, Prue acknowledges her debt to other foodwriters, including Elizabeth David and Jane Grigson, '. . . whose recipes we have unashamedly pinched for use in the School, and used for inspiration and reference in this book'. She knew them both well and admires their approach to food. 'They were both of the same ilk – that good food is fundamental to sensible society, it's truly important but not something you want to be pretentious about.'

Prue has also been influenced by the importance they placed on obtaining the best ingredients. 'I'd rather have good fresh pasta than poor-quality smoked salmon. Or a good quality baked potato than a second-class mock caviar. I suppose I get that from Jane and Elizabeth. Both of them wrote very well and didn't talk endlessly about food. I find conversation about food quite boring.'

Her own books are consequently practical and precise, constantly stressing the importance of sticking to the measurements in recipes. 'Elizabeth David's tends to say "take some coriander" . . . she also never tells you how to dish up anything, she always stops when it's still in the saucepan. I might be a little more pedantic saying, "this looks best in a shallow dish" or something.'

By the end of the first of Prue's 1980 trilogy, the beginner would be able to make a simple dish such as macaroni cheese or the more complicated roast pheasant with sauerkraut. The intermediate book stretches to yeast cookery, soufflé making and international dishes including Danish egg salad, stuffed vine leaves, Serbian roast carp and vegetarian meals such as nut cutlets with tomato sauce. The last is '. . . unashamedly written for the dedicated cook or enthusiastic amateur. It is not for the bachelor in a bedsitter or the overworked Mum on a tight budget.' But there is encouragement for the beginner too; once basic cooking methods have been mastered, advanced cookery is much like simple cookery. 'Someone who can make shortcrust pastry, custard, choux paste and caramel, and can whip cream, can also make that amazing pyramid of a French wedding cake, Gâteau St Honoré.'

Prue also advises on how to plan menus: if the main course needs last-minute work, choose a starter and pudding that can be done in advance. The amateur cook was relieved of this task in Prue's following books which put recipes into three-course menu formats. In *Prue Leith's Dinner Parties*, published in 1984, these range from Rich Mushroom and Parsley Soup, Chicken Curry with Yoghurt, followed by Tangerines in Caramel Sauce to 'the truly sensational, and horribly expensive' mix of *Soupe au Pistou*, Duck Breasts with Peppercorns, and Passionfruit Cream. She warns against combining too much rich food. 'Even if you do not drink at all, you can be horribly hungover after a meal consisting of taramasalata, roast pork, ratatouille and *crème brûlée* . . . all these dishes contain a much higher than average amount of fat.'

The dinner party came in to its own during the 1980s when it was often used to entertain employers or friends from work, and she provided advice in the book on avoiding embarrassing public panics. 'Only superwoman or the romantic male lead in the movies can whisk up dinner while the guests stand around the kitchen, glass in hand. In real life the best dinner parties are the ones with the best-laid plans. I unashamedly make lists and stick them on the refrigerator door so that even after a couple of drinks, I can move through the last-minute routine, "take salad out of fridge", "add pine nuts to casserole", "melt chocolate sauce", etc. without having to think.'

More menus followed with the publication of *Leith's Cookery School* in 1985, based on her own teaching programme. Some could be managed by beginners, such as Twice-baked soufflé, Navarin of Lamb with mashed potatoes and green salad, Treacle Tart and Yoghurt-and-custard. Others reflected recipes fashionable with top-flight chefs at that time: paper-thin raw beef with a mustard and horseradish sauce, Vinegar Chicken, Pommes Anna with broad beans, and Candied Lemon Tart. The demanding seafood and spinach *feuilleté* currently used to test her students' skills was coupled with a China tea sorbet in filigree baskets. But if the home cook reading these books was to achieve the same sort of success as Prue's students, they must obey her message and stick 'like a limpet' to the recipe. She explains in the introduction, 'My heart sinks like a stone when some amateur tells me, "Oh, I never use cookbooks, I like to create. I just fling in a bit of this and a bit of that, and I use my imagination. Cookbooks are for pedants." One knows at once what that cook's food tastes like – the product of heavy libations of wine from one hand and indiscriminate doses of herbs from the other. Good, even great cooks have devoted their lives to putting on paper the products of their own and their colleagues' experience. They have not been too proud to weigh and measure, to correct and adjust recipes, to make dishes again and again, just so less experienced cooks can, with their aid, turn out delicious food.'

It took Prue Leith and Caroline Waldegrave five years to produce their next joint book, *Leith's Cookery Bible*, published in 1991. It was the product of the school's sixteen years, with recipes and methods tested over and over again by 100 students and fifteen teachers. Over 600 pages long, the book has a more traditional format, organised into sections on first courses, fish, meat and vegetable dishes, puddings and cakes, with advice on healthy eating and nutrition. 'We threw recipes out, however classic and time-honoured, if the teachers and students did not like the results.' This meant the demise of rock buns and nut cutlets which were featured in Prue's first cookery course. Recipes are also borrowed from her other businesses: Leith's Good Food's Dauphinoise Potatoes and Leith's Restaurant's Artichoke and Green Olive Pie (see recipe at end of chapter). The remaining British classics such as Lancashire Hotpot and Bubble and Squeak have been supplemented by new dishes, particularly from the Orient, including Chicken and Spring Onion Wontons, Spring Pancake Rolls and Chinese Vegetables, and Gaeng Ped Nua, a Thai dish of spicy red beef.

New food trends, techniques and styles are constantly evaluated by the school, which runs courses ranging from one-day classes to the full six-month Credential Certificate for advanced students. About eighty per cent of the students are women and many want to return to paid employment after having children. 'They are much more serious about cooking, and one of the reasons is our fees are so high now. It costs five grand to come to us and more, which means that even for the rich it's no longer something you do just to send your daughter off to be finished. A lot of women pay for themselves anyway – they've been accountants, or lawyers or secretaries.'

Prue married in her thirties, has two children, and has often advised women to establish themselves in a career before getting married. Her husband has always been entirely supportive and is now her chairman and financial director. She also has the advantage of being her own boss. 'Most women in business have to make it against a sea of men – they're still in a male-dominated society. If you leave your work to have babies young, it's quite difficult from a confidence basis to get back into it. I've seen so many young women who've taken five or six years out, and who feel they've rotted and vegetated in that time, and have an incredible inferiority complex. In fact, what they've done in that time is learnt about management. I always say that if I had an equal man and a women, and the woman had brought up two children, I'd have the woman and risk that the kids would get chicken-pox or need someone to go to the carol concert. She will have managed, the chances are she'll have been doing three things at once all her adult life.'

She remembers one occasion as the perfect example of this. Two photographic sessions were taking place in Caroline Waldegrave's home; one for food photographs for a joint book; another for a Sunday newspaper colour supplement featuring their partnership. At the same time Caroline was finishing the monthly financial summary for the school, and her three year old was sick and off nursery school. 'She was sitting there with a calculator doing these figures, and she was on the phone, and talking to her daughter and to the photographer. She just got on with it, marvellously calm and organized. I know her well enough to know she freaks out too, just like I do, but women can be trusted with more balls in the air.'

Women chefs, she believes, can look forward more confidently to the future. Once one has been hired by a restaurant and proves her worth, it opens the way for others. The difficulty has been in getting women through the doors of the professional kitchens in the first place. 'In around 1970 I remember judging a competition at the Savoy, with Silvino Trompetto who used to be head chef there. I was trying to get our students placements or work experience but he said he would never have a woman in the Savoy kitchen. I asked him why, as we had women in the Dorchester and other places, and really wanted one in the Savoy. He said that they'd be absolutely useless for three days a month because at that certain time of the month women curdle the mayonnaise. I said he was talking about witchcraft but he insisted it was true, saying that in France women were banned from the mushroom sheds because the spores wouldn't germinate in their presence. If you're still dealing with attitudes as medieval as that in 1970, you've got a real problem.'

That attitude has changed at the Savoy, where the current Maître Chef des Cuisines, Anton Edelmann, regularly employs Prue's students. So do almost all of London's top restaurant kitchens. 'My original intention was to cream off the best students to work for me but what happens now is the Mosimanns and the Roux brothers of this world all come sniffing around our advanced students. Leith students are everywhere now and we have to compete for them. It's really irritating. But on the other hand because we want to run a professional school, all the top chefs do come and talk to the students.'

The results from her school have always been high; students taking the highest certificate from the Wine and Spirit Education Trust always achieve higher grades than the trade results. 'I think that's basically because we have well-educated, intelligent, middle-class people. It sounds snobby but in fact because they're paying, they're used to the idea of work. A lot of the college kids in the state catering colleges are there really for the wrong reasons. Their careers officers have despaired of them and thought they were only good enough for catering. It's a class thing. Middle-class women and men can be bright as buttons and it's perfectly respectable for them to be cooks.'

She believes that class is a factor not only in the attitudes towards the catering industry but also in the general enjoyment of food. 'I think one of the most difficult things the state colleges have to do is that if their students are less educated and working class, if you like, they've probably grown up with the idea of Kentucky Fried Chicken or a Big Mac as a treat. Their idea of eating out is, at most, a lasagne in the pub.'

Ironically, Prue was responsible for extending the high street hamburger culture into railway stations after she was put on the British Rail board in 1980 specifically to improve catering. 'I remember the first time I suggested we sell hamburgers on the stations there was a horrified silence. The then Chairman of British Transport Hotels, which at that time controlled Traveller's Fare, said, "Oh we don't want any of that, it would lower the tone."' Undeterred Prue sent representatives off to Hamburger University, run by McDonald's in the United States. She tried to do a deal with the burger chain but was unable to get the finances to work. 'So frankly I said, "Let's rip them off, we'll just copy the formula." So we analysed everything they did, and changed the colours, and upped the spec a tiny bit by putting more sesame seeds on the top of buns, a quarter of an ounce more beef in burgers, and made the milkshakes a tiny bit thicker. When Casey Jones opened in Waterloo, it was the most successful fast food outlet in the country by any measurement – sales per square foot or sales per staff member.'

Prue was also determined to improve the more traditional platform fare, the British Rail sandwich. 'It sounds silly now but we broke the white bread barrier. At that time Mother's Pride white bread was Britain's favourite bread, New Zealand cheddar the most popular cheese, and Anchor the most popular butter. So, put the three together and guess what you got? Britain's most popular sandwich. But that to me wasn't justification for selling nothing but it.' So she persuaded British Rail to branch out into brown bread on a trial basis. Ten per cent were made with brown, although not wholemeal as Prue had wanted because it failed to go through the butter spreader. On the first day, they had sold out by eleven o'clock and so the proportion was upped to twenty-five per cent. Now eighty per cent of sandwiches are made from granary bread. 'I remember suggesting salami and cheese as a filling, and more prawns, and everybody said "fancy foreign stuff, we can't have that". So I was pleased when we changed the sandwiches, and I think they're still very good.'

She was less happy with her attempts to improve the catering on board trains, initially trying to get Marks and Spencer to take it on, who declined her proposal. 'Train catering is basically a bad concept – a restaurant that doesn't always happen over mealtimes, or if the train is absolutely full nobody will go to the buffet for fear of losing their place. If the buffet is closed and people are in a rage it's usually because of something quite simple. The fridge may not be working or a member of staff is late. If that happens in a normal restaurant you open five minutes late but it's a different story on a train. So it's a horrible business, and I would like nothing to do with it!'

The problem is insoluble, she believes, unless management are prepared either to lose money or allow it to operate only on profitable lines as they do in France and Germany. 'I had to get off the British Railways Board because I realized I had become nobbled by them. I thought they were such a good band of guys trying so hard against impossible odds. I became so over-protective of them. I remember a railwayman in Derby asking why china cups weren't used in the buffet any more. And I started on about control, and how the staff would steal the coffee if it wasn't under control, and that passengers would steal the cups and saucers or throw them out of the window. He said I was giving the company line and that as a non-executive I was supposed to represent the passengers. He was quite right, of course.'

If transforming the food on trains was difficult because of varying timetables and facilities, Prue's next major project to improve catering for the masses had to cope with an element always uncertain – the weather. 'I suppose with hindsight, it was absolutely crazy to go into catering in the park' she says with a laugh, referring to the three-year contract she won to provide all the food in London's Hyde Park – from the humble ice-cream cornet to a full three-course restaurant meal. She started off by housing the new Serpentine Restaurant in a temporary structure while the old restaurant was being re-built. 'Originally the tender document suggested spending £100,000 on building a temporary flapping green tent. I simply would not have it. I realize now that's what I should have done because I'm now paying back a huge capital investment on a grand attempt at a semi-permanent building which has to come down in April. It was financially crazy, and if I was a public company with shareholders I'd never have been allowed to do it. One of the advantages and disadvantages of being your own boss is you get these lunatic ideas into your head and just do them.'

The weather had a dramatic effect on restaurant bookings. If it was wet, many cancelled; if it was sunny, the public strolling in the park became annoyed when it was fully booked. So after two years, Prue decided to turn it into a self-service bar and café. 'It's working much better, with more people coming in. You can still get the same charcoal grills and kebabs, smoked salmon on rye but you have to pick it up yourself.'

As at British Rail, improving sandwiches sold at the Park's Dell café became one of her targets. 'One day you have 25,000 people in the park because it's a lovely hot sunny day, and the next day it's wet and there are only twenty. The only way really to cope with that easily is to have huge freezers and a wrapped bought-in product. But that isn't what I went into the park to do. I wanted to show the world that customers would buy freshly made sandwiches that had lots of filling and were made with good Justin de Blanc's rye bread and crusty bloomers, and fresh home-made soup and freshly baked pizza, all of which we do. The waste factor is fantastic, we keep throwing food away but I'm glad we've stuck to it, although I think lesser people would have capitulated.'

Sales are good, higher than those of the previous caterers, but profits have been offset by the cost of collecting the litter generated by the catering operations. 'We will tender again, but on a less grand commission, and we probably won't get it because some other starry-eyed caterer will say Prue did it, it must be worth doing and offer more money, so I don't think we'll retain it.'

Her mission to improve the general quality of food sold in Britain extends to catering colleges which she visits regularly through her work as a member of the National Training Task Force that advises the Government. 'I've been to college kitchens where the boys can cook technically quite well, but they never taste anything. And you say to them, "Have you tasted it?", and they say, "Oh no, I wouldn't eat that, it's squid, yuk!" But the emphasis is changing and the colleges have got so much better. I used to judge these Chef of the Year competitions at Olympia, and in the old days the word "flavour" wasn't one of the criteria or, if it was, it was right at the end. They'd worry about presentation, skills, colour, but flavour – nobody tasted anything. These great amazing productions were just supposed to delight the eye and people forget that it's food.'

Prue believes that attitude developed after the great chef Escoffier died in 1935. He was known as the king of chefs and the chef of kings, creating dishes such as *pêche* Melba, *poularde* Adelina Patti and *salade* Tosca. Besides these creative new dishes for creative artists, he produced a definitive compendium of classic recipes and methods for the professional chef. 'He was so famous on both sides of the Channel that after he died his book, *Le Guide Culinaire*, became set in aspic. Nobody would say, "This is ridiculous, we can't do all this fancy food anymore." Nobody dared change a peppercorn. They tried to go on doing it but cut corners and it became the bible of every catering college. Even when I came to England in the 1950s people would say things like, "If it's not in Escoffier it's not cuisine."'

Her own philosophy is flavour first, with simple, attractive presentation, as she explains in the introduction to *Leith's Cookery Course*. 'The sight of food should make the mouth water, and induce feelings of positive greed and hunger. I think this is best achieved not by cutting radishes into roses or tomatoes into waterlilies, but by presenting food simply and freshly.'

She wants cooks to resist the temptation to turn food literally into an art form – a kind of edible sculpture. 'I think the British have a love affair with physical hobbies – putting ships into bottles and building things out of matches – and they put cooking in the same category, like making the Eiffel Tower out of woven potato or Snow White out of marzipan. That kind of cottage skill is very charming but it's not to do with cooking, with eating. We don't teach any of that, and I've got a campaign against it.'

A puritan ethic is at work she believes, which prevents the British from enjoying food free of guilt. 'People will say to me, "How can you bear it when the world is starving and you charge so much money?" My reply is that I have thirty waiters who would be starving if they didn't have jobs. I have to justify it, whereas in France nobody would ask that question. It is changing, and I remember Jane Grigson saying she refused to apologize for her hobby. Why should we have to excuse it as a hobby, when it's just a way of life for the Italians or French. It's the cement of society if you want to be pompous about it.'

So what has happened to the cement of British society? Prue passionately believes Britain potentially has an unparalleled advantage in the quality of ingredients on offer. 'I think our grouse is a million times better than any grouse that ever flapped in France; and Aberdeen Angus, two- to three-year-old beef, is just sensational.' Part of her empire includes Leith's Own Farm next to the family home in Oxfordshire, which supplies organically grown herbs and vegetables to Leith's restaurant and other parts of the business. She also has a policy of encouraging small suppliers and, as we spoke in her office, a telephone call came through from a grocer in Abergavenny in Wales who occasionally delivers fresh produce such as sea bass to her farm. 'I try to pump up his order to make it worthwhile for him to bring tuna steaks 200 miles by also ordering courgettes with flowers, and extra-virgin olive oil.'

But although good ingredients are available, many traditional dishes are no longer cooked in the home. She believes this decline in our 'cement of society' is due to the demanding methods used in these recipes. 'Funnily enough, English home cooking of the steak and kidney pie and Lancashire Hotpot variety is surprisingly difficult to do well, which is why it's largely died out. French cooking is quite easy, although grand cooking *"haute cuisine"* is much more difficult. But the simple salads you get in France with Steak Frites are much easier and it's not difficult to make a cassoulet. But to make a good pastry crust for steak and kidney pie takes one hell of a lot of skill. The pressures of time have knocked some of these dishes out. It's easier to grill a chicken breast, having dipped it in Teryaki sauce, for example.'

The style of cooking both in the home and commercially does seem to be developing into a more international cuisine often making use of easier imported techniques. But Prue emphasizes that British cooking has never developed in isolation. 'Even boiled beef and carrots exists as Pot au Feu and New England Boiled Dinner. Apple Pie is Danish Apple Cake, *Tarte Normande* and Deep South Apple Pie. These things are absolutely international.'

'The one thing that is truly English is the pudding. The English invented the pudding cloth in about 1690 and ingredients were wrapped up and boiled instead of having to be in a sealed pot. So I'm very keen to continue with that sort of thing; like Sticky Toffee Pudding, or Lemon Delight which is a lemon crusty top with curd underneath that bakes into two layers. I mean to try to hang on to the best of English and Scottish cooking.'

But this does not necessarily mean that she will follow her own advice and stick 'like a limpet' to the original recipe. 'People say "Do you do classic food, or ridiculous inventions?" We do classic *methods* but as Escoffier himself said, there's no dish that is sacred: if a better ingredient comes along or if a chef has a better way of doing it, the old recipes will be cast out and the new ones will take their place.'

MEDITERRANEAN GRILLED VEGETABLE SALAD

SERVES 8

1 head fennel
1 red pepper
1 yellow pepper
1 small aubergine, sliced into thin strips lengthwise
1 courgette, sliced into thin strips lengthwise
4 spring onions, trimmed and sliced in half lengthwise if thick
4 field mushrooms, tough stems removed and very thickly sliced
extra virgin olive oil
sea salt and freshly ground black pepper
balsamic vinegar
fresh basil leaves, to garnish
black olives, to garnish

Pre-heat grill, grill pan, barbecue or oven broiler.

Slice the fennel into thick slices, leaving some stalk-end on each slice to hold the leaves together. Use a swivel peeler to remove the thin outer membrane of the peppers. Then cut them into sections down the creases and peel any edges previously missed.

In a large bowl, turn all the vegetables in olive oil to coat.

Arrange all the vegetables on the grill, grill pan, in the grill basket or on a foil-covered grill tray. Grill at the maximum heat to char both sides, then grill more slowly to soften the pieces. Remove as they are done and allow to cool.

Serve cold, dressed with additional olive oil and a teaspoon of balsamic vinegar, season generously with sea salt and freshly ground black pepper. Garnish with sprigs of fresh basil and a few black olives.

LEITH'S RESTAURANT'S ARTICHOKE AND GREEN OLIVE PIE

Serves 4

10 fresh globe artichokes
25 g (1 oz) butter
10 shallots, finely diced
2 small garlic cloves, crushed
fresh thyme, chopped
fresh sage, chopped
60 ml (4 tablespoons) dry white vermouth or white wine
900 ml ($1\frac{1}{2}$ pints) double cream
175 g (6 oz) green olives, chopped
salt and freshly ground black pepper
225 g (8 oz) pastry, see following recipe
1 egg, beaten

Preheat oven to 190°C, 375°F or Gas Mark 5.

Peel the artichokes to the core and put them immediately into water containing a dash of lemon juice. Cut the artichokes into 5 mm ($\frac{1}{4}$ in) cubes and cook in the butter very slowly, with the shallots, garlic, thyme and sage, until soft.

Add the vermouth or wine. Add the cream and reduce, by boiling, to a coating consistency. Stir the sauce every so often to prevent it from catching on the bottom of the saucepan. Add the olives and season to taste. Leave to cool.

Line a 20 cm (8 in) flan ring with pastry. Pile in the artichoke and olive mixture and cover the pie with the remaining pastry. Brush with beaten egg and bake for 15-20 minutes or until golden brown.

PUFF PASTRY

If you have never made puff pastry before, use the smaller amount of butter: this will give a normal pastry. If you have some experience, more butter will produce a lighter, very rich pastry.

225 g (8 oz) plain flour
pinch of salt
30 g (1 oz) lard
150 ml ($\frac{1}{4}$ pint) icy water
150–200 g (5–7 oz) butter

Sift the flour with a pinch of salt. Rub in the lard. Add the icy water and mix with a knife to a doughy consistency. Turn on to the table and knead quickly until smooth. Wrap in polythene or a cloth and leave in the refrigerator for 30 minutes to relax.

Lightly flour the table top or board and roll the dough into a rectangle about 10 × 30 cm (4 × 12 in) long.

Tap the butter lightly with a floured rolling pin to get it into a flattened block about 9 × 8 cm ($3\frac{1}{2}$ × 3 in). Put the butter on the rectangle of pastry and fold both ends over to enclose it. Fold the third closest to you over first and then bring the top third down. Press the sides together to prevent the butter escaping. Give it a 90-degree anti-clockwise turn so that the folded, closed edge is on your left. Now tap the pastry parcel with the rolling pin to flatten the butter a little; then roll out, quickly and lightly, until the pastry is 3 times as long as it is wide. Fold it very evenly in 3, first folding the third closest to you over, then bringing the top third down. Give it a 90-degree anti-clockwise turn so that the folded, closed edge is on your left. Again press the edges firmly with the rolling pin. Then roll out again to form a rectangle as before.

Now the pastry has had 2 rolls and folds, or 'turns' as they are called. It should be put to rest in a cool place for 30 minutes or so. The rolling and folding must be repeated twice more, the pastry again rested, and then again given 2 more 'turns'. This makes a total of 6 turns. If the butter is still very streaky, roll and fold it once more.

GINGER SYLLABUB

SERVES 4

60–85 ml (4–5 tablespoons) Advocaat liqueur
30 ml (2 tablespoons) ginger marmalade
300 ml (½ pint) double cream
1–2 pieces preserved ginger

Mix the Advocaat and ginger marmalade together.

Whip the cream lightly and stir in the marmalade mixture.

Spoon into small glasses, little china pots or coffee cups.

Put 2–3 thin slivers of preserved ginger on top of each syllabub. Chill before serving.

* For a smoother texture the ginger marmalade and the Advocaat can be liquidised or sieved together.
** In the absence of ginger marmalade use orange marmalade well flavoured with finely chopped bottled ginger and its syrup.

TUILES À L'ORANGE

MAKES 25

2 egg whites
100 g (4 oz) caster sugar
50 g (2 oz) butter
50 g (2 oz) plain flour
grated rind of 1 orange

Set the oven to 190°C, 375°F or Gas Mark 5. Grease a baking sheet, or line with silicone paper.

Whisk the egg whites until stiff. Add the sugar and whisk thoroughly.

Melt the butter. Add it to the meringue mixture by degrees with the sifted flour. Fold in the orange rind.

Spread out teaspoonfuls very thinly on the prepared baking sheet, keeping them well apart to allow for spreading during cooking. Bake until golden brown (5–6 minutes).

Oil a rolling pin or the handle of a large wooden spoon. Loosen the tuiles from the baking sheet while still hot. While they are still warm and pliable curl them over the rolling pin or round the wooden spoon handle. When they are quite firm slip them off. When cold, store in an airtight container.

* Using silicone paper guarantees that the tuiles will not stick.

Blackened Fish and Spring Onion Salsa

new recipe

Serves 4

4 × 100 g (4 oz) tuna, salmon or any other fillets
melted butter
Cajun spice mixture, see below
spring onion salsa, see below

Dip the fish in melted butter, then into the spice mix. Press the spices into the fillets to form a crust.

Heat a dry heavy pan until smoking hot. Dry-fry steaks on both sides until very dark and crusty on the outside, still very moist and barely cooked inside. Serve with spring onion salsa.

Spring Onion Salsa

2 plum tomatoes, peeled, de-seeded and diced
4 spring onions, diced
1 clove garlic, crushed
60 ml (4 tablespoons) extra virgin olive oil
salt and freshly ground pepper

Mix all the ingredients together and season to taste.

CAJUN SPICE MIX

3 teaspoons salt
½ teaspoon cayenne pepper
½ teaspoon white pepper
¼ teaspoon black pepper
¼ teaspoon dried thyme
¼ teaspoon dried basil
¼ teaspoon dried oregano
2 teaspoons paprika

Mix all ingredients together. Store in a dry, cool place.

MADHUR JAFFREY

A Taste Palette

'The only way to eat superb Indian food, with a guarantee of variety, quality and freshness of ingredients, is to learn to cook it for yourself.' Jane Grigson called Madhur Jaffrey the Elizabeth David of India and, for many people in Britain, Jaffrey did the same for Indian cuisine that Elizabeth David had done for the Mediterranean. She has not just made the recipes accessible, removing the apparent mystery and complications, although that in itself is a huge change – she has made the reader want to read about India and discover its huge regional varieties through the delight that she herself takes in the subject.

At the end of a brief stopover for her in Britain, we are sitting in the Ritz hotel sipping coffee. Madhur Jaffrey has been in Britain filming a new television series and discussing book and television projects. She is dressed in a traditional sari and, although she looks tired after a hard filming schedule, when we begin talking about food, she immediately becomes enthusiastic and animated.

'Eating? I love eating. I do not like cooking when I am testing, I like cooking when I am doing it for myself and I can say, "Oh, I feel like pasta or

Chinese noodles." I just go with the stuff I have. I make it and we eat it and that is great fun.'

Madhur Jaffrey grew up in Delhi in India, and her childhood memories are full of evocations of food. Although she herself never cooked, she was always attracted to the goings on in the kitchen. There were always plenty of cooks and bearers in the kitchens, and one servant with a special role. As she explains in the introduction to her book *A Taste of India*, the *masalchi* was an underling to whose lot fell the tedious task of grinding on a heavy stone, twice a day, all the spices the cook deemed necessary. 'The *masalchi* would arrange little hills of yellows, browns and greens on a metal plate, sometimes single seasonings such as turmeric, fresh coriander and ginger, sometimes mixtures of, say, cloves, cinnamon, nutmeg, mace and black pepper, all ground in one lot for a specific dish.'

Although she did not cook as a child, Madhur had developed a sense of taste. 'I suppose I have come to believe that you are born with certain senses which are more developed than others and I suppose I always had a good eye and a good palate. Above all, the sense of taste is the ability to appreciate and remember.'

She believes that every good cook and especially good foodwriters need what she calls a 'taste memory'. In her introduction to *A Taste of India*, she explains that education of the palate comes early in India.

'From childhood onwards, an Indian is exposed to more combinations of flavours and seasonings than perhaps anyone else in the world. Our cuisine is based on this variety, which, in flavours, encompasses hot-and-sour, hot-and-nutty, sweet-and-hot, bitter-and-hot, bitter-and-sour and sweet-and-salty and in seasonings, it stretches from the freshness and sweetness of highly aromatic curry leaves to the dark pungency of the resin, asafetida, whose earthy aroma tends to startle Westerners just as much as the smell of strong, ripe cheese does Indians.'

These intense childhood memories of colour and taste explain her idea of the cooking palette. Each area right across the country has slightly different styles, tastes and traditions, '. . . the ingredients may be almost the same but the way they are used, what you might call the brush strokes, are different. So to an Indian it is immediately recognizable as Maharashtrian food or Kashmiri food because they mix them in a certain way. Every region of India takes colours and uses them in a different way.'

Coming from Delhi meant there was already a mix of influences: Muslim, Persian, Arabic traditions mixed with the vegetarian Hindu tradition. Each caste and subcaste has special traditions of its own and Madhur's family came from a mixed tradition. The men of the family all learnt the language of the courts and had virtually run the Mogul courts since the fifteenth and sixteenth centuries, and they all learnt Persian and ate meat. 'Since they were in the court all the time their traditions were very courtly, but in the Persian style and then they learnt and spoke Urdu.'

On her mother's side, the family was generally vegetarian and had kept up the traditions of the *Ramagana* and the *Mahabharata* and the telling of stories, '. . . which the men knew but they didn't read, because they read Persian and Arabic, so they didn't really read the scriptures in the way the women read the scriptures'.

The two traditions also brought separate food customs. 'If you went to my mother's family which was very traditional, a floor carpet would be spread on the floor at dinner time and then a white sheet would be put on it and all the food placed in the middle. Everyone would have their own plate and you would reach out in the middle to take whatever you wanted.

'In the muslim tradition of sharing, of brotherhood, the men eat first and the women eat afterwards. In the Hindu tradition it is purity, which is in the mind more than anything else and everyone had their own plate.'

India is now one giant country but before Independence there were 600 semi-independent kingdoms with fifteen major languages and more than 1000 minor languages and dialects. There were also five major religious faiths. It is a country proud of separate cultures and foods within borders.

'Each state is like a European nation with its own language, culture and foods, history and geography and own set of dominant religions.'

Religion and caste played an important part in daily food rituals. Upper-class Hindus, for example, would only eat meals which had been cooked and served by freshly bathed Brahmins, so there is no long tradition of fine public dining. Food that has been touched or eaten by someone else was considered 'unclean'. 'Even in my family where we were quite liberal, I never took a sip from my sister's glass or a bite from her apple. At least not without my mother's disapproval.'

At school Madhur did some cookery but only because she was not good at mathematics. 'You either did algebra, geometry and higher maths, or you did arithmetic, domestic science and needlework. I was forced into the cookery part of it. In the test they had a practical section, which I was not expecting. They gave us potatoes, ginger and spices and said, "Do something with it." I did not have a clue!'

The breadth and depth of Indian cuisine, the huge variety of flavours and cooking styles that the West is only just beginning to discover was a natural part of the taste palette for Madhur Jaffrey. Friends at school from different regions would bring their own specialities for lunch, to be eagerly swapped and tasted. This led to her delight in the differences and vitality of Indian food.

Madhur Jaffrey came to Britain in the late 1950s to study drama at the Royal Academy of Dramatic Art. It was in Britain that she learnt the twin skills of acting and cooking. As a student she was forced to cook and could not afford to buy what she wanted. So she began a correspondence cookery course with her mother back in India. The airmail letters from India, with their recipes and advice, brought back all the colours and smells of home. To a homesick student, shocked at the food offered to British students at the time, it was comforting to be able to experiment with these loved and remembered dishes.

'When my mother sent her recipes, even though they were very approximate, I knew what she was talking about because I could remember the taste of everything I had eaten. When I started cooking, if it wasn't right, I knew from the taste. I worked very hard and singlemindedly – so I was able then really to develop this over the years. If you ask me to chop onions, I do not chop onions like a chef, I do it like a housewife. But over the years I have developed expertise, though I always feel a bit of a fraud because it's not something I've been trained formally to do.' Particular favourites in her mother's letters were *kheema matar* (minced meat with peas), *rogan josh* (red lamb stew) and *phool gobi aur aloo ki bhaji* (cauliflower with potatoes).

Madhur's first book, *An Invitation to Indian Cookery*, was published in New York in 1973 and, like many events in her life, seems to have been the result of a happy accident. She had finished acting in a successful film, *Shakespeare Wallah*, and in the publicity for the film the *New York Times* printed a piece featuring her as the actress who likes to cook, and published some recipes. Indian food was still quite new in America and she was approached by a publisher to put together a book.

Madhur Jaffrey leans forward, takes a sip of coffee and laughs, 'It so happened that I had not got much work after *Shakespeare Wallah*. So I would be sitting around the home throwing fabulous dinner parties not knowing what else to do with myself. They would take two or three days to prepare and they'd be very grand and everybody would "ooh and aah". And that to me was almost like being an actress. So acting and entertaining were happening simultaneously. When it came to putting a book together I had already worked out a lot of recipes.'

First published in this country in 1976, *An Invitation to Indian Cookery* explains basic techniques of Indian cookery in a clear, friendly, readable style. Madhur is already preoccupied with the quality of ingredients, for example, buying spices in small enough quantities to know that they are fresh, and she emphasizes the importance of authenticity. In the introduction to the British edition she is delighted at the flourishing of so many Indian restaurants.

But she also sounds a note of caution. Quality and freshness of ingredients are vital but so is the connection with and respect for the past. She feels there is a danger of restaurants subsuming their individual and very different regional expertise to a severely reduced number of dishes that customers ask for again and again.

If they can sell tandoori chicken and lamb korma why experiment further? Customers like what they know and are perhaps afraid to experiment with different dishes. 'They still want the dishes they know, the korma, the tikka masala. But they would not be happy with vegetables cooked with a little coconut or steamed spinach, with just ginger because generally they want it very spiced.'

The temptation for the restaurateurs then is not to explore further the delights of their own region, 'The result is that sauces in such eating places inevitably have the same colour, taste and consistency; the dishes generally come "mild, medium or hot", which is an indication that the food is not being cooked with the spices, as it should be, but that something is being ladled on; mediocre chutney and relishes are piled on the table to fake an appearance of "a lot for your money", appetizers are suggested not because Indians eat them but because it is felt that the Western world cannot do without them.'

In the 1960s and 1970s many people in Britain tried to reproduce at home some of the flavours they had found in Indian restaurants. And most of them tried to do it with a jar labelled 'curry powder' found at the back of the cupboard. But Madhur stands firm against the use and abuse of the ubiquitous term 'curry' which, to many people before she came along and introduced the many and varied tastes of India, was all they knew of the food. If 'curry' is an oversimplified name for an ancient cuisine, then 'curry powder' attempts to oversimplify and destroy the cuisine itself. 'Curry powders are standard blends of several spices, including cumin, coriander, fenugreek, red peppers and turmeric – standard blends which Indians never use.'

Her openness to different foods from across the world goes back to childhood. As well as coming from two parental traditions, the overlay of the Raj meant that it was taken for granted that you mixed and matched the best from each culture.

'The Raj cooks at that time even in Indian homes were specially trained to know both traditions. Lunches were Indian but breakfast was a mix; we might eat a traditional English fried breakfast with egg, bacon and sausages or we might have an Indian breakfast.'

'When it came to dinner there was a mix of cultures. There would be a Western dish of some kind, cutlets of fried fish or something like that. Then we would have our Indian course – bread or rice and then a pudding at the end.'

The idea of mixing cultures and taking the best flavours from each has remained with her. The inherited mix of traditions and her extensive travelling all over the world have made Madhur suspicious of the currently fashionable idea of the purity of certain dishes. 'The most exciting thing for me is the intellectual exercise of linking foods. The first thing you learn, as you travel, is that nothing is authentic. People are absorbing recipes from each other at such a fast rate, and that has always been the case.'

She now lives in New York and is fascinated by the development of American cuisine. America is often criticised for having no national cuisine but to Madhur Jaffrey that is one of its strengths. 'You see cuisine in a flux, cuisine forming. It is a young country. If you want to look at cuisine forming, look at America. The same is happening there as previously happened round the world, only it is palpable there.'

What Madhur has done is to make Indian food easy. Some people are nervous of approaching Indian cuisine because of the different flavours, spices and herbs that can be mixed in a seemingly endless number of combinations.

She has shown that, if taken as a step-by-step process, the final meal is not as complicated as it might seem from the recipe. 'The Indian genius lies not only in squeezing several flavours out of the same spice by roasting it, grinding it or popping it whole into hot oil, but in combining seasonings.

We combine curry leaves with popped mustard seeds, ground roasted cumin seeds with mint, ginger and garlic with green chillies – to create a vast spectrum of tastes.'

Since the publication of her first book, Madhur has combined two careers – foodwriter and actress. She won a best actress award in Berlin for her part in Merchant Ivory's *Shakespeare Wallah*. She has also appeared in *Autobiography of a Princess* and *Heat and Dust* as well as theatrical parts such as the lead in the production of *Medea* at the Lyric, Hammersmith in London.

In 1978 the BBC invited her to present a television series based on *An Invitation to Indian Cookery*. In television she found a medium which combined both worlds, acting and food. 'Television presenting is a bit like acting. It's another form, you are selling yourself and something else to other people, holding their interest, trying to present it in as exciting a manner as possible.'

Part of her appeal on television is that she is obviously enjoying herself, even when things are going wrong. 'I enjoy it because I suppose I am a professional actress. So even if I'm finding it very hard, or if things go wrong, like once rice flew all over the place in one shot, as an actress your job is to put it all together.'

The series was an unexpected success and the entire print run of the book published to accompany the series sold out very quickly. Suddenly Indian cuisine had arrived. On one celebrated occasion she used fresh coriander in a recipe and the next day the whole of Manchester was ransacked for coriander! 'I do not see myself as a teacher. Like President Reagan, I am a communicator, the dreaded word, but I do think I can put things across to people.'

When we talked she had already finished filming a television series, *Firm Friends*, in Newcastle with Billie Whitelaw. It was about two women who set up an Indian catering business together. 'Wherever I went, when I was filming in Newcastle, people would come up to me and say they'd never tried Indian food before. And that, thanks to me, they did it for the first time, or that they were now more able to cook rice. And I got letters from people saying that seeing how I made eggs, they've never made eggs in the boring old way again.' She smiles broadly; the contact with readers and the television audience clearly gives her enormous pleasure.

Madhur attributes part of her success to the historical connections between Britain and India. This is partly reflected in the huge flowering of Indian, Pakistani and Bangladeshi restaurants in every town in Britain, so it sometimes seems that a visit to one is part of the Saturday night out. But it can also be seen in areas other than food; we seem to have a strong emotional pull for the links between India and Britain, which is why all the Raj books and films do so well here.

'There is an historical aspect which is deep in the souls of the British as colonisers. Maybe it is an historical echo. There is a hunger for that fun, that ambience and that food which has somehow trickled down to their children. Because I see that it is not there in America and I wonder what makes the British different. I think it is that link that somehow triggers a need and then a love.'

When asked about her own mentors in the food-writing world, Madhur Jaffrey quotes Elizabeth David, M.F.K. Fisher, as well as the American writers James Beard and Julia Child. Julia Child, sometimes known as the American Jane Grigson, has a thoroughness in her approach to food writing; and her television series has been a strong influence on Madhur.

'She pursues whatever it is to the end in terms of knowledge. If it is a fish, she will find out everything about the fish. She'll go and find out the best way of filleting it, how to store it. She manages to get all that information into her books and programmes. That is really important. A recipe for a hollandaise sauce is not enough by itself because it can go wrong in twenty different ways. In her book she will tell you what to do each time when it goes wrong, and I think that is the secret of a good cookery writer.

'I think I've always felt that you have to explain, even if you over-explain. I've had publishers who have said too many words, it will be too many pages, cut it down and I have tried to fight it as much as possible.'

Her concern with accuracy and thoroughness has resulted in a clear and straightforward approach which goes some way to explaining her popularity with readers and television fans, whatever their level of skill.

The recipe itself is only the starting point as far as she is concerned. 'The recipe is the functional element which you have to put in but the exciting element is how it came about and what people did with it, what was associated with it. A lot of Western cookery book writers say there is nothing original left. I don't believe that because I have done and found things which certainly do not appear in cookbooks.

'So, the recipe is not always "original" as someone, somewhere may have made it before, but it has not appeared before, and I take great pride in trying to put down things that have not appeared in print before.'

After the success of her book of Indian cookery, Madhur looked further east in her book *Eastern Vegetarian Cooking*, published in Britain in 1983. She has an uncanny knack of knowing in advance what people want to read about and cook next. *Eastern Vegetarian Cooking* hit the newly fashionable vegetarian nerve. The book was so successful it was reprinted twice in 1983 and 1984 and has been reprinted every year since.

In *Eastern Vegetarian Cooking* Madhur uses the same formula that was so successful in her books on Indian cuisine. It is a formula that she now uses with all her books. After an encouraging introduction which urges simplicity and experimentation, she takes each major group of foods: vegetables, beans and dried peas, noodles, pancakes and bread, and breaks them down into manageable, bite-sized pieces for the reader.

Each recipe has a little introduction, with an anecdote, a recommendation for serving, and historical or regional details. She demonstrates, for example, that tandoori, one of the most popular current styles of Indian cookery, was in fact brought to Delhi from the North-west and the Punjab by refugees after Partition in 1947. It quickly became a fashion in Delhi, then spread throughout India and abroad as one of the most 'typical' of Indian cuisines. Another example is that when an Indian sits down to eat meat, it is nearly always goat meat. 'The English in India translated this as mutton and it is still called this in Indian English today.'

Eastern Vegetarian Cooking closes with sample menus and a chapter of general information on herbs and spices and 'how-to' basics such as making coconut milk and finding the best fresh ginger. These chapters of general information serve as a well-laid-out reference section, giving hints and tips to the reader.

In 1985, Madhur returned to the Indian theme with *A Taste of India*, a look at regional Indian food in which she introduces us to the wonders of the different regions. The book is stuffed with childhood memories, chance meetings leading to wonderful meals, and historical anecdotes. The stunning photographs of both the regions and the dishes make this a book that one can pick up and read and muse on the different recipes.

In an introduction to a serialization of *A Taste of India* in the *Observer*, Jane Grigson wrote, 'How could we be so flannel swathed and impervious to such an extraordinarily ancient and richly layered civilization? How to account for it I do not know – and it was not just in matters of food either. Nor can I account for the fact that a Madhur Jaffrey has been so long in appearing. But here she is, we know her a little already and we must be grateful.'

Another book, *Food for Family and Friends*, followed in 1987, in which the emphasis is on entertaining with ease: preparing delicious food but having enough time to spend with your guests. The meals, whether simple or complicated, become an expression of the friendship; the emphasis is on making delicious dishes simple.

In the introduction she writes, 'Today when I go to the market and see, say, a pile of crisp, fresh green beans, dozens of possibilities start to buzz in my head. Should I cook them Szechwan style with garlic, red pepper and soy sauce or stir-fry them with a mound of shallots and strips of pork the way I had them on a beach in Bali? Of course, I could blanch them and douse them with a mustardy French vinaigrette, or, on the other hand, I could stir-fry them with cumin and ginger as we do in India.'

A second BBC television series accompanied the book *Far Eastern Cookery* in 1989. When travelling to the Far East for the first time twenty-five years ago, Madhur was struck by how well people ate and by the freshness of the ingredients. In the series, she concentrates on eight countries: Korea, Japan, Hong Kong, the Philippines, Vietnam, Thailand, Malaysia and Indonesia. All have a healthy emphasis on the importance of grains, 'wheat in the form of noodles, pancakes or steamed buns or it is given in rice'. One of her favourite seasonings, ginger, is found throughout the Far East.

In the introduction to this book she explains her enthusiasm for this part of the world. 'The culinary art of the Far East lies in the magical mingling and balancing of flavourings and textures. Western taboos just do not hold: fish and pork strips are thrown together in a fiery stew in Korea; a paste made of mince pork and crab meat is lathered on to triangles of bread before they are fried in Vietnam. The soft, the smooth, the crunchy and the slithery as well as the sweet, salty, hot and sour are all presented in a kaleidoscope of inventive permutations.'

Like most foodwriters she hates testing recipes and finds it hard to delegate. 'I have no secretaries, no help, because I just feel that nobody's going to be as thorough as I am! They are going to skip corners, they will not cut the cauliflower like I want it cut or they will buy the wrong cauliflower to begin with!'

Madhur Jaffrey has an acting and food-writing schedule that seems enough for three people. We had just managed to squeeze in time for an interview for this book before she flew back to New York that afternoon. She is booked up solidly for the next three years, with plans for another Far Eastern book, a big international vegetarian cookery book and a quick and easy Indian cookery book. For relaxation, she works in the garden, loves design magazines and going into kitchen shops. When we met, she was looking forward to going home to her new kitchen which she had just had built to her specifications.

'I have been cooking in a tiny kitchen all my life and now for the first time I have a big kitchen, with space, I love that.' She is also a collector of kitchen gadgets and will now have space for her favourite kitchen implements – a standard good-quality blender and two coffee grinders (one for spices), and an Indian grinding stone for small quantities of cumin and coriander. 'I have smaller gadgets which I can't live without, a Japanese ginger grater, for example. Sometimes you want to have a small finely grated amount – ginger should be like pulp, you can't throw a small amount into a machine, you won't get pulp. I am also not against a garlic press like a lot of foodwriters are.'

There's a lot of snobbery in food circles nowadays, the notion of the right gadgets to use, even the right foods to eat, but that goes against her whole credo. 'Iceberg lettuce used to be the bane of every food writer's existence in America. But I have always liked it. Food shouldn't be fashion. People who consider it a fashion are people who can't taste.' And not tasting in her book is the greatest crime. 'I was once on a chat show with a man in his eighties and he said, "Food is not important, eating is just something you have to do." I'm sure people do think of food as fuel and for those people it's right that they shouldn't bother. It's like admiring a painting; if you can't, don't go to art galleries!'

America is still a continent waiting to be converted to Indian food. Away from New York, in the heartland of America there are any number of Chinese restaurants but very few Indian restaurants. Madhur is a food consultant to a successful Indian restaurant in New York, *Dawat*, but with an entire country out there waiting for Indian food, there is a gleam in her eye when she says, 'I have a whole land to conquer and I am not doing too well!'

There are still many people who happily frequent Indian restaurants who would never try to reproduce the same food at home. Madhur Jaffrey is often approached and asked about how to get started in Indian cuisine. Her advice is characteristically straightforward, 'I always say, get a good cookbook. Look at the recipes and pick one that you think you want to make and just get the spices for that particular recipe. Do not get a million spices.'

'Make it a few times. If you enjoy it, look at another recipe. Then your spices will grow on the shelf as you go along and gradually you will build up a "spice wardrobe". Once you know what spices do, you will be able to improvise. That's the wonderful thing with Indian spices. If you have boiled potatoes sitting around and you want to do something with them and you take a few cumin seeds and you throw them into hot oil and throw in a few onions, put the potatoes in and stir them around, you get an Indiany potato which is very interesting.'

Madhur Jaffrey seems surprised at her own success, by the fact that people recognize her in the street and want to tell her about their attempts at cooking. 'I am an actress who has become a cook, who is playing the part of a cook, that is what I am!'

SAVOURY PORK AND CRAB TOASTS

Bánh mì chiên

MAKES ABOUT 32 TOASTS
(FROM THUY PELLISSIER)

You may serve these as a savoury at the end of a meal or as a first course. When I invite people over for drinks I find that these toasts are just the perfect nibble to pass around. Rather like the triangles of prawn toast that you might have eaten in Chinese restaurants, they are triangles of minced pork and shredded crab meat. They are simple to prepare. All that they require is that you fry them just before you serve them – usually for less than 2 minutes per batch.

If you are using frozen crab meat make sure you defrost it completely and squeeze out all of the moisture from it beforehand. If you are mincing the pork yourself, put the garlic and shallots into the mincer along with the meat.

2 large cloves garlic
15 g (½ oz) shallot or onion
75 g (3 oz) cooked crab meat, finely shredded
100 g (4 oz) lean pork, very finely minced
1 egg
freshly ground black pepper
1½ teaspoons sugar
1½ teaspoons fish sauce or salt to taste
about 8 average-sized slices white bread, about ½–¾ cm (¼–⅓ in) thick
vegetable oil for frying

Peel the garlic and shallot and mince or chop them finely. Combine the garlic, shallot, crab meat and minced pork in a bowl. Beat the egg in a separate bowl. Add 2 tablespoons of the beaten egg to the pork-crab mixture. (Save the remaining egg for use in another dish.) Add also a generous amount of black pepper, the sugar and the fish sauce. Mix well to form a paste. This mixture may be made ahead of time, covered and stored in the refrigerator.

Stacking a few slices of bread together at a time, cut off the crusts. Now cut the slices in half diagonally, making large triangles, then cut these triangles in half again to make small triangles. Using a knife, spread the prepared paste over one side of each triangle to a thickness of $\frac{1}{3}$ cm ($\frac{1}{8}$ in).

Pour the oil into a large frying pan to a depth of just under 1 cm ($\frac{1}{2}$ in) and set it over a medium low heat. When it is hot (a cube of bread dropped in should begin to sizzle immediately if the temperature is right), put in as many triangles of bread as will fit in a single layer, meat side down, and cook for $1\frac{1}{2}$ minutes or until the meat is golden brown. Turn the bread triangles over and cook on the second side for 30–60 seconds or until golden. Remove them with a slotted spoon and drain on kitchen paper. Fry all the triangles in this way. Serve hot.

RICE WITH PEAS

SERVES 6

Rice can be cooked with either fresh or frozen peas. In India, of course, it is always cooked with the fresh, hard, shelled variety, but I find that frozen peas work just as well for this dish.

2 tablespoons vegetable oil
$\frac{1}{2}$ teaspoon whole black mustard seeds
350 g (12 oz) long-grain rice
750 ml ($1\frac{1}{4}$ pints) chicken broth (fresh or tinned)
1 teaspoon salt
1 teacup shelled peas, fresh or frozen

Over a medium flame, heat the oil in a 3-quart heavy-bottomed pot (with tight-fitting lid – to be used later). When hot, add the mustard seeds and wait until they begin to darken (10–20 seconds). Put in the rice, and the peas if you are using fresh ones. Stir for a minute. Add the broth and salt. Bring to the boil. Cover and reduce the heat to very, very low. Leave to cook for 25–30 minutes.

If you are using frozen peas, defrost them by placing a cupful in colander and running under warm water. Leave to drain. When rice has cooked for 25 minutes, lift the cover off and quickly put defrosted peas on top of rice. Replace cover and cook about 5 minutes longer or until done.

Mix the rice and peas gently together and serve on a large platter.

This is a relatively bland dish. It goes well with Indian lentils and meats, and equally well with almost any English meat dish.

HARE MASALE WALI MURGHI

Lemony Chicken with Fresh Coriander

SERVES 6

Here is a delightful lemony, gingery dish that requires a lot of fresh coriander. It is a great favourite with our family. I generally serve it with spiced basmati rice.

2 × 2.5 cm (1 in) cubes of fresh ginger, peeled and coarsely chopped
4 tablespoons plus 150 ml (5 fl oz) water
6 tablespoons vegetable oil
1.25 kg (2½ lb) chicken parts, skinned
5 cloves garlic, peeled and very finely chopped
200 g (7 oz) fresh coriander (weight without roots and lower stems) very finely chopped
½–1 fresh, hot green chilli, very finely chopped
¼ teaspoon cayenne pepper
2 teaspoons ground cumin seeds
1 teaspoon ground coriander seeds
½ teaspoon ground turmeric
1 teaspoon salt – or to taste
2 tablespoons lemon juice

Put the ginger and 4 tablespoons of the water into the container of an electric blender. Blend until you have a paste.

Heat the oil in a wide, heavy, preferably non-stick pot over a medium-high flame. When hot, put in as many chicken pieces as the pot will hold in a single layer and brown on both sides. Remove the chicken pieces with a slotted spoon and put them in a bowl. Brown all the chicken pieces this way.

Put the garlic into the same hot oil. As soon as the pieces turn a medium brown colour, turn the heat to medium and pour in the paste from the blender. Stir and fry it for a minute. Now add the fresh coriander, green chilli, cayenne, ground cumin, ground coriander seeds, turmeric and salt. Stir and cook for a minute. Put in all the chicken pieces as well as any liquid that might have accumulated in the chicken bowl. Also add 150 ml (5 fl oz) water and the lemon juice. Stir and bring to the boil. Cover tightly, turn heat to low and cook for 15 minutes. Turn the chicken pieces over. Cover again and cook another 10–15 minutes or until chicken is tender. If the sauce is too thin, uncover the pot and boil some of it away over a slightly higher heat.

BANANA FRITTERS IN TEMPURA BATTER

SERVES 4–6

4 or 5 bananas
about 100 g (4 oz) flour for dredging
vegetable oil for deep frying

FOR THE BATTER:

1 large egg
300 ml (½ pint) ice cold water
115 g (4 oz) plain flour, sifted
with ½ teaspoon bicarbonate of soda

To make the batter, put the egg in a bowl and beat until smooth. Slowly add the iced water, beating as you do so. Now put in all the flour and bicarbonate of soda. Beat four or five times to mix. Do not overmix. The batter should be lumpy. Set the batter aside.

Cut the bananas crosswise into 2½ cm (1 in) chunks. Dredge lightly in flour. Heat the oil in a wok or frying pan over a medium flame to about 375°F (180°C). Dip the banana pieces a few times in the batter and then fry in the oil until golden. Remove with slotted spoon and drain on kitchen paper. Do all bananas this way. This much can be done ahead of time.

Just before you eat this sweet, heat the oil again over a medium flame. When hot, fry the bananas again. This will make them crisp. Shake icing sugar on the fritters and serve immediately.

Gingery Chicken Pieces

new recipe

Serves 4 (as a first course)

If you stick toothpicks into the chicken pieces, they may be served with drinks. If placed on a bed of lightly dressed salad greens, the chicken can be served as a first course. You may, of course, also eat it as part of your main meal.

350–450 g (¾–1 lb) boned and skinned chicken breasts
1 tablespoon tomato purée
2 tablespoons lemon juice
¾ teaspoon salt
Lots of freshly ground black pepper
1 clove garlic, peeled and crushed
1 teaspoon peeled and finely grated fresh ginger
⅛ teaspoon ground turmeric
1½ teaspoons ground cumin
1 teaspoon ground coriander
¼ teaspoon ground cayenne pepper
½ teaspoon garam masala*
1 teaspoon corn flour
3 tablespoons olive oil or other vegetable oil

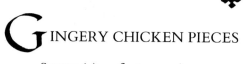

Cut the chicken into 2.5 cm (1-inch) cubes. Put into a bowl. Add the tomato purée, lemon juice, salt, pepper, garlic, ginger, turmeric, cumin, coriander, cayenne, *garam masala*, corn flour and 1 tablespoon of the oil. Mix well and set aside for 30–60 minutes.

Heat the oil in a non-stick frying pan over a high heat. When hot, put in all the chicken. Stir and fry for about 5 minutes or until chicken is just done. Serve as suggested above.

* For home-made *garam masala*, combine 1 tablespoon of cardamom seeds, 1 small stick of cinnamon, $\frac{1}{3}$ of a nutmeg, 1 teaspoon of black cumin seeds, 1 teaspoon of whole cloves and 1 teaspoon of whole black peppercorns and grind finely in a clean coffee-grinder or other spice-grinder. You may also buy ready-made *garam masala* from an Indian grocery.

JOSCELINE DIMBLEBY

The Art of Cooking

'When I'm working on a book I buy ingredients that I think are inspiring and I just stand in my kitchen thinking what shall I do? Sometimes I have waited and thought for two hours with nothing coming to me, and then it does.' For Josceline Dimbleby, creating recipes is as much an art form as painting a picture. Like an artist, she never wants to paint the same picture twice and, even with her own recipes, finds it almost impossible not to alter a dish each time she makes it.

Despite having no formal training and adopting a deliberately low profile, she is one of Britain's leading cookery writers, with book sales estimated to be in the region of two million. Her style is known for its highly individual blend of spices and herbs combined with the very best British cooking traditions, with dishes such as Roast Leg of Lamb with Cardamom Sauce, and Braised Beef in Walnut, Chilli and Chocolate Sauce. Her particular passion is puddings which she aims to be conversation stoppers. Placed on the dinner table might be a 'wild chocolate bowl with jagged edges' filled with fresh strawberries, or a hot lemon and passion fruit soufflé.

She loves to experiment and on arrival at her Putney home I was immediately offered her latest concoction – a mixture of apricot and elderflower jam. After digging in our teaspoons, she was full of enthusiasm. 'Don't you think it's absolutely delicious?' I had to agree it was – beautifully perfumed with the flavour of elderflower enhancing the succulence of fresh apricots.

As a seven-year-old in the Syrian capital Damascus, Josceline remembers seeing apricots from the garden drying on the flat roofs outside the kitchen and regularly watched the Armenian cook, Joseph, at work. Her stepfather was the British ambassador, and her mother often involved with diplomatic duties. 'I was always trying to escape from the rather strange governesses looking after me to the nicest place – the kitchen. The cook and his boy assistant were wonderful – they squeezed pomegranates for juice and made that very thin Arab bread with far more flavour than the pitta bread you buy now. So I got used to the idea of using mint, pine nuts and spices.' She also developed a life-long passion for lemon, using it to temper the sweetness of puddings and to add a tang to sauces, soups and stews.

The family regularly visited a weekend cottage in the hills, taking Joseph with them. 'It was a decaying but rather wonderful and romantic house, and we used to collect frogs – it sounds rather awful – from the stream at the end of garden and that was my first experience of eating frogs' legs. What terrible hardhearted children!'

Joseph made all kinds of meals from continental specialities such as frogs' legs to Middle Eastern dishes. Josceline's mother, like her grandmother, was a keen and imaginative cook and encouraged her cooks to produce local cuisine instead of the usual bland international food found in embassies. 'I never did any cooking there, I just absorbed and absorbed. It also developed my taste buds, more than if I'd been a child in England aged seven.'

Her taste buds, though, were regularly stretched in England. She was sent to boarding school in Dorset and during the holidays stayed with her grandmother, where she learnt to love puddings, sampling mixtures of lemon and egg, or gooey chocolate and caramel. 'My grandmother's rice pudding was better than anything. She made it with wholewheat rice and cooked it long and slowly. The result was very creamy, rich and nutty. It never stuck together and had a dark, wonderful skin. She and I used to walk what seemed like miles to one of the few health shops then to buy the rice and Barbados sugar, and my favourite – which I still love – dried bananas.'

Back at school, Josceline was struggling with the domestic science classes in spite, or probably because of, her unusual experiences of food. 'I was the worst person in the class. We had a very uninspired teacher and I couldn't bear having to do what I was told – given a recipe and having to stick to it. They were boring things like rock cakes, made in the most laborious way possible and not very nice at the end. I felt that through my instinct I could actually make something with a far better taste.'

With her instinct denied any expression, she lost all interest in food as an academic subject and began to concentrate on her music studies. She gained a place at the Guildhall School of Music to study singing and before the course began, went on a trip to Turkey with a friend. 'The Turks are brilliant cooks. When we arrived I had been given the name of an old man, an ex-diplomat who lived in a marvellous old traditional wooden house on the Bosporus. He was very keen on food and took us around the Istanbul restaurants, where they do all those wonderful stuffed dishes like mackerel with all the bones taken out and a stuffing put back.'

He insisted he should accompany the two girls, believing their planned trip to the south of the country was too dangerous on their own. 'We told him we wanted to travel cheaply and stay in very cheap places, so he was forced to travel on buses full of chickens. But it was brilliant that he came because he translated all the time.'

During this trip she rekindled her knowledge of aubergines, first tasted as a child in Damascus, and learnt the thousand different ways of frying and baking as well as grilling the vegetable, turning it black until it tastes smoky inside. She used this last technique to create her creamy aubergine purée which can be used as a dip or on toast.

She also noticed the unusual mixture of dill and pine kernels often mixed with rice, lamb and fish and uses the combination to make a moussaka with a Turkish flavour. This has a curd cheese topping dotted with pieces of aubergine and toasted pine kernels.

'The visit also got me very much on to stuffing vegetables and using vine leaves. It almost seemed as if every ingredient was stuffed.' The technique appealed as it provided an element of surprise and ingenuity, and she adapted the method to include it in a section in her 300-page bible, *The Cook's Companion*, published in 1991. As well as the more traditional Eastern Mediterranean dish of dolmades – vine leaves stuffed with rice and pine kernels – she demonstrates how to stuff a pumpkin using a spicy mixture of ginger, garlic, mace and cinnamon with spinach and soft white cheese.

Travelling is a constant pleasure, providing inspiration for her work, and she aims to spend a chunk of time away from Britain each year. She visited Turkey many more times and in one of her books included the traditional peasant dish of Turkish meatballs. This was given to her by a private chef in Istanbul, and the meatballs are served with an egg and lemon sauce.

Inspired after her first trip to Turkey, she began to cook in her shared student flat, with the usual lack of funds. 'Then I was living on very, very little money so I found it a terrific challenge. We used to get these things called cod's cheeks which were really a delicacy but only cost sixpence a pound, and tasted like a more delicate and tender form of scampi. Then I began to make things like shepherd's pie and that's where the Middle Eastern experience kept coming in as I experimented. I'd put in spices like cumin and coriander. Or I'd make the topping from a root vegetable like parsnip instead of potatoes.'

Pigeons were another cheap ingredient useful to the student cook. At her first real dinner party, Josceline made a pigeon casserole and thought it very grand to give each of the six guests a bird each. 'I filled the kitchen with terrible smoke trying to brown them. It was a tiny kitchen in a basement, with only one person able to stand in it. I remember I put some juniper berries in, which I thought would be good.'

She experimented with more casseroles and learnt her mother's way of making good roast potatoes but, as a full-time student, she had only limited time available for cooking. After marrying the broadcaster David Dimbleby, she knew she wanted to improve her culinary skills, as she confided in her book, *The Essential Josceline Dimbleby*, published in 1989. 'I remember feeling ashamed of the first meal I cooked for my husband – leathery steak and frozen peas – knowing I could do better.' She once more began to experiment when she knew people were coming to supper, her thoughts focusing on food. 'I used to go to bed at night thinking about what to cook the next day and I would actually dream ideas for meals in my sleep. For example, I would dream I was going to use stewing lamb and if I mixed it with this or that, and put a bit of spice in, then added some tomatoes, it would work well.' She would wake up with the recipe still in her head and then try it out. It sounds extraordinary, but her night-time thoughts were often an extension of her day. 'I used to spend an awful lot of time thinking and planning, just standing in front of a market stall looking at ingredients that inspired me. Sometimes if I'd already got the ingredients then I would continue the recipes in my sleep.'

Her friends who sampled these suppers began to urge her to write down her recipes and, after appearing in a *Harpers & Queen* article on private cooks, she was approached by a literary agent. Her first book *A Taste of Dreams*, published in 1976, was the result. 'I had these tiny children and it was terribly useful that I was able to use the night for thinking about food and even working out recipes because in the day I didn't have any time to think at all.'

She included dishes built upon her experiments in her student days, creating an oriental pie that was a mixture of shepherd's pie and Greek moussaka. She was already attracted to the spices and flavours of India, although she had yet to visit the country, and so added curry powder, cumin and spinach to the pie and topped it with mashed swede. Keen on using cheap ingredients, swede was also combined with carrot to create a soup, an unusual combination at that time; another soup made use of turnips with spring onions.

She overcame her aversion to beetroot to create a visually stunning dish of cod in a rich beetroot sauce flavoured with mustard and fresh ginger. Many of these ideas are widely used today but in 1976 the book was praised by Delia Smith for its personal and original touch.

As a busy mother, Josceline has always placed the highest priority on making dishes accessible and easy to make, and in *A Taste of Dreams* she uses ready-made pastry for dishes such as stuffed veal in a pastry case. 'I use a lot of bought puff pastry and do different things with it. I might smear some extra butter on it, or glaze it in a way that makes it taste delicious. Puff pastry is a rather skilled thing to make and most people just don't have the time to do it.' She experiments with traditional methods too, trying to make short cuts to cut down on the work; this created a favourite of hers – hot butter pastry. 'I was vaguely playing around and found that by just heating butter and either a little bit of water or juice, and stirring it into flour, you created a hot dough which could be pressed into the flan tin rather than rolling it out. You chill it in the fridge first and it makes a biscuity, firmer dough which doesn't shrink. It's very quick, with no rubbing in and rolling out, and terribly useful.' In more experiments she added flavourings such as orange rind, nuts and cocoa which created a 'wonderful dark chocolate pastry', and found that semolina added a crunchy texture.

This combination of simplicity and originality attracted the supermarket giant, Sainsbury. The wife of the chairman regularly used *A Taste of Dreams* for dinner parties and John Sainsbury was keen that the chain should start publishing cookbooks. 'He said they used my book, and asked if I'd like to do one for Sainsbury's, and would I think about what it should be about.' The first cookbook the store sold was her *Cooking for Christmas*, published in 1978. With her next book, *Cooking with Herbs and Spices*, she had to persuade the organization to experiment a little further. 'I wanted to do cooking with herbs and spices, and they were very worried because they thought their clientele would think it a little odd. This was in 1979, and then they still only stocked little drums of mixed spice, mixed herbs and thyme. The range was tiny.' She suggested she tell readers to get the other herbs from Indian grocers and Sainsbury agreed the book could go ahead. 'It was an act of faith, and they were amazed because the book sold very well. They suddenly realized everybody was longing for this type of food, and were more adventurous than they thought. So they began enlarging their range enormously. I really feel that I've played a part in that!'

Josceline used her love of herbs and spices to liven up a cheap ingredient for a Sainsbury's book published in 1982, *Marvellous Meals with Mince*. Coriander, cardamom and chillies were added to her spicy beef and coconut casserole with okra. Her chilli con carne was pepped up with cinnamon and a little dark chocolate – an ingredient used in Mexico, Spain and Italy to add richness and a touch of sweetness to spicy dishes. An intriguing technique shown in her first book was used in her recipe for vegetables in a pork case. Instead of pastry, the pie crust is made with minced pork, flavoured with garlic, mustard and rosemary, encasing a mixture of vegetables.

Experimentation with both techniques and ingredients is Josceline's trademark and creating recipes for books becomes a laborious process. It may take her a couple of hours to find inspiration for the ingredients she has in front of her. 'Sometimes, it's very drawn out. I do it step-by-step in my kitchen, and write down exactly what I'm doing in scribbly notes. If I see something is completely wrong, I do it another way and alter the recipe so I end up with these notes which I then decipher and put in a clearer way. Sometimes I only get one recipe a day.'

Her recipes for Sainsbury are then tested by an ordinary cook, not a home economist, who fills in a questionnaire which is returned to Josceline.

If one comes back with a comment that 'it seemed a bit runny' she re-tests the recipe.

'I sometimes realize things just don't taste quite right but I can usually work out how to improve them. I can somehow do that from my imagination.' Once a friend of hers made a lettuce soup that tasted quite bitter and was going to throw it away. 'I got it to taste all right by adding orange juice, black pepper and various things. I worked and worked and tasted and tasted until it was quite nice and my friend didn't have to throw it away.'

She prefers doing books covering a wide range of foods, even though many have been about specific types of dishes. 'I did a salads book for Sainsbury's and my family got extremely bored with these endless salads, especially as it was winter and they were longing for quite different things. I find it very difficult to think of doing very specific books because I always have so many very different ideas.'

Cooking for her husband and children has been a constant source of pleasure and, consequently, inspiration. She was keen to develop and influence her children's taste buds and doesn't believe in making children's food more bland than adults. 'I was a bit of a dragon with my children's friends when they were little. I was already doing books, and there were quite a lot of these odd things around instead of fish fingers. Lots of children really turned up their noses so I tried to make a rule that in our house, you didn't have to eat anything if you didn't like it but you had to taste, even if it was a tiny, tiny taste just to see if you did. And these children, with looks of disgust, would put something in their mouths and then quite often went on eating. This worked very well with cabbage, which they didn't like as it's usually overcooked and has a horrible stale smell but they got to like it as I made it fresh and slightly crispy, often with nutmeg and butter.'

Children can be notoriously faddy eaters and when her daughter became a vegetarian she had to decide whether to change her approach to family eating. 'I was rather fierce about not doing separate dishes for her because I felt it was entirely her choice, but I did make all the vegetables particularly nice.' She began to make more vegetable dishes and likes the general trend to have meat and fish in smaller quantities. 'Vegetables can almost be the main ingredient with maybe some tiny little slivers of chicken breast or fish among them and often no meat at all. I've always felt that I would never be a complete vegetarian because I don't want to limit my eating in any way. But I have found, like many people as they get older, I don't actually want meat so much, and I'm perfectly happy if I have meat only once a week.'

Her family are used to dishes never turning up the same twice, as she finds it difficult to resist changing recipes, and they often comment on the relative merits of the different versions. Over the last two years her son has developed a particular interest in the subject. 'It's completely changed our relationship. When he was at school he became a rugger player and I used to go and stand on the pitch with other parents and felt like sinking through the earth because they were hearty and cheering and I hated it. I just thought I couldn't follow the game and I'm a failure really as the mother of a sportsman. Then suddenly about two years ago or so he began being interested in cooking. Now we go out to meals together, and cook, and talk about food all the time and the other members of the family are rather amazed by this!'

Josceline works on her books in her large study at the top of her family home in Putney. It's a spacious room, originally designed for a billiard-table, with part of the roof made of glass to let in extra light. 'It's now become a full-time job. It was very convenient when the children were little because I didn't want it to be full-time – I didn't want to have proper nannies. When they got to school age I very much wanted to be there when they came back and to have proper school holidays with them. I'm very pleased that I did, and even now still try to have time for being with the children again on holidays or in Devon.'

The family has a cottage in Devon and on the whole Josceline does more of her work cooking in London and family cooking in Devon. 'Often I make a meal for perhaps ten people who're staying in Devon – we've been out all day, and there's not time to write down what I'm doing. Sometimes I do really wonderful things and it's terribly annoying. I try them again from memory but it's never exactly the same.'

The process of creating recipes is much easier if she has individuals in mind. 'I'm much more inspired when I know who I'm cooking for. When I'm doing a book, I feel torn as I often don't have time to keep arranging for people to come round. It's because I love pleasing people, and one of the absolute joys of cooking is the feeling that people are really enjoying it. I like them saying to me how nice it is, I've never grown out of wanting praise.'

Praise she wants in particular for her puddings. She considers them to be her 'thing', and adores cooking them to satisfy her sweet tooth. 'It seems to me they're a real indulgence because they're not completely necessary. They're always a treat and can be even more of a fantasy than savoury food.'

One of her favourites is a wild chocolate bowl with jagged edges, developed of course by experiment. 'I do it on crumpled-up greaseproof paper lining a bowl and all these folds just happen to take shape when you peel the paper off. And I fill it with ice-cream, fruit jellies or combinations of *crème fraîche* and yoghurt – whatever. I'm always thinking up endless fillings for it because it looks so dramatic!'

The bowl is designed to provoke a response from the diners, who have to acknowledge the pudding when it arrives. 'It really irritates me when I put something on the table and nobody notices. I can't bear it, and I have to say, "Do you think it looks it nice? Does it taste all right?" But my chocolate bowl never fails to stop the conversation.'

Chocolate is an inspirational ingredient for her puddings and she used it to extravagant effect in *A Taste of Dreams*, creating a chocolate mousse wrapped in cream cheese and hazelnuts. 'It looks like a creamily iced cake flecked with hazelnuts, but when you cut into it there's a rich fluffy chocolate mousse inside on a crunchy biscuit base.' She also began in this book to develop a recurrent theme – using fruit to balance the sweetness of chocolate, with desserts such as a blackcurrant and almond chocolate flan.

Another visually stunning pudding was raspberries wrapped in creamy cottage cheese on a meringue base. But although she adores the sight of grand desserts, her primary concern is for the taste. With this dish, the meringue is flavoured with rose water. 'It gives a deliciously subtle flavour both to the brittle meringue and the creamy filling.' She uses the ingredient to a greater extent in her rose petal tart, with the addition of crystallized petals from a scented red rose. As she explains in the book, 'If you have not discovered the subtle flavour of rose petals you have a treat in store. I first tried delicious, delicate rose petal jam in Istanbul and my luggage on the return flight was overweight because I could not resist cramming in several pots of jam. Since then I have realized it is easy to make one's own jam out of all those overblown roses which need snipping off throughout the summer.'

As well as using flowers, Josceline combines traditional English summer fruits such as rhubarb and gooseberries with a classic cake mix – Victoria sponge – to create a fresh fruit pudding. The raw fruit is placed over the uncooked cake mixture and baked in the oven. She enjoys experimenting with classic British puds too, and one of her old favourites is Sussex pond pudding. This contains a 'pond' of lemony juices which is revealed when the flaky crust is cut, and she adds fresh white breadcrumbs to create a lighter suet crust pastry.

She became friends with Jane Grigson who was keen on her use of English summer fruits and would often quote Josceline's recipes in her books. 'She was one of my earliest encouragers, who I'll never forget and I really loved her for it.' They met on a bus during a press trip to sample the food in Germany, when Josceline had recently written her first book. 'We used to get terribly excited by the food which was very rich with lots of goosefat, and we had long gluttonous conversations. A lot of the journalists on the trip from women's magazines used to look at us and say that they'd never heard food being talked about like that. It was almost obscene to them, our kind of orgiastic talk, and after that Jane became a huge friend and supporter.'

The issue of acknowledging other people's recipes is a tricky one. Writers such as Prue Leith and Jane Grigson have made it a point of principle but others have not been so honest. 'People get upset when recipes are re-published exactly – where every teaspoon is detailed and the wording is exactly the same. That's what plagiarism is. It does happen and it's very irritating if they're not acknowledged. If you're acknowledged, by someone like Jane Grigson, it's a wonderful compliment, of course!'

Although the creators of recipes own the copyright, the broad principles of their inventions can be easily and perhaps subconsciously borrowed. Once published, they are in the public arena and other cooks can learn and develop the idea. 'I remember in 1976 I was making a sauce out of red, yellow and green pepper purées, and then years later it became almost a cliché, that kind of red pepper purée. And I always wonder whether it was anything to do with me, just out of curiosity – I don't mind one bit – it may have been someone else had the same idea.'

General trends happen simply by a number of cooks developing a particular idea at the same time but Josceline has made a conscious effort to develop her ideas in isolation. 'I really don't care about trends. I love having conversations with other colleagues, and experiencing other foods often inspires me enormously to do different things. But I don't want to be influenced too much because I really want to go on feeling that it's my thing that I'm doing.'

Writing books and a regular column for the *Sunday Telegraph* for the last decade, it is impossible to avoid being influenced by trends and the latest ingredients. 'Sun-dried tomatoes, for example, are everywhere and you can't help experimenting with new things.' Josceline's visits to restaurants which are developing new trends also influence her as they may inspire her to try a similar kind of cooking. 'I always hope that my recipes aren't fashionable. But I looked back the other day and found a recipe for a nouvelle terrine with vegetables and I'd described it as typical of "the new style of cooking". I felt slightly embarrassed that I'd said that at all!'

Her study is lined with food books ranging from the latest publications which she needs for her journalistic work, to older editions about food. 'I find reading old cookery books – usually over fifty years old – quite inspires me. I never actually follow the recipes because the older they are, the less feasible they become. But I certainly benefit from ideas that have just been forgotten.' She gets particular inspiration from reading *The Gentle Art of Cookery* written in 1925 by Hilda Leyel, who founded the Culpepper House herb shops. The book includes a section on Dishes from Arabian Nights which uses some of Josceline's favourite ingredients such as mint, rosewater, and savoury and sweet spices. 'Many of the old English flavourings have simply been forgotten and, in fact, spices used to be used much more. Mrs Leyel's ideas were terribly interesting; she created really original recipes.'

The love of spices and travelling has lured Josceline to make frequent visits to India and its flavourings have always attracted her. Her first book, written before she had any experience of the country, used cardamom for savoury and sweet dishes, including a beef casserole and apricot apples baked with rum. 'I particularly love cardamom which I'm sure I've overused – but it's wonderful. It can be used with meat and fish, particularly combined with garlic and fresh ginger, and it also gives a scented flavour to puddings and ice-cream.'

Turmeric was used to 'Indianize' cold stuffed red peppers in her first book, and to flavour the pastry for pies filled with cream cheese, chilli powder and garlic. (See recipe for Turmeric Pies later in the chapter.) Josceline learnt how to bring out the aroma of spices by grinding them from whole, and often takes a central idea from a dish she ate in India and adapts it in a recipe back home. 'It's a fascinating country for food research as people are so interested in food there. You hear these passionate food discussions going on just as much as you would in France, and at all levels of society. Even if you ask very poor people what they're cooking, they'll launch forth into really enthusiastic explanations.'

Her most recent visit was to Gujarat where she wanted to explore the vegetarian food of the region. 'The people there are Jains and because of their religion they won't kill anything. They won't even eat root vegetables because it kills the insects on the roots if you pull them up. So a whole cuisine has developed which is rather delicate and uses beans, pulses and leafy things.'

She admires food writers such as Claudia Roden whose books combine recipes with descriptions of the region and its history. After visiting Gujarat, Josceline wrote an article in *Vogue* that was a new departure for her, combining both food and travel. 'It's the first thing I've written of that kind, and I had to do five recipes which were the proper versions of dishes we had during the visit. But I had to control myself not to change them!'

It is not without some irony that a cook who finds it difficult to resist changing recipes, was asked by Sainsbury to produce a definitive *Cook's Companion*, a step-by-step guide to cooking skills. Having had no formal training, she had to find out about some of the most basic methods. 'I've learnt a lot more now because I had to try out all these techniques that I hadn't really ever followed. But often I found that I had actually worked out the methods already. So what I did was to give a basic method and then add a personal note giving tips – on what may make the dish easier, or using different ingredients as an alternative.'

Stunning photographs of food often dismay home cooks when they compare their finished dish with the picture in the book. Keen to avoid intimidating her readers, Josceline dislikes food that looks too neat. 'Food looks more appetizing if it appears home-made, and I often say when a dish is being photographed for my books, "Don't make that look too perfect."'

Her readers often write to her and being 'hopeless' at typing she answers all of them by hand. 'Sometimes they're so pleased to get these handwritten letters back that they often write again! But over the years I've had lots of very nice letters. Occasionally they've had problems with a recipe, and it's often cakes. Cakes are just funny, people's ovens vary, and they do turn out differently every time.'

She has found that, for some unknown reason, her own baking at her holiday cottage in Devon is better than at her London home. As she explains in her books, 'My cakes are lighter, my bread rises better and my pastry is more delicate.' Notwithstanding this element of uncertainty, she takes a particular pleasure in baking cakes and biscuits which 'are not strictly necessary tasks and should therefore be pure pleasure.' One of her earliest recipes in *A Taste of Dreams* was for a 'Featherlight Flower Cake' – a fatless sponge to which either violet or rose essence is added for flavour. Her 'Unconventional Celebration Cake' is an alternative to the usual heavy fruit variety, and is a 'glorified carrot cake, packed with apricots and walnuts with a bite of crystallised ginger.' She also adores gooey chocolate cakes, often using her favourites, lemon and cardamom as flavourings.

From her contact with readers through letters and during roadshows, Josceline can gauge the general level of cooking skills. 'I suppose if it was in France there might be more people with an obvious sort of knowledge and expertise, but there's terrific enthusiasm and interest here. People sometimes though have strong prejudices.' She decided to use a recipe for parsnip and garlic purée which she thought 'delicious' to promote her latest book and spread it on biscuits for people to taste during the roadshows. 'If I told people what it was before they tried it, at least half of them would say they didn't like parsnips or they didn't like garlic and wouldn't taste it. Then sometimes I'd *force* them to try it and they found they liked it, and it sold more books than anything else because everyone loved it.'

Josceline has also had to force *herself* to get out of her kitchen and perform in public. Becoming a chef or running a restaurant has never appealed and, up until recently, she has steered clear of the now usual path to culinary fame – through television. 'It's quite unusual and I feel pleased I've reached a large number of people without it.' But when her *Cook's Companion* was launched in 1991 she felt duty-bound to accept an invitation to demonstrate in front of 800 people at a huge food show in Birmingham. 'I thought "I've got to conquer my shyness, I've got to do it", and was completely terrified. I did a dish made with mince and some of my puddings and the response of the audience was wonderful. I'm hopeless at saying what I'm doing – like "I'm now putting six ounces of so and so in . . ."; I can only do it as I really am, spontaneously. In fact this actually works quite well because the audience sympathizes with you!'

Josceline has also plucked up courage to perform live on television and, much to her surprise, discovered she liked it. 'I've broken through the shyness barrier – I just suddenly realized that being myself was the only way I can be. I'm sure that it all looks a bit chaotic with me, but then I think people feel that's how they are in their kitchen and, if I can make this food, they can.'

Turmeric Pies

Serves 6

These little yellow pies with a soft cream cheese and chilli filling make a pretty and unusual first course. Served warm with a cold, fresh-tasting soured cream sauce they melt in the mouth and are delicious.

For the pastry:

350 g (12 oz) plain flour
a pinch of salt
2 teaspoons turmeric
175 g (6 oz) butter or block margarine
75 g (3 oz) lard
a little very cold water

For the filling:

225 g (8 oz) full fat cream cheese
½ teaspoon chilli powder
1–2 cloves of garlic, crushed
salt and black pepper

For the sour-cream sauce:

150 ml (¼ pint) soured cream
150 ml (¼ pint) plain yogurt

Sift the flour, salt and turmeric into a mixing bowl. Cut in the fat and crumble the mixture with your fingertips until it resembles breadcrumbs. With a round-bladed knife mix in a very little cold water until the mixture just sticks together. Gather into a ball and put in the fridge for at least an hour.

Put the filling ingredients into a bowl and mix thoroughly together with a fork. To make the pies, roll out the pastry fairly thickly, about ½ cm (¼ in). Use a 7.5 cm (3 in) round fluted cutter and cut out 12 rounds, then a 5.5 cm (2¼ in) round cutter and cut another 12 rounds. Re-roll the pastry as necessary. Line some greased patty tins with the large rounds. Spoon some cheese filling into each round. Moisten the underside of the smaller rounds and put on top, pressing down lightly at the edges. Cut a small slit in each. Brush with milk and bake in the centre of the oven for about 20 minutes at 220°C, 425°F or Gas Mark 7. Leave them to cool in the tins for 5 minutes or so and then gently – as the pastry is deliciously crumbly – ease them out with a round-bladed knife. Serve warm, garnished with some watercress and parsley. Combine the soured cream and yoghurt in a bowl, sprinkle with a tiny pinch of chilli powder and pass the sauce round to spoon over the pies.

JAVANESE CHICKEN WITH AVOCADO

SERVES 4

We had taken the night train from Jakarta to Yogyakarta in the centre of Java. In the crush to board the train I had all my traveller's cheques stolen and we then had to sit up all night on wooden seats, stopping constantly. I began to hate Java. But soon after we arrived our luck changed when we went to visit an old lady whose daughter I had met in Jakarta. Mrs Sahir was tiny, with a neat black bun, humorous eyes and turned-up nose. She laughed a lot and took us everywhere. She also gave us some of the best food we had had so far on our trip. This chicken dish, made with spicy peanut sauce and coconut milk, is just a memory of the flavours we tasted, but it is a delicious one. Serve it with rice or Chinese noodles and a salad.

125 g (4 oz) desiccated coconut
450 ml (¾ pint) hot water
1 lemon
3 tablespoons groundnut oil
2 teaspoons ground cumin
4 teaspoons ground coriander
5–6 cloves of garlic, chopped
150 ml (¼ pint) water
2 level tablespoons smooth peanut butter
1 teaspoon oyster sauce
2–3 fresh green chillies, de-seeded and chopped
4 teaspoons brown sugar
4 chicken breast fillets, skinned and cut in half
2 small–medium onions, sliced
1 large avocado
salt
a few whole coriander leaves or continental parsley, to serve

Preheat the oven to 180°C, 350°F or Gas Mark 4. Put the coconut into a bowl and pour in the hot water. Leave on one side. Cut the lemon in half, squeeze out the juice and set it aside and then, using a sharp knife, cut the peel into thin strips. Put 2 tablespoons of the oil into a large iron or other flameproof casserole and heat it over a medium heat. Add the ground cumin and coriander, stir, and then add the chopped garlic. Stir for about a minute until the garlic just browns. Remove from the heat. Then add the water, the peanut butter, the oyster sauce, the lemon juice and peel, the chopped chillies, the brown sugar and a sprinkling of salt. Stir until the sauce is smoothly mixed. Now add the pieces of chicken and stir around to coat them with sauce. Put the casserole back on the heat, cover it and bring the sauce just to bubbling. Then put in the centre of the preheated oven for 1 hour.

Towards the end of the cooking, pour the coconut and the water into a food processor and whizz them for a minute or two; then pour them into a sieve over a bowl. Using your hands, squeeze out handfuls of the coconut mush as firmly as you can over the sieve, forcing out as much 'milk' as possible until you have squeezed out all the liquid. Keep the coconut milk on one side. Heat the remaining tablespoon of oil in a frying pan over a medium heat. Add the sliced onions and fry, stirring them around frequently for several minutes until they are completely soft. Turn off the heat, leaving the onions in the pan.

When the chicken is ready, remove from the oven and stir the coconut milk into the casserole. Put it back on the heat on top of the stove, bring to the boil and let it bubble for 2–3 minutes, stirring, to thicken it slightly. Remove the casserole from the heat and cover. Cut the avocado in half, peel it and remove the stone, and cut the halves across in thin slices. Add the slices to the casserole and gently stir them in. Then add the fried onions, leaving them mostly on top. Just before serving, scatter a few coriander leaves or some continental parsley on top.

BLUEBERRY TART WITH A CHOCOLATE CRUST

SERVES 6

This miraculous little tart can be adapted to any season by using any soft fruit which is available. Try it in particular with raspberries.

250 ml (8 fl oz) double cream
1 rounded tablespoon Greek yoghurt
225–350 g (8–12 oz) fresh blueberries
3 generous tablespoons bramble jelly
1 tablespoon lemon juice

FOR THE CHOCOLATE CRUST:

100 g (4 oz) plain flour
25 g (1 oz) cocoa powder
50 g (2 oz) icing sugar
½ teaspoon salt
75 g (3 oz) butter

To make the crust, sift the flour, cocoa, icing sugar and salt into a bowl and mix. Melt the butter and pour into the flour mixture a little at a time, stirring in to make a dough. Press evenly over the base and about 4 cm (1½ in) up the sides of a buttered 15 cm (6 in) loose-bottomed cake tin, leaving an uneven edge. Chill for 20–30 minutes.

Put a large piece of greaseproof paper inside the tin, coming up well above the rim. Fill with dried beans and bake blind in a preheated oven, 200°C, 400°F or Gas Mark 6 for 25 minutes. Remove the beans and grease-proof paper and put the crust back in the oven for another 5 minutes. Cool slightly then put the tin on to a jam jar and carefully push down the cake tin sides. Use a thin palette knife to transfer the crust on to a serving plate. Leave until cool.

Not more than 2 hours before serving, whip the cream until stiff, then fold in the yoghurt. Spoon the mixture into the crust and level the surface. Arrange the blueberries on top. Melt the jelly with the lemon juice until smooth, then boil for 2–3 minutes. Remove from the heat, let the bubbles subside and then trickle over the blueberries. Leave at room temperature or in a cool place (but not the refrigerator) until ready to eat.

Intense Chocolate Cake with Redcurrants

Serves 4–6

The popping sharpness of the redcurrant top goes wonderfully with this soft, intensely chocolaty cake. It is a pudding which no one resists. The cake is best made the day before the dinner party, with the topping put on a few hours before you eat. I serve it either with cream, or whipped cream mixed with yoghurt. It looks especially pretty if you bake the cake in a heart-shaped tin.

butter for greasing
225 g (8 oz) plain chocolate
2 tablespoons water
2 large eggs (size 1–2) separated
75 g (3 oz) soft dark brown sugar
1 tablespoon plain flour, plus extra for dusting

2 teaspoons natural yoghurt
100–175 g (4–6 oz) fresh redcurrants
icing sugar
salt

Butter a 15–18 cm (6–7 in) cake tin, line the base with a disc of buttered greaseproof paper and dust with flour. Break up three-quarters of the chocolate and put into the top of a double saucepan, or into a bowl set over barely simmering water. Add the water to the chocolate and stir until melted and smooth. Remove from the heat. Put the egg yolks in a mixing bowl and add the sugar and the melted chocolate. Whisk very thoroughly together. Then stir in the flour.

Heat the oven to 180°C, 350°F or Gas Mark 4. Whisk the egg whites with a good pinch of salt until they stand in soft peaks. Fold the egg whites into the chocolate mixture a little at a time, using a metal spoon, then pour the mixture into the prepared cake tin. Cook the cake in the centre of the oven for 25–30 minutes until a small knife inserted in the middle comes out clean.

Remove from the oven and leave in the tin for about 5 minutes (the cake will sink slightly – this is normal). Then loosen the edges carefully with a knife and turn the cake out on to a rack to cool, removing the greaseproof paper and turning the cake the right way up.

When the cake is cold, melt the remaining chocolate in a double saucepan over hot water, stirring in the yoghurt when melted. Spread this chocolate on top of the cake and then push the redcurrants off their stalks with a fork and put them on top of the chocolate. Leave in a cool place but not the fridge. Shortly before serving, sprinkle a very little icing sugar through a sieve on top of the redcurrants.

Baby Squid Stuffed with Salmon and Spinach in a Wine and Dill Sauce

new recipe

Serves 4

These little white torpedoes stuffed with a mosaic of pink and green look beautiful under their shiny translucent sauce. They create a fascinating fusion of flavours. To save time try to buy the ready prepared squid. This is a good dish for a light meal, accompanied by new potatoes and a mixed or tomato salad – and if you are looking for a low-fat recipe this is the one for you.

350 g (12 oz) fresh spinach
225 g (8 oz) skinned salmon fillet
finely grated rind and juice of 1 small orange
3–4 pinches of chilli powder
450–550 g (1–$1\frac{1}{4}$ lb) ready prepared baby squid
150 ml ($\frac{1}{4}$ pint) white wine
2 teaspoons dill vinegar
1 good handful fresh dill
1 rounded teaspoon arrowroot or cornflour

Wash the spinach and remove any thick stalks. Bring a saucepan of salted water to the boil, add the spinach and boil for 1–2 minutes until limp. Drain well, pressing out as much liquid as possible. Then chop the spinach fairly roughly and leave to cool. Slice the salmon fillet into small cubes. Mix the grated orange rind with the spinach and season with the chilli powder.

Remove the tentacle part of the prepared squid. Take a little bit of spinach and stick it down into the squid, pressing it in with one finger. Then insert a piece of salmon, then some more spinach followed by another piece of salmon and the same again until the squid is stuffed almost full. Lastly, stopper the stuffing by pressing the squid's tentacle part on top. Repeat the process with the other squid.

Now strain the orange juice into a wide shallow saucepan or deep sauté pan with a lid. Add the white wine, put over the heat and bring to simmering point. Carefully place in the stuffed squid, cover the pan and simmer very gently for only 1–2 minutes – just until the squid flesh has turned an opaque white. Remove from the heat, extract the squid using a slotted spatula (leaving the liquid in the pan) and arrange on a wide serving plate. Cover loosely with foil and keep warm in a very low oven while you make the sauce.

Chop the dill. Mix the arrowroot in a cup with about 2 teaspoons of water until smooth. Then stir this and the vinegar into the wine liquid and return to the heat. Bring up to bubbling, stirring all the time until thickened, then stir in the chopped dill and remove from the heat. If necessary, season the sauce with salt and a pinch or two of chilli. Pour over the squid just before serving.

Selected Bibliography

Marguerite Patten

What's Cooking? Recipes of a Lifetime, Hawker Publications, 1992
Cookery in Colour, Hamlyn, 1960
Eat Well, Stay Well, Mandarin, 1991
The Complete Book of Teas, Piatkus, 1989
500 Recipes for Main Meals, Hamlyn, 1963
500 Recipes for Slimmers, Hamlyn, 1962
500 Recipes for Suppers & Snacks, Hamlyn, 1963
500 Recipes for Working Wives, Hamlyn, 1970
House Making in Colour, Hamlyn, 1966
New Ways to Perfect Cooking, Hamlyn, 1989
We'll Eat Again, Hamlyn, 1985

Elizabeth David

A Book of Mediterranean Food, Dorling Kindersley, 1988
A Book of Mediterranean Food, Penguin, 1991
English Bread and Yeast Cookery, Penguin, 1979
French Provincial Cooking, Penguin, revised edition 1970
Italian Food, Penguin, revised edition 1989
Italian Food, Allen Lane, 1977
Spices, Salt and Aromatics in the English Kitchen, Penguin, 1975
Summer Cooking, Penguin, 1965
French Country Cooking, Dorling Kindersley, 1987

Jane Grigson

Charcuterie and French Pork Cookery, Michael Joseph, 1967
English Food, Ebury Press, 3rd revised edition 1992
Fish Cookery, Penguin, 1984 edition
Food with the Famous, Grub Street, 1979
Good Things, Penguin, 1991 edition

Jane Grigson's Fruit Book, Penguin, 1983 edition
Jane Grigson's Vegetable Book, Penguin, 1983 edition
The Mushroom Feast, Penguin, 1975

CLAUDIA RODEN

Coffee, Penguin, 1981
The Food of Italy, Chatto and Windus, 1989
A New Book of Middle Eastern Food, Penguin, 2nd revised edition 1986
Picnic The Complete Guide to Outdoor Food, Penguin, 1981

PRUE LEITH

Leith's Cookery Course 1. Basic, Fontana, 1979
Leith's Cooking Course 2. Intermediate, Fontana, 1980
Leith's Cookery Course 3. Advanced, Fontana, 1980
Leith's Cookery Bible, Bloomsbury, 1991
Leith's Cookery School, Macdonald, 1990
Prue Leith's Dinner Parties, Papermac, 1992

MADHUR JAFFREY

Eastern Vegetarian Cooking, Jonathan Cape, 1991
Food for Family and Friends, Pan, 1989
An Invitation to Indian Cookery, Jonathan Cape, 1991
Madhur Jaffrey's Far Eastern Cookery, BBC Books, 1989
A Taste of India, Pavilion, 1985

JOSCELINE DIMBLEBY

A Traveller's Tastes, J. Sainsbury, 1986
Josceline Dimbleby Book of Entertaining, J. Sainsbury, 1988
The Cook's Companion, J. Sainsbury, 1991
The Essential Josceline Dimbleby, Simon and Schuster, 1990
Marvellous Meals with Mince, J. Sainsbury, 1991
A Taste of Dreams, Sphere, 1984

Other cookery titles published by *BBC Books* include:

Michael Barry's Food & Drink Cookbook

Sarah Brown's Vegetarian Kitchen

Antonio Carluccio's Passion for Pasta

A Taste of Japan *Leslie Downer*

Floyd's American Pie *Keith Floyd*

Floyd on Britain and Ireland *Keith Floyd*

Floyd on Fire *Keith Floyd*

Floyd on Fish *Keith Floyd*

Floyd on France *Keith Floyd*

Valentina Harris's Complete Italian Cookery Course

Valentina's Italian Regional Cookery *Valentina Harris*

Ken Hom's Chinese Cookery

Madhur Jaffrey's Far Eastern Cookery

Madhur Jaffrey's Indian Cookery

Mireille Johnston's French Cookery Course, Part 1

Mediterranean Cookery *Claudia Roden*

At Home with the Roux Brothers *Albert & Michel Roux*

Spain on a Plate *María José Sevilla*

Delia Smith's Christmas

Delia Smith's Complete Cookery Course

Delia Smith's Complete Illustrated Cookery Course

Eating Out with Tovey *John Tovey*

Entertaining on a Plate *John Tovey*

Hot Chefs *Various*